The Book of Proverbs

A SOCIAL JUSTICE COMMENTARY

The Book of Proverbs

A SOCIAL JUSTICE COMMENTARY

Rabbi Dr. Shmuly Yanklowitz

with a foreword by
RABBI LAURA GELLER

CCAR
Press

CENTRAL CONFERENCE OF AMERICAN RABBIS

5782 NEW YORK 2022

Book of Proverbs translation: From *The JPS Tanakh: Gender-Sensitive Edition*
(RJPS), 2021–22. Used by permission of The Jewish Publication Society.

Cover image: *Mishnah: Women* by Isaac Brynjegard-Bialik. Used by permission of
the artist.

Published by Reform Judaism Publishing, a division of CCAR Press
355 Lexington Avenue, New York, NY 10017
(212) 972-3636 | info@ccarpress.org | www.ccarpress.org

Library of Congress Cataloging-in-Publication Data
Names: Yanklowitz, Shmuly, 1981– author. | Geller, Laura, 1950– author of
    foreword.
Title: The Book of Proverbs: a social justice commentary / Rabbi Dr.
    Shmuly Yanklowitz ; foreword by Rabbi Laura Geller.
Other titles: Bible. Proverbs. Selections. Hebrew. 2022.
Description: New York: Central Conference of American Rabbis, 2022. |
    "Book of Proverbs translation: From The JPS Tanakh: Gender-Sensitive
    Edition (RJPS), 2021–22"—Copyright page. | Includes bibliographical
    references. | Text in English with selection of verses from the Book of
    Proverbs in original Hebrew and English translation. | Summary: "The
    Book of Proverbs is a collection of Jewish wisdom, song, and
    inspiration. Using a blend of social justice practice and Jewish thought
    from throughout history, the books shows how Proverbs are pertinent to
    issues we face today. Using a wide range of sources, the books explores
    topics such as income inequality, feminism, animal rights,
    environmentalism, and more"—Provided by publisher.
Identifiers: LCCN 2021048777 (print) | LCCN 2021048778 (ebook) | ISBN
    9780881233766 (trade paperback) | ISBN 9780881233773 (ebook)
Subjects: LCSH: Bible. Proverbs—Criticism, interpretation, etc. | Social
    justice—Religious aspects—Judaism.
Classification: LCC BS1465.52 .Y36 2022 (print) | LCC BS1465.52 (ebook) |
    DDC 223/.706--dc23/eng/20211015
LC record available at https://lccn.loc.gov/2021048777
LC ebook record available at https://lccn.loc.gov/2021048778

Text design and composition by Scott-Martin Kosofsky
at The Philidor Company, Rhinebeck, NY

Printed in the United States of America

10 9 8 7 6 5 4 3 2 1 0

This book is dedicated to my amazing children,

Amiella Rachel

Meir Lev Kook

Maya Neshama

Shaya Or Nafshi Yosef

"My child, when your heart gains wisdom, my heart rejoices also."
—Proverbs 23:15

For you, my love knows no bounds.
Along with your beautiful and amazing mother, Shoshana, you are the dearest and most precious gifts in my life. Without you, I wouldn't be able to do the work I set out to carry out each day. I am so blessed to be your abba. You make even the most challenging days radiate with love and warmth. You reside in my heart, always.

May the Book of Proverbs guide you as you continue to grow and develop in all ways. As it says, "Speak up, judge righteously, champion the poor and the needy" (Proverbs 31:9). You will have many opportunities to use your God-given skills to help others. May you continue to be brave enough to accept these opportunities.

My children, may you each be blessed to always find the most precious pearls of wisdom within you, around you, and wherever else you may find them. May they fill you with joy and delight, all of your long days.

Contents

Foreword

Rabbi Laura Geller

YOU HOLD IN YOUR HANDS a commentary on the Book of Proverbs, that classic biblical collection of Jewish wisdom. But this volume is so much more. This is a book about contemporary life, a book about the Torah of our own lives as well as the Torah of tradition, a book that nourishes and challenges us by offering new ways of thinking about the questions we wrestle with as modern people. It's a book of theology as well as a commentary on the pressing social and political issues of our time, from environmentalism and sustainability to economic justice, worker rights, feminism, animal rights, and homelessness.

Our guide, Rabbi Dr. Shmuly Yanklowitz, an ordained Orthodox rabbi, brings us insights from his wide range of teachers: the Rabbis of the Talmud, the classical Jewish commentators, Chasidic rebbes, and modern Jewish thinkers, in addition to physicists, poets, psychologists, philosophers, artists, and contemporary thought leaders. *The Book of Proverbs: A Social Justice Commentary* opens up a classic biblical text that for so many of us has been easy to quote but hard to understand, a book that is not religious in the way religion is often understood, not God-centered yet deeply concerned with what makes a human life holy. As Rabbi Yanklowitz writes in the introduction, "As one might say today, the Book of Proverbs is 'spiritual but not religious.' It appears to have been written not for an intellectual elite interested in theology, but as a moral guide for all people. It is not an exclusively 'Jewish' book, but speaks to universal concerns. It does not address the needs, interests, and challenges of a specific community, but rather seeks to provide guidance for an individual— any individual."

Rabbi Yanklowitz's book is for all of us individuals who are spiritual seekers, wanting to discover in Jewish tradition both the tools to navigate the vicissitudes of our life and an experience of the Oneness and interconnectedness of life that leads to outward engagement with our broken world.

The book is also a critique of contemporary religious life. Rabbi Yanklowitz boldly argues that Jewish observance requires rebellion, not submission; protest, not obedience; and the space to develop our inner God-given capacities for moral reasoning, intuition, and conscience. For him, awe of the Divine is awe of the divine capacity for evolving, growing, and becoming; his commentary offers insights that can lead to our own evolving, growing, and becoming.

Rabbi Yanklowitz doesn't shy away from difficult passages. Instead, he offers the possibility of multiple readings. For example, consider Proverbs 13:24, "He who spares the rod hates his son, but he who loves him disciplines him early." How do you find a moral lesson in a vision of child-rearing so different from our contemporary one? He admits that it reflects a different sociocultural context and that it has been used over the past centuries to justify force and abuse against children. He acknowledges that even Maimonides believed that hitting children is appropriate because it instills fear in them, although that sage makes clear that corporal punishment should not be given in anger, not with sticks or straps, and not with the intention of embarrassing the child or causing harm. Rabbi Yanklowitz brings into the discussion other points of view, from Jewish sources as well as contemporary psychological insights, citing studies demonstrating that corporal punishment results in more aggressive behavior as a child grows up. What began as a commentary on a verse and a practice throughout Jewish history becomes a discussion about parenting and its challenges. Ultimately he suggests that a verse seeming to be a prescription is actually descriptive of the way parents sometimes act—and a reminder that successful parenting requires controlling our instincts.

The commentary that unfolds within this book is structured around specific verses. One could read it from beginning to end, or instead choose verses that call out to the reader for deeper exploration. Either way, the commentary offers a journey into the world of Jewish thought and tradition and the personal and social challenges of our time. Not surprisingly, it ends with the most well-known passage from the Book of Proverbs, *Eishet Chayil*, "A Woman of Valor." Here too Rabbi Yanklowitz offers multiple readings, from a feminist critique to a mystical reimaging, leaving it up to us, his readers, to ask not only what the passage means to us, but also how it calls to us to transform our own lives.

Rabbi Yanklowitz concludes with a prayer: "May we have the strength to recognize the infinite wisdom contained within these verses, this book, and these ideas. Through them, we are handed the potential needed to actualize deep and true wisdom throughout the world and in ourselves. How we choose to wield this potential is left entirely up to us."

Quite a challenge—and quite an opportunity.

Rabbi Laura Geller, rabbi emerita of Temple Emanuel of Beverly Hills, was the third woman in the Reform Movement to become a rabbi. Named one of *Newsweek*'s 50 Most Influential Rabbis in America and by PBS's Next Avenue as a 2017 Influencer in Aging, she was a cofounder of ChaiVillageLA and is the chair of the Synagogue Village Network. She served on the Corporation of Brown University and on the boards of the Jewish Women's Archive, Encore.org, and B3: The Jewish Boomer Platform. Coauthored with her husband Richard Siegel (*z"l*), her book *Getting Good at Getting Older* was named a National Jewish Book Award finalist in the category of Contemporary Jewish Life and Practice.

Acknowledgments

JEWISH WISDOM is not something one acquires lightly. It is a pursuit that takes a lifetime of rigorous study, guidance, perspicacity, and openheartedness. On the other hand, Jewish literature is not necessarily just a means to achieve intellectual glory—studying Jewish texts is a journey with infinite steps and no end in sight, a pleasurable pursuit for its own sake.

The opportunity to study and to write about the Book of Proverbs has been a delight. In all my years as a Jewish educator, I have never encountered ideas quite like these. It was both a challenging and an illuminating experience to approach these ancient ideas and apply them to this fraught contemporary moment. It has been a revelatory encounter with the timeless totality of Jewish wisdom.

The book you hold in your hands was perhaps my most difficult one to write to date, and I could not have done it without the support of many partners. I would like to start by saying how grateful I am to my publisher, CCAR Press, for allowing me to publish another book in this Social Justice Commentary series. My previous books—a commentary on the Book of Jonah and a commentary on *Pirkei Avot*—were made all the more special thanks to the dedication of the CCAR Press team to ensure that the final product was of the highest quality. To Rabbi Hara Person and Rafael Chaiken, thank you for continuing to be my guides and biggest proponents at the CCAR. Many thanks as well to Rabbi Dr. Sonja Pilz, Rabbi Jan Katz, Raquel Fairweather, Debbie Smilow, Chiara Ricisak, and the whole CCAR Press team for their support throughout all the steps it took to get this book into your hands. I thank copy editor Debra Hirsch Corman, book designer Scott-Martin Kosofsky, proofreader Michelle Kwitkin, and cover designer Barbara Leff as well. I am truly grateful for everything the CCAR does.

I am also grateful for the work of Abraham J. Frost, who pitched ideas for the book and offered helpful edits. I am so grateful for his hard work throughout the years. To Judry Subar, who added enormous insight with his contributions and editing acumen, and to Dani Satlow, who contributed suggestions as well, thank you so much for your attentiveness to this work. The assistance from these esteemed colleagues was invaluable as I made my way through my spiritual and intellectual journeys with the Book of Proverbs.

Most importantly, writing this book would not have been possible without the everlasting love of my beautiful and brilliant wife, Shoshana, and our wonderful children, Amiella, Lev, Maya, and Shay. Whenever I found myself in need of inspiration, I thought of my family. Thank you for all the joy and light you share with me every day. I love you with all my heart!

Finally, I give my humble thanks to the Creator—the light and joy of my soul—for giving me life, for giving me hope, for giving me curiosity, for giving me trials and tasks to conquer, and for giving me the ability to pursue a life dedicated to holiness.

—

Introduction

THE RABBIS TAUGHT that most of the Israelites did not leave Egypt during the Exodus. Indeed, for some—perhaps most—people, the familiar state of "slavery" is much more comfortable than unknown "freedom." Today, our world changes faster than ever before in human history. There is a lot of fear of change, fear of loss. We need to weather these storms together and hold each other closer. Only together, with grace and humility, can we courageously evolve. As spiritual seekers, we have unique opportunities each day to continue to reflect on the ancient wisdom of our tradition and how it can be made relevant to our moment.

Spirituality is not simply "fun" or "meaningful." There is far too much at stake. If we do not elevate our spiritual consciousness, we will destroy ourselves. More than a political revolution, we need a global spiritual awakening to the oneness and the interconnectedness of all life! How will we get there? What intellectual and spiritual resources will help us all move forward? Which of those resources will be brand-new and which ones will be ancient?

The Book of Proverbs in the Hebrew Bible

The Book of Proverbs—a book of ancient wisdom—is one of the most profound works found within the Hebrew Bible, but one that is not often explored in a truly spiritual, accessible, and relevant way. The language of the book is often vague, and its words and lessons are often open-ended and shrouded with literary ambiguity, qualities that make it hard to digest for the contemporary reader. Still, the wisdom that is contained within the Book of Proverbs is timeless, and readers have much to gain by learning from its ancient precepts.

Those of us who live in a world of paradox might find the Book of Proverbs—known as *Sefer Mishlei* in Hebrew—to seem a bit binary and simplistic. However, the book pushes us to remember that actually much of life is quite binary! We are confronted with good and evil, life and death, joy and sorrow. The challenge is to see which moments require us to view situations with nuance and embrace paradox—and which moments require our fervent and robust moral and spiritual action. In the latter moments, we should not try to find intellectual excuses, but rather respond with clarity and courage. In the Book of Proverbs, we find the productive and the lazy, the wise and the foolish, the just and the unjust—and we know where we want to find ourselves on that map!

The Book of Proverbs is the second book of *K'tuvim* ("Writings," the third section of the Hebrew Bible) and consists of only thirty-one chapters. As part of the biblical "wisdom literature," the book discusses moral values and proper conduct. The collection is divided according to its different authors.[1] In fact, one might divide the book into seven different books merged into one, similar to a contemporary anthology consisting of seven chapters written by different authors. Other books in the Hebrew Bible of the same wisdom literature genre include Ecclesiastes and Job.[2]

Due to the lack of references to the Divine, the content of the Book of Proverbs is accessible to a broad readership, believers and non-believers alike. Proverbs is not a typical biblical book. God is mentioned here and there, but the content of the book is mostly focused on human learnings and wisdom. As one might say today, the book is "spiritual but not religious." It appears to have been written not for an intellectual elite interested in theology, but as a moral guide for all people. It is not an exclusively "Jewish" book, but speaks to universal concerns. It does not address the needs, interests, and challenges of a specific community, but rather seeks to provide guidance for an individual—any individual.

According to Jewish tradition, the book was written by King Solomon, the assumed author of other wisdom books like the Song of Songs and the Book of Ecclesiastes.[3] The Malbim suggests that Solomon is referred to in three different ways in the Book of Proverbs corresponding to three different paths to truth:[4]

- "Solomon": prophecy
- "Son of David": tradition (passed from parent to child)
- "King of Israel": intelligence and intellectual discernment

The Book of Proverbs as a Source of Ethics and Jewish Sprituality
Dating this book is difficult, primarily because this genre of wisdom writings lasted over a millennium throughout the ancient Near East.[5] However, the wisdom found in the Hebrew Bible is quite distinct from Greek writings in that it mostly does not engage with abstract philosophical concepts rooted in metaphysics, epistemology, or ontology, but instead offers practical advice for the human life.[6] Scholars suggest that parts of the Book of Proverbs were written during the Persian or Hellenistic periods (sixth through first centuries BCE).

On the one hand, Proverbs seems to offer a rather simplistic theology: "Follow the rules and you'll be rewarded." This simplicity is countered by the complexity of the messages in Ecclesiastes and Job. On the other hand, when viewed within the entirety of Hebrew Bible, Proverbs is anything but simple. It is radically subversive in choosing new points of emphasis, ignoring older depictions of God, values, and ethics. At no point does the book mention the miracles in Egypt or the revelation at Sinai. The book draws upon a new center: the self. Indeed, the Book of Proverbs was such a theologically challenging book that the Rabbis considered excluding it from the canon.[7] Its possible exclusion likely had to do with its many self-contradictions—characteristic to an anthology. Consider, for example, Proverbs 26:4, "Do not answer a dullard in accord with their folly," in contrast to the next verse in 26:5, "Answer a dullard in accord with their folly."

The book speaks in short, elliptic, and often aphoristic maxims or *m'shalim*, "allegories," captured in a story or teaching. Its ideas are more easily expressed in Hebrew than in English, which often requires double the number of words. The assumption of the compiler of Proverbs is that its words contain simple moral truths that are worth memorizing. About half the book is made up of wisdom sayings. The other half uses a more poetic style. The poetry is not brilliantly clever and deep, but rather accessible and easy to memorize. Bible scholar Robert Alter explains:

> If there were in fact Wisdom schools in ancient Israel, it is easy enough to imagine how the formulation of ethical and pragmatic principles in poetry helped students to memorize them. . . . The line "Cheating scales are the Lord's loathing / and a true weight-stone His pleasure" . . . occurs several times with minor variations. Unlike the sundry claims about the righteous and the wicked, it is unassailable as an ethical principle. One would hardly call it great poetry, but the poetic parallelism does service to inscribe the saying in memory with the aim of being a kind of ethical prophylaxis: should you ever be tempted to enhance your profits in a sale of goods by using a crooked scale or an underweight marked stone, this saying is meant to come to mind and dissuade you.[8]

A common recurring theme is that "the fear of God" is "the beginning of wisdom," promoting submission to the divine will. The pious path to that end is primarily to seek wisdom and to work on morally refining one's character. As a second step, the fool is contrasted with the wise.

We are taught not only the ways of the foolish, but also the path of the virtuous. We should walk in the good and just ways (Proverbs 2:20), cultivate wisdom in the heart and knowledge in the soul (2:10). There are countless teachings on poverty (6:30, 16:8, 17:5, 19:4, 22:22, 28:3, 28:6, 28:27, 29:7, 31:8, 31:9) and how wealth should be justly acquired and understood. We learn about how horrific violence is to all (16:29, 29:10). We are told to love wisdom (Proverbs 3), seek happiness through wisdom (3:13–14, 8:32), act ethically in business (11:1, 20:10, 20:14, 22:26–27, 28:13) and in inheritance (20:21), consider our speech carefully (11:11, 15:23), choose with whom we walk in the world very carefully (13:20, 14:7, 24:19–22), choose more vegetables over meat (15:17, 23:20), control our fear (3:25), care for the widow (15:25) and the vulnerable child (23:10), protect the righteous (17:26), and cultivate the ethic of humility (22:4). We are adjured to do all we can to save life (14:25, 24:11). We are warned not to show favoritism in judgment (24:23, 28:21). In addition to all of this, we are reminded that each day we should resist tyranny (29:26), avoid vain testimony (19:5, 24:28), be mindful of boundaries (22:28, 23:10), rule ethically (29:4), have ethical boundaries within argumentation and conflict (20:3, 24:29, 25:9, 25:21), be a good spouse (12:4, 18:22, 25:24), keep in mind countless teachings on parenting, and avoid praise of the wicked (24:24).

Proverbs is not about self-understanding, but rather instructs about wisdom beyond the self. "Fools do not desire understanding / But only to air their thoughts" (Proverbs 18:2). The self is not the center in this intellectual and spiritual quest. We must learn to listen to others instead of meditating and thinking in isolation: "To answer before listening / This is foolish and disgraceful" (18:13). The book notes, however, that we must learn to know our own soul as well (Proverbs 24:14).

However, the Book of Proverbs addresses not only our behavior but also our inner, spiritual lives. We are invited to trust others in their self-understanding: "The heart alone knows its bitterness" (Proverbs 14:10). We are instructed to be emotionally alive (28:14), to cultivate our spiritual lens concerning both God and humans (3:4, 16:7), to contemplate hell (15:11, 15:24) but also how "those who die without judgment [are] swept away unjustly" (13:23), to be concerned with mental illness (referred to as "a sad heart," 15:13), to raise each other up (25:7), and to cultivate moral perseverance (expressed in the notion that the righteous fall seven times, 24:16). We can refine our everyday interactions, Proverbs tells us, by ensuring we do not cause others to struggle unnecessarily (3:28). We should strive to be givers, not takers, the book emphasizes, even to the point of hating gifts (15:27).

To the modern ear, even in translation biblical language is archaic; no less so with the Book of Proverbs. Consequently, when it comes to gender references, for example, we need to remember that the work was written thousands of years ago, far in time from modern feminist sensitivities. The book does, though, recognize that gender does not dictate moral standing; it contrasts the "stupid woman" (Proverbs 9:13–18) with the "capable wife" ("woman of substance") (31:10–31).

While most of the book deals with either ethical principles or inner moral growth, it certainly also contains a message about connecting with the Divine. Interesting enough, in the Torah, we learn of *halachta bidrachav* ("you shall walk in God's ways," Deuteronomy 28:9), also known as *imitatio Dei*. The Book of Proverbs teaches an expansion of that axiom: "In all your ways acknowledge God" (Proverbs 3:6). Not only are we created holy, we must strive to make holy whatever we are doing.[9] Based on this verse, the Rabbis teach, "Social responsibility is great, for whoever has achieved it has befriended both the Holy and Blessed One and human beings."[10]

How to Use This Book

Throughout this commentary on the Book of Proverbs, we will explore ethical issues such as natural morality (Proverbs 6:6), human responsibility (1:2), justice (2:9), moral rebuke (9:8), wealth and charity (11:4, 13:7–8, 13:11), and the engagement with enemies (11:10, 24:17–18), as well as closely related issues of spirituality and human growth such as maintaining relationships (17:1, 17:17), parenting (1:8, 13:24), death (5:11), managing character traits (4:27, 14:29, 19:15), spirituality (6:23, 13:9), and so much more. If you would like to skip from chapter to chapter, rather than reading the book linearly, that is perfectly acceptable. Create your own path and move ahead at your own speed.

This volume sets out the Hebrew and JPS English translation for each chapter of the Book of Proverbs, followed by several commentaries (fifty-seven in total) on particular verses or themes in that chapter. Consequently, you as the reader can learn the full text of the Book of Proverbs on your own and then engage more deeply with this and other commentaries. In a few cases, my translation for a particular verse will differ from JPS. The teachings of the Book of Proverbs are often quite simple and can be used as meditative mantras as part of one's ethical and meditative practices. One can read the text of the Book of Proverbs, but one can also sing or chant it as a way to reflect and internalize chosen messages.

As a good complement, one might study the Rabbinic texts compiled in *Pirkei Avot* along with the Book of Proverbs. Written in different eras of Jewish history, both works strive to make daily lived ethics a primary focus. In fact, *Pirkei Avot* seems, at times, to use Proverbs as a starting place, quoting the book no fewer than twenty-two times. One mishnah, in fact, consists entirely of a quote from Proverbs.[11] Two *mishnayot* include three quotes from Proverbs each,[12] and one mishnah even includes seven quotes from Proverbs.[13]

As you proceed through this book, read other commentaries too, and compare how thinkers throughout the centuries have approached these texts. There are so many social issues that we might be able to tackle through the wisdom found in these ancient holy words. The axioms of Proverbs are meant to be lived and to be applied to everyday life. Go! And begin to allow these teachings to inspire you to actualize your holy potential.

About the Translation
Rabbi David E. S. Stein, PhD

THE TRANSLATION OF THE BOOK OF PROVERBS in this volume is adapted from the New Jewish Publication Society version (NJPS) that was first published in 1982. In the words of the instigator of NJPS, Professor Harry Orlinsky, *z"l*, the original translation team's goal was "to render the Hebrew text as they believed the original author of that text meant it to be understood"—that is, to render the text's plain sense and to do so in the idiom of contemporary English.

Our adaptation effort, which did not deviate from the aforementioned goal, is part of a reworking of the entire *Tanach* (Hebrew Bible) translation that JPS aims to publish in 2022. Its impetus is the evolution in English usage in the intervening decades, particularly with regard to the pronouns "he/him/his" and the noun "man." Because those terms are seldom used with gender-inclusive force anymore, our adaptation focuses on representing the text's gender implications both clearly and precisely. That is, the translators strive to give the contemporary audience the same picture regarding gender as was evoked for the text's original ancient audience, given the predictable interactions between the text and each audience's likely assumptions of what went without saying.

As depicted in wisdom literature, the Deity engages with human behavior mainly as judge, and not in a specifically gendered manner. Hence this translation avoids masculine pronouns for references to God, and its default representation of God's ineffable personal name (*YHVH* in Hebrew) is the familiar non-gendered term GOD, that is, with small capitals to signal that it should be regarded as a name.

In its references to human beings, the Book of Proverbs deals in social stereotypes. Its conceit is to educate young minds toward what is *conventional*. In that world, the Deity engaged with human behavior as judge, but not in a particularly gendered manner—as this translation reflects. Mothers were often the teachers of ethical and practical wisdom for both daughters and sons (see Proverbs 1:8, 6:20, 31:26). Conceivably some Israelite young women learned to be scribes (as is attested in Mesopotamia) and thus were educated with wisdom teachings. Nonetheless, in its final form the Book of Proverbs addresses a young male student/son, who is being groomed to govern a household successfully and perhaps even for an advisory role in the king's court. Whenever a social or religious role is in view in this book, it either is not specifically gendered, or is manly, or is viewed from a man's point of view. As the commentator Michael V. Fox underscores, "Proverbs speaks to males and their concerns."[1]

We therefore translate according to that presumed communication context—while noting that this focus on the lot of a young man is a matter of specification of the topic; it does not imply that only males were deemed worthy of wisdom education. Our adaptation uses gendered terms where the context seems to require it, with enough frequency so that the audience will recall that its dramatic voice is directed at a young man.

This ancient book repeatedly employs three pedagogic or rhetorical devices that affect how gender considerations are rendered into English. One device is the aforementioned recourse to social stereotypes. When a certain type of person is brought into view, it often suggests a specific associated gender within Israelite society. If it cannot be assumed that the contemporary audience will reliably recognize the implicit gender, the translation gives hints of varying explicitness, as needed. Non-gendered renderings thus can mean either that gender is not restricted or that the intended restriction of gender goes without saying—just as in normal English parlance.

The second relevant device in Proverbs is the reinforcement of an intended contrast in human behaviors via grammatical means: a paired singular-versus-plural distinction. More so than NJPS and even other gender-sensitive Bible translations, the present adaptation strives to convey those contrasts in grammatical number. As a result, when the topic is a general observation about life in human society or an aspect of the human condition, phrases in the singular often need to be recast (relative to NJPS) in order to avoid masculine pronouns (rather than presented with gender-inclusive plural forms). Meanwhile in other cases, when a contrast in number was not germane, we rendered some singular terms in the plural—as NJPS had done—not only for the sake of gender neutrality but also because it often yielded a more natural English expression.

The third relevant literary device is the lifting up of various types of people as a role model, both positive and negative. The pedagogic goal appears to be that the student psychically *identify with* such figures—so that he pictures himself in that role. Because the student is presumed to be male, this device gives such references to role models a specificity that is implicitly gendered as manly. To the extent that such a gender distinction would not be obvious to the contemporary audience, we adopted an explicitly gendered rendering.

The Book of Proverbs

Chapter 1

1   The proverbs of Solomon son of David, king of Israel:

2   For learning wisdom and discipline;
    For understanding words of discernment;

3   For acquiring the discipline for success,
    Righteousness, justice, and equity;

4   For endowing the simple with shrewdness,
    The young with knowledge and foresight.

5   —The wise, hearing them, will gain more wisdom;
    The discerning will learn to be adroit;

6   For understanding proverb and epigram,
    The words of the wise and their riddles.

7   The fear of GOD is the beginning of knowledge;
    Fools despise wisdom and discipline.

8   My son, heed the discipline of your father,
    And do not forsake the instruction of your mother;

9   For they are a graceful wreath upon your head,
    A necklace about your throat.

10 My son, if sinners entice you, do not yield;

11 If they say, "Come with us,
    Let us set an ambush to shed blood,
    Let us lie in wait for the innocent
    (Without cause!)

12 Like Sheol, let us swallow them alive;
    Whole, like those who go down into the Pit.

13 We shall obtain every precious treasure;
    We shall fill our homes with loot.

פרק א

1 מִשְׁלֵי שְׁלֹמֹה בֶן־דָּוִד מֶלֶךְ יִשְׂרָאֵל:

2 לָדַעַת חָכְמָה וּמוּסָר לְהָבִין אִמְרֵי בִינָה:

3 לָקַחַת מוּסַר הַשְׂכֵּל צֶדֶק וּמִשְׁפָּט וּמֵישָׁרִים:

4 לָתֵת לִפְתָאיִם עָרְמָה לְנַעַר דַּעַת וּמְזִמָּה:

5 יִשְׁמַע חָכָם וְיוֹסֶף לֶקַח וְנָבוֹן תַּחְבֻּלוֹת יִקְנֶה:

6 לְהָבִין מָשָׁל וּמְלִיצָה דִּבְרֵי חֲכָמִים וְחִידֹתָם:

7 יִרְאַת יְהֹוָה רֵאשִׁית דָּעַת חָכְמָה וּמוּסָר אֱוִילִים בָּזוּ:

8 שְׁמַע בְּנִי מוּסַר אָבִיךָ וְאַל־תִּטֹּשׁ תּוֹרַת אִמֶּךָ:

9 כִּי | לִוְיַת חֵן הֵם לְרֹאשֶׁךָ וַעֲנָקִים לְגַרְגְּרֹתֶךָ:

10 בְּנִי אִם־יְפַתּוּךָ חַטָּאִים אַל־תֹּבֵא:

11 אִם־יֹאמְרוּ לְכָה אִתָּנוּ נֶאֶרְבָה לְדָם נִצְפְּנָה לְנָקִי חִנָּם:

12 נִבְלָעֵם כִּשְׁאוֹל חַיִּים וּתְמִימִים כְּיוֹרְדֵי בוֹר:

13 כָּל־הוֹן יָקָר נִמְצָא נְמַלֵּא בָתֵּינוּ שָׁלָל:

14 Throw in your lot with us;
   We shall all have a common purse."
15 My son, do not set out with them;
   Keep your feet from their path.
16 For their feet run to evil;
   They hurry to shed blood.
17 In the eyes of every winged creature
   The outspread net means nothing.
18 But they lie in ambush for their own blood;
   They lie in wait for their own lives.
19 Such is the fate of all who pursue unjust gain;
   It takes the life of its possessor.

20 Wisdom cries aloud in the streets,
   Raises her voice in the squares.
21 At the head of the busy streets she calls;
   At the entrance of the gates, in the city, she speaks out:
22 "How long will you simple ones love simplicity,
   You scoffers be eager to scoff,
   You dullards hate knowledge?
23 You are indifferent to my rebuke;
   I will now speak my mind to you,
   And let you know my thoughts.
24 Since you refused me when I called,
   And paid no heed when I extended my hand,
25 You spurned all my advice,
   And would not hear my rebuke,
26 I will laugh at your calamity,
   And mock when terror comes upon you,
27 When terror comes like a disaster,
   And calamity arrives like a whirlwind,
   When trouble and distress come upon you.
28 Then they shall call me but I will not answer;
   They shall seek me but not find me.

גּוֹרָלְךָ תַּפִּיל בְּתוֹכֵנוּ כִּיס אֶחָד יִהְיֶה לְכֻלָּנוּ: 14

בְּנִי אַל־תֵּלֵךְ בְּדֶרֶךְ אִתָּם מְנַע רַגְלְךָ מִנְּתִיבָתָם: 15

כִּי רַגְלֵיהֶם לָרַע יָרוּצוּ וִימַהֲרוּ לִשְׁפָּךְ־דָּם: 16

כִּי־חִנָּם מְזֹרָה הָרָשֶׁת בְּעֵינֵי כָל־בַּעַל כָּנָף: 17

וְהֵם לְדָמָם יֶאֱרֹבוּ יִצְפְּנוּ לְנַפְשֹׁתָם: 18

כֵּן אָרְחוֹת כָּל־בֹּצֵעַ בָּצַע אֶת־נֶפֶשׁ בְּעָלָיו יִקָּח: 19

חָכְמוֹת בַּחוּץ תָּרֹנָּה בָּרְחֹבוֹת תִּתֵּן קוֹלָהּ: 20

בְּרֹאשׁ הֹמִיּוֹת תִּקְרָא בְּפִתְחֵי שְׁעָרִים בָּעִיר אֲמָרֶיהָ תֹאמֵר: 21

עַד־מָתַי | פְּתָיִם תְּאֵהֲבוּ־פֶתִי וְלֵצִים לָצוֹן חָמְדוּ לָהֶם
וּכְסִילִים יִשְׂנְאוּ־דָעַת: 22

תָּשׁוּבוּ לְתוֹכַחְתִּי הִנֵּה אַבִּיעָה לָכֶם רוּחִי אוֹדִיעָה דְבָרַי
אֶתְכֶם: 23

יַעַן קָרָאתִי וַתְּמָאֵנוּ נָטִיתִי יָדִי וְאֵין מַקְשִׁיב: 24

וַתִּפְרְעוּ כָל־עֲצָתִי וְתוֹכַחְתִּי לֹא אֲבִיתֶם: 25

גַּם־אֲנִי בְּאֵידְכֶם אֶשְׂחָק אֶלְעַג בְּבֹא פַחְדְּכֶם: 26

בְּבֹא (כשאוה) [כְשׁוֹאָה] | פַּחְדְּכֶם וְאֵידְכֶם כְּסוּפָה יֶאֱתֶה
בְּבֹא עֲלֵיכֶם צָרָה וְצוּקָה: 27

אָז יִקְרָאֻנְנִי וְלֹא אֶעֱנֶה יְשַׁחֲרֻנְנִי וְלֹא יִמְצָאֻנְנִי: 28

29 Because they hated knowledge,
And did not choose fear of GOD;

30 They refused my advice,
And disdained all my rebukes,

31 They shall eat the fruit of their ways,
And have their fill of their own counsels.

32 The tranquility of the simple will kill them,
And the complacency of dullards will destroy them.

33 But the one who listens to me will dwell in safety,
Untroubled by the terror of misfortune."

29 תַּחַת כִּי־שָׂנְאוּ דָעַת וְיִרְאַת יְהֹוָה לֹא בָחָרוּ:

30 לֹא־אָבוּ לַעֲצָתִי נָאֲצוּ כָּל־תּוֹכַחְתִּי:

31 וְיֹאכְלוּ מִפְּרִי דַרְכָּם וּמִמֹּעֲצֹתֵיהֶם יִשְׂבָּעוּ:

32 כִּי מְשׁוּבַת פְּתָיִם תַּהַרְגֵם וְשַׁלְוַת כְּסִילִים תְּאַבְּדֵם:

33 וְשֹׁמֵעַ לִי יִשְׁכָּן־בֶּטַח וְשַׁאֲנַן מִפַּחַד רָעָה:

On Human Responsibility for a Moral World

For learning wisdom and discipline;
For understanding words of discernment.
　　　—Proverbs 1:2

WE ARE MERELY A VERSE into the Book of Proverbs when we are presented with a statement by King Solomon, the book's suggested author, who presents the first in a series of statements on what it means to receive wisdom and truly imbibe it within one's soul. But herein lies the paradox of Proverbs' earliest chapters: What does it mean to "learn wisdom and discipline"? The book has just begun! At this point, nothing of substance has been presented for us, as faithful readers, especially in terms of wisdom and discipline!

Or has there?

For the purposes of expanding our potential and actualizing it to improve our communities and ourselves, pure intellectual interaction with the world is not enough. Behavioral modification is not enough. Identity work is not enough. Rather, what we need to "learn wisdom and discipline" in realizing the precious nature of moral wisdom is the understanding that human growth is essentially a constant transformation, a transformation that affects people to the core of their being. To embrace transformation is to embrace human responsibility.

And human responsibility is the foundation of morality.

We are free. We are responsible. We are the ones we have been waiting for. We cannot look only to God to save us from our human predicaments. Of course, that sounds like we would give up on God.

Did not God create humans to rely on God for support and guidance during times of great travail? Well, we do not give up on God. However, maybe the question of the ways in which God saves us does not have as simple an answer as we like to imagine.

In his book *Who Needs God?* Rabbi Harold Kushner shares a story precisely about this spiritual disjunction. In this tale, which Rabbi Kushner learned from Elie Wiesel, an imaginary conversation takes place between the human and God. The two parties are in disagreement about the extent of their respective suffering from existence.

> [The human] came before God on His heavenly throne and said to Him, "Which do you think is harder, to be man or to be God?" "Being God is much harder," God answered. "I have a whole universe to worry about, planets and galaxies. All you have to worry about is your family and your job." "True enough," said [the human]. "But You have infinite time and infinite power. The hard part is not doing the job, but doing it within the limits of human strength and human life span." God answered, "You don't know what you're talking about. It's much harder to be God." [The human] replied, "I don't know how You can say that so confidently when You've never been human and I've never been God. What do You say we change places for just one second, so You can know the feeling of being [a human] and I can know what it feels like to be God. Just for one second, that's all, and then we'll change back."[1]

God did not want to change, but the human kept begging and pleading, and finally God relented. They changed places. The human became God, and God became human. And the story goes on to say that once the human sat on the divine throne, the human refused to give God back God's place, and ever since then the human has ruled the world and God has been in exile.

Let's take a look at what could be considered a later "sequel" to this story, namely the later life and development of Moses into a leader. Now, Moses, our teacher, never needs an introduction. But it is important to consider that one of the greatest legacies of Moses's leadership is that unlike the human in Elie Wiesel's story who was simply greedy for power, Moses did the opposite. Moses approached

Pharaoh with trepidation and humility. Indeed, Moses's prophetic innovation was making humility his foremost trait. He was a reluctant leader. If left up to him, Moses would have most likely remained a shepherd in Midian for the remainder of his days tending sheep and livestock, without caring too much about the destiny of an entire people—his people. But the call from the Divine was too great, the task too righteous to ignore.

Yet Moses knew that once his task was assigned, he would have to grow into his role as a leader. It did not come overnight for him—but it came. And when he finally approached the most powerful human leader in the world, Moses was prepared to speak truth to rebut Pharaoh's lies and chicanery, to call Pharaoh out on his callous oppression of the Hebrews, and to demand freedom and justice for a people that deserved to be free to control their destiny.

If Moses had never grasped onto this moment of moral clarity and mission from God, what would the world look like today? If not for his bravery and the courageous leap of faith into true spiritual and ethical responsibility and leadership, would we even have the precepts of moral living that we take for granted on a daily basis?

We have so much to learn from Moses. Moses was alienated and lonely, yet throughout his years as a leader he led with faith. Even in doubt, he cradled faith within him with vigor. Moses had neither military strength nor wealth, but he carried moral truth. Moses had no formal authority; he didn't even possess an ounce of charisma, if we are to believe the biblical descriptions of him, nor did he care for maintaining easy popularity over what was the right course of action. Throughout his tenure as the leader of the Israelites during their wanderings, Moses was steadfast in his moral vision of liberation of and full agency for the Hebrew people.

One thing that we can learn from this characterization of Moses is the importance of unpretentiousness and meekness of ego. Moses has no tombstone where we can honor him. Such a tombstone would ascribe to him a material identity that we might attempt to use as a moral shortcut to come closer to him and the ideals he represents.

However, instead of visiting his grave, we honor him and the One who sent him on his holy mission by speaking moral truth to power, by daring not to prioritize comfort and conformity at the expense of constant ethical growth, and by acknowledging the deepest truths we have inherited: we are ambassadors for love and dignity, paving a path for a redeemed world.

On the theme of female leadership during the time of the Exodus, Rabbi Jonah Pesner writes:

> It would seem that the Torah includes the brief story of Shiphrah and Puah into the longer narrative of the Exodus in order to juxtapose their response to Pharaoh's cruel act of injustice with Egyptian complicity. The presence and power of Puah and Shiphrah make the point clear: resistance to injustice is *always* possible. In the case of our Exodus, even the least powerful are able to thwart a seemingly omnipotent tyrant.[2]

Our spiritual inheritance from Moses, Shiphrah, and Puah calls upon each of us to exercise moral leadership in our own way. "If there is no Torah, there is no worldly occupation [read: social responsibility]."[3] The spirit of this prophetic responsibility is alive within each of us. The Book of Proverbs amplifies this responsibility as part of its opening credo: we are called upon to pursue moral wisdom. This call is heard frequently throughout the Book of Proverbs, as we will see. It is a quiet voice calling us to actualize our individual potential in bringing light to any dark space we encounter. It inspires us to be humble. And it inspires us to be courageous.

Rabbi Rick Jacobs, the president of the Union for Reform Judaism, and Ruth W. Messinger, the former president of American Jewish World Service, write:

> So, we are called upon to act, to do what we can, both at home and abroad, to be that light unto the nations even—or perhaps, particularly—in hard times. We must pursue justice at home, in our own communities, in our own country, in Israel, and throughout the world. Before millions starve in East Africa or new violence erupts in Sudan, we, as Jews, motivated by text, by tradition, and

by history, must heed the call to accept responsibility, to act, and to protest these transgressions. Only in these ways can we take up fully our intended role on this planet, helping to create a world in which we toil for equity and fairness and hope that encourages others so that more and more of us each day are working for the good of the entire globe.[4]

We take responsibility because we know that small actions can have a huge impact. Robert F. Kennedy inspired us to imagine a new future and work to achieve those dreams:

> Some believe there is nothing one man or one woman can do against the enormous array of the world's ills. Yet many of the world's great movements, of thought and action, have flowed from the work of a single man. A young monk began the Protestant reformation, a young general extended an empire from Macedonia to the borders of the earth, and a young woman reclaimed the territory of France. It was a young Italian explorer who discovered the New World, and the thirty-two-year-old Thomas Jefferson who proclaimed that all men are created equal. These men moved the world, and so can we all.[5]

We begin by realizing that we are free and that our freedom gives us a responsibility. This is our subjective freedom. We must recall that in addition to objective freedom, we can work each day for our subjective freedom. One path toward holy internal liberation is to dismiss more and more how others experience us and to deepen our own internal self-cultivated experiences. Such subjective freedom liberates us to work more deeply on matters of objective freedom that concern us all. Together, can we redeem a broken world.

Teachings from a Father and Mother

My son, heed the discipline of your father,
And do not forsake the instruction of your mother.
　　—Proverbs 1:8

THE MITZVAH to honor one's father and mother, commonly listed as the fifth of the Ten Commandments (Exodus 20:12 and Deuteronomy 5:16), is one of the best-recognized moral teachings found within the whole of the Jewish legal canon—partly because honoring one's parents and respecting older generations is an almost universal value, cherished also in societies not influenced by Abrahamic religious values. The need to respect one's parents goes beyond obeying their commands or revering them. The bond between parents and children is potentially sacrosanct, and when tended to with the greatest love, it is akin to the highest levels of the Divine's love of the world.

Yet, as human beings, we are susceptible to being deficient in following this mitzvah as much as any other. Take, for example, the well-known fact that millions of elderly Americans are neglected at that most vulnerable time in the lives. The Book of Proverbs, using the words from the Torah as its base, exhorts us to honor and learn from our parents.[6] Giving up on them is antithetical to the Torah, but an even more pronounced aspect of this ethical precept is the Jewish legal emphasis not only to care for them, but also to honor our parents. This commandment requires us to invest a significant amount of time and energy into caring for and learning from those who brought us into this world.[7]

The ancient mitzvah to honor one's parents, codified into law around the world, impacts the current moment. For example, in July

2013, China required that adult children take care of their parents. The law mandates that they must visit their elderly relatives and are prohibited from insulting, mistreating, or abandoning them, under pain of lawsuit.[8] Wu Ming, who acted as deputy department head in China's Ministry of Civil Affairs, said, "Family members should not ignore and isolate the elderly. And they should come often to visit."[9] Despite the fact that millions of Chinese workers live thousands of miles away from their parents and the reality that the traditional values of filial piety have become more challenging to put into practice, those who fail to take care of their parents are subject to a fine.

In Japan, another country with a long-standing culture of familial reverence, modern legislation assists families to pay for hired caregivers (although they cannot be family members), and many other nations mandate some level of care for the elderly too.[10] For example, in much of the former Soviet Union, the elderly may sue their children for support, and siblings may sue each other to make sure the money is raised and the burden shared.[11] In Western Europe, much is done to help the elderly, typically ensuring that support is available through social insurance programs. The most effective example of this policy is in Norway, where every person who is elderly is guaranteed long-term care.[12]

How do those of us in United States, which has traditionally been reluctant to implement social welfare policies that are taken for granted in Europe, compare to the rest of the industrial world? Unfortunately, the answer is not so well. The state does not provide for long-term care for our elders, and even though a non-trivial number of adult children provide care for their aging parents,[13] the provision of such care usually imposes significant financial, emotional, and physical burdens on the adult children as caregivers.[14]

One bright spot is that many adults can take up to twelve weeks off from work to care for an ill parent (or any other family member) without losing their job under the Family and Medical Leave Act of 1993. But this leave is often without pay. Indeed, much of the cost of elder care is borne privately, rather than through government-funded programs.[15] Therefore, the policies that were meant to ensure protection for those who take care of an elderly parent (or another sick relative) provide an unaffordable option for a vast number of hardworking Americans. It is also lamentable that over half of all nursing home residents pay nursing home costs out of their own savings.[16] After these savings and other resources are spent, many people who stay in nursing homes for long periods eventually become eligible for Medicaid, funds provided by the government to those below the poverty line. While the United States remains a wealthy nation and many Americans can still afford their own care (though frequently with great strain), we should heed the teachings of the Torah and Proverbs and truly honor our parents and provide for them.

The Rabbis accentuate the importance of caring for one's parents in the following story, the message of which was later codified as binding:[17]

> They inquired of Rav Ula, "How far does honoring parents extend?" He said to them, "Go out and see what one [non-Jew] did in Ashkelon. His name was Dama ben Netinah. Once the Sages sought merchandise for a price of sixty myriads, but the key was resting under his father's head, and he did not disturb him. . . . When Rav Dimi came, he said, "Once he was wearing a gold diadem and sitting among the greats of Rome, when his mother came and tore it off him, and hit him over the head and spit in his face, but he did not humiliate her."[18]

Even when mistreated and shamed by a parent, many demands to honor parents still remain,[19] taking the verse of the proverb to its logical end. There are limits, however. As the *Shulchan Aruch* states:

> One whose mother or father breaks down mentally—they must make the effort to behave with them in accordance with their condition until [God] has mercy on them; but if it is not possible for them to stand it, because they have become greatly insane—they may go and leave them behind, so long as they command others to treat them properly.[20]

The Jewish tradition wisely—and prophetically—notes the mental and physical strain that an elderly parent with dementia can impose on a family. However, the same tradition also mandates that we provide some degree of proper care for them. To express this notion in more contemporary terms, we should not force families to go into bankruptcy in order to avoid placing their parents in virtual warehouses where their parents may be neglected and mistreated, but we must provide for affordable, dignified care for our elders, as we see it modeled around the world—in China, in Norway, and beyond, as previously described. Such a notion of honoring and caring for one's parents is also emphasized in *Sefer HaChinuch*, which states:

> Among the bases of this mitzvah [honoring one's father and mother] is the fact that it is proper that a person recognize and bestow kindness upon one who has done them good. A person should realize that their mother and father are the cause of their being in the world, and therefore it is truly proper that they render them all the honor and do them all the service they can.[21]

Indeed, honoring parents is akin to honoring the Divine:

> The Rabbis say: "Three combine in the making of each person: God, the father, and the mother. If people honor their father and mother, God says, 'I ascribe merit to them as if I dwelled among them as if they honored Me.'"[22]

Furthermore, honoring one's parents is tied to obedience to the divine will. Consider a profound midrash where we learn how God and parents partner in creating a child:

> There are three partners in making a person: the Holy One, the father, and the mother. The father supplies the seed of the white substance out of which are formed the child's bones, sinews, nails, the brain in the head, and the white of the eye; the mother supplies the seed of the red substance out of which is formed the skin, flesh, hair, blood, and the black of the eye; and the Holy One gives the child spirit [*ruach*], and soul [*n'shamah*], beauty of features, eyesight and the power of hearing, and the ability to speak and to walk, understanding, and discernment. When one's time to depart from the world approaches, the Holy One takes away one's share and leaves the shares of one's father and mother with them.[23]

If we are unable to honor our parents out of pure love, we should still do it out of self-care. Rabbi Laura Geller explains:

> "Honor your father and your mother, that you may long endure on the land that the Eternal your God is assigning to you" (Exodus 20:12). The Torah doesn't tell us that it is easy or that all the solutions will be elegant. But it does suggest that there is a reward. For me the reward is not that I will necessarily have a longer life, but that I will have a more peaceful heart.[24]

Each person must express gratitude to God and to their parents for their existence. The Malbim suggests that our learning from our parents is so rich because it was our earliest possible experience for the cultivation of our moral character and thus formative on both conscious and unconscious levels.[25]

When the Book of Proverbs reminds us to look after our parents, it is being extremely literal: we must do all we can to look after those who set us on our paths to becoming adults, finding protection and shouldering responsibilities in this world, and developing the necessary tools to become whoever we are today and supposed to be tomorrow. Therefore, we should do all we can to ensure that our parents are venerated through deeds of duty, deeds of compassion, and deeds of true love. With respect, we can learn from them and pass their deepest virtues and wisdom forward to the next generation.

Chapter 2

1 My son, if you accept my words
   And treasure up my commandments;
2 If you make your ear attentive to wisdom
   And your mind open to discernment;
3 If you call to understanding
   And cry aloud to discernment,
4 If you seek it as you do silver
   And search for it as for treasures,
5 Then you will understand the fear of GOD
   And attain knowledge of God.
6 For GOD grants wisdom;
   Knowledge and discernment are by God's decree.
7 Ability is reserved for the upright
   And [God] is a shield for those who live blamelessly,
8 Guarding the paths of justice,
   Protecting the way of those who are loyal.
9 You will then understand what is right, just,
   And equitable—every good course.
10 For wisdom will enter your mind
   And knowledge will delight you.
11 Foresight will protect you,
   And discernment will guard you.
12 It will save you from an evildoer's ways,
   From a man who speaks duplicity—
13 Those who leave the paths of rectitude
   To follow the ways of darkness,
14 Who rejoice in doing evil
   And exult in an evildoer's duplicity,

פרק ב

1 בְּנִי אִם־תִּקַּח אֲמָרֵי וּמִצְוֺתַי תִּצְפֹּן אִתָּךְ:

2 לְהַקְשִׁיב לַחָכְמָה אָזְנֶךָ תַּטֶּה לִבְּךָ לַתְּבוּנָה:

3 כִּי אִם לַבִּינָה תִקְרָא לַתְּבוּנָה תִּתֵּן קוֹלֶךָ:

4 אִם־תְּבַקְשֶׁנָּה כַכָּסֶף וְכַמַּטְמוֹנִים תַּחְפְּשֶׂנָּה:

5 אָז תָּבִין יִרְאַת יְהוָה וְדַעַת אֱלֹהִים תִּמְצָא:

6 כִּי־יְהוָה יִתֵּן חָכְמָה מִפִּיו דַּעַת וּתְבוּנָה:

7 (וצפן) [וְצָפַן] לַיְשָׁרִים תּוּשִׁיָּה מָגֵן לְהֹלְכֵי תֹם:

8 לִנְצֹר אָרְחוֹת מִשְׁפָּט וְדֶרֶךְ חֲסִידָו יִשְׁמֹר:

9 אָז תָּבִין צֶדֶק וּמִשְׁפָּט וּמֵישָׁרִים כָּל־מַעְגַּל־טוֹב:

10 כִּי־תָבוֹא חָכְמָה בְלִבֶּךָ וְדַעַת לְנַפְשְׁךָ יִנְעָם:

11 מְזִמָּה תִּשְׁמֹר עָלֶיךָ תְּבוּנָה תִנְצְרֶכָּה:

12 לְהַצִּילְךָ מִדֶּרֶךְ רָע מֵאִישׁ מְדַבֵּר תַּהְפֻּכוֹת:

13 הַעֹזְבִים אָרְחוֹת יֹשֶׁר לָלֶכֶת בְּדַרְכֵי־חֹשֶׁךְ:

14 הַשְּׂמֵחִים לַעֲשׂוֹת רָע יָגִילוּ בְּתַהְפֻּכוֹת רָע:

15 All whose paths are crooked
   And who are devious in their course.
16 It will save you from the forbidden woman,
   From the alien woman whose talk is smooth,
17 Who forsakes the companion of her youth
   And disregards the covenant of her God.
18 Her house sinks down to Death,
   And her course leads to the shades.
19 All who go to her cannot return
   And find again the paths of life.

20 So follow the way of the good
   And keep to the paths of the just.
21 For the upright will inhabit the earth,
   The blameless will remain in it,
22 While the wicked will vanish from the land
   And the treacherous will be rooted out of it.

15 אֲשֶׁר אָרְחֹתֵיהֶם עִקְּשִׁים וּנְלוֹזִים בְּמַעְגְּלוֹתָם:

16 לְהַצִּילְךָ מֵאִשָּׁה זָרָה מִנָּכְרִיָּה אֲמָרֶיהָ הֶחֱלִיקָה:

17 הַעֹזֶבֶת אַלּוּף נְעוּרֶיהָ וְאֶת־בְּרִית אֱלֹהֶיהָ שָׁכֵחָה:

18 כִּי שָׁחָה אֶל־מָוֶת בֵּיתָהּ וְאֶל־רְפָאִים מַעְגְּלֹתֶיהָ:

19 כָּל־בָּאֶיהָ לֹא יְשׁוּבוּן וְלֹא־יַשִּׂיגוּ אָרְחוֹת חַיִּים:

20 לְמַעַן תֵּלֵךְ בְּדֶרֶךְ טוֹבִים וְאָרְחוֹת צַדִּיקִים תִּשְׁמֹר:

21 כִּי־יְשָׁרִים יִשְׁכְּנוּ־אָרֶץ וּתְמִימִים יִוָּתְרוּ בָהּ:

22 וּרְשָׁעִים מֵאֶרֶץ יִכָּרֵתוּ וּבוֹגְדִים יִסְּחוּ מִמֶּנָּה:

On Righteousness and Justice

You will then understand what is right, just,
And equitable—every good course.
For wisdom will enter your mind
And knowledge will delight you.
—Proverbs 2:9–10

IT IS NOT A SECRET that the Hebrew Scriptures, in passages well beyond our verse, are obsessed with justice. Not only does Deuteronomy demand a communal pursuit of justice (Deuteronomy 16:20), but even in an early story describing a classic confrontation between Abraham and God regarding the future of the city of Sodom (Genesis 18:20–32), the Torah has Abraham remind the Divine of the centrality of divine rectitude and the concomitant need for God to mete out justice justly. Postbiblical Jewish tradition is also focused tightly on the need to pursue and seek justice. So focal is the concept of justice in Jewish learning and practice that it has become the dominant trope for the dialogue of prayers between humans and the Divine on the holiest days of the Jewish year. Jewish thought even presumes that the sense of justice that God demands of humans is inherently divine—that our sense of justice is a gift from God.

But even justice without righteousness behind it is only an aspirational, abstract form of justice. The verse from the Book of Proverbs here seals the bond between the two values of justice and righteous action. A just society is dependent upon the actions and behavior of each individual, as well as upon the actions and behaviors of the society as an interconnected whole. On this idea, Rabbi Abraham Isaac HaKohen Kook writes:

> The essence of the entire Torah in all its expansiveness is found
> in the individual soul, in its perfected aspects and its flaws, in its
> ascents and descents, and after that, the individual soul is found
> interwoven with the whole; then the essence of the whole, in the
> entire world and in being is recognized as dependent on the perfec-
> tion of each individual's moral behavior.[1]

The refined soul is needed to have a clear moral compass. In addition
to the soul, it is the action and souls of others that guide us. As Rabbi
Kook explains, the individual and collective are connected: "The
same happens on a larger scale in all of creation, in all the worlds and
what happens to all the worlds happens to every [person] as well."[2]

The Vilna Gaon, one of the most highly regarded Jewish minds of
all time, argued that the totality of one's worship of God is made up
by a person's ability to refine their character.[3] This is to say that the
basis of our everyday spiritual work is character development. In this
way the motivation for moral and just action emerges from our very
being. The way we walk in the world is as important as the direction
in which we are walking. Taking this point even further, Maimonides
argues that it is not an ordinary meta-ethical principle but a "biblical
commandment" (*mitzvah d'oraita*) to emulate the compassionate
ways of God.[4] Cultivating a kind and compassionate soul is not only
helpful for our relationships, but it is the basis of the Jewish enter-
prise and constitutes the foundation of righteous action.

We should not only consult traditional sources to learn how to
cultivate compassionate and kind souls in the world; we must also
look to the Torah of our time. Revelation is ongoing; it is a constant
process. This can be experienced observing our scientific progress,
intellectual developments, new spiritual understandings, and the
shifts of our social paradigms. A midrash says that there were parts of
the Torah that were not revealed to Moses but that were revealed to
Rabbi Akiva over a millennium later.[5] At each moment, we have new
opportunities to learn truth and refinement; each new and unique
situation provides an opportunity for learning and refinement and
impacts our relationship to God and God's word. If we look only to

the traditional sources, how can we understand contemporary issues such as capitalistic conundrums, issues of trans rights, housing laws, internet privacy, and the potential ethical dilemmas of the future? We must expose ourselves to contemporary understandings and reflections to be able to make sense of the current moment. After all, Jewish wisdom instructs that the path to the Divine is through ethics, through human relationships, through a dialogue with the world. Rabbenu Asher, for example, writes, "The Holy and Blessed One values more those mitzvot through which the needs of people are satisfied than those that are strictly between a person and the Creator,"[6] and we also learn that "stealing from another person is worse than stealing from the Temple."[7] The prioritization of social justice is pervasive throughout Jewish literature.

> Rabbi Yochanan taught, "See how powerful are the sins of personal violence; for the generation of the Flood committed every transgression possible, but their sentence was not sealed until they got involved in larceny, as it says: 'For the earth is filled with lawlessness because of them: I am about to destroy them with the earth'" (Genesis 6:13).[8]

As the first part of our verse in Proverbs states, we must be tireless advocates for what is "right, just, and equitable." At the same time, we have to seek the wisdom and knowledge of our souls and minds, so that our souls will delight and our hearts will be compassionate and kind.

Chapter 3

1 My son, do not forget my teaching,
   But let your mind retain my commandments;
2 For they will bestow on you length of days,
   Years of life and well-being.
3 Let fidelity and steadfastness not leave you;
   Bind them about your throat,
   Write them on the tablet of your mind,
4 And you will find favor and approbation
   In the eyes of God and human beings.
5 Trust in GOD with all your heart,
   And do not rely on your own understanding.
6 In all your ways acknowledge [God],
   And your paths will be made smooth.
7 Do not be wise in your own eyes;
   Fear GOD and shun evil.
8 It will be a cure for your body,
   A tonic for your bones.
9 Honor GOD with your wealth,
   With the best of all your income,
10 And your barns will be filled with grain,
   Your vats will burst with new wine.
11 Do not reject the discipline of GOD, my son;
   Do not abhor [God]'s rebuke.
12 For whom GOD loves, [God] rebukes,
   As a father the son whom he favors.

פרק ג

1 בְּנִי תּוֹרָתִי אַל־תִּשְׁכָּח וּמִצְוֹתַי יִצֹּר לִבֶּךָ:

2 כִּי אֹרֶךְ יָמִים וּשְׁנוֹת חַיִּים וְשָׁלוֹם יוֹסִיפוּ לָךְ:

3 חֶסֶד וֶאֱמֶת אַל־יַעַזְבֻךָ קָשְׁרֵם עַל־גַּרְגְּרוֹתֶיךָ כָּתְבֵם עַל־לוּחַ לִבֶּךָ:

4 וּמְצָא־חֵן וְשֵׂכֶל־טוֹב בְּעֵינֵי אֱלֹהִים וְאָדָם:

5 בְּטַח אֶל־יְהֹוָה בְּכָל־לִבֶּךָ וְאֶל־בִּינָתְךָ אַל־תִּשָּׁעֵן:

6 בְּכָל־דְּרָכֶיךָ דָעֵהוּ וְהוּא יְיַשֵּׁר אֹרְחֹתֶיךָ:

7 אַל־תְּהִי חָכָם בְּעֵינֶיךָ יְרָא אֶת־יְהֹוָה וְסוּר מֵרָע:

8 רִפְאוּת תְּהִי לְשָׁרֶּךָ וְשִׁקּוּי לְעַצְמוֹתֶיךָ:

9 כַּבֵּד אֶת־יְהֹוָה מֵהוֹנֶךָ וּמֵרֵאשִׁית כָּל־תְּבוּאָתֶךָ:

10 וְיִמָּלְאוּ אֲסָמֶיךָ שָׂבָע וְתִירוֹשׁ יְקָבֶיךָ יִפְרֹצוּ:

11 מוּסַר יְהֹוָה בְּנִי אַל־תִּמְאָס וְאַל־תָּקֹץ בְּתוֹכַחְתּוֹ:

12 כִּי אֶת־אֲשֶׁר יֶאֱהַב יְהֹוָה יוֹכִיחַ וּכְאָב אֶת־בֵּן יִרְצֶה:

13 Happy is the one who finds wisdom,
   The one who attains understanding.
14 Her value in trade is better than silver,
   Her yield, greater than gold.
15 She is more precious than rubies;
   All of your goods cannot equal her.
16 In her right hand is length of days,
   In her left, riches and honor.
17 Her ways are pleasant ways,
   And all her paths, peaceful.
18 She is a tree of life to those who grasp her,
   And whoever holds on to her is happy.

19 GOD founded the earth by wisdom
   And established the heavens by understanding;
20 By GOD's knowledge the depths burst apart,
   And the skies distilled dew.
21 My son, do not lose sight of them;
   Hold on to resourcefulness and foresight.
22 They will give life to your spirit
   And grace to your throat.
23 Then you will go your way safely
   And not injure your feet.
24 When you lie down you will be unafraid;
   You will lie down and your sleep will be sweet.
25 You will not fear sudden terror
   Or the disaster that comes upon the wicked,
26 For GOD will be your trust
   And will keep your feet from being caught.

אַשְׁרֵי אָדָם מָצָא חׇכְמָה וְאָדָם יָפִיק תְּבוּנָה: 13

כִּי טוֹב סַחְרָהּ מִסְּחַר־כָּסֶף וּמֵחָרוּץ תְּבוּאָתָהּ: 14

יְקָרָה הִיא (מפניים) [מִפְּנִינִים] וְכׇל־חֲפָצֶיךָ לֹא יִשְׁווּ־בָהּ: 15

אֹרֶךְ יָמִים בִּימִינָהּ בִּשְׂמֹאולָהּ עֹשֶׁר וְכָבוֹד: 16

דְּרָכֶיהָ דַרְכֵי־נֹעַם וְכׇל־נְתִיבוֹתֶיהָ שָׁלוֹם: 17

עֵץ־חַיִּים הִיא לַמַּחֲזִיקִים בָּהּ וְתֹמְכֶיהָ מְאֻשָּׁר: 18

יְהֹוָה בְּחׇכְמָה יָסַד־אָרֶץ כּוֹנֵן שָׁמַיִם בִּתְבוּנָה: 19

בְּדַעְתּוֹ תְּהוֹמוֹת נִבְקָעוּ וּשְׁחָקִים יִרְעֲפוּ־טָל: 20

בְּנִי אַל־יָלֻזוּ מֵעֵינֶיךָ נְצֹר תֻּשִׁיָּה וּמְזִמָּה: 21

וְיִהְיוּ חַיִּים לְנַפְשֶׁךָ וְחֵן לְגַרְגְּרֹתֶיךָ: 22

אָז תֵּלֵךְ לָבֶטַח דַּרְכֶּךָ וְרַגְלְךָ לֹא תִגּוֹף: 23

אִם־תִּשְׁכַּב לֹא־תִפְחָד וְשָׁכַבְתָּ וְעָרְבָה שְׁנָתֶךָ: 24

אַל־תִּירָא מִפַּחַד פִּתְאֹם וּמִשֹּׁאַת רְשָׁעִים כִּי תָבֹא: 25

כִּי־יְהֹוָה יִהְיֶה בְכִסְלֶךָ וְשָׁמַר רַגְלְךָ מִלָּכֶד: 26

27 Do not withhold good from those who deserve it
   When you have the power to do it [for them].

28 Do not say to your fellow, "Come back again;
   I'll give it to you tomorrow," when you have it with you.

29 Do not devise harm against your fellow
   Who lives trustfully with you.

30 Do not quarrel with someone for no cause,
   When they have done you no harm.

31 Do not envy a lawless man,
   Or choose any of his ways;

32 For the one who goes astray is an abomination to GOD,
   But the straightforward are intimates.

33 GOD's curse is on the house of the evildoer,
   But the abode of the righteous is blessed.

34 At scoffers [God] scoffs,
   But the lowly are shown grace.

35 The wise shall obtain honor,
   But dullards get disgrace as their portion.

27 אַל־תִּמְנַע־ט֑וֹב מִבְּעָלָ֑יו בִּהְי֥וֹת לְאֵ֖ל [יָדְךָ֣] (ידיך) לַעֲשֽׂוֹת׃

28 אַל־תֹּ֘אמַ֤ר [לְרֵעֲךָ֨] (לרעיך) ׀ לֵ֣ךְ וָ֭שׁוּב וּמָחָ֣ר אֶתֵּ֑ן וְיֵ֣שׁ אִתָּֽךְ׃

29 אַל־תַּחֲרֹ֣שׁ עַל־רֵעֲךָ֣ רָעָ֑ה וְהֽוּא־יוֹשֵׁ֖ב לָבֶ֣טַח אִתָּֽךְ׃

30 אַל־[תָּרִ֣יב] (תרוב) עִם־אָדָ֣ם חִנָּ֑ם אִם־לֹ֖א גְמָלְךָ֣ רָעָֽה׃

31 אַל־תְּ֭קַנֵּא בְּאִ֣ישׁ חָמָ֑ס וְאַל־תִּ֝בְחַ֗ר בְּכָל־דְּרָכָֽיו׃

32 כִּ֤י תוֹעֲבַ֣ת יְהֹוָ֣ה נָל֑וֹז וְֽאֶת־יְשָׁרִ֥ים סוֹדֽוֹ׃

33 מְאֵרַ֣ת יְ֭הֹוָה בְּבֵ֣ית רָשָׁ֑ע וּנְוֵ֖ה צַדִּיקִ֣ים יְבָרֵֽךְ׃

34 אִם־לַלֵּצִ֥ים הֽוּא־יָלִ֑יץ [וְ֝לַעֲנָוִ֗ים] (ולעניים) יִתֶּן־חֵֽן׃

35 כָּ֭בוֹד חֲכָמִ֣ים יִנְחָ֑לוּ וּ֝כְסִילִ֗ים מֵרִ֥ים קָלֽוֹן׃

The Creation and Application of Wisdom

GOD founded the earth by wisdom
And established the heavens by understanding.
    —Proverbs 3:19

WHEN THE WORLD WAS CREATED, was it created entirely as matter ("earth," "waters," etc.), or was there something else infused into this divine sculpture of place and space? A reading of the verse here in Proverbs seems to suggest that God used God's wisdom to create the world, the heavens, and the intangible ether that connects every atom to each other. The *Tanya*, however, interprets this verse to mean that rather than having God using wisdom to create the world, wisdom is both something within God and something that is featured in all of God's creations, including human beings.[1] As a result, wisdom is found within both God *and* human beings. And it is precisely *that* wisdom within the human being—any human being—that brings us back to the wisdom of the Creator.

This is a vision of the universe based on similarity and partnership between humans and God. It seems like the Chasidic masters merged Spinozian philosophy with quantum mechanics, telling us that since we are all created by God using and sharing a sense of order and holiness—call it "wisdom," call it "a never-ending chain of cosmic coincidences"—even the most foolish among us, in some way or another, experiences the Divine.

The question, then, is how each of us taps into our own wisdom to experience God. For me, as a rabbi, as a teacher, and as a human, the starting place for realizing the potential of inner wisdom lies *within*.

Human development and moral life depend on our ability to pause, reflect, and gain clarity of our affective and cognitive selves. A recent study showed that when confronted with clear choices of right and wrong, people who take the time to think about the issue rather than making a quick, rash decision are five times more likely to pick the *right* thing.[2] By pausing to reflect, we provide ourselves with moral clarity.

We use our power of reflection, our ability to pause, and our considerations of the risks and challenges that we face to shoulder our biggest task in life: to gain control over our emotions as we react to the unknown and unpredictable. While we are not in control of all that life brings us, we are in control of our reactions. Our main task is to break free from the negative emotions of fear, anger, resentment, jealousy, and hate so that we can actualize ourselves in joy, positivity, hope, and love.

A potential strategy to acquire this ability is to become more self-aware. Ronald Heifetz, a professor of leadership at the Harvard Kennedy School, writes, "Knowing how the environment is pulling your strings and playing you is critical to making responsive rather than reactive moves."[3] In other words, becoming aware of your instinctive emotional responses to the circumstances surrounding you is the first step to controlling your emotions. Each moment is an opportunity to learn and prepare for the future. Becoming aware of negative emotions can lead to increased control over them. Rabbi Joseph B. Soloveitchik teaches that negative emotions—once noticed and controlled—can become stimuli for good:

> Of course, love is a great and noble emotion, fostering the social spirit and elevating man, but not always is the loving person capable of meeting the challenge of harsh realities. In certain situations, a disjunctive emotion, such as anger or indignation may become the motivating force for noble and valuable action.[4]

A related challenge is to understand how emotions interconnect. One may, for example, suppress feelings of anger, but how will that affect one's resentment or sadness? One may release one's jealousy, but how will that affect one's yearning? Rabbi Lawrence Kushner writes about the relationship between love and humility in his book *God Was in This Place*:

> The opposite of love is not hate but self-love. Indeed, the paradox of loving seems to be that you get bigger from making yourself smaller. Love cannot be acquired but only given. The love you give is the love you have. And the more people you love, the more love you have.[5]

In other words, as Kushner describes, only by making conscientious sacrifices can one increase love. Often in our daily lives, however, we forget this fact. We find ourselves stuck on cruise control, unable to see beyond the surface. Consider Maimonides's example of when our ignorance of underlying emotions leads us to err. In his *Mishneh Torah*, he claims that "accepting hospitality from someone who does not have enough for oneself verges on stealing. Yet, the recipient might think that one has done nothing wrong, saying, 'Didn't I take only what they offered me?'"[6]

There are certainly times when we are caught in disputes. We get overwhelmed by emotional passion, unaware of the needs of others or even of our surroundings. During these instances we lose the bigger perspective.

What is the kind of wisdom acquired through pausing, controlling our emotions, and growing self-awareness? A parable: Rabbi Chaim of Volozhin, a devout opponent to the spread of Chasidism who led one of the most prominent European yeshivot in the early nineteenth century, was approached with a question regarding a dispute over land. He told the rivals that the land did not belong to either of them and that ultimately they both would belong to it.

Another example demonstrating the gap that might lie between our subjective emotions and the truths found in our immediate surroundings is captured powerfully by the ritual gesture at the end of every Jewish wedding when, at the pinnacle of utmost joy, the groom breaks a glass. The broken glass serves as a reminder to everyone present that material possessions break and are ultimately valueless and that every human story, even the most joyous, includes trauma and loss.

Even though we can never know the full workings of the world around us, through pausing and reflecting we might at least grow more emotionally aware of the needs of others. A Tibetan lama teaches how important it is to be emotionally scrupulous at the bed of the dying:

> I advise everyone to do their best to work out attachment and grief with the dying person before death comes: Cry together, express your love, and say goodbye, but try to finish with this process before the actual moment of death arrives. If possible, it is best if friends and relatives do not show excessive grief at the moment of death, because the consciousness of the dying person is at that moment exceptionally vulnerable.[7]

Indeed, we all yearn to understand something deeper, something beyond ourselves. Rabbi Samson Raphael Hirsch taught that the blessing *HaMalach HaGo-eil*, "the saving angel," traditionally given to children on the festival of Simchat Torah, asks us to be like fish that swim to great depths. Humans who always remain on the surface of things cannot see their whole. Rabbi Jonathan Sacks teaches that "secular wisdom" (his translation of *chochmah*) descibes a mere philosophical education, while true Torah learning teaches "moral wisdom." In his words:

> *Chokhmah* is the truth we discover; Torah is the truth we inherit. *Chokhmah* is the universal language of humankind; Torah is the specific inheritance of the Israel. *Chokhmah* is what we attain by being in the image of God; Torah is what guides Jews as the people of God. *Chokhmah* is acquired by seeing and reasoning; Torah is received by listening and responding. *Chokhmah* tells us what is; Torah tell us what ought to be.[8]

What Rabbi Sacks does not acknowledge is that it is difficult to achieve intellectual synergy of philosophical and moral wisdom, as there are many different and sometimes contradicting kinds of philosophies and perspectives available to us. Not all of these are merely subjective—many are culturally given and hard to transcend. The French-born author Anaïs Nin writes, "We do not see things as they are, we see things as we are."[9] Nin touches on the larger point that for human beings there is no unfiltered reality. All objective data must pass and be processed through the subjective mind to be experienced. This processing is what philosopher Erich Fromm refers to as our "frame of orientation."[10]

While understanding each other may be a societal problem, it is also an individual opportunity. American dancer/choreographer Martha Graham wrote to Agnes DeMille, another American dancer/choreographer, about the importance of individually cultivating our unique wisdom and energy:

> There is a vitality, a life force, a quickening that is translated through you into action. And because there is only one of you in all time, this expression is unique. If you block it, it will never exist through any other medium and be lost. The world will not hear it. It is not your business to determine how good it is; nor how valuable it is; nor how it compares with other expressions. It is your business to keep it yours, clearly and directly, to keep the channel open. You do not even need to believe in yourself or your work. You have to keep open and aware directly to the urges that motivate you. Keep the channel open. . . . There is no satisfaction at any time. There is only a divine dissatisfaction, a blessed unrest that keeps us marching and makes us more alive than others.[11]

Some of us hide from attaining wisdom for this reason—because it is challenging, unsettling, and even disturbing to understand others and ourselves. Others refrain from transformative learning because of the moral responsibilities that would emerge with such new understanding. These concerns are well founded. Once we understand both ourselves and others, once we are able to see the whole of things, including ourselves, we may become very "powerful"—and, that is, very responsible. Consider the wisdom of Marianne Williamson:

Our deepest fear is not that we are inadequate. Our deepest fear is that we are powerful beyond measure. It is our light, not our darkness that frightens us. Actually, who are you not to be? You are a child of God. Your playing small doesn't serve the world. There's nothing enlightened about shrinking so that other people won't feel insecure around you. We were born to make manifest the glory of God that is within us.[12]

When we come to understand our unique position and potential in the world, we can become terrified by how much needs to be done.

To stay focused on learning and growing, we need the positive support of others and to take good care of ourselves. The great philosopher Maimonides teaches that there are two different types of "healing wisdom" that can help to heal a person from sadness and alienation. First, Maimonides suggests reliance on others:

What is a remedy for sicknesses of the soul? Go next to wise people, for they are healers of the soul, healing it by means of temperaments that they teach until they have returned the soul to the good ways. Concerning those who recognize in themselves bad temperaments but do not go to the wise to be cured by them, among them wise Solomon said, "Fools despise wisdom and discipline" (Proverbs 1:7).[13]

And the second kind of "healing wisdom" is found in solitary contemplation:

If one is afflicted with melancholy, one should cure it by listening to songs and various kinds of melodies, by walking in gardens and fine buildings, by sitting before beautiful forms, and by things like this that delight the soul and make the disturbance of melancholy disappear from it. In all this one should aim at making one's body healthy, the goal of one's body's health being that one attain knowledge.[14]

Maimonides teaches that we should put ourselves in beautiful natural environments that elevate the soul sensually and surround ourselves with people of wisdom, positioning ourselves for a lifelong journey of learning.

For the sake of our own health, our most precious relationships, and our success over the course of our all-too-short lives, we must learn to understand and embrace our emotional lives, be it through writing, therapy, or prayer. Only then can we master the emotional cultivation that helps us actualize our moral and spiritual values. We must search for the understanding of others, as well as our moral responsibilities—while embracing our intellectual capabilities, mental faculties, and spiritual yearnings. Through consistent transformative learning, we can develop our intellect, empathy, and dedication to service that subsequently lead each of us to fulfill our unique roles enhancing the world through wisdom.

Chapter 4

1 Sons, heed the discipline of a father;
  Listen and learn discernment,
2 For I give you good instruction;
  Do not forsake my teaching.

3 Once I was a son to my father,
  The tender darling of my mother.
4 He instructed me and said to me,
  "Let your mind hold on to my words;
  Keep my commandments and you will live.
5 Acquire wisdom, acquire discernment;
  Do not forget and do not swerve from my words.
6 Do not forsake her and she will guard you;
  Love her and she will protect you.
7 The beginning of wisdom is—acquire wisdom;
  With all your acquisitions, acquire discernment.
8 Hug her to you and she will exalt you;
  She will bring you honor if you embrace her.
9 She will adorn your head with a graceful wreath;
  Crown you with a glorious diadem."

10 My son, heed and take in my words,
  And you will have many years of life.
11 I instruct you in the way of wisdom;
  I guide you in straight courses.
12 You will walk without breaking stride;
  When you run, you will not stumble.
13 Hold fast to discipline; do not let go;
  Keep it; it is your life.

פרק ד

1 שִׁמְעוּ בָנִים מוּסַר אָב וְהַקְשִׁיבוּ לָדַעַת בִּינָה:

2 כִּי לֶקַח טוֹב נָתַתִּי לָכֶם תּוֹרָתִי אַל־תַּעֲזֹבוּ:

3 כִּי־בֵן הָיִיתִי לְאָבִי רַךְ וְיָחִיד לִפְנֵי אִמִּי:

4 וַיֹּרֵנִי וַיֹּאמֶר לִי יִתְמָךְ־דְּבָרַי לִבֶּךָ שְׁמֹר מִצְוֹתַי וֶחְיֵה:

5 קְנֵה חָכְמָה קְנֵה בִינָה אַל־תִּשְׁכַּח וְאַל־תֵּט מֵאִמְרֵי־פִי:

6 אַל־תַּעַזְבֶהָ וְתִשְׁמְרֶךָּ אֱהָבֶהָ וְתִצְּרֶךָּ:

7 רֵאשִׁית חָכְמָה קְנֵה חָכְמָה וּבְכָל־קִנְיָנְךָ קְנֵה בִינָה:

8 סַלְסְלֶהָ וּתְרוֹמְמֶךָּ תְּכַבֵּדְךָ כִּי תְחַבְּקֶנָּה:

9 תִּתֵּן לְרֹאשְׁךָ לִוְיַת־חֵן עֲטֶרֶת תִּפְאֶרֶת תְּמַגְּנֶךָּ:

10 שְׁמַע בְּנִי וְקַח אֲמָרָי וְיִרְבּוּ לְךָ שְׁנוֹת חַיִּים:

11 בְּדֶרֶךְ חָכְמָה הֹרֵתִיךָ הִדְרַכְתִּיךָ בְּמַעְגְּלֵי־יֹשֶׁר:

12 בְּלֶכְתְּךָ לֹא־יֵצַר צַעֲדֶךָ וְאִם־תָּרוּץ לֹא תִכָּשֵׁל:

13 הַחֲזֵק בַּמּוּסָר אַל־תֶּרֶף נִצְּרֶהָ כִּי־הִיא חַיֶּיךָ:

14 Do not enter on the path of the wicked;
   Do not walk on the way of evildoers.

15 Avoid it; do not pass through it;
   Turn away from it; pass it by.

16 For they cannot sleep unless they have done evil;
   Unless they make someone fall they are robbed of sleep.

17 They eat the bread of wickedness
   And drink the wine of lawlessness.

18 The path of the righteous is like radiant sunlight,
   Ever brightening until noon.

19 The way of the wicked is all darkness;
   They do not know what will make them stumble.

20 My son, listen to my speech;
   Incline your ear to my words.

21 Do not lose sight of them;
   Keep them in your mind.

22 They are life to those who find them,
   Healing for the whole body.

23 More than all that you guard, guard your mind,
   For it is the source of life.

24 Put crooked speech away from you;
   Keep devious talk far from you.

25 Let your eyes look forward,
   Your gaze be straight ahead.

26 Survey the course you take,
   And all your ways will prosper.

27 Do not swerve to the right or the left;
   Keep your feet from evil.

14 בְּאֹרַח רְשָׁעִים אַל־תָּבֹא וְאַל־תְּאַשֵּׁר בְּדֶרֶךְ רָעִים:

15 פְּרָעֵהוּ אַל־תַּעֲבָר־בּוֹ שְׂטֵה מֵעָלָיו וַעֲבֹר:

16 כִּי לֹא יִשְׁנוּ אִם־לֹא יָרֵעוּ וְנִגְזְלָה שְׁנָתָם אִם־לֹא
(יכשולו) [יַכְשִׁילוּ]:

17 כִּי לָחֲמוּ לֶחֶם רֶשַׁע וְיֵין חֲמָסִים יִשְׁתּוּ:

18 וְאֹרַח צַדִּיקִים כְּאוֹר נֹגַהּ הוֹלֵךְ וָאוֹר עַד־נְכוֹן הַיּוֹם:

19 דֶּרֶךְ רְשָׁעִים כָּאֲפֵלָה לֹא יָדְעוּ בַּמֶּה יִכָּשֵׁלוּ:

20 בְּנִי לִדְבָרַי הַקְשִׁיבָה לַאֲמָרַי הַט־אָזְנֶךָ:

21 אַל־יַלִּיזוּ מֵעֵינֶיךָ שָׁמְרֵם בְּתוֹךְ לְבָבֶךָ:

22 כִּי־חַיִּים הֵם לְמֹצְאֵיהֶם וּלְכָל־בְּשָׂרוֹ מַרְפֵּא:

23 מִכָּל־מִשְׁמָר נְצֹר לִבֶּךָ כִּי־מִמֶּנּוּ תּוֹצְאוֹת חַיִּים:

24 הָסֵר מִמְּךָ עִקְּשׁוּת פֶּה וּלְזוּת שְׂפָתַיִם הַרְחֵק מִמֶּךָּ:

25 עֵינֶיךָ לְנֹכַח יַבִּיטוּ וְעַפְעַפֶּיךָ יַיְשִׁרוּ נֶגְדֶּךָ:

26 פַּלֵּס מַעְגַּל רַגְלֶךָ וְכָל־דְּרָכֶיךָ יִכֹּנוּ:

27 אַל־תֵּט־יָמִין וּשְׂמֹאול הָסֵר רַגְלְךָ מֵרָע:

The Middle Path:
The Obligation to Avoid Extremism

Do not swerve to the right or the left;
Keep your feet from evil.
        —Proverbs 4:27

WITH THIS VERSE, the Book of Proverbs plainly encourages us to follow the middle path of moderation and to avoid walking on the paths toward extremes. The verse is an exhortation that is meant to dissuade us from embracing any kind of extremism as a manifestation of holiness. Judaism, which mostly rejects both asceticism and excessiveness, asks us to embrace the holiness of moderation—in essence, to embrace a middle path toward holiness.

We tend to think of clergypersons, Torah scrolls, and synagogue buildings as the realm of the holy. But how do we make our lives holy? What is our holy work?

1. **Pride:** Maimonides, in the middle of his introduction to his commentary on *Pirkei Avot*, writes about the "golden mean" of pride as the path toward a life of holiness. On one hand, too much pride might lead to someone forgetting the needs of others; on the other hand, not enough pride will cause someone to be exploited by others. Only by walking the middle path will one live a life of meaning and service to God.

2. **Coming Close to "the Holy Other":** Many kabbalistic and Chasidic rabbis are known as *hakadosh*—"the holy one"—since they achieved a spiritual and cognitive level that allowed them to draw close to the Divine. Some of us

might perceive of holiness in spiritual proximity to God. Others, like the French philosopher Emmanuel Levinas, understand holiness as the spiritual proximity to other humans, through which we are able to experience and practice a "horizontal" theology. As Levinas puts it, "Holiness represents the moment at which, in the human . . . the concern for the other breaches the concern for the self."[1]

3. **Separatism and Asceticism:** For Nachmanides, attaining holiness is about going "beyond the letter of the law"—*lifnim m'shurat hadin*.[2] He tells us to avoid even those morally ambiguous behaviors that the tradition does not formally prohibit.[3] The Vilna Gaon was another exemplar of individual asceticism, following the concept of *pat b'melach tochal*, that one should "subsist on bread and salt."[4] Social separatism on a communal level may include the spiritual or spatial separating from the nations of the world, based on the biblical argument that the Jewish people should be considered "holy"—"different"—having their own unique mission (Leviticus 20:26).

4. **Communal Ethics:** To me, holiness is about community. Jewish prayer requires a minyan, a "quorum of ten," to recite prayers evoking holiness (the *Kaddish* and the *K'dushah*, for example). Moses tells the Israelite people, *V'lihyot'cha am kadosh l'Adonai Elohecha*—that we are to be "a holy nation to God" (Deuteronomy 26:19). There is an individual level to the communal holiness too, of course: each individual should participate in the collective effort to be a holy nation.

5. **The Good for Its Own Sake:** Many have claimed that the holy Land of Israel was promised to the Jews, who must fully own and possess it. Professor Moshe Halbertal has made the opposite claim, arguing that because the land is holy, it is God's and no person or group of people can ever fully take ownership of it.[5] Halbertal maintains that the holy

is that which cannot be used for any type of gain. The holy is good for its own sake; one should not use what is holy to gain personal benefits. For example, Jewish tradition says that one cannot pass through a synagogue as a shortcut. The holy must be an end in itself, not an instrument for gain. One commits a *chilul* (desecration) when emptying the holy of its sanctity, and one performs a *kiddush* (sanctification) when filling a profane void with that which is "holy"—true and good.[6]

Now, these various models are not mutually exclusive. We can buy into all of them, we can favor some of them over others, or we can ignore them all. Most of us seek to achieve a synthesis of different approaches to holiness.

How should we engage with extremists? Do we ignore them? Should we debate them? What is the right course of action?

To answer this question, I would like to provide a brief story. Over thirty years ago, Rabbi Avi Weiss staged a curious event. He invited Harvard Law School professor Alan Dershowitz to debate the right-wing activist Rabbi Meir Kahane at Weiss's synagogue, the Hebrew Institute of Riverdale. It was, and remains, a fascinating display of contrasts: a liberal law professor and a reactionary politician. In his opening remarks, Dershowitz responded to those who criticized him for debating Kahane:

> I am debating Rabbi Meir Kahane because too few blacks debated and responded to Rev. Jesse Jackson and Louis Farrakhan. I am debating Rabbi Kahane because virtually no Arabs are willing to debate Yasser Arafat. I think it is imperative that the world understand not only that the vast majority of Jews repudiate Rabbi Kahane's views, but also why we repudiate those views.[7]

While Dershowitz's actions in the many years since the debate have come under greater scrutiny, his words are still relevant today. In addition to explaining one's core position, debating violent extremists can, if done with precision, point out the ugliness of those extremist views. And if one has the courage to explain and stand by one's conviction, one can truly undermine the extremist view.

Douglas Murray, founder of the Centre for Social Cohesion in the United Kingdom, writer for the *Spectator*, and currently associate director of the Henry Jackson Society, is a gay, atheist, and neoconservative defender of Western institutions. He accepted a debate, nevertheless, with a radical Muslim group that supported terrorism, subjecting himself to verbal and physical intimidation. After the debate, he stated that free speech is not an easy process and that many audiences would be hostile. Yet, Murray believes that some members of those audiences may be affected in a positive way: "Even if it is just one member of the audience who is receptive to the anti-totalitarian possibility it is vital to do this. It is the reason why I debate." In addition, he noted that debate brings out just how violent extremists are:

> Yesterday showed why bringing them out in the open and challenging their ideas is necessary. It reminds the government, the press and British citizens of the true nature of these fundamentalist thugs who are not just going to disappear. Not since Oswald Mosley's British Union of Fascists (BUF) have we seen intimidation like this on the streets of London. Like the BUF, they will resort to violence the moment their fascist views are challenged.[8]

The failure to debate, or at least debunk, outrageous positions may be perilous. In 2004, John Kerry, who was the Democratic nominee for president during that campaign year, was smeared by the "Swift Boat" campaign that diminished Kerry's experience as a Vietnam War veteran. Although the campaign was funded by partisan extremists and had no factual credence, Kerry's reluctance to face this campaign (and most likely his underestimation of the damage it caused) turned a minor annoyance into a major problem and probably contributed to his defeat.

To engage with someone of a completely different ideology does not need to be viewed as validating their views. In fact, Jewish tradition suggests the opposite: *sh'tikah k'hodaah*, "silence is like assent." It is not engaging but rather disengaging that is viewed as validating.[9]

If not to persuade others, we are to speak up to mark our disagreement with false contentions and harmful propositions. There is a lot at stake in the marketplace of ideas. We must learn to determine when to simply ignore faulty marginal ideas and when to openly confront them.

All of us sometimes find ourselves in narrow places of conformity and agreement. Often we must step out of our respective comfort zones to learn about those who view things differently from us. At specific times, we seem to have no choice other than to debate fundamentalists and extremists. During these times, we must ensure our own safety—physical and emotional—while standing by our convictions. In the famous biblical story of the Exodus, Moses could have merely waged war and led a slave uprising. Alternatively, he could have advocated having the Israelites avoid the risk of resistance by simply remaining slaves. Instead of adopting either extreme, he approached Pharaoh and engaged him in the pursuit of justice. He looked evil in the face without flinching. He took the golden mean.

We, like Moses, can trust in truth and moral values to triumph over vehement extremism if we live our lives in holiness.

Chapter 5

1 My son, listen to my wisdom;
  Incline your ear to my insight,
2 That you may have foresight,
  While your lips hold fast to knowledge.
3 For the lips of a forbidden woman drip honey;
  Her mouth is smoother than oil;
4 But in the end she is as bitter as wormwood,
  Sharp as a two-edged sword.
5 Her feet go down to Death;
  Her steps take hold of Sheol.
6 She does not chart a path of life;
  Her course meanders for lack of knowledge.
7 So now, sons, pay heed to me,
  And do not swerve from the words of my mouth.
8 Keep yourself far away from her;
  Do not come near the doorway of her house
9 Lest you give up your vigor to others,
  Your years to a ruthless one;
10 Lest strangers eat their fill of your strength,
  And your toil be for the house of another;
11 And in the end you roar,
  When your flesh and body are consumed,
12 And say,
  "O how I hated discipline,
  And heartily spurned rebuke.
13 I did not pay heed to my teachers,
  Or incline my ear to my instructors.

פרק ה

1 בְּנִי לְחָכְמָתִי הַקְשִׁיבָה לִתְבוּנָתִי הַט־אָזְנֶךָ:

2 לִשְׁמֹר מְזִמּוֹת וְדַעַת שְׂפָתֶיךָ יִנְצֹרוּ:

3 כִּי נֹפֶת תִּטֹּפְנָה שִׂפְתֵי זָרָה וְחָלָק מִשֶּׁמֶן חִכָּהּ:

4 וְאַחֲרִיתָהּ מָרָה כַלַּעֲנָה חַדָּה כְּחֶרֶב פִּיּוֹת:

5 רַגְלֶיהָ יֹרְדוֹת מָוֶת שְׁאוֹל צְעָדֶיהָ יִתְמֹכוּ:

6 אֹרַח חַיִּים פֶּן־תְּפַלֵּס נָעוּ מַעְגְּלֹתֶיהָ לֹא תֵדָע:

7 וְעַתָּה בָנִים שִׁמְעוּ־לִי וְאַל־תָּסוּרוּ מֵאִמְרֵי־פִי:

8 הַרְחֵק מֵעָלֶיהָ דַרְכֶּךָ וְאַל־תִּקְרַב אֶל־פֶּתַח בֵּיתָהּ:

9 פֶּן־תִּתֵּן לַאֲחֵרִים הוֹדֶךָ וּשְׁנֹתֶיךָ לְאַכְזָרִי:

10 פֶּן־יִשְׂבְּעוּ זָרִים כֹּחֶךָ וַעֲצָבֶיךָ בְּבֵית נָכְרִי:

11 וְנָהַמְתָּ בְאַחֲרִיתֶךָ בִּכְלוֹת בְּשָׂרְךָ וּשְׁאֵרֶךָ:

12 וְאָמַרְתָּ אֵיךְ שָׂנֵאתִי מוּסָר וְתוֹכַחַת נָאַץ לִבִּי:

13 וְלֹא־שָׁמַעְתִּי בְּקוֹל מוֹרָי וְלִמְלַמְּדַי לֹא־הִטִּיתִי אָזְנִי:

14 Soon I was in dire trouble
   Amidst the assembled congregation."

15 Drink water from your own cistern,
   Running water from your own well.

16 Your springs will gush forth
   In streams in the public squares.

17 They will be yours alone,
   Others having no part with you.

18 Let your fountain be blessed:
   Find joy in the wife of your youth—

19 A loving doe, a graceful mountain goat.
   Let her breasts satisfy you at all times;
   Be infatuated with love of her always.

20 Why be infatuated, my son, with a forbidden woman?
   Why clasp the bosom of an alien woman?

21 For everyone's ways are before the eyes of GOD,
   Who surveys their entire course.

22 The wicked man will be trapped in his iniquities;
   He will be caught up in the ropes of his sin.

23 He will die for lack of discipline,
   Infatuated by his great folly.

14 כִּמְעַט הָיִיתִי בְכָל־רָע בְּתוֹךְ קָהָל וְעֵדָה:

15 שְׁתֵה־מַיִם מִבּוֹרֶךָ וְנֹזְלִים מִתּוֹךְ בְּאֵרֶךָ:

16 יָפוּצוּ מַעְיְנֹתֶיךָ חוּצָה בָּרְחֹבוֹת פַּלְגֵי־מָיִם:

17 יִהְיוּ־לְךָ לְבַדֶּךָ וְאֵין לְזָרִים אִתָּךְ:

18 יְהִי־מְקוֹרְךָ בָרוּךְ וּשְׂמַח מֵאֵשֶׁת נְעוּרֶךָ:

19 אַיֶּלֶת אֲהָבִים וְיַעֲלַת־חֵן דַּדֶּיהָ יְרַוֻּךָ בְכָל־עֵת בְּאַהֲבָתָהּ תִּשְׁגֶּה תָמִיד:

20 וְלָמָּה תִשְׁגֶּה בְנִי בְזָרָה וּתְחַבֵּק חֵק נָכְרִיָּה:

21 כִּי נֹכַח | עֵינֵי יְהֹוָה דַּרְכֵי־אִישׁ וְכָל־מַעְגְּלֹתָיו מְפַלֵּס:

22 עַווֹנוֹתָיו יִלְכְּדֻנוֹ אֶת־הָרָשָׁע וּבְחַבְלֵי חַטָּאתוֹ יִתָּמֵךְ:

23 הוּא יָמוּת בְּאֵין מוּסָר וּבְרֹב אִוַּלְתּוֹ יִשְׁגֶּה:

On Death: The Quest for Material Wealth Is Ultimately Meaningless

And in the end you roar,
When your flesh and body are consumed.
—Proverbs 5:11

ONE OF THE CRUEL REALITIES of being human is the foreknowledge that we will one day no longer exist in our physical form. Death is coming for all of us.

The Book of Proverbs does not shy away from this truth. We will all eventually die, and most of us will be forgotten. When we do not fully come to terms with this reality and we fail to be moved by the fact that we have no idea of what to expect after death, contemplating the end of life only invokes deep anxiety and fear. Yet, when we live in accordance with the truths revealed through the deepest embracing of this inevitable reality, we can discover a sublime joy and freedom that is liberating and refreshing.

I have seen death. I have held hands with people who were close to leaving their physical selves. I have also been there when they transcended their earthly bonds. At many deathbeds, I have sensed that the dying person deeply regretted pursuing so much vanity during their limited years of life. So many people expressed belated sorrow that they prioritized fleeting mundane desires over that which was sacred in their lives. While I have given countless sermons decrying the problematic obsession with material wealth in our society, the difficulty posed by this preoccupation only becomes most painful in those last moments when a soul's sparks are already tugging for the eternal bonfire. Throughout the Torah, we witness powerful polemics against materialism, especially at times when there are many people who suffer from poverty. For example, Moses smashes the holy tablets with the word of God written upon them because the tablets lost their sanctity the moment that the receivers had become obsessed with vanity, worshiping a Golden Calf and giving up faith (Exodus 32). The midrash explains that Moses really smashed only empty rocks because the holy letters had already risen from the tablets to the heavens, so that that which was holy was not desecrated by the sight of something unholy.[1]

I believe that the message of this midrash is applicable to today. When some of the most vulnerable human beings on the planet beg for refuge and are instead shamed for being stateless, the earth below us becomes unholy. Their shame is a testimony to our materialism, maintained at the expense of the sanctity of life. To be sure, each day we can and must choose the world of the mundane in order to go about our daily tasks of work, paying our bills, and taking care of our families. But the sacred must be right before our eyes, guiding our actions. If we choose gold instead of holiness, the sanctity simply disappears. Holiness is subjective, relative, and elusive, and it evaporates when one's life priorities are out of order.

Death is coming for us. We need not be paralyzed by fear. We just need to align our life priorities with our deepest values.

The greatest idolatry today appears to be the worship of wealth—an obsession with material possessions. We do not just miss the sacred right before our eyes; we drain the world of its sacred material. Nothing is sacred to us anymore. The holy letters have ascended back to the heavens.

A famous parable that Rabbi Simchah Bunim of Peshischa used to tell his followers also decries materialism.[2] The story tells of a poor Jew from Galicia who dreamed that there was gold under a bridge in Prague, hundreds of miles away. After much thought and anguish, he decided to saddle his horse and head off alone from his house in search of that gold, which would sustain him for the rest of his life. The Jew—let's call him Yankel—got to Prague and found that the bridge about which he dreamed several times was heavily guarded. With no idea what else to do, he simply went underneath the bridge with a shovel and began to dig. Before he broke ground, however, he felt a tap on the shoulder. Yankel turned around and saw a soldier glaring intimidatingly at him. "What are you doing?" said the soldier. Knowing that any evasion was useless, Yankel said, "I dreamed that there was a chest of gold buried here, and I am hoping that it could sustain me and the rest of my family for the remainder of my life." The soldier stared at Yankel with disbelief. "You will not find any treasure here, but I dreamed that there was a large pot of gold under the stove of a poor Jew called Yankel!" Yankel looked at the soldier and said, "I am Yankel!" He rushed back to his house, removed the stove, and began digging. Lo and behold, after a half hour, he found a large chest filled with gold, which helped sustain his family for the rest of his life.

While there are manifold ways to interpret this story, one way is to see Yankel as selfishly absorbed with his family's well-being. Rather than stay in his house and take care of his family on a daily basis, Yankel abandoned them for an extended period of time, forcing his wife and children to fend for themselves with limited means. The irony of the story can be seen as exacerbated by the likelihood that Yankel would have to replace his oven before too long, allowing him then to find the gold buried underneath as a matter of course. And if he had found the gold in Prague, would Yankel ever have returned to his family? We can easily imagine that much of Yankel's drive came from greed and the pursuit of material success. If he were to have stayed with his family and embraced their presence, everything might have turned out just fine, too.

Yankel's tale serves as a story of hope: by searching inside one's house and being committed to one's family, we come across the greatest treasures. May we embrace the sacred values of family and community, putting them before any pursuit of wealth.

Chapter 6

1 My son, if you have stood surety for your fellow,
Given your hand for another,
2 You have been trapped by the words of your mouth,
Snared by the words of your mouth.
3 Do this, then, my son, to extricate yourself,
For you have come into the power of your fellow:
Go grovel—and badger your fellow;
4 Give your eyes no sleep,
Your pupils no slumber.
5 Save yourself like a deer out of the hand [of a hunter],
Like a bird out of the hand of a fowler.

6 Lazybones, go to the ant;
Study its ways and learn.
7 Without leaders, officers, or rulers,
8 It lays up its stores during the summer,
Gathers in its food at the harvest.
9 How long will you lie there, lazybones;
When will you wake from your sleep?
10 A bit more sleep, a bit more slumber,
A bit more hugging yourself in bed,
11 And poverty will come calling upon you,
And want, like a man with a shield.

12 A scoundrel, an evil man
Lives by crooked speech,
13 Winking his eyes,
Shuffling his feet,
Pointing his finger.

פרק ו

1 בְּנִי אִם־עָרַבְתָּ לְרֵעֶךָ תָּקַעְתָּ לַזָּר כַּפֶּיךָ:

2 נוֹקַשְׁתָּ בְאִמְרֵי־פִיךָ נִלְכַּדְתָּ בְּאִמְרֵי־פִיךָ:

3 עֲשֵׂה זֹאת אֵפוֹא | בְּנִי וְהִנָּצֵל כִּי בָאתָ בְכַף־רֵעֶךָ לֵךְ הִתְרַפֵּס וּרְהַב רֵעֶיךָ:

4 אַל־תִּתֵּן שֵׁנָה לְעֵינֶיךָ וּתְנוּמָה לְעַפְעַפֶּיךָ:

5 הִנָּצֵל כִּצְבִי מִיָּד וּכְצִפּוֹר מִיַּד יָקוּשׁ:

6 לֵךְ־אֶל־נְמָלָה עָצֵל רְאֵה דְרָכֶיהָ וַחֲכָם:

7 אֲשֶׁר אֵין־לָהּ קָצִין שֹׁטֵר וּמֹשֵׁל:

8 תָּכִין בַּקַּיִץ לַחְמָהּ אָגְרָה בַקָּצִיר מַאֲכָלָהּ:

9 עַד־מָתַי עָצֵל | תִּשְׁכָּב מָתַי תָּקוּם מִשְּׁנָתֶךָ:

10 מְעַט שֵׁנוֹת מְעַט תְּנוּמוֹת מְעַט | חִבֻּק יָדַיִם לִשְׁכָּב:

11 וּבָא־כִמְהַלֵּךְ רֵאשֶׁךָ וּמַחְסֹרְךָ כְּאִישׁ מָגֵן:

12 אָדָם בְּלִיַּעַל אִישׁ אָוֶן הוֹלֵךְ עִקְּשׁוּת פֶּה:

13 קֹרֵץ בְּעֵינָו מֹלֵל בְּרַגְלָו מֹרֶה בְּאֶצְבְּעֹתָיו:

14 Duplicity is in his heart;
   He plots evil all the time;
   He incites quarrels.
15 Therefore calamity will come upon him without warning;
   Suddenly he will be broken beyond repair.

16 GOD hates six things—
   And abominates seven:
17 A haughty bearing,
   A lying tongue,
   Hands that shed innocent blood,
18 A mind that hatches evil plots,
   Feet quick to run to evil,
19 A false witness testifying lies,
   And one who incites siblings to quarrel.

20 My son, keep your father's commandment;
   Do not forsake your mother's teaching.
21 Tie them over your heart always;
   Bind them around your throat.
22 When you walk it will lead you;
   When you lie down it will watch over you;
   And when you are awake it will talk with you.
23 For the commandment is a lamp,
   The teaching is a light,
   And the way to life is the rebuke that disciplines.
24 It will keep you from an evil woman,
   From the smooth tongue of a forbidden woman.
25 Do not lust for her beauty
   Or let her captivate you with her eyes.
26 The last loaf of bread will go for a harlot;
   A married woman will snare a person of honor.
27 Can anyone rake embers into their bosom
   Without burning their clothes?

14 תַּהְפֻּכ֨וֹת ׀ בְּלִבּ֗וֹ חֹרֵ֣שׁ רָ֣ע בְּכָל־עֵ֑ת (מדנים) [מִדְיָנִ֥ים]
יְשַׁלֵּֽחַ:

15 עַל־כֵּ֗ן פִּ֭תְאֹם יָב֣וֹא אֵיד֑וֹ פֶּ֥תַע יִ֝שָּׁבֵ֗ר וְאֵ֣ין מַרְפֵּֽא:

16 שֶׁשׁ־הֵ֭נָּה שָׂנֵ֣א יְהוָ֑ה וְ֝שֶׁ֗בַע (תועבות) [תּוֹעֲבַ֥ת] נַפְשֽׁוֹ:

17 עֵינַ֣יִם רָ֭מוֹת לְשׁ֣וֹן שָׁ֑קֶר וְ֝יָדַ֗יִם שֹׁפְכ֥וֹת דָּם־נָקִֽי:

18 לֵ֗ב חֹ֭רֵשׁ מַחְשְׁב֣וֹת אָ֑וֶן רַגְלַ֥יִם מְ֝מַהֲר֗וֹת לָר֥וּץ לָרָעָֽה:

19 יָפִ֣יחַ כְּ֭זָבִים עֵ֣ד שָׁ֑קֶר וּמְשַׁלֵּ֥חַ מְ֝דָנִ֗ים בֵּ֣ין אַחִֽים:

20 נְצֹ֣ר בְּ֭נִי מִצְוַ֣ת אָבִ֑יךָ וְאַל־תִּ֝טֹּ֗שׁ תּוֹרַ֥ת אִמֶּֽךָ:

21 קָשְׁרֵ֥ם עַל־לִבְּךָ֣ תָמִ֑יד עָ֝נְדֵ֗ם עַל־גַּרְגְּרֹתֶֽךָ:

22 בְּהִתְהַלֶּכְךָ֨ ׀ תַּנְחֶ֬ה אֹתָ֗ךְ בְּֽ֭שָׁכְבְּךָ תִּשְׁמֹ֣ר עָלֶ֑יךָ וַ֝הֲקִיצ֗וֹתָ
הִ֣יא תְשִׂיחֶֽךָ:

23 כִּ֤י נֵ֣ר מִ֭צְוָה וְת֣וֹרָה א֑וֹר וְדֶ֥רֶךְ חַ֝יִּ֗ים תּוֹכְח֥וֹת מוּסָֽר:

24 לִ֭שְׁמָרְךָ מֵאֵ֣שֶׁת רָ֑ע מֵֽ֝חֶלְקַ֗ת לָשׁ֥וֹן נָכְרִיָּֽה:

25 אַל־תַּחְמֹ֣ד יָ֭פְיָהּ בִּלְבָבֶ֑ךָ וְאַל־תִּ֝קָּחֲךָ֗ בְּעַפְעַפֶּֽיהָ:

26 כִּ֤י בְעַד־אִשָּׁ֥ה זוֹנָ֗ה עַֽד־כִּכַּ֫ר לָ֥חֶם וְאֵ֥שֶׁת אִ֑ישׁ נֶ֝֗פֶשׁ
יְקָרָ֥ה תָצֽוּד:

27 הֲיַחְתֶּ֤ה אִ֓ישׁ אֵ֬שׁ בְּחֵיק֑וֹ וּ֝בְגָדָ֗יו לֹ֣א תִשָּׂרַֽפְנָה:

28 Can anyone walk on live coals
   Without scorching their feet?

29 It is the same with the man who sleeps with his fellow's wife;
   No one who touches her will go unpunished.

30 A thief is not held in contempt
   For stealing to appease his hunger;

31 Yet if caught he must pay sevenfold;
   He must give up all he owns.

32 He who commits adultery is devoid of sense;
   Only one who would destroy himself does such a thing.

33 He will meet with disease and disgrace;
   His reproach will never be expunged.

34 The fury of the husband will be passionate;
   He will show no pity on his day of vengeance.

35 He will not have regard for any ransom;
   He will refuse your bribe, however great.

28 אִם־יְהַלֵּךְ אִישׁ עַל־הַגֶּחָלִים וְרַגְלָיו לֹא תִכָּוֶינָה׃

29 כֵּן הַבָּא אֶל־אֵשֶׁת רֵעֵהוּ לֹא יִנָּקֶה כָּל־הַנֹּגֵעַ בָּהּ׃

30 לֹא־יָבוּזוּ לַגַּנָּב כִּי יִגְנוֹב לְמַלֵּא נַפְשׁוֹ כִּי יִרְעָב׃

31 וְנִמְצָא יְשַׁלֵּם שִׁבְעָתָיִם אֶת־כָּל־הוֹן בֵּיתוֹ יִתֵּן׃

32 נֹאֵף אִשָּׁה חֲסַר־לֵב מַשְׁחִית נַפְשׁוֹ הוּא יַעֲשֶׂנָּה׃

33 נֶגַע־וְקָלוֹן יִמְצָא וְחֶרְפָּתוֹ לֹא תִמָּחֶה׃

34 כִּי־קִנְאָה חֲמַת־גָּבֶר וְלֹא־יַחְמוֹל בְּיוֹם נָקָם׃

35 לֹא־יִשָּׂא פְּנֵי כָל־כֹּפֶר וְלֹא־יֹאבֶה כִּי תַרְבֶּה־שֹׁחַד׃

On Natural Morality

Lazybones, go to the ant;
Study its ways and learn.
Without leaders, officers, or rulers,
It lays up its stores during the summer,
Gathers in its food at the harvest.
　　　—Proverbs 6:6–8

THE INDIVIDUAL BEING addressed in this passage—the "lazy-bones"—is neither a scholar nor the most reflective of people, but one who wanders through life without thinking too much about its structure or following any guidance. The text points out that by simply observing the world around us, we can learn about ourselves and for ourselves. What are the characteristics and mechanisms of what we call "Jewish learning"?

Religiosity has two crucial components: outward engagement with the world and spiritual introspection. The external component must be the dominant one: we are to observe, study, and learn intellectually from our texts, ritual, community, and social problems; but in addition to this outward element of religious practice, we must look inside ourselves, cultivate spirituality, and nurture our own reason and faith.

Each of us has to find our authentic calling. In the twenty-first century, the most crucial need for the Jewish people is to learn how to connect an outer religious life with an inner religious life more deeply. We can only do the messy work of the world if we have done the messy work inside ourselves. This work requires respect and nourishment for our natural morality—the potential that was placed within us at Creation. However, each of us also has to study the ways of Creation—of nature and its inherent morality and laws—itself.

This perspective dominates the work of Rabbi Y'hudah HaLevi. HaLevi, an influential medieval Jewish philosopher and poet, proposed that spiritual practices and virtues are distinct from natural or intellectual ones, and he argued that the natural law, which all humans can comprehend without revelation, precedes the divine law. It cannot be neglected in religious life; instead, it must be seen as part of religious life and thought. For HaLevi, complying with revealed law but not with norms of natural morality constitutes a failure to fulfill core human responsibilities. He explains that God gets upset with people who ignore the obligations of natural law:

> When Israel's rebelliousness reached the point of disregarding even the indispensable intellectual and governmental laws . . . but held fast to the ritual acts pertaining to the sacrifices and the other divine and traditional laws, God became satisfied with less from them.[1]

To be sure, human intellectual reasoning pales in comparison with the moral understanding one can gain through spiritual revelation, but HaLevi believed in the primacy of what he called intellectual law: "For the divine law can only be fulfilled completely after perfect adherence to the governmental and intellectual law has been achieved."[2]

HaLevi ends by referencing what is perhaps our most noble religious imperative: "What does the Eternal require of you but to do justice, to love kindness, and to walk humbly with your God?" (Micah 6:8). According to HaLevi, Jewish tradition and law demand us to follow basic, natural, and intellectually sensible moral guidelines.

Now, HaLevi was not the first to suggest the connection between Jewish religious law and natural morality; the Sages of the Talmud preceded him by centuries. To quote a Talmudic saying ascribed to Rabbi Yochanan, "Had the Torah not been given, we would have learned modesty from a cat, [the prohibition of] theft from an ant, [the prohibition of] adultery from the dove, the proper [sexual] conduct from a rooster."[3] Already in one of the earliest passages in the Torah, in the story of Creation, God calls the human being, above all other creatures, "very good" (Genesis 1:31). Humans are good because they can constantly grow their capacity for moral intuition, conscience, reason, and empathy. "The laws of our Torah must agree with reason and common sense."[4]

Throughout our spiritual lives, we encounter opportunities to engage on four primary levels of "repair," *tikkun*: repair of the self (*tikkun atzmi*), repair of the home (*tikkun bayit*), repair of the community (*tikkun kahal*), and, perhaps the best known, *tikkun olam* (repair of the world).[5] Religious life without all four of these levels of religious repair lacks spiritual efficacy and authenticity. Rabbi HaLevi's reminder of the significance of a natural and sensible morality compels us to tackle the task of observance, studying, learning, and engaging with the natural and material world. This will allow us to truly change ourselves, the Jewish community, and the world. Once we have allowed our learning to become internalized, we must have the courage to allow ourselves to be guided by the internal moral compass that God has placed inside of us.

Perhaps the greatest modern proponent of natural morality was Rabbi Abraham Isaac HaKohen Kook (1865–1935), the first chief rabbi of British Mandatory Palestine, who writes:

> Morality, in its natural state, with all its profound splendor and might, must be fixed in the soul, so that it may serve as a substratum for the great effects emanating from the strength of Torah. . . . Every element of Torah must be preceded by *derech eretz* [basic ethical decency].[6]

Rabbi Avraham Yeshaya Karelitz, known as the Chazon Ish (1878–1953, Belarus and Israel), focused on the following distinction in his book, *Emunah uBitachon* (faith and trust): There is an important distinction between the Torah's will (*r'tzon haTorah*) and God's will (*r'tzon HaShem*): God's will encompasses more than simply the Torah's will. There are clear ethical mandates that cannot be found in biblical verses. Even though the Torah does not expressly forbid harming animals, the medieval rabbis, wise leaders, knew that it had to be *r'tzon HaShem* even if it was not explicitly *r'tzon haTorah*. Our natural morality helps us to discover *r'tzon HaShem*.

When, as Jews, we do not cultivate our internal moral compasses, we risk becoming irrelevant as a people. Rabbis and educators encouraging a "slide to the right" that prioritizes ritual observance over social responsibility not only misrepresent the Torah; they put the future relevance of Jewish law and morality at risk.[7] The most remarkable calling of Judaism is to engage in the world as exemplary moral beings—to strive toward the betterment of ourselves and toward the betterment of all humanity.

While there are certainly elements of Jewish thought supporting the view that Jewish ritual observance aims at nothing other than teaching us obedience, there are also those arguing that the principal concern of Jewish ritual law is the cultivation of one's moral character and that the development of personal conscience must be more central than pure obedience.[8] Rabbinic lore emphasizes that the purpose of the mitzvot is to refine our character.[9] That refinement is not some mysterious mystical process achieved through blind obedience and submission to authorities, but rather a process of intellectual and spiritual deliberation.

When we feel desperate for guidance and simple solutions, we might want to turn to experts whose wisdom we can rely on. However, it is important for us to exercise great caution not to conceive of these people as infallible beings whom we unthinkingly follow. Some religious authorities today claim that there would be great nobility in blindly outsourcing our life decisions, invoking a legal innovation called *daat Torah*, "the wisdom or opinion of Torah," according to which we are bound by God to accept the divinely inspired rulings of rabbinic authority regarding all aspects of our lives; this, however, is not a traditional path. We do not need rabbinic approval to, for example, lease a new car, take a new job, or join a new educational program. We need not believe that any authority knows the will of God regarding our personal lives outside of the synagogue better than we ourselves do.

In contrast to the approach of *daat Torah*, there are many teachings that tell us to act in direct contravention of the rulings of those authorities whenever they deviate from the paths of righteousness. When an exegetical source says something as radical as "human dignity is so important that it supersedes even a biblical prohibition,"[10] we are asked to exercise our moral and emotional intelligence to arrive at the righteous path and to ignore traditional authority. This principle is supported by Nachmanides, who writes:

> God says that with respect to what God has not commanded, you should likewise take heed to do the good and the right in God's eyes, for God loves the good and the right. And this is a great matter. For it is impossible to mention in the Torah all of a person's actions toward one's neighbors and acquaintances, all of one's commercial activity, and all social and political institutions.[11]

We have to assume that not every possible case or question is explicitly debated in the Torah—and whenever that is the case, we must judge and answer each question based on the principles of righteousness.

I am expanding Nachmanides's views to state that we might need to act contrary to even traditional Jewish practice whenever we arrive at the conclusion that it does not adhere to principles of righteousness. The Rabbis themselves were willing to apply principles of Jewish ethics in order to resolve religious and moral matters. For example, they ruled in favor of employees over the employer, not because it was the *law* but because it was the just thing to do.[12] Various additional sources support this approach, empowering us to exercise our intellectual and spiritual sensitivity to navigate our lives.

To engage ethically with the rules of religious life—religious commitment, community, and structure—requires us to stay conscious of the fact that human understandings of the Infinite are imperfect. No religion represents a perfect truth, though all of them attempt to achieve it in their own noble ways. The ways of world religions are largely reflections and constructions of humanity, even when springing forth from divine revelation. The spirit of religion speaks through the human spirit revealing the word of God, and that word sounds different to every single one of us. One cannot hide behind religious teachings or behind another's religious authority as a means to avoid the heavy intellectual lifting of moral decision-making. Whenever we choose to settle for easy truths—the truths of someone else—it is as if we have not yearned for truth at all. Each of us must stand before God on our own. Each of us is accountable for our own morality. We are not allowed to rely on the direction of others. That would be a false idealization of authority in a world in which we are called to pursue our own intellectual and spiritual knowledge.

In a letter to his father-in-law, Rabbi Joseph B. Soloveitchick,[13] Rabbi Aharon Lichtenstein (1933–2015), a prominent Israeli American *rosh yeshivah*, writes that he was deeply disturbed after witnessing two young religious boys who failed to help someone in need because they were engaged in a textual analysis. He raises the following question:

> Can't we find children who would have helped him and still know the *gemara*? Do we have to choose? I hope not; I believe not. If forced to choose, however, I would have no doubts where my loyalties lie: I prefer that they know less *gemara* but help him.[14]

For reference, Rabbi Lichtenstein dedicated his life to Torah learning. Yet, he still believed fervently that adhering to our moral conscience and inner sense of morality must, at times, outweigh even the religious vale of studying Torah.

At times, blind adherence to religious principles may render us not only insensitive and egoistic, but overtly violent. The Talmud records an incident in which the scholars of the School of Shammai ambushed and killed many scholars of the rival scholar camp, the School of Hillel, so that they could outvote them and put in place their own laws.[15] The story reminds us that at times we must denounce some of our greatest sages, should they become religious fanatics or even murderers.

An example: While we may revere Maimonides as one of the greatest philosophers in Jewish history, we must also acknowledge that he taught a rule that must be rejected. Regarding those who deny a fundamental Jewish belief or disobey a Jewish law, Maimonides problematically instructed, "If it is within one's power to kill them with a sword in public view, then kill them. If that is not possible, one should devise schemes that can bring about their deaths."[16] Another example of Maimonides's moral fallibility can be found in his recommendation regarding domestic violence: "A wife who refuses to perform any kind of work that she is obligated to do may be compelled to perform it even by scourging her with a rod."[17] My point is not that we should stop revering Maimonides as a great scholar. However, we should not submit totally to him and make him our ultimate authority, never to be contradicted. He lived in a different time and had different understandings of religious tolerance, gender roles, and violence against women. We cannot merely adapt the ideas and rules of someone else. In each generation, situation, and life, we must reinterpret our sacred sources anew and do the work of revealing their meaning in our moment and in the relationship to the past and the future. We should revere Maimonides as a great scholar—and we should be brave enough not to submit to him unthinkingly, making him into an ultimate authority over our own lives' decisions.[18]

Another example, a little closer to our time—relatively: The community of the Vilna Gaon attributed to their teacher a statement calling for the persecution of Chasidic Jews. In 1772, they went so far as to excommunicate all Chasidim in Vilna.[19] Should we learn the Vilna Gaon's brilliant insights? Unequivocally yes. Should we submit to him as an authority we are bound by on all matters? Unequivocally no.

For too long, countless religious teachers have pretended that Jewish tradition never gave rise to serious moral problems—or they have offered very peculiar apologetics. Those of us committed to Jewish tradition as well as to social progress must be open and honest about these traditional teachings and take responsibility for them. There are indeed many Jewish rulings that are morally problematic. We must be wary of any school of thought that posits that the Rabbis express the pure word and will of God. Indeed, Jewish theology is adamant in its acknowledgment that all human beings are fallible and products of their time.[20] Will each of us, as mortal and fallible beings, make more mistakes when we take responsibility for our religious and moral lives than when we outsource that responsibility? Perhaps. But we were given free will, intellectual capacity, spiritual yearning, and an inner morality to exercise exactly this responsibility. We have one shot at life. We cannot give up this opportunity to cultivate our inner world and to make the best choices we can. The Talmud teaches that "Jerusalem was only destroyed because . . . they judged solely by the Torah's law and did not act beyond the letter of the law."[21] There is a tension between the letter of the law and a personal, natural, moral sensibility. If we quiet the divine voice speaking within our souls, then our awe of heaven is no longer pure.[22] We must stop treating individuals as "too weak" and "too ignorant" to make their own decisions. We must encourage people to pursue their own moral and spiritual decision-making.

However, there will always be those who throw off their responsibility of refining their character, intellectual deliberations, and spiritual growth. They spend their lives in the stock market, watching sports, and enjoying good food and never seek more. They might be happy to adhere blindly to religious authorities. However, most American Jews today are not those types of people. They seek an intellectually stimulating and rigorous Judaism. For such a Judaism to thrive, we must take a step forward. Jewish observance requires rebellion, not submission; protest, not obedience. In committing to the tradition (in whatever ways we commit), we are engaging in a subversive act: we vow not to conform with society.

And yet, let me add a word of caution. We cannot make our moral decisions all by ourselves, either. Rabbi Kook explains that we need something called "holy arrogance" (gaavah d'kedushah) to come close to God:

> Often a person's heart will feel full of strength. At first glance this feeling will seem similar to a feeling of arrogance. But after clarifying the matter, the reality is that one's heart is filled with courage from the divine light that shines in one's soul. What one sees is the greatness of HaShem. If this person subdues themself and distances

themself from this pride, not only will they not do themself any good. They will also weaken all of their spiritual powers.[23]

We must make sure that we are walking on God's path of righteousness. From Genesis onward, it might seem as if God is continually disappointed with humanity. Creation, with all its moral potential, never lives up to divine expectations. From the expulsion from Eden, to Cain killing his brother Abel, the failings of the generation of the Flood, and the necessary dispersion at Babel, humans, from the beginning, fail repeatedly. One might assume that it would be enough to simply rely upon our own reason, conscience, and intuition. However, God saw early on that we needed more, and thus we received the gift of godly revelation—to reinforce what humans already and deep down know. But the revelation of a body of guiding laws is a dangerous step to take, dangerous even (and maybe especially) for God. Creating a mandate inevitability leads to rebellion, as we see early in the narrative when humans commit their first error (the eating of the fruit from the Tree of Knowledge). With the revelation of the Torah, God makes a compromise: God reveals to us what we already know while constantly asking us to pursue higher levels of moral and spiritual consciousness.

The Rabbis of the Talmud state explicitly that studying Torah merely reinforces what people could have learned from intuition and experience. As already quoted above, "If we had not received the Torah, we would have learned modesty from watching a cat, honesty from the ant, and fidelity from the dove."[24] There were the chosen few who understood the holy and true path before the rest of humanity. We call these learned few the Patriarchs and Matriarchs, and indeed, the Rabbis taught that these great ancestors already knew the Torah on their own without the need for revelation. "Abraham our Father fulfilled the entire Torah before it was given, even the laws of the Sabbath food preparation on a festival."[25] In a related explication of this thought centuries later, Rabbi Levi Yitzchak of Berditchev, a Chasidic commentator who lived from 1740 to 1810, explains in his book *K'dushat Levi*, that the Patriarchs knew the Torah intimately through their limbs: "248 positive mitzvot of the Torah parallel our 248 spiritual limbs; the Torah's 365 prohibitions are parallel to our 365 spiritual sinews."[26] It is through the corporeality of the body and incorporeality of the consciousness that we can already know Torah without external revelation.

The medieval Jewish philosophers, such as Saadyah Gaon and Maimonides, also stated clearly that reason and revelation do not contradict each other. Humans were not reaching the moral and spiritual level God expected them to reach through reason alone, so divine mercy provided for an adapted plan: thunderbolts, lightning, and the direct word of God at Sinai. Rabbi Levi Yitzchak of Berditchev teaches that God is "clothed" at Sinai—as compared to being "unclothed" at the miracles of the Red Sea—pointing out that revelation calls for intellectual and moral comprehension rather than for an emotional and experiential connection to the Divine.[27]

It is also noteworthy that it was not God's wish that revelation would happen to one particular people. Initially, God had attempted to form a universal covenant through Noah. However, this universal covenant did not create true moral commitment. Thus, God gifted one single people with the gift of revelation. We, as this people, are tasked to share this gift—and to evolve morally and intellectually from particularism to universalism.

And yet. Only moments after divine revelation, confusion and the fragmentation of truths might occur again. While we always have access to the truth within, we are still prone to confusion, struggling through historical discrepancies and seeming contradictions. The laws and principles of historical revelation seem to compete with the ongoing revelation of now. We are stuck with this tension. We must embrace both the historical and the ongoing revelations, allowing them to refine one another. The Chasidic masters conveyed to us that there are sparks of light and truth, however fragmented and garbed, to be found everywhere.

The revelations within are often more powerful than any text we can study. Ultimately, we should transcend the boundaries of historical religious thought and move into a greater spiritual realm. This is the purpose of our rich spiritual inheritance. Every time we engage with tradition, we become attuned to the manifold realities of the Divine. When we are religiously engaged (emboldened for actualization yet still humbled by self-doubt), we are transformed into spiritual beings yearning for truth.

In *Models of Revelation*, Avery Dulles lays out five different models of revelation:[28]

1. Revelation as Doctrine
2. Revelation as History
3. Revelation as Inner Experience
4. Revelation as Dialectical Presence
5. Revelation as New Awareness

Each faith tradition (and each denomination within each faith tradition) will emphasize a different model of these five, and individuals may be seeking an understanding of the term "revelation" that is coherent, meaningful, intellectually consistent, and useful to them personally.

Let's get back to our original passage from Proverbs. An ant is not so much a thinking creature, but one that moves and works together with its community at all times. When times become dire, the group of ants have the resources they need to ensure their survival. As we, as religious persons, engage with both the historical and the ongoing revelation, we too must make sure to gather strength and resources for dire times. We are the ants, and the Divine in the world is "the group." For the word of God to survive in the world, it must be alive within us, in our minds and souls. Religious life today is becoming less meaningful because we too often fail to develop our inner, God-given capacities: moral reason, intuition, and conscience. We simply obey historical revelation, when indeed our first priority should be to follow our inner divine revelation, to guard and cultivate the holiness of our inner world, and to be grateful for that divine consciousness implanted within us to reinforce the just and the holy.

Religiously and spiritually, we need to rely less on authorities and more on our conscience, which needs to be continuously cultivated. Our task in the world is to navigate each situation with great care, morality, and spiritual integrity—in dialogue with, but not blindly obeying, tradition. We cannot afford to outsource our most crucial decisions to those who are distant from the matter at hand—our lives—and merely interpret external sources.[29] While it is certainly good to consult with trusted rabbinic experts, their central role is to act as educators and not as ultimate authorities. The final decisions for our most essential choices can only be our own. We are called to embrace a hermeneutic of suspicion and engage in critical interpretation of ideas and of texts. We are to bring our full understanding to our encounter with revelation, be it of the past or be it of the current time.

Does God Hate What God Hates?

> GOD hates six things—
> And abominates seven:
> A haughty bearing,
> A lying tongue,
> Hands that shed innocent blood,
> A mind that hatches evil plots,
> Feet quick to run to evil,
> A false witness testifying lies,
> And one who incites siblings to quarrel.
> —Proverbs 6:16–19

THESE VERSES of the Book of Proverbs are very interesting because it seems that in *Pirkei Avot*, the opposite is claimed! It says there, "Who is mighty? One who subdues one's [evil] inclination, as it is said: "One who is slow to anger [slow to hate] is better than the mighty; and one who rules one's spirit than one who takes a city.""[30] How is it possible that God criticizes us for being hateful when God seems to feel hatred too? Indeed, the notion of God "hating" is theologically complex, not only because it implies that God experiences emotions, but also because feeling hatred seems to be a vice, while generally held conceptions of God claim that God is a perfect, and therefore vice-free, God.

Many of us may feel uncomfortable with the notion of God being "hateful." The idea of a benevolent, omniscient God hating anything certainly is anathema to many in Western Europe and the United States today. However, in recent years, we have seen seen fringe groups use the phrase "God hates . . ." to sow social division and create toxicity. In centuries past, employing the idea that God hates certain groups of people has proved to be disastrous, as innumerable populations were destroyed because demagogues used fear of a vengeful god to wipe out vulnerable communities.

Jewish tradition, too, does not shy away from recognizing that God hates certain elements of this world. As stated in the verses above, God despises negative traits: lies, murder, violence, and false testimony. This list cannot be surprising, as all virtuous people would agree that those human acts are deleterious to a moral life. Passages found in the Talmud[31] reiterate the stance found in Proverbs: "God hates the one who speaks one thing with their mouth and another thing in their heart."[32] With the knowledge that in some manner or another, God wishes to see human beings overcome certain of their all-too-human traits, specific questions arise for us: Should we fight for justice and righteousness with hearts full of love or hearts full of anger? Which is more rewarding? Which is more productive? Which must we cultivate as conscientious people of faith?

According to Rabbi Joseph B. Soloveitchik, the "hate" that God feels diverges from the emotion we humans feel. "Hate" in godly terms is not as much a feeling of deep disgust as it is a divine longing for a return to a world where love and peace are the highest values for humankind. Rabbi Soloveitchik's major caveat is that humanity cannot generally achieve these heavenly ideals. As he writes:

> Love is a great and noble emotion, fostering the social spirit and elevating man, but not always is the loving person capable of meeting the challenge of harsh realities. In certain situations, a disjunctive emotion, such as anger or indignation, may become the motivating force for noble and valuable action.[33]

The conflicting nature of love and hate, both at times in the service of the good, has flummoxed and inspired philosophers throughout the ages. Nietzsche writes, "He who cannot hate also cannot love."[34] The French writer George Sand espouses in her first novel, *Indiana*, that hate itself may at times be an expression of love and that indignation over oppression and injustice is indeed the highest expression of love. It seems that we humans cannot be commanded or persuaded to suppress an emotion as strong as hatred, but that we must obey our ontological situations and affective destinies. Could it be that the emotional life that accompanies our service in the world is simply a matter of our personal character, good enough as long as it serves the right purposes?

Lewis Goldberg, emeritus professor of psychology at the University of Oregon and leader in the field of personality traits, addresses this issue. He promotes a personality schema of five distinct traits.[35] This model, nicknamed the "Big Five," is a good starting point for attempting to understand how a specific human being may react to the world surrounding them:

1. Extraversion: outgoing and stimulation-oriented versus quiet and stimulation-avoiding
2. Neuroticism: emotionally reactive, prone to negative emotions versus calm, imperturbable, optimistic
3. Agreeableness: affable, friendly, conciliatory versus aggressive, dominant, disagreeable
4. Conscientiousness: dutiful, planful, and orderly versus laidback, spontaneous, and unreliable
5. Openness to experience: open to new ideas and change versus traditional and oriented toward routine

Are a "dominant" person and a "conciliatory" person equally capable of bringing about great revolutions? A spontaneous and an orderly person? Might we need different personalities involved to evoke true change? Do we need all of them? Stripping away our shame for our emotional lives and personality traits we find ourselves made of, we are able to embrace and elevate our personalities and emotional realities to become who we are destined to be and fight for whom we must champion. They cry out to us. Momentarily, we might be able to outgrow ourselves with exhilaration—but then we inevitably retreat to find ourselves within our own familiar souls. Ultimately, each of us has only one heart, and this heart is here to stay.

While we may be different, we must unite in our love, thereby actualizing the human spirit and giving merit to our creation—only then will we be able to evoke true change.

Rabbi Meir Simcha HaKohen of Dvinsk, known as the Meshech Chochmah (1843–1926, Lithuania/Latvia), argued that we are no longer permitted to hate others. Before the Golden Calf, he suggests, people were allowed to hate someone for their deeds. But since that moment, we have been prohibited from judging others. Instead, we should focus on a humble awareness of our flaws. Rather than hating another, we must invest our time and spiritual energy to examine and work on our *own* traits. He takes into consideration that there may be some people righteous enough to hate another, but suggests that we will have a lot of difficulty finding anyone on this spiritual level. Almost all of us are called upon to use our discomfort—or anger—toward others as a mirror to our own souls to grow morally and come closer to God.

And yet the question remains: If God can hate and we are to emulate God, are we not also called to emulate God's hatred? The answer seems to be that our ability to emulate this particular godly trait must be cultivated with great caution and sensitivity due to the extreme harm it can cause to ourselves and others. This is what *Pirkei Avot* teaches: if we allow our hate to translate into anger, we may harm ourselves and others.

While we do not rejoice at the downfall of our enemies, we *do* rejoice at the downfall of evil. As is recorded in the Talmud:

> Rabbi Y'hudah the son of Rabbi Shimon ben Pazi said: "David composed a hundred and three chapters [of psalms], and he did not say 'Halleluyah' until he saw the downfall of the wicked, as it says, 'Let sinners cease out of the earth, and let the wicked be no more. Bless the Eternal, O my soul. Hallelujah' (Psalm 104:35)."[36]

Hate the sin but not the sinner—this is one of the key lessons the great Talmudic sage B'ruriah teaches her husband.[37]

Indeed, we should combat injustice, oppression, and wickedness wherever possible. Yet, at the same time, we must be aware that some of that evil exists closer to home (within us and those we love) than we like to think—and that some virtues might be found within our enemies more than we might like to acknowledge. May we work hard to get rid of evil—within us and others—while controlling our own anger.

Holy Illumination

For the commandment is a lamp,
The teaching is a light...
—Proverbs 6:23

TODAY, PEOPLE OFTEN CHOOSE only one aspect of Judaism to focus on and mistakenly take it as the entirety of the Jewish experience. Some people choose to focus their attention solely on the State of Israel. For them, the most meaningful expression of Judaism is Zionism, and that is the totality of their Jewish identity. Others prioritize *tikkun olam*[38] and volunteerism as their main expression of Judaism. Still others appreciate prayer and meditation but ignore the social justice component. And, of course, many people hold onto their Judaism in the memory of the Holocaust while forgoing active participation in the present community. It is only natural for each of us to gather spiritual strength in a particular way.

The Torah and its 613 mitzvot are ever present and available to all those who seek its wisdom. Many Jews embrace this spiritual potential, while many do not choose to follow this path.

The Book of Proverbs leaves us with the ultimate hope: that this set of writings, which has sustained the Jewish people through the millennia, is always there to enlighten our way.

Torah not only nourishes but also challenges us. It forces us to focus on a more diverse set of Jewish practices and texts. Describing the phenomenon of compartmentalizing Jewish identity, Rabbi David Wolpe[39] uses a metaphor suggested by the 1950s intellectual Will Herberg. Wolpe is worried that our tendency to focus on one kind of Judaism exclusively might undermine the strength and survival of Judaism as a whole:

> Herberg once spoke of "cut-flower ethics." He argued that Jewish
> ethical norms will last for a brief while, even apart from Jewish
> teachings, just as flowers uprooted from the soil stay in bloom for
> a short time after cutting. But soon the flowers fade. Behaviors,
> too, disintegrate if cut from the soil in which they were nourished.
> All those teachers and scientists and musicians and artists are the
> bloom of Jewish spirituality; given time, without the soil, that
> bloom will fade.[40]

Indeed, for flowers to live and grow, they have to remain connected
to the earth. Rabbi Noa Kushner[41] shared a similar idea, noting that
a bird needs her forest. If we take the bird, the one part of the forest
that we like, out of the forest, she will die.[42]

Against all odds, Jews have survived to this day. According to leading archaeologists, the first record of the Jewish people in history
(outside our own Bible) is in the Merneptah Stele.[43] It states, "Israel
is laid waste—his seed is no more." This first allusion to Jews in history boasts that they are destroyed. And yet, here we are—here in this
contemporary moment, stronger than ever, in the homeland and in
the Diaspora as well.

What has enabled the Jewish people to survive the harshest perse-
cutions? A commitment to all our values. Torah study *and* mitzvot,
understood in today's most pluralistic sense, have been our lights in
the darkness of the world.

In light of the Torah's great strength, it is remarkable how much
of Jewish thought has taken a humble, non-triumphalist approach.
Consider the notion that Balaam, a gentile prophet whose story can
be found in the Torah portion of *Balak* (Numbers 22–24), might have
equal—or even greater—access to God than our greatest prophet
(Moses)![44] We can be proud that our biblical theology already models
spiritual modesty, boldly ascribing godliness to potentially everyone. We and our Torah are appreciative, even curious, of the spiritual
potentials outside of our own.

The Rabbis debated the essence of Torah:

"Love your neighbor as yourself": Rabbi Akiva says, "This is the encompassing principle of the Torah." Ben Azzai says, "'This is the book of the generation of Adam' (Genesis 5:1) is a still more encompassing principle."[45]

Many rabbis have offered interpretations of the nature of Rabbi Akiva's and Ben Azzai's disagreement. Here is what the Raavad offers:

"Love your neighbor as yourself":

Rabbi Akiva said: "This is a great rule in Torah: as that which is hateful to you, you should not do to your friend."

Ben Azzai said: "This is the book of the generation of *adam* [man]: In the day the God created humankind, in the likeness of God God made him—this is an even greater rule."

It was interpreted as follows: They asked, "From the first verse we only heard 'as yourself'—if he was humiliated or cursed, or robbed or injured, should his friend be humiliated, cursed, and injured with him?!"

Therefore, it says: "He was made in the likeness of God." Who are you humiliating and cursing? God's likeness!

This second rule is superior to the first.[46]

To keep Jewish ethical values alive, we must invest not only in the values themselves but in the entire Jewish system: the social, spiritual, communal, ethical, and intellectual elements and general infrastructure that allow for our "family" to survive. The Torah is the light; the mitzvot are our lamp; our deeds are our way of spreading Jewish wisdom through peace and radical love.

Perhaps the greatest way to open up our inner channels of light is to improve our character. Rabbi Lisa L. Goldstein writes, "When we work on our *middot*, we are clearing away the blockages that prevent us from radiating the inner divinity that is our human birthright."[47]

The Rabbis taught that fire was created on *Motza-ei Shabbat* (Saturday night after Shabbat ends). "God gave intellect to the first human, comparable to the divine intellect, and he grounded two rocks together until fire came out from them."[48] Humans are partners of

God in creation. They too create and share their light with the world. That is why, when making *Havdalah*, we say, "The Jews had light." Commenting on this phrase, the Rabbis explain, "Light is Torah."[49] Indeed, each day, in learning our tradition's stories and values and passing them forward, we spread light.

Coveting in Our Time

Do not lust for her beauty
Or let her captivate you with her eyes.
　　　—Proverbs 6:25

ONE OF THE MOST WELL-KNOWN MITZVOT—due to its placement in the Ten Commandments—is the prohibition to covet. Though most people are able to heed the warnings not to murder and not to steal, it seems that the act of coveting is ubiquitous—and that is understandable. There are times in our lives when we look at our friends and colleagues and think, "I wish I had what they have," whether it is material items, a relationship, a well-paying job, or connections to well-established industry figures. These desires often lure us into the wrong direction, destroying elements of our souls, and keeping us from engaging for the sake of the less fortunate. They form the basis of a covetous existence.

Why does the Torah prohibit coveting? Why should a matter of emotional regulation be part of the Ten Commandments?

The Rabbis taught that the prohibition of covetousness was a preventative measure. The notion and prevention of coveting could lead to less theft (Deuteronomy 5:18). The belief was that if we lost control of our feelings to the point of wanting something that someone else owned, we might not be able to control ourselves and would take it from them. The prohibition was put in place to prevent the emotion that might lead us to act improperly.

Another way to think about coveting is by considering the harmful way in which it affects how we think about economic and financial matters. In an ideal, equitable society, resources and labor are shared evenly within the community, and there is enough for everyone.

While this notion is unrealistic due to capital and resource scarcity, it is a worthy aspirational vision on which to base our actions.

Indeed, the emotion of covetousness is so harmful to our inner selves and actions that its prohibition might well be considered most important among the commandments and prohibitions of the Torah. According to Rabbi Yakum, "One who violates the tenth commandment [prohibiting coveting] violates them all."[50]

Rabbi Michal of Zolotchov, a Chasidic master, explained that the tenth obligation is not so much a command as it is an assurance of a divine reward. If we fulfill the first nine commandments with all of our heart, God promises us that we will not want anything else and thus not succumb to coveting. While we may choose to work harder to attain more, we must also learn our limits and to be content with what we have. An additional argument against covetousness is that when we act in this way, we affect not only our own, but others' emotions. Our pulse rates, our joy, our stress, and other physiological conditions can travel via "emotional contagion." Daniel Goleman writes, "When three strangers sit facing each other in silence for a minute or two, the one who is most emotionally expressive transmits his or her mood to the other two—without speaking a single word."[51] This process, known as mirroring, is not only tragic but also the basis of empathy. We seek attunement with one another. Our emotions, positive and negative, impact others deeply.

The Book of Proverbs—along with the Torah, generally—does not want to impugn success. People often work hard to attain success in their chosen fields. And those who have worked diligently throughout their lives and have supported their communities deserve our respect. But it is not right when those who rig the game for themselves in the pursuit of an ever-rising net worth have greater influence over others.

Today, we look for an end to unbridled greed and a society in which the bottom line is not the only line. In recent history, coveting has not only taken hold; it has proceeded to theft and a regressive redistribution of wealth from the poor and middle class to the wealthiest by methods that border on immoral. It has fed on itself and threatens to disrupt society as we know it. Paying heed to the need to avoid coveting expressed both in the Ten Commandments and in our verse can help us keep society on the proper path. Indeed, this commandment can be the basis for pursuing economic justice. As Rabbi Isaac Mayer Wise wrote in the nineteenth century, "There can be no favored classes before God."[52]

Chapter 7

1   My son, heed my words;
    And store up my commandments with you.

2   Keep my commandments and live,
    My teaching, as the apple of your eye—

3   Bind them on your fingers,
    Write them on the tablet of your mind.

4   Say to Wisdom, "You are my sister,"
    And call Understanding a kinswoman.

5   She will guard you from a forbidden woman;
    From an alien woman whose talk is smooth.

6   From the window of my house,
    Through my lattice, I looked out

7   And saw among the simple,
    Noticed among the youths,
    A young man devoid of sense.

8   He was crossing the street near her corner,
    Walking toward her house

9   In the dusk of evening,
    In the dark hours of night.

10 A woman comes toward him
    Dressed like a harlot, with set purpose.

11 She is bustling and restive;
    She is never at home.

12 Now in the street, now in the square,
    She lurks at every corner.

13 She lays hold of him and kisses him.
    Brazenly she says to him,

פרק ז

1 בְּנִי שְׁמֹר אֲמָרֶי וּמִצְוֺתַי תִּצְפֹּן אִתָּֽךְ:

2 שְׁמֹר מִצְוֺתַי וֶחְיֵה וְתוֹרָתִי כְּאִישׁוֹן עֵינֶֽיךָ:

3 קָשְׁרֵם עַל־אֶצְבְּעֹתֶיךָ כָּתְבֵם עַל־לוּחַ לִבֶּֽךָ:

4 אֱמֹר לַחָכְמָה אֲחֹתִי אָתְּ וּמֹדָע לַבִּינָה תִקְרָֽא:

5 לִשְׁמָרְךָ מֵאִשָּׁה זָרָה מִנָּכְרִיָּה אֲמָרֶיהָ הֶחֱלִֽיקָה:

6 כִּי בְּחַלּוֹן בֵּיתִי בְּעַד אֶשְׁנַבִּי נִשְׁקָֽפְתִּי:

7 וָאֵרֶא בַפְּתָאיִם אָבִינָה בַבָּנִים נַעַר חֲסַר־לֵֽב:

8 עֹבֵר בַּשּׁוּק אֵצֶל פִּנָּהּ וְדֶרֶךְ בֵּיתָהּ יִצְעָֽד:

9 בְּנֶשֶׁף־בְּעֶרֶב יוֹם בְּאִישׁוֹן לַיְלָה וַאֲפֵלָֽה:

10 וְהִנֵּה אִשָּׁה לִקְרָאתוֹ שִׁית זוֹנָה וּנְצֻרַת לֵֽב:

11 הֹמִיָּה הִיא וְסֹרָרֶת בְּבֵיתָהּ לֹא־יִשְׁכְּנוּ רַגְלֶֽיהָ:

12 פַּעַם בַּחוּץ פַּעַם בָּרְחֹבוֹת וְאֵצֶל כָּל־פִּנָּה תֶאֱרֹֽב:

13 וְהֶחֱזִיקָה בּוֹ וְנָשְׁקָה לּוֹ הֵעֵזָה פָנֶיהָ וַתֹּאמַר לֽוֹ:

14 "I had to make a sacrifice of well-being;
   Today I fulfilled my vows.
15 Therefore I have come out to you,
   Seeking you, and have found you.
16 I have decked my couch with covers
   Of dyed Egyptian linen;
17 I have sprinkled my bed
   With myrrh, aloes, and cinnamon.
18 Let us drink our fill of love till morning;
   Let us delight in amorous embrace.
19 For the man of the house is away;
   He is off on a distant journey.
20 He took his bag of money with him
   And will return only at mid-month."

21 She sways him with her eloquence,
   Turns him aside with her smooth talk.
22 Thoughtlessly he follows her,
   Like an ox going to the slaughter,
   Like a fool to the stocks for punishment—
23 Until the arrow pierces his liver.
   He is like a bird rushing into a trap,
   Not knowing his life is at stake.
24 Now, sons, listen to me;
   Pay attention to my words;
25 Let your mind not wander down her ways;
   Do not stray onto her paths.
26 For many are those she has struck dead,
   And numerous are her victims.
27 Her house is a highway to Sheol
   Leading down to Death's inner chambers.

זִבְחֵי שְׁלָמִים עָלָי הַיּוֹם שִׁלַּמְתִּי נְדָרָי: 14

עַל־כֵּן יָצָאתִי לִקְרָאתֶךָ לְשַׁחֵר פָּנֶיךָ וָאֶמְצָאֶךָּ: 15

מַרְבַדִּים רָבַדְתִּי עַרְשִׂי חֲטֻבוֹת אֵטוּן מִצְרָיִם: 16

נַפְתִּי מִשְׁכָּבִי מֹר אֲהָלִים וְקִנָּמוֹן: 17

לְכָה נִרְוֶה דֹדִים עַד־הַבֹּקֶר נִתְעַלְּסָה בָּאֳהָבִים: 18

כִּי אֵין הָאִישׁ בְּבֵיתוֹ הָלַךְ בְּדֶרֶךְ מֵרָחוֹק: 19

צְרוֹר־הַכֶּסֶף לָקַח בְּיָדוֹ לְיוֹם הַכֵּסֶא יָבֹא בֵיתוֹ: 20

הִטַּתּוּ בְּרֹב לִקְחָהּ בְּחֵלֶק שְׂפָתֶיהָ תַּדִּיחֶנּוּ: 21

הוֹלֵךְ אַחֲרֶיהָ פִּתְאֹם כְּשׁוֹר אֶל־טֶבַח יָבֹא וּכְעֶכֶס 22
אֶל־מוּסַר אֱוִיל:

עַד יְפַלַּח חֵץ כְּבֵדוֹ כְּמַהֵר צִפּוֹר אֶל־פָּח וְלֹא־יָדַע 23
כִּי־בְנַפְשׁוֹ הוּא:

וְעַתָּה בָנִים שִׁמְעוּ־לִי וְהַקְשִׁיבוּ לְאִמְרֵי־פִי: 24

אַל־יֵשְׂטְ אֶל־דְּרָכֶיהָ לִבֶּךָ אַל־תֵּתַע בִּנְתִיבוֹתֶיהָ: 25

כִּי־רַבִּים חֲלָלִים הִפִּילָה וַעֲצֻמִים כָּל־הֲרֻגֶיהָ: 26

דַּרְכֵי שְׁאוֹל בֵּיתָהּ יֹרְדוֹת אֶל־חַדְרֵי־מָוֶת: 27

Moral Reminders

Bind them on your fingers,
Write them on the tablet of your mind.
　　　—Proverbs 7:3

ONE OF THE BEAUTIFUL literary elements of the Book of Proverbs is how it treats intangible, spiritual objects as part of our tangible reality. The "them" in the phrase "Bind them on your fingers" refers to the mitzvot, based on the previous verse. On one level, a mitzvah cannot literally be bound on anything, as it is an idea and an aspiration. However, on another level and in the words of the verse, it seems that a mitzvah is a physical and tangible thing. The verse reminds us that the mitzvot aren't only black ink on a white page.

One can easily wrap *t'fillin* on one's hands and across one's head. But how do we write things on our minds? What does that entail?

Every day we need reminders to stay on track morally, spiritually, and philosophically. The world contains a cacophony of negative emotions that permeate into all sectors of our lives. Be it racism, baseless hatred, war, and other deeds of ill intent, there is so much that we face on a day-to-day basis that it is difficult to keep our minds focused on the good—and it is not even enough to merely "know" the good! Beyond merely knowing what appears to be good, we must do the challenging work of conditioning ourselves to stay on the proper course of action every day, avoiding the divergences caused by desire, temptation, and the inclination to conform.

Although we are not exactly sure where we are supposed to tie and to write "on the tablets of our minds," the message suggested by the verse as a whole is unambiguous: we need to be morally on track both physically and mentally. We woke up this morning, but did we really *wake* up? Or are we drifting between cycles of waking and sleeping? To be awake, to truly see the world with our eyes open, our body erect, and our mind clear, we must stir our inner being and be prepared to encounter all that comes before us. Only then will we be free to make a difference.

Consider that the Torah tells us that Adam, the first person created, went to sleep (Genesis 2:21), yet the Torah never tells us that he woke up. Was it all a dream? Is he still sleeping? Is all of humanity still asleep, waiting for our great collective awakening?

The key to being fully awake is to understand that our time on earth is limited—that every breath, every action, and every day counts. A tragedy of humanity is the knowledge that one day our lives will cease. The body that we inhabit in the world will no longer exist in its corporeal form. Our sinews will return to the earth in one way or another. Our lives are remarkably short. And yet we need spiritual activities to constantly remind us of the truth of our own fragility.

Consider this mind-clearing fact: A person who lives to be eighty years old will take about 672,768,000 breaths in a lifetime. The shofar only makes its sound if someone blows their precious breath into it. So, too, our soul prays only if we allow God to breathe through us. The divine breath breathes through you like a divine shofar.

Feel the gratitude and intimacy.

Feel the love.

Then the soul will start to shake, to dance, to sing!

To rejoice!

Being aware of the preciousness of our breath, of the fragility of our lives, can be a source of alertness and joy. When we encounter others, we must see beyond the surface. Rabbi Alexandri teaches:

> If a common person uses a broken vessel, it is considered a disgrace. But not the Holy One, blessed be God. All of God's vessels are broken. "The Eternal is close to the brokenhearted" (Psalm 34:19).[1]

To emulate the Divine, we should pay attention to the most power-less rather than the most powerful, the most broken rather than the most privileged and fortunate; we must witness the suffering right before our eyes. We have to break from what the eyes want to see to what the heart needs to see. A Chasidic story rings true, reinforcing this valuable message:

> The Sassover Rebbe entered a hotel and sat beside two local peas-ants. As the two peasants sat at the bar and drank, they began to fall into a drunken stupor. One turned to his friend and said, "Tell me, friend, do you love me?" His colleague responded, "Of course I love you. We're drinking companions. Naturally I love you." Then the first one said to his friend, "Then tell me, friend, what causes me pain?" His colleague said, "How should I know what hurts you? I'm just your drinking buddy." He said, "If you loved me, you would know what causes me pain."[2]

Rabbi Abraham Isaac HaKohen Kook explains that there are intelligent slaves whose being is full of freedom, and there are free individuals whose being consists of the spirit of a slave. A real slave is one who lives only in conformity with others, seeking to be honored by others. The free individual experiences inner freedom, focusing on the eternal illumination of the image of God within.[3] Many con-sider themselves free even though, from the Torah's perspective, they are still enslaved. Only those truly free can truly see—only those can see the pain of others. To achieve a level at which we truly understand what causes pain to those in pain, we must gain an elevated freedom. The opportunities to truly see ourselves and others are right before our eyes. Our freedom, indeed our dignity, lies in our choice to truly see.

Chapter 8

1   It is Wisdom calling,
      Understanding raising her voice.
2   She takes her stand at the topmost heights,
      By the wayside, at the crossroads,
3   Near the gates at the city entrance;
      At the entryways, she shouts,
4   "O human race, I call to you;
      My cry is to all mortals.
5   O simple ones, learn shrewdness;
      O dullards, instruct your minds.
6   Listen, for I speak noble things;
      Uprightness comes from my lips.
7   My mouth utters truth;
      Wickedness is abhorrent to my lips.
8   All my words are just,
      None of them perverse or crooked;
9   All are straightforward to anyone with intelligence,
      And right to those who have attained knowledge.
10   Accept my discipline rather than silver,
      Knowledge rather than choice gold.
11   For wisdom is better than rubies;
      No goods can equal her.

12   "I, Wisdom, live with Prudence;
      I attain knowledge and foresight.
13   To fear GOD is to hate evil;
      I hate pride, arrogance, the evil way,
      And duplicity in speech.

פרק ח

1 הֲלֹא־חָכְמָה תִקְרָא וּתְבוּנָה תִּתֵּן קוֹלָהּ׃

2 בְּרֹאשׁ־מְרוֹמִים עֲלֵי־דָרֶךְ בֵּית נְתִיבוֹת נִצָּבָה׃

3 לְיַד־שְׁעָרִים לְפִי־קָרֶת מְבוֹא פְתָחִים תָּרֹנָּה׃

4 אֲלֵיכֶם אִישִׁים אֶקְרָא וְקוֹלִי אֶל־בְּנֵי אָדָם׃

5 הָבִינוּ פְתָאיִם עָרְמָה וּכְסִילִים הָבִינוּ לֵב׃

6 שִׁמְעוּ כִּי־נְגִידִים אֲדַבֵּר וּמִפְתַּח שְׂפָתַי מֵישָׁרִים׃

7 כִּי־אֱמֶת יֶהְגֶּה חִכִּי וְתוֹעֲבַת שְׂפָתַי רֶשַׁע׃

8 בְּצֶדֶק כָּל־אִמְרֵי־פִי אֵין בָּהֶם נִפְתָּל וְעִקֵּשׁ׃

9 כֻּלָּם נְכֹחִים לַמֵּבִין וִישָׁרִים לְמֹצְאֵי דָעַת׃

10 קְחוּ־מוּסָרִי וְאַל־כָּסֶף וְדַעַת מֵחָרוּץ נִבְחָר׃

11 כִּי־טוֹבָה חָכְמָה מִפְּנִינִים וְכָל־חֲפָצִים לֹא יִשְׁווּ־בָהּ׃

12 אֲנִי־חָכְמָה שָׁכַנְתִּי עָרְמָה וְדַעַת מְזִמּוֹת אֶמְצָא׃

13 יִרְאַת יְהוָה שְׂנֹאת־רָע גֵּאָה וְגָאוֹן | וְדֶרֶךְ רָע וּפִי תַהְפֻּכוֹת שָׂנֵאתִי׃

14 Mine are counsel and resourcefulness;
   I am understanding; courage is mine.
15 Through me kings reign
   And rulers decree just laws;
16 Through me princes rule,
   Great men and all the righteous judges.
17 Those who love me I love,
   And those who seek me will find me.
18 Riches and honor belong to me,
   Enduring wealth and success.
19 My fruit is better than gold, fine gold,
   And my produce better than choice silver.
20 I walk on the way of righteousness,
   On the paths of justice.
21 I endow those who love me with substance;
   I will fill their treasuries.

22 "I was created at the beginning of GOD's course
   As the first of the works of old.
23 In the distant past I was fashioned,
   At the beginning, at the origin of earth.
24 There was still no deep when I was brought forth,
   No springs rich in water;
25 Before [the foundations of] the mountains were sunk,
   Before the hills I was born.
26 Earth and fields had not yet been made,
   Or the world's first clumps of clay.
27 I was there when the heavens were set into place;
   When the horizon was fixed upon the deep;
28 When the heavens above were made firm,
   And the fountains of the deep gushed forth;
29 When the sea was assigned its limits,
   So that its waters never transgress God's command;
   When the foundations of the earth were fixed,

14 לִי־עֵצָה וְתוּשִׁיָּה אֲנִי בִינָה לִי גְבוּרָה׃

15 בִּי מְלָכִים יִמְלֹכוּ וְרֹזְנִים יְחֹקְקוּ צֶדֶק׃

16 בִּי שָׂרִים יָשֹׂרוּ וּנְדִיבִים כָּל־שֹׁפְטֵי צֶדֶק׃

17 אֲנִי (אהביה) [אֹהֲבַי] אֵהָב וּמְשַׁחֲרַי יִמְצָאֻנְנִי׃

18 עֹשֶׁר־וְכָבוֹד אִתִּי הוֹן עָתֵק וּצְדָקָה׃

19 טוֹב פִּרְיִי מֵחָרוּץ וּמִפָּז וּתְבוּאָתִי מִכֶּסֶף נִבְחָר׃

20 בְּאֹרַח־צְדָקָה אֲהַלֵּךְ בְּתוֹךְ נְתִיבוֹת מִשְׁפָּט׃

21 לְהַנְחִיל אֹהֲבַי | יֵשׁ וְאֹצְרֹתֵיהֶם אֲמַלֵּא׃

22 יְהֹוָה קָנָנִי רֵאשִׁית דַּרְכּוֹ קֶדֶם מִפְעָלָיו מֵאָז׃

23 מֵעוֹלָם נִסַּכְתִּי מֵרֹאשׁ מִקַּדְמֵי־אָרֶץ׃

24 בְּאֵין־תְּהֹמוֹת חוֹלָלְתִּי בְּאֵין מַעְיָנוֹת נִכְבַּדֵּי־מָיִם׃

25 בְּטֶרֶם הָרִים הָטְבָּעוּ לִפְנֵי גְבָעוֹת חוֹלָלְתִּי׃

26 עַד־לֹא עָשָׂה אֶרֶץ וְחוּצוֹת וְרֹאשׁ עַפְרוֹת תֵּבֵל׃

27 בַּהֲכִינוֹ שָׁמַיִם שָׁם אָנִי בְּחֻקוֹ חוּג עַל־פְּנֵי תְהוֹם׃

28 בְּאַמְּצוֹ שְׁחָקִים מִמָּעַל בַּעֲזוֹז עִינוֹת תְּהוֹם׃

29 בְּשׂוּמוֹ לַיָּם | חֻקּוֹ וּמַיִם לֹא יַעַבְרוּ־פִיו בְּחוּקוֹ מוֹסְדֵי אָרֶץ׃

30 I was with [God] as a confidant,
   A source of delight every day,
   Rejoicing before [God] at all times,
31 Rejoicing in God's inhabited world,
   Finding delight with mortals.

32 Now, children, listen to me;
   Happy are they who keep my ways.
33 Heed discipline and become wise;
   Do not spurn it.
34 Happy is the one who listens to me,
   Coming early to my gates each day,
   Waiting outside my doors.
35 For one who finds me finds life
   And obtains favor from GOD.
36 But one who misses me self-destructs;
   All who hate me love death."

וָאֶהְיֶה אֶצְלוֹ אָמוֹן וָאֶהְיֶה שַׁעֲשֻׁעִים יוֹם | יוֹם מְשַׂחֶקֶת 30
לְפָנָיו בְּכָל־עֵת:

מְשַׂחֶקֶת בְּתֵבֵל אַרְצוֹ וְשַׁעֲשֻׁעַי אֶת־בְּנֵי אָדָם: 31

וְעַתָּה בָנִים שִׁמְעוּ־לִי וְאַשְׁרֵי דְּרָכַי יִשְׁמֹרוּ: 32

שִׁמְעוּ מוּסָר וַחֲכָמוּ וְאַל־תִּפְרָעוּ: 33

אַשְׁרֵי אָדָם שֹׁמֵעַ־לִי לִשְׁקֹד עַל־דַּלְתֹתַי יוֹם | יוֹם לִשְׁמֹר 34
מְזוּזֹת פְּתָחָי:

כִּי מֹצְאִי (מצאי) [מָצָא] חַיִּים וַיָּפֶק רָצוֹן מֵיהֹוָה: 35

וְחֹטְאִי חֹמֵס נַפְשׁוֹ כָּל־מְשַׂנְאַי אָהֲבוּ מָוֶת: 36

Seeking Closeness with God

Those who love me I love,
And those who seek me will find me.
　　—Proverbs 8:17

ONE OF THE EARLY Chasidic masters conveys the true power of seeking and holding onto the presence of God in all things. This master writes, "I heard from my master [the Baal Shem Tov, the founder of Chasidism] that where a person places one's thoughts, that is where all of oneself is."[1] One possible answer to the modern question of "What is the self?" is presented by the Baal Shem Tov: a person consists of that person's thoughts. We are, existentially, what we think. The "I" is located where the mind is. When our thoughts—the precious contents of our minds and hearts—are with God, we are united with God. If we *seek* God, we will *find* God; this notion is an unbreakable promise. And if we love God, God loves us.

To be united with God, however, requires exposing one's self and becoming vulnerable. Moses wore a veil when he stood before the people, yet when he stood before God, he removed his veil (Exodus 33:34–35). We can learn from Moses's behavior that God is not interested in our clothes, our social media presence, or our prestige, but rather cares about what happens in our souls.

In fact, looking specifically at the issue of clothes, the Torah indicates that they are deceptive, for example when Jacob is dressing up as his brother to deceive his father Isaac. In Hebrew, *beged* (clothes) is linked to *b'gidah* (betrayal), *m'il* (overcoat) to *m'ilah* (treachery), and *k'sut* (covering, like clothes) to *kisui* (concealment).

Deepak Chopra, one of the most widely influential spiritual thinkers of the last half-century, relates a story about the power of seeking

God even when one's faith is low:

> "How do I find God?" a young disciple once asked a famous guru in India. "I can't see any evidence that He is anywhere around us, and millions of people live very well without him."

> "Everything without God happens in space and time. This is the world you are used to," his guru replied. "Space and time are like a net that has trapped you, but nets always have holes. Find such a hole and jump through it. Then God will be obvious." Every religious tradition contains such loopholes, escape routes into a world beyond ours.[2]

Some of the most poignant spiritual practices for finding God in the Jewish tradition are contemplation, spiritual seeking, and doing justice. Indeed, seeking to serve others, when conducted with a spiritual consciousness, can be a path to finding God. Together, as servants, we serve God by healing the world. Rabbi Ariana Silverman, a Reform rabbi in Detroit, writes:

> God inspires my pursuit of social justice. God is the power that makes me, in the words of one of my teachers, tremble with prophetic rage. . . . In the vein of predicate theology, regardless of whether an interventionist God heals the sick, healing the sick is godly. We elevate the sacred when we work toward *shalom*, toward wholeness.[3]

One can be moral and effective in work to serve the vulnerable and not embrace God, just as one can be devout religiously and not create any serious impact through social action. As a guiding principle, however, embracing God offers us the opportunity to raise the bar we set for what we want to achieve and for how we must achieve it. God is the most powerful reality ever encountered, and like no other idea, embracing the Divine can inspire humankind to ideal goodness and transformative justice. To idolize our own human authority represents a failure to recognize the power and truth of our calling, destiny, and command; embracing the humility to acknowledge a power beyond us demands social protest, never submission.

Rabbi Dr. Michael Marmur writes about how we must seek

intellectual integrity in our search for God. We do not need to hold on to the images that comforted us as children. Instead, we need to grow into a full understanding and a mature practice of what it means "to be called":

> Many experience as a crisis the realization that they can no longer accept the idea of God presented to them from childhood. Having read Karl Marx (socialism) or Sigmund Freud (psychoanalysis) or Nietzsche (nihilistic philosophy) or Maly Daly (feminism) or Richard Dawkins (science-based atheism), or simply having listened to the world news, they must abandon the God of old. The "ought" of old, the "should" of tradition, is rejected.[4]

Each of us must find the rituals and spiritual practices that will help us find God. God is not hiding on some mountaintop or at the bottom of the sea. As the Torah tells us, "It [that is, God's message to humans] is not in the heavens. . . . Neither is it beyond the sea. . . . The thing is very close to you" (Deuteronomy 30:12–14). God is right here, but we always need tools to seek.

The Torah of Heaven, the Torah of Earth

I was created at the beginning of God's course
As the first of the works of old.[5]
　—Proverbs 8:22

TRADITIONAL JEWISH THOUGHT takes as axiomatic the overarching concept of *Torah min hashamayim*, the proposition that the totality of "Torah originates from the heavens." This philosophical framework is distinct from the more concrete notion of *Torah miSinai*, the idea that the "Torah was delivered and received at Sinai." The former thought implies that there is a spiritual element to the Torah that transcends the realities of this earthly existence as we know it, while the latter places the Torah firmly in the hands of the Children of Israel.

The Book of Proverbs, being a wisdom book and not a narrative, discusses the concepts of Creator and creation, nobility and commonality, wealth and penury. The book presents cycles of arguments about who deserves praise and who deserves criticism, challenging social norms and assumptions. The juxtaposition of these concepts tears at the heart of what it means to be a spiritual creation.

Does wisdom, does Torah, originate from the human mind or does it have a metaphysical progenitor? Can human beings ever truly reconcile with an entire universe of ideas when we only occupy a speck of dust and ash hurtling through infinity? Finding answers to these questions is not only a spiritual struggle, but an existential yearning. Since before written history, human beings have wanted to understand more about their environment. Consider how the

Rabbis engage with the eighth chapter of Proverbs to suggest that the Torah originated in heaven and not on earth:

> Rabbi Chananya said, "Originally the Torah was in heaven, as it is written: 'I was with God as a confidant, a source of delight every day, rejoicing before God at all times' (Proverbs 8:30). Then Moses ascended, took the Torah, and brought it down to earth and gave it to humankind, as it is written, 'Rejoicing in God's inhabited world, / Finding delight with mortals" (Proverbs 8:31).[6]

Earlier in the eighth chapter of Proverbs, a case is made for the idea that an untethered primordial wisdom existed before Creation:

> I was created at the beginning of God's course
> As the first of the works of old.
> In the distant past I was fashioned,
> At the beginning, at the origin of earth.
> There was still no deep when I was brought forth,
> No springs rich in water;
> Before [the foundations of] the mountains were sunk,
> Before the hills I was born.
>   (Proverbs 8:22–25)

Then again, in the ninth chapter, the book reads, "Wisdom has built her house" (Proverbs 9:1). The Rabbis explain, using this verse, "This refers to the King of Kings of Kings, who built the entire world with wisdom."[7] Based on Proverbs 8:30, which refers to "a source of delight every day," Rabbi Shimon ben Lakish teaches that the Torah existed for two thousand years before the creation of the world[8] and that God used it as a blueprint in the act of Creation.

The Rabbis go far to wonder: on a very practical level, how could the Torah have been written in heaven without any earthly materials? What follows is a remarkable exchange on the ontological reverberations of wisdom in creation:

> On what was the primordial Torah written? On parchment? But the animals had not been created yet, so how could one use their skins for parchment? Maybe on gold or silver? But the metals had not been created, refined, or unearthed! Maybe on wooden tablets?

But the trees had not yet been created! So, what was it written on? It was written with black fire on white fire and wrapped around the right arm of the Holy One, as it is written: "On God's right arm fiery law" (Deuteronomy 33:2).[9]

Furthermore, based on a verse in Proverbs 23:5, "You see it, then it is gone," Rabbi Akiva argues that "when a person learns a chapter [of Torah] and forgets it, it returns to heaven."[10] Such an approach implies that there is a dynamic, ongoing experience between heaven and earth in our studying. We learn. Torah is revealed. We forget what we've learned and the Torah goes back up to heaven, to wait until Creation is in need of it again. We relearn, remember, and reengage in the flow between heaven and earth, between divine consciousness and human consciousness, that continues dynamically.

In a phenomenally creative and significant Talmudic passage, Rabbi Y'hoshua says we do not listen to heavenly voices anymore, based on the verse in Deuteronomy 30:12, "The Torah is not in heaven!"[11] But, what exactly does this pronouncement mean? As the Talmud passage records:

> What did he mean by this? Said Rabbi Yirm'yah, "That the Torah had already been given at Mount Sinai; we pay no attention to a Heavenly Voice, because You have long since written in the Torah at Mount Sinai: 'A case must be decided on the basis of the majority.'"
>
> Rabbi Natan met Elijah (the Prophet) and asked him, "What did the Holy One be blessed do in that hour [that is, at the hour that Rabbi Yirm'yah provided his insight]?" He replied, "God laughed [with joy], saying, 'My children have defeated Me, My children have defeated Me.'"[12]

Do we have true access to the Torah and to the wisdom it contains? In one sense, we may never know. The mind of God is a mysterious entity that has never been penetrated by any living person throughout history. On the other hand, by reading the Torah, by studying the commentaries, and by engaging each other in lively, courteous debate, we gain a fractional glimpse into the mind of Infinity. So yes, in one sense, the Torah is still in heaven. Revelation continues. The

Divine-human relationship continues. But the Torah is no longer in heaven. It is here. It is for the people to access at a moment's notice for comfort, for healing, and for spiritual revitalization. This means that religion and ethics are our responsibility. We do not look for a miracle or listen for the voice of God to emerge. We must do the challenging, but rewarding, work of textual interpretation, of reasoning, of dialogue, and of moral deliberation.

It is also for this reason that we embrace humility within narrative wars. Yossi Klein Halevi argues that in supporting dual narratives we never allow for "absolute justice for either side." He then explains that *tzedek*, "justice" is repeated twice in "Justice, justice, you shall pursue" (Deuteronomy 16:20) because "sometimes, the pursuit of justice means fulfilling two claims to justice, even when they clash."[13] Today, we shoulder the responsibility for the Torah but only with humility and radical uncertainty. This leads us not to moral relativism, but to bold action that has an underlying humility to it.

Chapter 9

1 Wisdom has built her house,
She has hewn her seven pillars.
2 She has prepared the feast,
Mixed the wine,
And also set the table.
3 She has sent out her maids to announce
On the heights of the town,
4 "Let the simple enter here."
To those devoid of sense she says,
5 "Come, eat my food
And drink the wine that I have mixed;
6 Give up simpleness and live,
Walk in the way of understanding."

7 To correct a scoffer,
Or rebuke an evildoer regarding a blemish,
Is to call down abuse on oneself.
8 Do not rebuke scoffers, for they will hate you;
Reprove the wise, and they will love you.
9 Instruct the wise, and they will grow wiser;
Teach the righteous, and they will gain in learning.
10 The beginning of wisdom is fear of GOD,
And knowledge of the Holy One is understanding.
11 For through me your days will increase,
And years be added to your life.
12 If you are wise, you are wise for yourself;
If you are a scoffer, you bear it alone.
13 The stupid woman bustles about;
She is simple and knows nothing.

פרק ט

1 חׇכְמוֹת בָּנְתָה בֵיתָהּ חָצְבָה עַמּוּדֶיהָ שִׁבְעָה:

2 טָבְחָה טִבְחָהּ מָסְכָה יֵינָהּ אַף עָרְכָה שֻׁלְחָנָהּ:

3 שָׁלְחָה נַעֲרֹתֶיהָ תִקְרָא עַל־גַּפֵּי מְרֹמֵי קָרֶת:

4 מִי־פֶתִי יָסֻר הֵנָּה חֲסַר־לֵב אָמְרָה לּוֹ:

5 לְכוּ לַחֲמוּ בְלַחֲמִי וּשְׁתוּ בְּיַיִן מָסָכְתִּי:

6 עִזְבוּ פְתָאיִם וִחְיוּ וְאִשְׁרוּ בְּדֶרֶךְ בִּינָה:

7 יֹסֵר | לֵץ לֹקֵחַ לוֹ קָלוֹן וּמוֹכִיחַ לְרָשָׁע מוּמוֹ:

8 אַל־תּוֹכַח לֵץ פֶּן־יִשְׂנָאֶךָּ הוֹכַח לְחָכָם וְיֶאֱהָבֶךָּ:

9 תֵּן לְחָכָם וְיֶחְכַּם־עוֹד הוֹדַע לְצַדִּיק וְיוֹסֶף לֶקַח:

10 תְּחִלַּת חָכְמָה יִרְאַת יְהֹוָה וְדַעַת קְדֹשִׁים בִּינָה:

11 כִּי־בִי יִרְבּוּ יָמֶיךָ וְיוֹסִיפוּ לְּךָ שְׁנוֹת חַיִּים:

12 אִם־חָכַמְתָּ חָכַמְתָּ לָּךְ וְלַצְתָּ לְבַדְּךָ תִשָּׂא:

13 אֵשֶׁת כְּסִילוּת הֹמִיָּה פְּתַיּוּת וּבַל־יָדְעָה מָּה:

14 She sits in the doorway of her house,
   Or on a chair at the heights of the town,

15 Calling to all the wayfarers
   Who go about their own affairs,

16 "Let the simple enter here";
   And to those devoid of sense she says,

17 "Stolen waters are sweet,
   And bread eaten furtively is tasty."

18 He does not know that the shades are there,
   That her guests are in the depths of Sheol.

14 וַיָּשְׁבָה לְפֶתַח בֵּיתָהּ עַל־כִּסֵּא מְרֹמֵי קָרֶת:

15 לִקְרֹא לְעֹבְרֵי־דָרֶךְ הַמְיַשְּׁרִים אֹרְחוֹתָם:

16 מִי־פֶתִי יָסֻר הֵנָּה וַחֲסַר־לֵב וְאָמְרָה לּוֹ:

17 מַיִם־גְּנוּבִים יִמְתָּקוּ וְלֶחֶם סְתָרִים יִנְעָם:

18 וְלֹא־יָדַע כִּי־רְפָאִים שָׁם בְּעִמְקֵי שְׁאוֹל קְרֻאֶיהָ:

The Power of Loving Rebuke

Reprove the wise, and they will love you.
—Proverbs 9:8

THE IDEA OF A LOVING REBUKE repeatedly appears in the Book of Proverbs,[1] emphasizing the importance of recognizing that peers, friends, and even detractors often effectively point out our blind spots and mistakes with the intention of correcting them. The positive evaluation of these rebukes is not an idea that originates in Proverbs, as there is a much earlier biblical mitzvah to offer "rebuke" (*tochachah*): "You shall not hate your kinsfolk in your heart. Rebuke your kin but incur no guilt on their account" (Leviticus 19:17). The verse in the Book of Proverbs teaches that we offer reproof for two reasons: so that our resentments do not lead to hate, and so that wrongs are not carried out—wrongs for which we too would be responsible. Rather than speaking *lashon hara* and *r'chilut*—"speaking negatively about another" and "spreading gossip"—we are to confront the individual about whom we have something to say directly. We care about the moral and spiritual welfare of others; thus, it is vital that we give feedback when we see others going astray.

There is a position according to which the mitzvah of rebuke only applies when the recipient of rebuke will be open to hearing our reproof. If not, it is considered counterproductive. As the Talmud teaches, "Just as there is a mitzvah for a person to say words of rebuke that will be accepted, so too there is a mitzvah for a person not to say words of rebuke that will not be accepted."[2] It's only a mitzvah when one suspects the other has the integrity and emotional intelligence to truly open their eyes to their blind spot and to correct the wrong that flows from that blindness. The goal of rebuke, according to this position, is not just to express righteous indignation, but to create change and stop a wrong or abuse that is occurring before our eyes.

Rabbi Zeira, on the other hand, teaches that one should offer rebuke whether or not one believes it will be accepted.[3] We simply cannot stand idly by while others do wrong in our midst. As Rabbi Abraham Joshua Heschel (1907–1972) teaches, "We are a generation that has lost its capacity for outrage. We must continue to remind ourselves that in a free society all are involved in what some are doing. *Some are guilty, all are responsible.*"[4] According to Heschel, even if our rebuke might not create change, it is still on us and our moral integrity to protest and not remain silent. Silence, in the face of injustice, would damage our character—indeed, even our souls.

A heavy charge, but a necessary one.

To ensure that justice is achieved in this world, we have to express outrage about actions that are morally wrong. Building off this axiom, the Rabbis teach, "Everyone who can protest a wrong in one's midst and does not [in public] is responsible for those people. [Someone who fails to protest the wrongs committed by] the people of his city is [held] responsible for the people of the city. For the whole world, one is responsible for the whole world."[5] If we do not speak up, our own moral integrity is in jeopardy. The Rabbis teach the concept of *sh'tikah k'hodaah*—that when we stay silent, we are considered to be in agreement.[6] According to this view, even if we cannot correct the wrong, we must not stand idly by.

Of course, in most cases, any feedback should be given gently, in private, at the right time, and in the appropriate environment. Most importantly, we should be sure not to shame anyone when challenging them. This is a difficult skill to learn. Abuses must be addressed. Some acts require whistleblowing when they become harmful or reach a level of illegality. Other acts require constructive feedback more than rebuke.

Sadly, we do not always have personal access to public figures, and so we must indeed bring our knowledge of evil into the public sphere. We cannot simply write private letters that will not be read. We must make the public aware so that we can collectively act in opposition to injustice.

The obligation to give *tochachah*, "rebuke," is not a simple command. The Rabbis teach that no one today is on the spiritual level necessary to engage in rebuke in a proper manner, as few are self-aware and humble enough to give *tochachah* appropriately, and few are humble enough to hear and accept it effectively. For this reason, *Sefer Chasidim*, a twelfth-century work ascribed to the German pietist Rabbi Yehudah HeChasid, suggests that we can only give rebuke to someone whom we love. Clearly, we have to be careful to check our motives before challenging another's conduct.

This is a reminder that yelling in the wind, even with the most righteous intentions, has its limits. Indeed, we must not only speak about issues at hand. We need to organize, build power, and create lasting change. There are limits to the efficacy of rebuke.

We must learn the art and ethics of critique (and protest) so that we can build a stronger society committed to truth, human dignity, and transparency. We can start by checking our own practices, holding ourselves accountable, and inviting others to reproach us if we ourselves ever cross boundaries. While we also need to discuss moral rebuke in families, social circles, the workplace, and broader communities, we also have to reflect on the moral limits of speech.

The Basis of Human Wisdom

The beginning of wisdom is fear of GOD,
And knowledge of the Holy One is understanding.
　　—Proverbs 9:10

T'CHILAT CHOCHMAH YIRAT HASHEM! Here, God is rendered as *yod, hei, vav,* and *hei (Adonai),* frequently just called *HaShem,* "The Name," to honor the sacred nature of God's ineffable nature. When God is revealed before Moses at the Burning Bush, the name that is given is *Ehyeh-Asher-Ehyeh* ("I will be what I will be"; Exodus 3:14). This is to say that our awe of "God" can also be understood as our awe of the divine capacity for evolving, growing, and becoming. Through wisdom, we invite ourselves to take the slightest glimpse into the Divine correlative to the human mind—the mind-like essence of the Infinite Creator of the universe. Through wisdom, we stand on the edges of the universe looking for clarity into life's greatest mysteries. And through wisdom, we are allowed to taste awe, realizing that the human mind is a speck compared to the wisdom-center of God.

But how do we approach wisdom? Where does it come from? Where will it lead to? These are questions that arise between the lines of the verse in Proverbs. And, to be sure, they lead us on an incredible journey through infinity, spirituality, and history.

In his work *Ehyeh: A Kabbalah for Tomorrow,* Rabbi Dr. Arthur Green, a contemporary scholar of Kabbalah and Chasidism, writes that "Kabbalah teaches that *Ehyeh* (pronounced *eh-yeh*), or 'I shall be,' is the deepest, most hidden name of God."[7] Indeed, the name *Ehyeh* has sparked spiritual curiosity among scholars and laypeople for millennia, with each generation exploring the tension between the simpler notion that the name points to God's quality of being self-evident in the world and the far more complex idea that the name *Ehyeh* points to God's quality of what we might call "extreme holiness," a holiness that can never be fully understood. As a result, each interpretation, despite never reaching the ultimate truth, is valid, each with its own strengths and weaknesses.

The ambiguity found in the linguistic construction of the phrase *Eyheh-Asher-Eyheh*, the title God gives God's self when God introduces God's self, is, perhaps, one of the greatest gifts of the Torah and Jewish thought generally. What other line has inspired so many Jewish thinkers to go beyond the ordinary and reach for the heavens? Indeed, what is most pertinent to the discussion of this verse is the examination of the inspiration that the term *Ehyeh* has provided for some of the brightest minds throughout history. Where did their thinking lead them? What does their thinking tell us about the mysteries and wonders of Torah? How do we apply these ancient words to our contemporary lives and societies?

But how can we interpret this verse in a way that is consistent with and relevant to our contemporary lives today when our relationship to God—and religion generally—is ever dynamic and not static, evolving and not stagnant? Traditional conceptions demanded fidelity to the past, loyalty to authority, and commitment to the unchanging. As a result, we now will need to engage in a completely new, constructive theology to identify an authentic Jewish model of dynamic theology. We are exploring a theology of radical divine presence, as the prophet articulated: "God's presence fills all the earth" (Isaiah 6:3)—and of a God who is at the center of all life and existence, as the "Ever-Living One" (Daniel 12:7). Everything is new, everything is refreshed and renewed, and everything is in a state of dynamic transformation.

We cannot know the God of the future without knowing the God of our ancestors. We must know our past in order to create a vision for our future. The Hebrew word *kodem* (before) has the same root as *kadimah* (forward), because in the Jewish tradition there is no moving forward without looking back. God is the one constant throughout history, but the "face" of God appears differently in each era and to each generation; the "voice" of God is spoken (and heard) differently in each era and by each generation.

The word *Ehyeh* points to a subject so expansive that we should begin by breaking down the meaning of the word. Martin Buber's explanation of the scene at the Burning Bush is succinct as well as insightful:

> Moses is told: *Ehyeh asher ehyeh*. This [phrase] is usually understood to mean I am that I am, in the sense that YHVH[8] describes himself as the Being One or even the Everlasting One, the one unalterably persisting in His being. But that would be abstraction of a kind which does not usually come about in periods of increasing religious vitality; while in addition the verb in the Biblical language does not carry this particular shade of meaning of pure existence. It means: happening, coming into being, being there, being present, being thus and thus; but not being in the abstract sense.[9]

Buber's explication is compelling, to be sure. His exegetical analysis points to the fact that the *Ehyeh* metonym is among the deepest, most mysterious, and most profound names of God in the Jewish canon. But following both Buber's and Green's suppositions: What is it about this name that makes it "the deepest"? What makes this name one of the most important of God's many names?

Let's go back to the biblical text of the Book of Exodus. Rabbi Harold Kushner, a leading contemporary Jewish thinker, writes:

> To overcome Moses' understandable reluctance, God answers him in a sentence that is often overlooked but that I consider to be one of the most important verses in all of Scripture. When Moses says, "Who am I that I should go to Pharaoh?" God answers not by telling Moses who he is, but by telling him who God is, saying, "I will be with you" (Exodus 3:12). When Moses, in the next verse, asks God, "What is Your name?"—that is, what is Your nature? What kind of God are you?—God replies, "*Ehyeh asher ehyeh*," three words so vague as to be virtually untranslatable, usually rendered somewhat mystifyingly as "I am who I am" or "I will be what I will be." But the Hebrew word *ehyeh* is the same word God used two verses earlier, "I will be with you."

> As I understand it, that is God's name. That is what God is all about. God is the One who is with us when we have to do something we do not think we are capable of doing.[10]

Reading into Kushner then, this name may be considered "the deepest" precisely because it portrays God as a mother (a quite subversive rendering in contrast to more normative notions of God as "Father"), as a caregiver with a feminine quality of a bedside nurse, in contrast to a sideline coach. According to this understanding, the most immediate meaning of the name *Ehyeh* is that God is present.

God may not be the great intervener who saves us from future calamities, but God is next to us—holding our hand, crying with us—in times of pain and sorrow. This is indeed a powerful theological and pastoral model. The Talmud corroborates this narrative:

> "In all their affliction, God was afflicted" (Isaiah 63:9). Rabbi Meir says, "When a person suffers, what does the *Shechinah* [the feminine side of the Divine] say? 'My head hurts! My arm hurts!' If God suffers at the blood of the wicked that is shed, how much more so at the blood of the righteous!"[11]

Such an idea envisioning God as an entity with human qualities would not work for those like Maimonides who envision God as incorporeal—how, for example, could God shed tears without physical tear ducts?—and thus also lacking in pure emotion. For others such as the narrator in the Mishnaic narrative above, liberation theology with its emphasis on welfare for the poor and vulnerable is another legitimate and powerful Jewish spiritual option. The Talmud suggests that even God sheds tears: "When God remembers God's children who dwell in misery among the nations of the world, God causes two tears to descend to the ocean, and the sound is heard from one end of the world to the other."[12]

The concept of the Divine as a present force in the world surrounding us is called panentheism, the notion that God penetrates everything that exists in the universe (and beyond as well).[13] Panentheism posits that God is found in all things, but more than comprising of all things; God is the Creator of this world but still more than this world. A typical example of this theology would be demonstrated in the well-known Rabbinic saying "God is the place of the world, but the world is not God's place."[14] Buber explained this notion of panentheism in more detail. In his view:

> God can be beheld in each thing and reached through each pure deed. But this insight is by no means to be equated with a pantheistic world view, as some have thought. In the Hasidic teaching, the whole world is only a word out of the mouth of God. Nonetheless, the least thing in the world is worthy that through it God should reveal Himself to the man who truly seeks Him; for no thing can exist without a divine spark, and each person can uncover and redeem this spark at each time and through each action, even the most ordinary, if only he performs it in purity, wholly directed to God and concentrated in Him.[15]

Centuries before Buber, the kabbalist Rabbi Moshe Cordovero (1522–70) wrote about the same notions, expressing himself in more traditional Jewish terms:

> The essence of divinity is found in every single thing—nothing but it exists. Since it causes everything to be, no thing can live by anything else. It enlivens them; its existence exists in each existent. Do not attribute duality to God. Let God be solely God. If you suppose that Ein Sof [a kabbalisitic concept of God's never-ending qualities] emanates until a certain point, and that from that point on is outside of it, you have dualized. God forbid! Realize, rather, that Ein Sof exists in each existent. Do not say, "This is a stone and not God." God forbid! *Rather, all existence is God, and the stone is a thing pervaded by divinity.*[16]

One reason that these ideas are comforting and spiritually energizing today lies in their radical approach that one need not go to synagogue to commune with God. We can, literally, experience the fullness of God's presence at any place and at any moment during our lives. The challenge, however, is recognizing this divinity and letting it permeate every aspect of our being. Why should we? Because we assume that not only does God influence the events of the world, but we also influence God, based on our assumption that there is an interconnectedness of the Divine and human realms. An anthology of teachings attributed to the Baal Shem Tov (ca. 1700–1760) and his student Rabbi Dov Baer ben Avraham of Mezeritch (d. 1772), known as the Maggid (preacher) of Mezeritch, explain this notion as follows: "Whatever you lack, that same deficiency is in the Shekhinah. For a person is a 'part of God from on high' (Job 31:2). Any deficiency in a part, therefore, applies to the Whole as well, and the Whole senses the deficiency of the part."[17]

The weakness in this view lies in the presupposition that evil exists in the world and there is a reason for its existence. This presupposition leads to a theological dilemma: If God is the cause of everything and is within everything, is God also found within evil? How does one make sense of the notion that God is all good when evil is allowed not only to exist but even, at times, to flourish throughout the world? The Chasidic masters continue to ponder this theologically problematic notion later in the text where they say:

> Everything in the universe contains holy sparks. Nothing is devoid of sparks, even wood and stones. There are sparks from the "breaking of the vessels" even in all of a person's deeds, even in a sin he commits.[18]

We see that it is not that we encounter God outside of ourselves, but rather that we find God within ourselves—and with that knowledge we can enter the divine realm. As Rabbi Nachman of Bratzlav (1772–1810), a great-grandson of the Baal Shem Tov and a significant early Chasidic master in his own right, taught, "The essence of a person is consciousness and therefore wherever one is conscious, there is the whole person. And likewise, one who knows and attains an understanding of God is actually in God. The greater a person's knowing, the more that person is included in the Root, in God."[19]

Teaching that God is to be found within each individual, Rebbe Nachman offers a rich pedagogy about the relationship between people and the Divine: the more conscious and mindful of the Divine a person is, the closer they are to God. This idea is reflected in later Jewish thought as well. For example, another Chasidic thinker explained:

> "You will find the Eternal your God, if only you seek with all your heart and soul" (Deuteronomy 4:29). That is to say: all wisdom and [the use of philosophical] analysis to comprehend God and His unity is called "there": that is to say, from somewhere else. But the real truth is literally in its place—that is to say, in one's heart. For when a person properly purifies his character traits, he will find the Divine in his heart. And that is the "finding," for you should know that you don't need to inquire about God, to seek and search from anywhere else, except in your heart and in your soul.[20]

Put into other words, at some point the concepts of God entering human beings and human beings entering God conflate. When the distinction between self and Other dissipates, the Divine dominates the non-divine aspect of human identity to an ultimate degree. Who is inside of Whom (or whom) is no longer a relevant question. Indeed, once we awaken our deepest inner self, we find a window between the terrestrial and celestial worlds that can be looked through from either direction. As the Christian mystic Eckhart von Hochheim (known as Meister Eckhart, ca. 1260–ca.1328), wrote, albeit for a completely different audience, "The eye with which I see God and the eye with which God sees me are the same eye."[21]

Such spiritual consciousness may create confusion about the authenticity of our perceptions. Addressing this potential problem, Arthur Green writes:

> We may project a God-image that reflects us, but God may also project a human image that reflects God. We may have projected a God who reflects our own cultural and historical setting, but we did so because we felt within us the stirring of a deeper reality in which we ourselves are mere projections. The human brain conceives of a Cosmic Mind of which the brain itself is a tiny copy. Or does the Cosmic Mind, the "mainframe" of intellect in the universe, replicate itself in some minuscule way in that mini-wonder called the human brain? Who can determine where this hall of mirrors begins?[22]

Anticipating that one might choose to embrace this type of radical spiritual consciousness, Rabbi Abraham Isaac HaKohen Kook explained that "in the flow of the holy spirit, one feels the divine life force coursing the pathways of existence, through all desires, all worlds, all thoughts, all nations, all creatures."[23] Furthermore, for Rabbi Kook, such divine dynamism leads people toward what some see as process theology—God is in the process of becoming rather than in a state of being. God—and God's will—evolves in synchronicity with humanity. It is for this reason then that we should not be traditionalists looking to the past but we should also be progressives ready to adapt to future possibilities. Rabbi Kook writes:

> And in general, this is an important rule in the struggle of ideas: we should not immediately refute any idea that comes to contradict anything in the Torah, but rather we should build the palace of Torah above it; in so doing we are exalted by the Torah, and through this exaltation the ideas are revealed, and thereafter, when we are not pressured by anything, we can confidently also struggle against it.[24]

Put slightly differently, the Torah expands as it incorporates new ideas that are good, wise, and just; democracy, egalitarianism, and pluralism, for example, are postbiblical manifestations of important biblical and Rabbinic values. However, how shall we approach Jewish rituals embedded in the past? Maimonides, the medieval rabbinic scholar, addressed this question when he explained how the will of God evolves over time:

> It was in accordance with the wisdom and plan of God, as displayed in the whole Creation, that God did not command us to give up and to discontinue all these manners of service; for to obey such a mitzvah it would have been contrary to the nature of a human being, who generally cleaves to that to which one is used; it would in those days have made the same impression as a prophet would make at present if he called us to the service of God and told us in God's name that we should not pray to God, not fast, not seek God's help in time of trouble; that we should serve God in thought, and not by any action.[25]

Here, Maimonides explains that animal sacrifice was not desirable, but that it would have been too radical to ask a people living in the ancient world to abandon the most basic way they knew of worshiping a divinity. The teachings of the Torah were not intended to be eternal per se. Instead, the purpose of the Torah was to maintain a mechanism ensuring ethical progress. Maimonides's thinking is consistent with Rav Kook's thinking that *midat chasidut*, "the trait of gentle piety," is embodied not in the technicalities of Jewish tradition, but rather in the spirit of morality that has its roots in traditional norms but that goes beyond the requirements of legal minutia.[26]

Not only do we as humans help the Torah to grow and change, but God Godself is also present in the dynamic evolution of human civilization through the application of Jewish tradition. The Talmud even suggests that God evolves with humans during these processes, most often through the form of the *Shechinah* (often understood as "the feminine side of the Divine")—at least to the extent of also going in and out of exile. One example is given in a story in Tractate *M'gillah*:

> Rabbi Shimon ben Yochai says, "Come and see how beloved the people Israel are before God! For wherever they were exiled, the *Shechinah* was with them. When they were exiled to Egypt, the *Shechinah* was with them, as it is said: 'Was I not revealed to your father's house when they were in Egypt?' (I Samuel 2:27). When they were exiled to Babylon, the *Shechinah* was with them, as it is said: 'For your sake have I been sent to Babylon' (Isaiah 43:14). And also, at the time when they are destined to be redeemed, the *Shechinah* will be with them, as it is said: 'And God will return with your returning exiles' (Deuteronomy 30:3). [The verse just cited] does not say 'God will bring back,' but 'God will return [*t'shuvah*].' [The Torah thus] teaches that God will return with them from the exiles."[27]

Another, more radical Talmudic passage goes so far as to suggest that God Godself does *t'shuvah* (engages in repentance):

> Rabbi Shimon ben Pazi posed the following contradiction. It is written, "And God created the two great luminaries" (Genesis 1:16)

[which implies that the sun and moon were created equally great], and it is written right afterward that "the great luminary [to dominate the night," meaning the sun is greater than the moon. How are these statements to be reconciled?]

[Initially both luminaries were created equal, but then] the moon said before God, "Sovereign of the universe! Is it possible for two kings to utilize the same crown? God said to it [the moon], "Indeed, go and diminish yourself!" [The moon] then said, "God, because I said a correct thing before You, I must diminish myself?!" God said to the moon [in consolation], "Go and rule by day and by night." The moon then said to God, "What is the greatness in that—for of what use is a candle in the daytime?" God said, "Go and let Israel reckon the days and years through you." The moon said to God, "But the sun also serves this capacity, for they cannot but reckon the seasons [by the sun], as it is written: 'And they [the two large luminaries] shall serve for signs and for festivals and for days and years' (Genesis 1:14)." God replied, "Go, and the righteous will be called by your name." . . . Nevertheless, God saw that [the moon] was not mollified. Therefore, God said, "Bring an atonement on My behalf for having diminished the moon!"[28]

While God might go out of God's way to help those surrounding God, when we do not embrace God, it is as if God does not truly exist. This notion finds apt expression in the following Rabbinic homily:

"You are My witnesses—says the Eternal—and I am God" (Isaiah 43:12). Rabbi Shimon bar Yochai said, "If you are My witnesses, then I am God. If you are not My witnesses, then I am not God."[29]

Furthermore, God's presence manifests differently at different times—God's identity and name are transformed at the given moment:

When I judge my creatures, I am called *Elohim*. When I wage war against the wicked, I am called *Tz'vaot*. When I suspend judgment for a person's sins, I am called *El Shaddai*. When I have compassion upon my world, I am called *YHVH* [the Eternal].[30]

Rabbi Y'hudah Aryeh Leib Alter (1847–1905), known as the S'fat Emet, articulates concisely how this theology expands one's religious service:

All people can become attached to God wherever they are, through the holiness that exists in every single thing, even corporeal things. . . . This is the foundation of all the mystical formulations in the world.[31]

Additionally, Rabbi Kalonymus Kalman Shapira (1889–1943, known as the Piaseczner Rebbe) writes about this spiritual approach as a response to despair in his moving work *Eish Kodesh*:

> Make it a regular practice, as you go about your day, to notice your sense of distraction and despair as you remind yourself that the entire world is God. The specks of sand underfoot are God. The air in my lungs is God. Why am I flung from the Holy Presence to this distant exile, to become a separate entity, a kingdom of one? My will and awareness are encased in this body, my very spirit is subject to this materiality, God help me.[32]

Emmanuel Levinas takes a slightly different approach to envisioning God in the world around us, explaining that we can only relate to a God that is felt, particularly in living interpersonal moments:

> The God of the Bible cannot be defined or proved by means of logical predications and attributions. Even the superlatives of wisdom, power, and causality advanced by medieval ontology are inadequate to the absolute otherness of God. It is not by superlatives that we can think of God, but by trying to identify the particular interhuman events that open toward transcendence and reveal travels where God has passed. The God of ethical philosophy is not God the almighty being of creation, but the persecuted God of the prophets who is always in relation with man and whose difference from man is never indifference. This is why I have tried to think of God in terms of a desire, a desire that cannot be fulfilled or satisfied—in the etymological sense of satis, measure.[33]

For many (especially those influenced by Maimonidean thought), the entire premise of this theological outlook will seem blasphemous. God is unknown, unfelt, indescribable—without corporeality and emotions—and is completely unreachable through normal human means. God is in the heavens and people are here on earth. It is mere arrogance to think we can touch, feel, or talk with God. It is heretical to think God can cry, or go into exile, or repent. However, as has been demonstrated here, Jewish tradition also embraces a theology of divine presence, of panentheism, of process theology, and of liberation theology, and these approaches all have roots in ancient Jewish thought.[34]

While there are many sources of light from the past—such as *or B'reishit* (the light of Creation), *or haTorah* (the light of Torah), and *or haMikdash* (the light of the Temple), to name a few—it is also true that by looking forward, we can access the most important lights, that of *or haMashiach* (the light of the Messiah) and *or haG'ulah* (the light of redemption). As the Chasidic thinker Rabbi Pinchas of Koretz explains:

> Imagine one is walking in a very dark place and sees from the distance a very bright light or torch. There are those whose eyes are very strong and who can therefore make use of the light even at a distance. And there are those whose legs are very strong, and who can therefore run closer to the light in order to make use of it. Similarly, the *Tannaim* [the sages of the Mishnaic period] and the *Amoraim* [the sages of the Talmudic period] were close to the destruction of the Temple, and they could still get illumination from its only recently departed light. And the latter-day tzaddikim of our own time are close to the light of the Messiah, and thus it is not surprising that they can also comprehend the truth.[35]

Our spiritual challenge is to maintain a constant awareness, presence, and willingness to listen and to react, even in uncertain moments—called "sacred attunement" by University of Chicago theology professor Michael Fishbane.[36] In fact, we must reobserve the ways of the world and gain new skills as we evolve, in order to be able to respond to contemporary challenges, especially in our human relationships. We cannot just be coasting, without growing and evolving; this is most certainly true with our relationship with the Divine. If we hold onto an immature, childish relationship with God, we condemn ourselves to relate to God in an infantile manner throughout our entire adult lives. By the same token, when we allow our appreciation of the Divine to develop and mature over the course of our lives, we will mirror the development inherent in the idea of the Divine.

For those of us who fully adapted to the humble uncertainty of postmodernity, the challenge of engaging with God to address our contemporary challenges becomes even more pressing. Rabbi Shimon Gershon Rosenberg (1949–2007), known by his initials as Rav Shagar, explains:

> I have already suggested that postmodernism expresses the perspective of *soveiv kol almin*, or "surrounding all the worlds"—the divinity that transcends the universe. The other perspective, *m'mallei kol almin*, or "filling all worlds," is the opposite way of *soveiv*, in that it describes a reality that is not random but is instead steeped in meaning, and even generates a powerful mutual responsibility based on a perception of the unity of creation and of the other's godliness. On its own, however, the *m'mallei* point of view poses great danger. In the spiritual context, it can give rise to stagnation and dogmatism, because it "contains" divinity in limited, constricted vessels; in the social context, it can create a suffocating embrace of the Other that overlooks the other's uniqueness.
>
> That is why *soveiv*—with its equanimity and the reflexivity that generates relativism—must augment the *m'mallei* point of view. *Soveiv* may be corrosive, but it engenders tolerance. Spirituality, forgoing the need to constrict God in a vessel, leads to a sense of release and ecstasy, to a true encounter with the divine infinitude.[37]

As our tradition teaches, "*Ehyeh*, I am: I am with you, I am by your side, I am here." And as the world evolves, as we evolve—indeed, perhaps, as God evolves with us— we must reconnect and revisit with one another. This is not always easy work. For those of us who consider ourselves traditionalists and progressives at the same time, theological models offer an exciting opportunity for embracing God more deeply in our work to repair the world. In our defeats, we can experience divine tears. In our triumphs, we can sense divine participation. In striving for equality, peace, and justice, we can feel the quiet voice of God urging us forward. Let us listen intently to determine the most intimate path of wisdom.

Chapter 10

1 The proverbs of Solomon:
   A wise son brings joy to his father;
   A dull son is his mother's sorrow.
2 Ill-gotten wealth is of no avail,
   But righteousness saves from death.
3 GOD will not let a righteous person go hungry,
   But denies the wicked what they crave.
4 Negligent hands cause poverty,
   But diligent hands enrich.
5 He who lays in stores during the summer is a capable son,
   But he who sleeps during the harvest is an incompetent.
6 Blessings light upon the head of a righteous person,
   But lawlessness covers the mouths of the wicked.
7 The name of a righteous person is invoked in blessing,
   But the fame of the wicked rots.
8 Whoever has a wise heart accepts commands,
   But one whose speech is foolish comes to grief.
9 Whoever lives blamelessly lives safely,
   But one who walks a crooked path will be found out.
10 Whoever winks causes sorrow;
   One whose speech is foolish comes to grief.
11 The mouth of a righteous person is a fountain of life,
   But lawlessness covers the mouths of the wicked.
12 Hatred stirs up strife,
   But love covers up all faults.
13 Wisdom is to be found on the lips of the intelligent,
   But a rod is ready for the back of the senseless.

פרק י

1 מִשְׁלֵי שְׁלֹמֹה בֵּן חָכָם יְשַׂמַּח־אָב וּבֵן כְּסִיל תּוּגַת אִמּוֹ׃

2 לֹא־יוֹעִילוּ אוֹצְרוֹת רֶשַׁע וּצְדָקָה תַּצִּיל מִמָּוֶת׃

3 לֹא־יַרְעִיב יְהֹוָה נֶפֶשׁ צַדִּיק וְהַוַּת רְשָׁעִים יֶהְדֹּף׃

4 רָאשׁ עֹשֶׂה כַף־רְמִיָּה וְיַד חָרוּצִים תַּעֲשִׁיר׃

5 אֹגֵר בַּקַּיִץ בֵּן מַשְׂכִּיל נִרְדָּם בַּקָּצִיר בֵּן מֵבִישׁ׃

6 בְּרָכוֹת לְרֹאשׁ צַדִּיק וּפִי רְשָׁעִים יְכַסֶּה חָמָס׃

7 זֵכֶר צַדִּיק לִבְרָכָה וְשֵׁם רְשָׁעִים יִרְקָב׃

8 חֲכַם־לֵב יִקַּח מִצְוֺת וֶאֱוִיל שְׂפָתַיִם יִלָּבֵט׃

9 הוֹלֵךְ בַּתֹּם יֵלֶךְ בֶּטַח וּמְעַקֵּשׁ דְּרָכָיו יִוָּדֵעַ׃

10 קֹרֵץ עַיִן יִתֵּן עַצָּבֶת וֶאֱוִיל שְׂפָתַיִם יִלָּבֵט׃

11 מְקוֹר חַיִּים פִּי צַדִּיק וּפִי רְשָׁעִים יְכַסֶּה חָמָס׃

12 שִׂנְאָה תְּעוֹרֵר מְדָנִים וְעַל כָּל־פְּשָׁעִים תְּכַסֶּה אַהֲבָה׃

13 בְּשִׂפְתֵי נָבוֹן תִּמָּצֵא חָכְמָה וְשֵׁבֶט לְגֵו חֲסַר־לֵב׃

14 The wise store up knowledge;
   The mouth of a fool is an imminent ruin.

15 For someone rich, wealth is a fortress;
   For the poor, poverty is a ruin.

16 The labor of the righteous makes for life;
   The produce of the wicked makes for want.

17 One who follows discipline shows the way to life,
   But one who ignores reproof leads astray.

18 One who conceals hatred has lying lips,
   While one who speaks forth slander is a dullard.

19 Where there is much talking, there is no lack of transgressing,
   But one who curbs the tongue shows sense.

20 The tongue of a righteous person is choice silver,
   But the mind of the wicked is of little worth.

21 The lips of a righteous person sustain many,
   But fools die for lack of sense.

22 It is the blessing of GOD that enriches,
   And no toil can increase it.

23 As mischief is sport for the dullard,
   So is wisdom for the man of understanding.

24 What an evildoer plots backfires;
   What the righteous desire is granted.

25 When the storm passes a wicked person is gone,
   But the righteous person is an everlasting foundation.

26 Like vinegar to the teeth,
   Like smoke to the eyes,
   Are sluggards to those who send them on a mission.

27 The fear of GOD prolongs life,
   While the years of the wicked will be shortened.

28 The righteous can look forward to joy,
   But the hopes of the wicked are doomed.

29 The way of GOD is a stronghold for a blameless person,
   But a ruin for evildoers.

14 חֲכָמִים יִצְפְּנוּ־דָעַת וּפִי־אֱוִיל מְחִתָּה קְרֹבָה:

15 הוֹן עָשִׁיר קִרְיַת עֻזּוֹ מְחִתַּת דַּלִּים רֵישָׁם:

16 פְּעֻלַּת צַדִּיק לְחַיִּים תְּבוּאַת רָשָׁע לְחַטָּאת:

17 אֹרַח לְחַיִּים שׁוֹמֵר מוּסָר וְעוֹזֵב תּוֹכַחַת מַתְעֶה:

18 מְכַסֶּה שִׂנְאָה שִׂפְתֵי־שָׁקֶר וּמוֹצִא דִבָּה הוּא כְסִיל:

19 בְּרֹב דְּבָרִים לֹא יֶחְדַּל־פָּשַׁע וְחֹשֵׂךְ שְׂפָתָיו מַשְׂכִּיל:

20 כֶּסֶף נִבְחָר לְשׁוֹן צַדִּיק לֵב רְשָׁעִים כִּמְעָט:

21 שִׂפְתֵי צַדִּיק יִרְעוּ רַבִּים וֶאֱוִילִים בַּחֲסַר־לֵב יָמוּתוּ:

22 בִּרְכַּת יְהוָה הִיא תַעֲשִׁיר וְלֹא־יוֹסִף עֶצֶב עִמָּהּ:

23 כִּשְׂחוֹק לִכְסִיל עֲשׂוֹת זִמָּה וְחָכְמָה לְאִישׁ תְּבוּנָה:

24 מְגוֹרַת רָשָׁע הִיא תְבוֹאֶנּוּ וְתַאֲוַת צַדִּיקִים יִתֵּן:

25 כַּעֲבוֹר סוּפָה וְאֵין רָשָׁע וְצַדִּיק יְסוֹד עוֹלָם:

26 כַּחֹמֶץ | לַשִּׁנַּיִם וְכֶעָשָׁן לָעֵינָיִם כֵּן הֶעָצֵל לְשֹׁלְחָיו:

27 יִרְאַת יְהוָה תּוֹסִיף יָמִים וּשְׁנוֹת רְשָׁעִים תִּקְצֹרְנָה:

28 תּוֹחֶלֶת צַדִּיקִים שִׂמְחָה וְתִקְוַת רְשָׁעִים תֹּאבֵד:

29 מָעוֹז לַתֹּם דֶּרֶךְ יְהוָה וּמְחִתָּה לְפֹעֲלֵי אָוֶן:

30 The righteous person will never be shaken;
    The wicked will not inhabit the earth.
31 The mouth of a righteous person produces wisdom,
    But the treacherous tongue shall be cut off.
32 The lips of a righteous person know what is pleasing;
    The mouth of the wicked [knows] duplicity.

30 צַדִּיק לְעוֹלָם בַּל־יִמּוֹט וּרְשָׁעִים לֹא יִשְׁכְּנוּ־אָרֶץ:

31 פִּי־צַדִּיק יָנוּב חָכְמָה וּלְשׁוֹן תַּהְפֻּכוֹת תִּכָּרֵת:

32 שִׂפְתֵי צַדִּיק יֵדְעוּן רָצוֹן וּפִי רְשָׁעִים תַּהְפֻּכוֹת:

The Memory of the Righteous

The name of a righteous person is invoked in blessing,
But the fame of the wicked rots.
　　—Proverbs 10:7

THE PHRASE THAT WE INVOKE so often after the name of the deceased, *zeicher tzaddik livrachah*, is derived from the first line of this verse in the Book of Proverbs. Why does Judaism place so much emphasis on creating such language around the notion of a "righteous person"? Why is it so important for us to keep a "righteous person" in our memory? Let's bracket these questions for a moment. Later in this chapter of Proverbs, we learn, "But the righteous person is an everlasting foundation" (Proverbs 10:25). Indeed, the world would collapse if it were run purely on greed. Those who take care of others sustain not only individual human lives but the foundation of societal trust that connects us all.

But it is not only the righteous people themselves, living and deceased, who are a blessing to us. Also our mere memory of them is a blessing. The objective (the person) and the subjective (our experience of the person) are intertwined, and the inner life of subjectivity is given force. Our memory of the other reminds us of our capacity to live up to our deepest potential, realizing that the impact of our work lasts well past the time of our death. We never complete the larger goals. We never become whole. Until the day that we pass from this earth, we are unable to fully step back and "throw in the towel." As the sage Rabbi Tarfon teaches, "You do not bear the burden of finishing the task, even as you are not free to distance yourself from it."[1] On this point of never giving up on our missions, Rabbi Judah Loew ben Bezalel—also known as the Maharal of Prague—teaches:

One is not created in their final wholeness. One was created to actualize their wholeness. That is the meaning of the verse 'One was born to toil.'[2] One is born and exists for the aim of this toil, which is the actualization of their potential. One can, however, never attain the state of actualized being. One must toil forever, to actualize their wholeness. That is the essence of their final wholeness. Even when one attains a certain level of actualization, one still remains potential, and will forever have to go on actualizing oneself.[3]

Born to toil: we must constantly strive to actualize a sense of wholeness in our soul. This human need for a sense of completion and wholeness, one might suggest, can only be achieved through the kind of partnership where finite souls embrace one another in search of love, care, and justice. Wholeness is found in the uniting of disparate souls.

The late James Fowler, a theologian and professor, attempts to describe the highest stage of faith that one could reach in one's spiritual development:

Fascinated with the charisma, the authority and frequently the ruthlessness of such leaders, we must not fail to attend to the . . . criteria of inclusiveness of community, of radical commitment to justice and love and of selfless passion for a transformed world, a world made over not in their images, but in accordance with an intentionality both divine and transcendent.[4]

In addition to working to improve the world, as spiritual wrestlers, we also crave feeling whole and spiritually fulfilled. This spiritual yearning furthers our attachments to justice, to seeking peace and equity for all people. The Talmud says that one only learns Torah in areas where one's heart has desire (interest).[5] So too in our leadership-justice work! Too often, we choose service that deadens us rather than awakens us. Our obligation, our opportunity, lies right before us. We must pursue the work that our souls crave. We must build our spiritual activist communities allowing this diversity of desire.

Awaken!

Awaken today!

Awaken every day!

Getting to this point of spiritual activism is not easy; it will never be. As Rabbi Joseph B. Soloveitchik argues, it is only when we are unprepared to lead and take initiative that God comes to us:

> A person is summoned to serve God by serving his fellow man when he is least inclined to place himself at the disposal of others, when he is preoccupied with himself and the only service to which he attributes any value is self-service. He is contented with himself; he has been successful, he rejoices at his own great achievements, and he is ready to shut out the world in his exultation over his marvelous self. Exactly then, the call to service sounds.[6]

While there are many ways to interpret this passage from Proverbs, my sense is that we are never allowed to be fully comfortable and content with our lives because once we are, God will challenge us to do more and to work harder. We need to keep the memory of the righteous in our hearts so that we have spiritual role models to look up to. To keep the memory of a righteous person alive, even the memory of someone relatively unknown in the world, is to take advantage of a valuable, infinite gift. Such a challenge should be interpreted not as a cause for despair, but rather as an opportunity to work continually to make the world a better place, helping those around us. May we continue to hear the call of others and always be willing to help.

Chapter 11

1   False scales are an abomination to GOD,
    Who finds an honest weight pleasing.
2   When arrogance appears, disgrace follows,
    But wisdom is with those who are unassuming.
3   The integrity of the upright guides them;
    The deviousness of the treacherous leads them to ruin.
4   Wealth is of no avail on the day of wrath,
    But righteousness saves from death.
5   The righteousness of the blameless smooths their way,
    But the wicked fall by their wickedness.
6   The righteousness of the upright saves them,
    But the treacherous are trapped by their malice.
7   At death the hopes of a wicked person are doomed,
    And the ambition of evildoers comes to nothing.
8   A righteous person is rescued from trouble
    And it comes to the wicked instead.
9   An impious person destroys a neighbor through speech,
    But through knowledge the righteous are rescued.
10 When the righteous prosper the city exults;
    When the wicked perish there are shouts of joy.
11 A city is built up by the blessing of the upright,
    But it is torn down by the speech of the wicked.
12 One who speaks contemptuously of neighbors is devoid of sense;
    A prudent man keeps his peace.
13 A base fellow gives away secrets,
    But a trustworthy soul keeps a confidence.
14 For want of strategy an army falls,
    But victory comes with much planning.

פרק יא

1 מֹאזְנֵי מִרְמָה תּוֹעֲבַת יְהוָה וְאֶבֶן שְׁלֵמָה רְצוֹנוֹ:

2 בָּא־זָדוֹן וַיָּבֹא קָלוֹן וְאֶת־צְנוּעִים חָכְמָה:

3 תֻּמַּת יְשָׁרִים תַּנְחֵם וְסֶלֶף בּוֹגְדִים (ושדם) [וְשַׁדֵּם]:

4 לֹא־יוֹעִיל הוֹן בְּיוֹם עֶבְרָה וּצְדָקָה תַּצִּיל מִמָּוֶת:

5 צִדְקַת תָּמִים תְּיַשֵּׁר דַּרְכּוֹ וּבְרִשְׁעָתוֹ יִפֹּל רָשָׁע:

6 צִדְקַת יְשָׁרִים תַּצִּילֵם וּבְהַוַּת בֹּגְדִים יִלָּכֵדוּ:

7 בְּמוֹת אָדָם רָשָׁע תֹּאבַד תִּקְוָה וְתוֹחֶלֶת אוֹנִים אָבָדָה:

8 צַדִּיק מִצָּרָה נֶחֱלָץ וַיָּבֹא רָשָׁע תַּחְתָּיו:

9 בְּפֶה חָנֵף יַשְׁחִת רֵעֵהוּ וּבְדַעַת צַדִּיקִים יֵחָלֵצוּ:

10 בְּטוּב צַדִּיקִים תַּעֲלֹץ קִרְיָה וּבַאֲבֹד רְשָׁעִים רִנָּה:

11 בְּבִרְכַּת יְשָׁרִים תָּרוּם קָרֶת וּבְפִי רְשָׁעִים תֵּהָרֵס:

12 בָּז־לְרֵעֵהוּ חֲסַר־לֵב וְאִישׁ תְּבוּנוֹת יַחֲרִישׁ:

13 הוֹלֵךְ רָכִיל מְגַלֶּה־סּוֹד וְנֶאֱמַן־רוּחַ מְכַסֶּה דָבָר:

14 בְּאֵין תַּחְבֻּלוֹת יִפָּל־עָם וּתְשׁוּעָה בְּרֹב יוֹעֵץ:

15 Harm awaits one who stands surety for another;
   One who spurns pledging shall be secure.

16 A graceful woman obtains honor;
   Ruthless men obtain wealth.

17 A kindly man benefits himself;
   A cruel one makes trouble for himself.

18 A wicked person earns illusory wages,
   But one who sows righteousness has a true reward.

19 Righteousness is a prop of life,
   But to pursue evil leads to death.

20 Crooked minds are an abomination to GOD,
   But those whose way is blameless are pleasing.

21 Assuredly, the evildoer will not escape,
   But the offspring of the righteous will be safe.

22 Like a gold ring in the snout of a pig
   Is a beautiful woman bereft of sense.

23 What the righteous desire can only be good;
   What the wicked hope for [stirs] wrath.

24 Some give generously and end with more;
   Others stint on doing the right thing and incur a loss.

25 A generous person enjoys prosperity;
   One who satisfies others shall likewise be sated.

26 Whoever withholds grain earns the curses of the people,
   But blessings are on the head of the one who dispenses it.

27 One who earnestly seeks good pursues what is pleasing;
   Evil comes to someone who is bent on it.

28 One who trusts in wealth shall fall,
   But the righteous shall flourish like foliage.

29 He who makes trouble for his household shall inherit the wind;
   A fool is a slave to the wise-hearted.

30 The fruit of the righteous is a tree of life;
   The wise captivate people.

31 If the righteous on earth get their deserts,
   How much more evildoers and sinners.

רַע־יֵרוֹעַ כִּי־עָרַב זָר וְשֹׂנֵא תֹקְעִים בּוֹטֵחַ׃ 15

אֵשֶׁת־חֵן תִּתְמֹךְ כָּבוֹד וְעָרִיצִים יִתְמְכוּ־עֹשֶׁר׃ 16

גֹּמֵל נַפְשׁוֹ אִישׁ חָסֶד וְעֹכֵר שְׁאֵרוֹ אַכְזָרִי׃ 17

רָשָׁע עֹשֶׂה פְעֻלַּת־שָׁקֶר וְזֹרֵעַ צְדָקָה שֶׂכֶר אֱמֶת׃ 18

כֵּן־צְדָקָה לְחַיִּים וּמְרַדֵּף רָעָה לְמוֹתוֹ׃ 19

תּוֹעֲבַת יְהוָה עִקְּשֵׁי־לֵב וּרְצוֹנוֹ תְּמִימֵי דָרֶךְ׃ 20

יָד לְיָד לֹא־יִנָּקֶה רָּע וְזֶרַע צַדִּיקִים נִמְלָט׃ 21

נֶזֶם זָהָב בְּאַף חֲזִיר אִשָּׁה יָפָה וְסָרַת טָעַם׃ 22

תַּאֲוַת צַדִּיקִים אַךְ־טוֹב תִּקְוַת רְשָׁעִים עֶבְרָה׃ 23

יֵשׁ מְפַזֵּר וְנוֹסָף עוֹד וְחוֹשֵׂךְ מִיֹּשֶׁר אַךְ־לְמַחְסוֹר׃ 24

נֶפֶשׁ־בְּרָכָה תְדֻשָּׁן וּמַרְוֶה גַּם־הוּא יוֹרֶא׃ 25

מֹנֵעַ בָּר יִקְּבֻהוּ לְאוֹם וּבְרָכָה לְרֹאשׁ מַשְׁבִּיר׃ 26

שֹׁחֵר טוֹב יְבַקֵּשׁ רָצוֹן וְדֹרֵשׁ רָעָה תְבוֹאֶנּוּ׃ 27

בּוֹטֵחַ בְּעָשְׁרוֹ הוּא יִפֹּל וְכֶעָלֶה צַדִּיקִים יִפְרָחוּ׃ 28

עֹכֵר בֵּיתוֹ יִנְחַל־רוּחַ וְעֶבֶד אֱוִיל לַחֲכַם־לֵב׃ 29

פְּרִי־צַדִּיק עֵץ חַיִּים וְלֹקֵחַ נְפָשׁוֹת חָכָם׃ 30

הֵן צַדִּיק בָּאָרֶץ יְשֻׁלָּם אַף כִּי־רָשָׁע וְחוֹטֵא׃ 31

Workers and the Dignity of a Stable Income

Wealth is of no avail on the day of wrath,
But righteousness saves from death.
    —Proverbs 11:4

THE THEME OF CHARITY (*tzedakah,* "righteousness," in the above translation) rescuing vulnerable people from death is repeated throughout the Book of Proverbs.[1] While we can most easily see that charitable giving can rescue a needy recipient of charity from impoverished circumstances, the act of giving can also rescue the soul of the giver from their own greed or from an inability to empathize with tragedy right before their eyes. Additionally, in the United States, many thinkers, from Henry David Thoreau to Martin Luther King, have objected to, and even defied, laws that deprive people who lack resources of the basic necessities of life. It is not adequate to provide meager soup kitchens to which the poor must travel. Many members of our communities need more and find themselves so desperate that they beg in the streets.

We must respond earnestly and with compassion. The Jewish people need to be at the forefront of this call to action, applying the teachings of the Torah to help make the world a better, more just place.

A Rabbinic teaching from Rabbi Meir asks how we can balance justice manifested in support of the oppressed with righteousness that calls for equality before the law. His answer is not to change the law or the tools that allow for the practice of procedural justice, but to alter our perceptions of charity so that we can make sure that the poor, needy, and marginalized are better cared for.[2] Other Rabbinic teachings provide an alternative view. In a teaching drawn from two sources found in the Book of Proverbs, we learn that at times the law actually embodies ethics that go beyond the letter of the law:

> Some porters working for Rabah bar bar Chanan broke a jug of wine. He seized their clothes. They came before Rav, and Rav said to Rabah bar bar Chanan, "Give them their clothing." Rabah bar bar Chanan said to him, "Is this the law?" Rav said, "Yes, because of the principle 'You should walk in the ways of the good.'" He gave them back their clothes. They said to him, "We are poor, and we troubled ourselves to work all day and we are needy—do we receive nothing? Immediately, Rav said to Rabah bar bar Chanan, "Go, give them their wages." He said to Rav, "Is this the law?" Rav said, "Yes—'you should keep the ways of the righteous.'"[3]

The Malbim explains that "the ways of the good" means general kindness and compassion, and the second part of the verse, "keep the ways of the righteous," is more specific to laborers.[4] Part of what is fascinating here is that the Book of Proverbs is quoted in a legal dispute. The Rabbis typically draw from verses in the Torah to support their legal opinions, but not from the *Tanach* at large. In quoting the Book of Proverbs, they display their commitment to the crucial principle that the law includes that which goes beyond the law. The verse cited by Rav is about general righteousness and is not specifically about one prescriptive law. The metaethics of Proverbs serve as the proof text for a law requiring us to support the vulnerable. Rabbi Meir thinks that charity is outside of the law. However, Rav explains that charity must be a part of justice.

The Baal Shem Tov teaches:

> I heard in the name of Rabbi Yisroel Baal Shem Tov that if you do a good deed, but have an ulterior motive, it is better not to do it at all. The only exception is charity. Even though it is not as good as doing it with a pure motive, it is still a good deed, since you sustain the poor no matter what your motive.[5]

Rabbi David Jaffe, a progressive Orthodox Mussar teacher, writes that we must habituate ourselves more deeply in our *tzedakah* commitments:

The sacrificial system, so prominent in Leviticus and Numbers, is a model for being in relationship, for drawing close. *Ratzon*, "desire," may be the most important element of becoming close to God and others. However, *ratzon* can be fleeting. We may feel a connection one day and not on the next. Through concrete acts of thoughtfulness, giving, and love, *n'divut*, "generosity," helps us turn our *ratzon* for closeness into habitual behavior. From this internalized sense of responsibility for each other and for God, we create real closeness.[6]

Indeed, Proverbs 10:2 indicates that "*tzedakah* [righteousness] saves from death." It is the greatest force. The Talmud then interprets:

> He [Rabbi Y'hudah] used to say: "Ten strong things were created in the world: A mountain is strong, but iron cuts through it. Iron is strong, but fire can make it bubble. Fire is strong, but water puts it out. Water is strong, but clouds contain it. Clouds are strong, but the wind can scatter them. Breath is strong, but the body holds it in. The body is strong, but fear breaks it. Fear is strong, but wine dissipates its effects. Wine is strong, but sleep overcomes its power. Death is stronger than all of them. But *tzedakah* saves from death, as it is written, 'And *tzedakah* saves from death' (Proverbs 10:2)."[7]

What does it mean that *tzedakah* saves lives? Here are a few possibilities:

1. In the most literal sense, it can save the life of people who are dependent upon the financial support.
2. It saves the giver morally.
3. We need righteous connection with others to be saved from isolation and depression (a form of spiritual death).
4. "True life" is achieved through compassionate oneness. Selfish living leads one to be detached from the Source of Life.

One aspect of justice must be to ensure that workers can live off their wages. Lessening the gap between the rich and the poor is one of the most crucial moral issues to address in America today. Much of the problem has to do with fair wages. While some progress has been made, we still have a long way to go. In 2012, eight states raised their minimum wage, yet the federal wage floor for most workers many years later remains $7.25 an hour, well below what could be considered a livable wage.[8] The integrity of our labor system is broken, and we must respond to this brokenness.

While some may argue that raising the cost of labor will hurt workers because employers might then need to hire fewer workers, many have shown this argument to be false.[9] Speaking to this issue, Nobel Prize–winning economist Robert Solow stated that "the evidence of job loss is weak. And the fact that the evidence is weak suggests that the impact on jobs is small."[10] Furthermore, there is evidence suggesting that when low-wage workers have more spending power, more jobs and an increased demand for labor are created. For example, in 2019, a report published by the Economic Policy Institute stated that raising the federal minimum wage to $15 an hour would lift the wages of 33 million workers, 6.2 million of whom live in poverty.[11] Proverbs teaches, "The labor of the righteous makes for life" (Proverbs 10:16).

At the end of the day, minimum wage reform is still not enough. Even if wage rates are raised, that will not be enough to push low-wage-earning families above the poverty line and enable them to support themselves without needing help from others. While the Book of Proverbs doesn't have anything to say about the issue in a literal sense, these verses certainly support the notion that we have to remain watchful and defend those teetering on the brink of poverty. We need to turn the raise of minimum wages from a partisan issue to a moral imperative. To promote a raise of the minimum wage is itself a mitzvah. Maimonides says that ensuring that others have work that can sustain them is the highest rung of the hierarchy on how to give *tzedakah*.[12] What is important to note in this interpretation is that according to Jewish tradition, *tzedakah* means not only "charity" but also "justice." We rectify social wrongs and fulfill our obligations through the giving of *tzedakah*. With a raise in the minimum wage, people who work are given the chance to escape deep poverty.

Maimonides is interested in private voluntary giving; however, this value is all the more true when applied to a system of legislation that transforms individually accepted norms into fixtures of an entire social system. The mission of the Jewish people is to perpetuate our most precious values of the good and the just and to inculcate them into broader society. Our messianic dream is the creation of a society where Torah values are actualized in the world to create a more just and holy civilization. The Jewish vision for a messianic age is one in which there will be no more war (Isaiah 2:4), peace and harmony with our nature (Isaiah 4:2), an end to human fear (Micah 4:4), and justice for the oppressed and dignity for those in poverty (Isaiah 11:4).

Raising the minimum wage helps underprivileged families move out of poverty, spurs job creation, and stimulates economic growth; thus it is our Jewish obligation to lead the fight for economic justice. The Rema teaches that when one is involved in an issue regarding public monies, one must engage in these issues *l'shem shamayim*, "for the sake of heaven"—that is, for the right reasons, not based on self-interest.[13] It is crucial that Jews position themselves on the right side of this national debate as advocates for systemic change for the poor.

The Rabbis already limited the wealth of owners selling essential food to help the poor through the laws of *onaah* (misappropriation; price gouging). An owner should not keep more than one-sixth of the profit in order that others could be sustained as well.[14] For the Rabbis, the value of maintaining an orderly, just society where the needs of all can be met outweighs the full autonomy of owners to maximize their profits.

The primary wage responsibilities fall upon employers. Jewish legal authorities, such as Rabbeinu Yonah in *Sefer HaYirah*, teach:

> Be careful not to afflict a living creature, whether animal or fowl, and even more so not to afflict a human being, who is created in God's image. If you want to hire workers and you find that they are poor, they should become like poor members of your household. You should not disgrace them, for you shall command them respectfully, and should pay their salaries (1:7).

In the above passage, Rabbeinu Yonah teaches that when we hire a worker and find that they are still poor after we pay them, we must treat them as "members of [our] households"—*b'nei beitecha*. If we choose to become employers, we must take responsibility to ensure that our workers do not live in poverty.

The patchwork of minimum wage rules currently in place across the country is a collective violation of the biblical prohibition of *oshek* (worker oppression), as workers remain poor while they so frequently work to their full capacity. Our verse informs us that we must not be enablers of social wrongs—*lifnei iveir* (we are admonished in Leviticus 19:14 not to place a stumbling block "before a person who is blind")—linking the two responsibilities of fair wages and Jewish activism. Now is the time for a collective Jewish intervention to ensure that those who work can live.

Workers should not be forced by unreasonably low wage rates to work multiple jobs, only to pile on debt, and to take handouts. It is unjust that a person who works all day, every day, should live in poverty. There is no theory that outweighs the imperative for basic justice in a nation with soaring corporate profits. As Barbara Ehrenreich, who described her attempt to survive on a wage (above the minimum) in *Nickel and Dimed* (2002), wrote later in 2007, "There is no moral justification for a minimum wage lower than a living wage. And given the experience of the . . . states that have raised their minimum wages, there isn't even an amoral economic justification."[15]

Furthermore, Jews are commanded against following laws that do the opposite of denying humanity to others, since we are obligated to feed and tend to the most vulnerable in our midst. For example, as the *Shulchan Aruch* says:

> If someone comes and says, "Feed them," you do not check them to see if they are an imposter, but you feed them right away. If there is a naked person who comes and says, "Give me clothing," you check them to see if they are an imposter. And if you know them, you give them clothing right away.[16]

In the Torah, a society that punishes those that feed the homeless is analogous to Sodom, a city that was riddled with moral perversion.[17] The story encourages us to engage in hospitality and acts of kindness; we are warned that there will be punishment for those who mistreat guests and those in need. We see this in the paradigmatic failing of the value of *hachnasat orchim* (hosting guests) in Sodom and the resulting destruction of society (Genesis 19). As the Talmud further elaborates, "They had beds [in Sodom] upon which travelers slept. If one [the guest] was too long, they shortened them [by lopping off their feet]; if too short, they stretched them out."[18] They not only avoided welcoming guests, they also abused them—and they punished those who reached out to others. As the midrash explains, "They issued a proclamation in Sodom saying: 'Everyone who strengthens the hand of the poor and the needy with a loaf of bread shall be burnt by fire!'"[19]

Maimonides teaches, "We are required to be more scrupulous with the mitzvah of charity than with any other positive mitzvah, for charity is emblematic of the righteous descendants of Abraham, our father, as it says: 'For I have singled him out, that he may instruct his children and his posterity to keep the way of the Eternal by doing what is just' (Genesis 18:19)."[20]

Charity is not purely about giving, but to a significant degree it is about empowering. Today, using the Book of Proverbs as a guide and a motivator, we can act to create change to ensure that all who work are afforded dignity in what they do. The worker rights movement need not take place solely in street marches. Rather, each of us, in our own ways, can add support to those working hard and enhance the dignity of the workers in our midst.

Do We Rejoice at the Downfall of Our Enemies?

When the righteous prosper the city exults;
When the wicked perish there are shouts of joy.
—Proverbs 11:10

THE BOOK OF PROVERBS entails a contradiction: on the one hand, we learn about the "shouts of joy" when the wicked die; yet, later in the book, we also learn, "If your enemies fall, do not exult; / If they trip, let your heart not rejoice" (Proverbs 24:17). One way to resolve the contradiction might be to say that the first verse is descriptive (people will naturally rejoice) and that the second verse is prescriptive (we should try not to rejoice).

When the Israelites cross the Reed Sea and reached redemption after generations of enslavement, they sing to celebrate their freedom from bondage, as any free people would do. At that same moment of liberation, the walls of the Reed Sea come crashing back down, killing the Egyptian pursuers, who so desperately wanted to recapture their former human chattel. Picture yourself in the moment. After a lifetime of being treated cruelly, suffering from lost dignity and individuality, and being told and shown that your life is worth less than mud, would you not feel the need to release decades of pent-up anger and righteous fury too? A song of victory over a fallen enemy: the sweetest, most cathartic, taste of revenge.

However, even though the Torah records that a song was sung after the defeat of the Egyptian hordes, it is up to debate who actually sang the song on the other side of the sea. The Talmud provides three different answers to this question:

1. Moses sang and the people replied with a refrain.
2. Moses sang and the people responded verse by verse.
3. Moses and the people sang together.[21]

The Sages of the Talmud record in their conversations that it wasn't only the living who cried out in song, but even the fetuses in the mothers' wombs participated in joyous song![22] Think of such a scene when even the unborn have such a strong spiritual connection to the downfall of their enemy that a miracle occurs and even they join their families in song. The Sages go so far as to suggest that the mothers' bellies even had a window through which the fetuses could peer out to witness the redemption of the Israelite people.[23]

Over the millennia, the primal human notion of revenge and vendetta have spurred conflicts and cost countless lives. Yet, humans go to war. We see people perish and body counts rise; we see societies lust for weapons that destroy bodies and souls. When we look back to the biblical scene at the Reed Sea, we are given an ethical Rorschach test: Are the Hebrews rejoicing over their freedom or are they celebrating the brutal death of the Egyptians in the sea? The brilliant but ambiguous treatment of the text by the Rabbis and their different interpretations leave unanswered the profound question of whether we should celebrate the deaths of our enemies. The Rabbis debated the question elsewhere vociferously, with various sages choosing one viewpoint over the other. As a passage in the Mishnah reads:

> Do not rejoice when your enemy falls, and let not your heart be glad when he stumbles, lest God see it and be displeased, and God turn away God's wrath from your enemy.[24]

In demonstrating the problematic nature of the mirth at the death of a fellow creature of God, the Rabbis suggest in a truly moving midrash that the angels in the heavenly court were rebuked by God for wanting to join the newly freed Israelites in their song:

> In that hour the ministering angels wished to utter the song [of praise] before the Holy One, blessed be God, but God rebuked them, saying, "My handiwork [the Egyptians] is drowning in the sea; would you utter song before Me?!"[25]

Every year during the Passover seder, we perform a most peculiar ritual. After filling our wine glasses, we recite the order of the Ten Plagues, some of the darkest and most horrible miracles that ever occured on earth. As we recite the plagues, we spill out some of the wine from our glasses. The plagues were a constant plea for mercy, yet Pharaoh refused to budge. Pharaoh's heart was so hardened against the idea of showing clemency for the Hebrews under his rule that he caused his own people to suffer. They suffered horribly, experiencing countless atrocities such as boils, relentless hail, the death of crops, the death of livestock, and a heavy darkness. The Egyptians suffered so that the Hebrews could taste freedom.

If Jewish thought shows us anything, it's that empathy for the oppressed is a value above all other. Yet, it seems odd that the Jewish people would show empathy for an empire that treated the ancient Israelites as nothing more than property—and yet, we reject blood-lust for compassion and disown the need to celebrate the downfall of enemies. One of the primary reasons given for why we remove ten drops of wine from our seder cups is that the act constitutes a gesture of mourning over the loss of life of Egyptians. They enslaved us, beat us, robbed us, but we still mourn their death? Indeed, a midrash says that we recite only a partial *Hallel*[26] on Passover instead of a full one because of the fact that we made the Egyptian people suffer:

> Another explanation for not writing joyousness in regard to Passover is because of the death of the Egyptians. We thus find that all seven days of Sukkot we say *Hallel*, whereas on Passover we only say *Hallel* on the first day and its night. Why? As Sh'muel [a rabbi from the time of the Mishnah] said, "Do not rejoice when your enemy falls."[27]

We are a better and stronger people precisely because we recognize that pain is a human condition. God created all of humanity, not only the Jews, and thus, in the Jewish tradition, the downfall of any person means that a creation of God is lost. This theological realization influenced Jewish thought in profound ways, and ironically, those ways have set us apart morally.

At the same time, the Rabbis of the Talmud were not moral relativists. While they did not condemn the non-Jew as a category, they did condemn evil wherever they found it, including among themselves. They believed we should celebrate ridding the earth of evil. As noted in the Talmud:

> When the wicked enter the world, wrath enters, for it is written, "Along with the wicked comes derision, / And with rogues, contempt" (Proverbs 18:3). When the wicked perish from the world, good comes to the world. . . . When the righteous departs from the world, evil enters, as it is written, "The righteous perishes, / And no one considers; / Pious men are taken away, / And no one gives thought / That because of evil / The righteous was taken away" (Isaiah 57:1).[28]

Consider also this moving passage from the Talmud:

> Rabbi Y'hudah the son of Rabbi Shimon ben Pazi said, "King David composed a hundred and three chapters [psalms], and he did not say 'Halleluyah' until he saw the downfall of the wicked, as it says, 'May sinners disappear from the earth, / and the wicked be no more. / Bless the Eternal, O my soul. / Hallelujah' (Psalm 104:35–36)."[29]

So, how do we balance these two positions to, on the one hand, despise evil and vanquish it from the earth but, on the other hand, not celebrate the death of anyone, even our enemies? The Talmud relates a story featuring B'ruriah, the greatest female sage of the Talmud, on this notion:

> There were some boors in Rabbi Meir's neighborhood, who caused him great distress. Rabbi Meir would pray that they would die. His wife B'ruriah said to him, "What are you thinking?" [He responded,] "Because it says, 'Sinners will cease'" (Psalm 104:35). [She responded,] "Does it say 'sinners'? 'Sins' is what it says. [End the evil, not evildoers.] Furthermore, go down to the end of the verse, 'The wicked be no more.' Since their sinning will stop, will there 'no longer be sinners'? Rather, you should pray that they repent, then 'they will be wicked no more.'" [Rebbi Meir] prayed for mercy upon them, and they repented.[30]

Hate the sin, love the sinner—a mantra that sustains and nourishes Jewish wisdom. Rabbi Meir Simcha HaKohen of Dvinsk,
known as the Meshech Chochmah (1843–1926, Latvia) goes so far
as to write, "There is no festival or holiday in Israel celebrating the
downfall of enemies." But what about holidays and texts that clearly
seem to demonstrate a celebration? He continues:

> For all [other] nations make the day of victory, the day of their
> enemies' downfall, into a victory holiday. Not so for Israel! They
> do not rejoice over their enemies' downfall. They will not celebrate
> that joy. . . . A superior man does not rejoice at his enemy's down-
> fall, since such rejoicing is evil in the eyes of the Eternal, and one
> should hate that which is evil in the Eternal's eyes.[31]

Indeed, if a holiday or a ritual seems to celebrate death, we might
have misinterpreted it. We must understand that violence and death
have always been a part of the world, but they have never been something to be celebrated. We must fight for good and passionately
express gratitude when good overcomes evil. We must remain humble and recognize God within everything, even if God is at times hidden (and suppressed) deep within the oppressor. We must go even
further and help our enemy. "When you see the ass of your enemy
lying under its burden and would refrain from raising it, you must
nevertheless help raise it" (Exodus 23:5). Is this about turning an
enemy into a friend? Is this about caring about the animal's plight?
Whatever it is, the Talmud, commenting on this verse, suggests that
if we encounter our friend and enemy on the road at the same time,
both in need of help, we should choose to help our enemy to overcome our "evil inclination" (yetzer hara; Genesis 6:5) that drives us
toward those we already love.[32] That is true righteousness.

Chapter 12

1 One who loves discipline loves knowledge;
   Whoever spurns reproof is a brute.
2 A good person earns the favor of GOD,
   A man of intrigues, God's condemnation.
3 No one can be established in wickedness,
   But the root of the righteous will not be shaken loose.
4 A woman of substance is a crown for her husband,
   But an incompetent one is like rot in his bones.
5 The purposes of the righteous are justice,
   The schemes of the wicked are deceit.
6 The words of the wicked are a deadly ambush,
   But the speech of the upright saves them.
7 Overturn the wicked and they are gone,
   But the house of the righteous will endure.
8 A man is commended according to his intelligence;
   A twisted mind is held up to contempt.
9 Better to be lightly esteemed and have a servant
   Than to put on airs and have no food.
10 A righteous person knows the needs of their beast,
   But the compassion of the wicked is cruelty.
11 He who tills his land shall have food in plenty,
   But one who pursues vanities is devoid of sense.
12 A wicked man covets the catch of evildoers;
   The root of the righteous yields [fruit].
13 Sinful speech is a trap for the evildoer,
   But a righteous man escapes from trouble.
14 A man gets his fill of good from the fruit of his speech;
   One is repaid in kind for one's deeds.

פרק יב

1 אֹהֵב מוּסָר אֹהֵב דָּעַת וְשֹׂנֵא תוֹכַחַת בָּעַר:

2 טוֹב יָפִיק רָצוֹן מֵיהֹוָה וְאִישׁ מְזִמּוֹת יַרְשִׁיעַ:

3 לֹא־יִכּוֹן אָדָם בְּרֶשַׁע וְשֹׁרֶשׁ צַדִּיקִים בַּל־יִמּוֹט:

4 אֵשֶׁת־חַיִל עֲטֶרֶת בַּעְלָהּ וּכְרָקָב בְּעַצְמוֹתָיו מְבִישָׁה:

5 מַחְשְׁבוֹת צַדִּיקִים מִשְׁפָּט תַּחְבֻּלוֹת רְשָׁעִים מִרְמָה:

6 דִּבְרֵי רְשָׁעִים אֱרָב־דָּם וּפִי יְשָׁרִים יַצִּילֵם:

7 הָפוֹךְ רְשָׁעִים וְאֵינָם וּבֵית צַדִּיקִים יַעֲמֹד:

8 לְפִי־שִׂכְלוֹ יְהֻלַּל־אִישׁ וְנַעֲוֵה־לֵב יִהְיֶה לָבוּז:

9 טוֹב נִקְלֶה וְעֶבֶד לוֹ מִמִּתְכַּבֵּד וַחֲסַר־לָחֶם:

10 יוֹדֵעַ צַדִּיק נֶפֶשׁ בְּהֶמְתּוֹ וְרַחֲמֵי רְשָׁעִים אַכְזָרִי:

11 עֹבֵד אַדְמָתוֹ יִשְׂבַּע־לָחֶם וּמְרַדֵּף רֵיקִים חֲסַר־לֵב:

12 חָמַד רָשָׁע מְצוֹד רָעִים וְשֹׁרֶשׁ צַדִּיקִים יִתֵּן:

13 בְּפֶשַׁע שְׂפָתַיִם מוֹקֵשׁ רָע וַיֵּצֵא מִצָּרָה צַדִּיק:

14 מִפְּרִי פִי־אִישׁ יִשְׂבַּע־טוֹב וּגְמוּל יְדֵי־אָדָם
(יָשׁוּב) [יָשִׁיב] לוֹ:

15 The way of fools is right in their own eyes;
   But those who are wise accept advice.

16 Fools' vexation is known at once,
   But the clever conceal their humiliation.

17 A faithful witness tells the truth,
   But a false witness, deceit.

18 There is blunt talk like sword-thrusts,
   But the speech of the wise is healing.

19 Truthful speech abides forever,
   A lying tongue for but a moment.

20 Deceit is in the minds of those who plot evil;
   For those who plan good there is joy.

21 No harm befalls a righteous person,
   But the wicked have their fill of misfortune.

22 Lying speech is an abomination to GOD,
   But those who act faithfully are pleasing.

23 A clever person conceals knowledge,
   But the mind of dullards cries out folly.

24 The hand of the diligent wields authority;
   The negligent are held in subjection.

25 If there is anxiety in someone's mind, let them quash it,
   And turn it into joy with a good word.

26 A righteous person gives friends direction,
   But the way of the wicked leads astray.

27 A negligent person never has game to roast;
   A diligent one has precious wealth.

28 The road of righteousness leads to life;
   By way of its path there is no death.

15 דֶּרֶךְ אֱוִיל יָשָׁר בְּעֵינָיו וְשֹׁמֵעַ לְעֵצָה חָכָם:

16 אֱוִיל בַּיּוֹם יִוָּדַע כַּעְסוֹ וְכֹסֶה קָלוֹן עָרוּם:

17 יָפִיחַ אֱמוּנָה יַגִּיד צֶדֶק וְעֵד שְׁקָרִים מִרְמָה:

18 יֵשׁ בּוֹטֶה כְּמַדְקְרוֹת חָרֶב וּלְשׁוֹן חֲכָמִים מַרְפֵּא:

19 שְׂפַת־אֱמֶת תִּכּוֹן לָעַד וְעַד־אַרְגִּיעָה לְשׁוֹן שָׁקֶר:

20 מִרְמָה בְּלֶב־חֹרְשֵׁי רָע וּלְיֹעֲצֵי שָׁלוֹם שִׂמְחָה:

21 לֹא־יְאֻנֶּה לַצַּדִּיק כָּל־אָוֶן וּרְשָׁעִים מָלְאוּ רָע:

22 תּוֹעֲבַת יְהֹוָה שִׂפְתֵי־שָׁקֶר וְעֹשֵׂי אֱמוּנָה רְצוֹנוֹ:

23 אָדָם עָרוּם כֹּסֶה דָּעַת וְלֵב כְּסִילִים יִקְרָא אִוֶּלֶת:

24 יַד־חָרוּצִים תִּמְשׁוֹל וּרְמִיָּה תִּהְיֶה לָמַס:

25 דְּאָגָה בְלֶב־אִישׁ יַשְׁחֶנָּה וְדָבָר טוֹב יְשַׂמְּחֶנָּה:

26 יָתֵר מֵרֵעֵהוּ צַדִּיק וְדֶרֶךְ רְשָׁעִים תַּתְעֵם:

27 לֹא־יַחֲרֹךְ רְמִיָּה צֵידוֹ וְהוֹן־אָדָם יָקָר חָרוּץ:

28 בְּאֹרַח־צְדָקָה חַיִּים וְדֶרֶךְ נְתִיבָה אַל־מָוֶת:

Know Your Animal Soul

A righteous person knows the needs of their animal soul,
But the compassion of the wicked is cruelty.
        —Proverbs 12:10

THOUGH THE BOOK OF PROVERBS is known primarily for its wisdom and not for its poetry, there is a unique poetry to be found within the book. Consider the language used in this verse: "know your animal soul." Indeed, as human beings created in the image of God, we have nobility yet are also a part of the animal kingdom. Why do we have that animal dimension? Why should we struggle between our higher angels and our lower, more base instincts? And are those really two separate things, one higher and better than the other?

The Rabbis teach that just as one blesses God for the good, so too one must bless God for the bad.[1] The source for this Rabbinic dictum is the verse "And you shall love the Eternal your God with all your heart and with all your soul and with all your might" (Deuteronomy 6:5). The Rabbis suggest that as hard as it may be, we should accept both the good and the bad with joy,[2] as we do not know what will determine our lives in the end; we are to learn to accept God's will.[3] Yet, who among us is capable of doing this?

A famous story about an early Chasidic master illustrates this specific point:

> Chasidic lore recounts the attitude of the beloved Rabbi Meshulam Zusha of Annopol (1718–1800). His teacher Rabbi Dov Baer (d. 1772), the Maggid (preacher) of Mezeritch, was once asked: How is it possible to accept the good and the bad with true equanimity, thanking the Almighty for both to the same extent?
>
> The Maggid responded, "Go and ask my student Reb Zusha." The questioners sought Reb Zusha and found him sitting in a corner, in torn rags, a picture of pain and suffering. They addressed

him: "Reb Zusha, the Maggid sent us to you. How is it possible to accept the good and the bad with true equanimity?"

Hearing the question, Reb Zusha was surprised. He responded, "You must be mistaken; I am not the person to ask. Thank God, I have never experienced anything bad!"[4]

Now, not many people have reached the level of Rabbi Zusha. And in a society consumed with accruing wealth at an avaricious and unsustainable rate, there is little chance that most people would consider living in rags and filth to be a mark of happiness. Indeed, many people among us are very aware of their suffering, and it might be this self-awareness of our vulnerability and pain that makes us the most human. As if to illustrate the point, Charles Darwin was once asked, according to the writer Mark Twain, about how humans are linked to the animals and, with all of our knowledge about evolution, whether there was still anything unique about being a human. Darwin answered, "Man is the only animal that blushes." Twain retorted to Darwin's answer, saying, "Sure, man is the only animal with good reason to blush."[5]

Meditating on the importance of the blush is a spiritual exercise. What are the physiological and spiritual dimensions of this physical and emotional reaction? Blushing indicates that human beings experience their own vulnerability in recognizing failings and deficiencies. We have been endowed with such enormous mental capacities that we can feel embarrassed and ashamed of ourselves.

While we may—and should—blush at our misgivings, it is also crucial to develop self-respect and perhaps even a healthy sense of self-love. *New York Times* columnist and commentator David Brooks, in his book *The Road to Character*, explores this tension in philosophical terms:

> Around the eighteenth century, moral realism found a rival in moral romanticism. While moral realists placed emphasis on inner weakness, moral romantics like Jean-Jacques Rousseau placed emphasis on our inner goodness. The realists distrusted the self and trusted institutions and customs outside the self; the

romantics trusted the self and distrusted the conventions of the outer world. The realists believed in cultivation, civilization, and artifice; the romanticists believed in nature, the individual, and sincerity.[6]

In contrast to the differentiation Brooks draws between realism and romanticism, Jewish philosophy embraces both the emotional self and the institutionalized public life; both our inner weakness and our inner strength. It is our custodianship of a "good inclination" (*yetzer tov*) that we must cultivate and the "evil inclination" (*yetzer hara*) that we must either destroy or channel toward righteousness (see more in a moment). We build off of our own inner divine light and goodness to go out and make our world more compassionate and holy.

As if to anticipate Brooks by many decades, Rabbi Kook's poem "Or HaNer" speaks about *how* unique and precious each of our spiritual capabilities can be:

> Everyone must know and understand
> that within burns a lamp or candle.
> No one's candle is like another's,
> and no one lacks his or her own candle.
> Everyone must know and understand
> that it is their task to work to reveal the light of
> that candle in the public realm.
> And to ignite it until it is a great flame
> And to illuminate the whole world.[7]

But how do we deal with people who come off as vindictive, vituperative, and downright cruel; who do not care about the consequences of their actions? How does Jewish tradition approach the question of people's animal, dark soul?

We know that we are commanded to *dan l'chaf z'chut*, "give the benefit of the doubt," and assume that others are good and innocent. However, we also learn at the beginning of the Torah, "The human mind inclines to evil from youth onward" (Genesis 8:21).

The *Tanya*, an eighteenth-century mystical Chasidic text, teaches that we are not innately good or evil but that our good and evil inclinations are perpetually at war with one another. Through our free will, we choose how to act. We must exercise and strengthen our capacity to choose good or our righteous inclinations will be defeated. The Sages taught that the *yetzer hara*, our "evil inclination," exists in a person from the time of birth[8] and renews itself each day,[9] but that the *yetzer tov*, or "good inclination," does not take effect until one reaches thirteen years of age.[10]

Most of us still do not generally distrust others, notwithstanding the teachings of the *Tanya*. Rabbi Aharon Lichtenstein explains:

> Judaism shares the view of classical religious humanism, according to which man is not inherently good but is capable of great good, provided that he is trained properly. . . . [This idea] demands that we sharpen our awareness of the evil that lurks within us, and stand guard with greater vigilance against it. When I say "within us," I refer to the world at large, to the intimate society that surrounds us, and to the depths of the individual soul.[11]

Essentially, there is a basic goodness to all people, but each person has a shadow as well. That innate potential for evil can and must be overcome with training so that that our goodness and decency can shine forth. And, indeed, we see the basic goodness of workers, our neighbors, our friends, and our family members win out over the inclination toward laziness, selfishness, and fear time and time again. A few recent examples come to mind:

- In December 2013, postal worker Jermaine Shirley was on his way to work when he noticed that there was a fire in a Bronx apartment building. He alerted many of the residents, but on the third floor, Everdean and Nikalia Codner, and their eleven-month-old twin boys, Israel and Ishmael, were unable to get through the smoke and could only get to the rear window. Shirley then sprang into action, climbing up on the roof of a first-floor shed, after which he was able to catch each of the twin infants as their father dropped them to safety. The parents then partially climbed down the fire escape ladder and had to jump themselves. As Shirley said later, "I have a family, too. I would want somebody to do the same for me."

- In January 2014, in yet another school shooting, a twelve-year-old boy shot two students with a sawed-off shotgun. At that point, a social studies teacher walked up to the boy. The boy pointed the shotgun at the teacher, but nevertheless the teacher persuaded him to put the shotgun down, after which the teacher pinned the student down until he could be taken by authorities.

It would have been much easier for the postal worker to go to work, to assume that firefighters would take care of the situation, and to move on with his day, but he thought about what it was like to have family members in danger. Similarly, it would have been easy for the teacher to flee from the dangerous environment and ensure the preservation of his own life. Instead, he, like so many other teachers and staff in similar situations who have risked, and often lost, their lives to protect the children in their care, acted bravely and altruistically.

People with bad intentions hurt others; almost everyone has suffered this kind of pain. After each painful experience of being wronged, we can find ourselves becoming less trusting of others; this reaction is natural. However, cynicism is fatal from a spiritual perspective. Judaism demands that we keep our hope in the human potential and remain open and forgiving in interpreting others' motives; we can abide by faith even while protecting ourselves and abstaining from naiveté.

The Sages taught, "Since the Temple was destroyed, prophecy has been taken from prophets and given to fools and children."[12] No one has perfect wisdom, nor does anyone have total virtue. No one is entirely evil, and no one is entirely good. We need to work continuously to illuminate the world—together.

We have the ability to blush because we have the ability to be ashamed of the moments when our evil inclination drove our choices. We possess the gift to realize our wrongs and repair the world. We all may make mistakes and stumble, and it is healthy and emotionally prudent to retain a degree of skepticism regarding our own behavior and that of others. May we continue to strive to see the good in others.

The Value of Toil

He who who tills his land shall have food in plenty,
But one who pursues vanities is devoid of sense.
—Proverbs 12:11

EACH FALL after the High Holy Days pass, Jews move from comfortable homes into impermanent huts in their backyards, driveways, and on their balconies to celebrate the festival of Sukkot. Sukkot is a beautiful holiday that presents a meaningful contrast to the contemporary experience. The vast majority of people living in America today live indoors in structures built by others,[13] in houses that are stationary and usually do not have large skylights to the skies above. However, during Sukkot, we are invited to build a sukkah, a structure that reminds us of the Israelites' wanderings in the desert. Originally, these harvest sukkahs were meant only to provide temporary shelter while being on the journey. Each night, they were built. And each morning, they were torn down again.

Nothing lasts forever.

By eating and living in these fragile shelters, we remember the Israelites' struggles in the desert, but we also train ourselves to temporarily subordinate our *gashmiyut* (materialism) to our *ruchaniyut* (spirituality). We step out of our comfortable homes to think broadly about the future—for our families, for our community, for ourselves. On one level, we learn from the verse above about the value of work and of the focus on what really matters. However, we also learn about the deep relationship people have to the soil, to the earth. I offer this parable to those who have forgotten how interconnected our existence is with the earth:

Three people on a rowboat.

The one in front is rowing as fast as possible.

The one in the middle is drilling a hole in the boat.

The one in the back is enjoying a burger, hoping the one in front will stop the one drilling in the middle.

One in front: "Hey, stop drilling that hole. You're going to sink us all!"

One in the middle: "This is a free society. Mind your own business. This is my part of the boat and I can do what I please."

One in the back (takes another bite of the burger, losing his paddle as it falls into the water): "Oh man, I really hope that guy in the front does something about this."[14]

To be sure, most of Jewish tradition is not keen on asceticism, according to which retreating from the physical is a celebrated ideal. Rather, we hope that by removing ourselves from our customary comforts for the week of Sukkot, we will reach a heightened ethical and spiritual sensitivity regarding our materialism and consumption. We hope to learn to act with greater integrity once we return to our daily routine.

Indeed, the renewed awareness resulting from observing Sukkot is essential in protecting the world for future generations.[15]

We learn from the Talmudic tale of Choni the Circle-Maker about the importance of protecting our world for our descendants. One day Choni happened upon an old man planting a carob tree. Curious, Choni asked the man how long it would take for the tree to bear fruit. When the man replied that it would take seventy years, Choni reproached him: "Silly old man, do you really think you'll live to see its fruit?" The old man answered, "I found this world planted with carob trees; as my parents planted for me, so I will plant for my children."[16]

Unfortunately, in contemporary America—and much of the globe—we live with too little concern for the world around us. To cite just one example of our unsustainable consumption practices, American meat intake has soared to unprecedented levels, while a reduction in the overall amount of meat eaten could have a massively positive impact on the issue of global hunger (not to mention enhance human health, reduce animal suffering, and protect the environment for all).[17]

These global issues can be addressed not only during the holiday of Sukkot, but every time we consume, whether it's food or clothes or anything else. When one says a blessing over food, the intention is to enhance our spiritual consciousness of the factors that led to that sustenance on our plates: it came from our Creator, was prepared in a ritually fitting manner, and isn't environmentally or morally damaging. The blessing is the affirmation that we have investigated what this food is, where it came from, and that it is fully fit for consumption.

Our tradition goes so far as to call unethical consumption a "sin." For example, the *Sefer HaChinuch*, a thirteenth-century Spanish work summarizing the Jewish mitzvot, considers consuming something produced unjustly to be an act of idolatry, the worship of selfish desire over the good.[18] So, too, purposeless destruction is viewed as violating biblical ethics.[19] In today's interconnected economy and ecology, unethical consumption affects us all. If we truly want to embrace the myriad values of our tradition, we should not only observe kashrut, but also demonstrate a general respect for human dignity, for the sentience of animals, and for the upkeep of our planet. In this globalized and decentralized age, we must be fully aware of the impact we have as consumers in the marketplace, as well as of the conditions under which our products are produced and shipped.

In fact, our votes as consumers may matter even more than our political votes, as large corporations have overtaken many nation-states in budget. For example, of the hundred largest economies in the world, fifty-one are corporations, while forty-nine are nation-states, making it so that the largest hundred corporations now control around 20 percent of the global assets. The products we purchase are manifestations of our values. We live in a precarious time, with low costs taking precedence among consumers over such moral imperatives as supporting worker justice, the humane treatment of animals, and the protection of the environment. Such a mentality is also present in the Jewish community. I recall sitting on a panel with a leading ultra-Orthodox rabbi, who suggested "no one cares if the poet stinks," explaining: readers want good poetry, not hygiene; kosher consumers want good taste at a low price, not ethically produced foods. Such a mentality is foreign to the texts of our tradition, specifically relating to food consumption, and has to change in order to enable our great-great-great-grandchildren to enjoy the shade and beauty of the carob trees.

Our planet is in a perilous state, and we look to both our leaders and our traditions to ensure the sustainability of the human people. For many years, scientists have warned of the consequences of climate change and its impact on humanity. Unfortunately, at conferences at Kyoto (1997) and Copenhagen (2009), world leaders largely failed to address this looming crisis in a meaningful way.[20] In August 2019, the world's leading climate scientists (through the Intergovernmental Panel on Climate Change, a United Nations–sponsored group) issued a dire warning concerning the level of carbon emissions and its potential to bring about cataclysmic climate change. Unfortunately, unless there is a radical reduction of greenhouse gas emissions, this level may be reached within a few decades.

The Book of Proverbs reminds us of our responsibility to take care of the land and enjoy its beauty. Its exploitation for gain and profit is truly an affront to the ideal of Torah. It is our duty to use the Jewish tradition as a way to fight against human exploitation of other humans, the limitation of resources, and insufficient respect for our environment. While it will certainly not be easy, our deep engagement with the Jewish sources should serve as a springboard to inspire us to action and help us bear the metaphorical fruit from the textual soil we worked so hard to till.

The Book of Proverbs realigns the prophetic with the practical. If this world is to continue spinning and supporting life, then we have to work hard to ensure that there is no disruption. We have the blessed opportunity to sit in our sukkah—and out in nature, during other times—to remind ourselves that we have always been and continue to be wanderers and to connect deeply to our ancestors who lived in these rough huts as they traveled the desert with no room for superfluous fancy. At our core, we are akin to undocumented workers struggling to make it in America today. All of us are short-term visitors to this world, charged with the great task of leaving the universe more whole and less broken than we received it.

Chapter 13

1 A wise son—it is through the discipline of his father;
A scoffer—he never heard reproof.

2 A man enjoys good from the fruit of his speech;
But out of the throat of the treacherous comes lawlessness.

3 Those who guard their tongue preserve their life;
Those who open wide their lips, it is their ruin.

4 A sluggard craves, but has nothing;
The diligent shall feast on rich fare.

5 The righteous hate lies;
The wicked are vile and disgraceful.

6 Righteousness protects the one whose way is blameless;
Wickedness subverts the sinner.

7 Some pretend to be rich and have nothing;
Others profess to be poor and have much wealth.

8 Riches are ransom for a person's life,
The poor never heard a reproof.

9 The light of the righteous is radiant;
The lamp of the wicked is extinguished.

10 Arrogance yields nothing but strife;
Wisdom belongs to those who seek advice.

11 Wealth may dwindle to less than nothing,
But one who gathers little by little increases it.

12 Hope deferred sickens the heart,
But desire realized is a tree of life.

13 One who disdains a precept will be injured thereby;
One who respects a command will be rewarded.

14 The instruction of the wise is a fountain of life,
Enabling one to avoid deadly snares.

פרק יג

1 בֶּן חָכָם מוּסַר אָב וְלֵץ לֹא־שָׁמַע גְּעָרָה:

2 מִפְּרִי פִי־אִישׁ יֹאכַל טוֹב וְנֶפֶשׁ בֹּגְדִים חָמָס:

3 נֹצֵר פִּיו שֹׁמֵר נַפְשׁוֹ פֹּשֵׂק שְׂפָתָיו מְחִתָּה־לֽוֹ:

4 מִתְאַוָּה וָאַיִן נַפְשׁוֹ עָצֵל וְנֶפֶשׁ חָרֻצִים תְּדֻשָּֽׁן:

5 דְּבַר־שֶׁקֶר יִשְׂנָא צַדִּיק וְרָשָׁע יַבְאִישׁ וְיַחְפִּֽיר:

6 צְדָקָה תִּצֹּר תָּם־דָּרֶךְ וְרִשְׁעָה תְּסַלֵּף חַטָּֽאת:

7 יֵשׁ מִתְעַשֵּׁר וְאֵין כֹּל מִתְרוֹשֵׁשׁ וְהוֹן רָב:

8 כֹּפֶר נֶפֶשׁ־אִישׁ עָשְׁרוֹ וְרָשׁ לֹא־שָׁמַע גְּעָרָה:

9 אוֹר־צַדִּיקִים יִשְׂמָח וְנֵר רְשָׁעִים יִדְעָֽךְ:

10 רַק־בְּזָדוֹן יִתֵּן מַצָּה וְאֶת־נוֹעָצִים חָכְמָֽה:

11 הוֹן מֵהֶבֶל יִמְעָט וְקֹבֵץ עַל־יָד יַרְבֶּֽה:

12 תּוֹחֶלֶת מְמֻשָּׁכָה מַחֲלָה־לֵב וְעֵץ חַיִּים תַּאֲוָה בָאָֽה:

13 בָּז לְדָבָר יֵחָבֶל לוֹ וִירֵא מִצְוָה הוּא יְשֻׁלָּֽם:

14 תּוֹרַת חָכָם מְקוֹר חַיִּים לָסוּר מִמֹּקְשֵׁי מָֽוֶת:

15 Good sense wins favor;
   The way of treacherous men is unchanging.
16 Those who are clever act knowledgeably,
   But dullards expose their stupidity.
17 Harm befalls a wicked messenger;
   A faithful courier brings healing.
18 Poverty and humiliation are for the one who spurns discipline;
   But one who takes reproof to heart gets honor.
19 Desire realized is sweet to the soul;
   To turn away from evil is abhorrent to the stupid.
20 One who keeps company with the wise becomes wise,
   But one who consorts with dullards comes to grief.
21 Misfortune pursues sinners,
   But the righteous are well rewarded.
22 A good man has what to bequeath to his grandchildren,
   For the wealth of sinners is stored up for the righteous.
23 The tillage of the poor yields much food;
   But substance is swept away for lack of moderation.
24 He who spares the rod hates his son,
   But he who loves him disciplines him early.
25 The righteous person eats to satiety,
   But the belly of the wicked is empty.

שֵׂכֶל־טוֹב יִתֶּן־חֵן וְדֶרֶךְ בֹּגְדִים אֵיתָן: 15

כָּל־עָרוּם יַעֲשֶׂה בְדָעַת וּכְסִיל יִפְרֹשׂ אִוֶּלֶת: 16

מַלְאָךְ רָשָׁע יִפֹּל בְּרָע וְצִיר אֱמוּנִים מַרְפֵּא: 17

רֵישׁ וְקָלוֹן פּוֹרֵעַ מוּסָר וְשׁוֹמֵר תּוֹכַחַת יְכֻבָּד: 18

תַּאֲוָה נִהְיָה תֶּעֱרַב לְנָפֶשׁ וְתוֹעֲבַת כְּסִילִים סוּר מֵרָע: 19

(הלוך) [הוֹלֵךְ] אֶת־חֲכָמִים (וחכם) [יֶחְכָּם] וְרֹעֶה 20
כְסִילִים יֵרוֹעַ:

חַטָּאִים תְּרַדֵּף רָעָה וְאֶת־צַדִּיקִים יְשַׁלֶּם־טוֹב: 21

טוֹב יַנְחִיל בְּנֵי־בָנִים וְצָפוּן לַצַּדִּיק חֵיל חוֹטֵא: 22

רָב־אֹכֶל נִיר רָאשִׁים וְיֵשׁ נִסְפֶּה בְּלֹא מִשְׁפָּט: 23

חוֹשֵׂךְ שִׁבְטוֹ שׂוֹנֵא בְנוֹ וְאֹהֲבוֹ שִׁחֲרוֹ מוּסָר: 24

צַדִּיק אֹכֵל לְשֹׂבַע נַפְשׁוֹ וּבֶטֶן רְשָׁעִים תֶּחְסָר: 25

On Wealth and Poverty

Some pretend to be rich and have nothing;
Others profess to be poor and have much wealth.
  —Proverbs 13:7

EARLY IN THE DRAMAS of the Torah, the Book of Genesis discusses the wealth that is divided between Abraham and his nephew Lot: "Now Lot, who had gone with Abram, also had flocks and herds and tents, so that the land could not support them both; they had so much property that they could not remain together" (Genesis 13:5–6). In this brief passage, we already begin to form a sense that class issues, access to resources, and inherent inequality are problems that stem back to time immemorial. Struggles for equity are responses to systemic injustice that dates back to the earliest recorded moments of human history. Yet, it seems that already millennia before social movements, philosophers, and politicians placed their ambitions in exploring the intrinsic problems of wealth, the Torah laid out a critical view of excessive wealth and its impact on a human's development.

Wealth and financial safety are very subjective but central elements in every person's life, and the Book of Proverbs acknowledges this. One can have little and feel they have much. Others can have much and feel they have little. However, there is also an objective moral reality to wealth: "Wealth may dwindle to less than nothing, but one who gathers little by little increases it" (Proverbs 13:11). The Rabbis teach, "Whoever wishes to live in sanctity, may they live according to the true laws of commerce and finance."[1] This teaching may seem curious because one might have expected holiness to primarily be related to matters of prayer and study. However, the Rabbis teach that it is precisely the way we handle issues of money and financial gains that determines the level of holiness and morality on which we live. The Torah expresses great concern and clear displeasure over the heavy financial burdens that many endure. This is evident in the Talmudic principle *chasah al mamonam shel Yisrael*, "the Torah protects the property of Israel." That is, Jewish law seeks to spare us unnecessary expense in the observance of mitzvot. Rabbinical adjudicators' (*poskim*) find leniencies in the law when a more stringent conclusion would involve significant financial loss.[2]

How we relate to wealth—the amount or lack of it—reveals much about our character. The Talmud teaches that a person shows their character in three ways: *koso*, *kaaso*, and *kiso* (literally, "his cup," "his anger," and "his pocket," referring to what emerges when one drinks, how one handles one's anger, and how one relates to money).[3] Over the last several years, a growing body of research has been conducted on the topic of how humans treat one another in any given situation and the factors that impact our behavior. Psychologists have been able to find more and more evidence of just how powerfully our subjective sense of our individual financial well-being determines the way we treat others.

For example, social psychologists from the University of Amsterdam and the University of California at Berkeley observed how people of various socioeconomic statuses listened to one another and found that more powerful individuals were less compassionate toward the suffering of the less powerful.[4] In yet another study, Dacher Keltner and Michael Kraus found that those with power in society tend to pay little attention to those with less power *even when* those with less power work for them.[5] This attitude has had catastrophic political consequences, as the wealthy blame the poor for their own misfortune. In October 1964, Ronald Reagan gave a speech reflecting this view: "We were told four years ago that seventeen million people went to bed hungry each night. Well, that was probably true. They were all on a diet." When Reagan later became president and was in a position to do something about the needs of the poor across the United States, he failed to do so. Rather, he severely undermined their interests. While drastically cutting taxes for the wealthy,[6] he cut domestic spending by about 25 percent[7] and reduced the number of federal housing units.[8] When more than one million people became homeless, President Reagan again denied there was a problem, saying, "People who are sleeping on the grates . . . are homeless, you might say, by choice."[9] By the time President Reagan left office, the nonpartisan Government Accounting Office took the unprecedented step of issuing a warning that the number of homeless had ballooned to three million and was steadily increasing.[10] The government's failure to protect the poor—which sometimes comes in the form of the active undermining of their interests—continues to this day.

Many Jewish teachings remind us that our primary responsibility is to protect and prioritize the most vulnerable individuals and parties: "God seeks the pursued" (Ecclesiastes 3:15). God does not want us to withhold support from anyone who suffers. This is what it means to be Jewish: to prioritize the suffering of others at our own expense.

As we see in the Book of Proverbs, every individual should have the same and fair opportunities to reach their full potential. We must be committed to truth, justice, and equity for all to achieve their goals in this world. This vision is not reality; it must be our aspiration. And even if it were true already in theory, Judaism teaches that we must go above and beyond the law (*lifnim mishurat hadin*) to support those more vulnerable than ourselves.[11] We learned that God created and destroyed many worlds that were built upon the foundation of *din* (judgment) until, finally, our world was built upon *rachamim* (mercy).[12] Our world cannot exist on the basis of pure judgment. Instead, as fallible beings, we rely upon the grace, empathy, and kindness of God toward humanity.

Consider this scenario: many of us have become accustomed to walking by the homeless as they shiver on our city streets, paying as little attention as we can, attempting to avoid eye contact. In fact, many of us view the homeless, as they beg for help, as a sort of bother or annoyance—a depressing obstacle on the way to our intended destinations. Though many of us are not among the highest income earners in this country, our relative wealth and comfort should allow us to offer assistance, yet most of us do not. Our behavior toward the neediest among us begs the question: Do the wealthy *see* the poor? Do we know how to help, and do we decide to help?

A midrash explains that typically people in poverty should not live separately from the wealthy because extreme poverty has the potential to lead to violence. Those with extreme wealth, however, who use it to support a regressive treatment of those who have nothing, are violating Judaism's commitment to fairness and impartiality, making extreme wealth as dangerous as extreme poverty.[13]

One strategy to create a warm and welcoming society for all is to address the underlying problems of poverty. Lavishness often grows a sense of entitlement, which leads to corruption, which leads to an exploitation of those without access to the same resources—be they institutional, educational, or political. Consider how Egypt's prosperity factored into the devaluing of their Israelite slaves, or how America's growth into a superpower was largely dependent on slave labor. Being charitable, in an effort to remove guilt, does not erase the oppression that made that charity possible. When one views those with fewer means as transactional objects, tools on the path toward one's personal fulfillment, then one loses their integrity to lavishness.

There is much pain to be found in poverty. On the other hand, Judaism does not condemn wealth. While there are serious risks that come along with being wealthy, wealth by itself, when earned with integrity, is not objectionable. However, wealth comes with moral obligations, individually and collectively, to ensure that wealth adds dignity rather than destroys spirits. Deuteronomy 15:11 reminds us that there will always be people who are poor and that we must always work to support them. In the case of Lot and Abraham, one might argue that "the land could not support them" precisely because "they had so much property" and that this is not a space issue, but a relationship issue. This is, the problem is not about whether Abraham and Lot had enough land but about how they *viewed* that land. The family can no longer remain a family due to greed and jealousy. It was precisely their relationship to wealth that made it impossible for them to dwell together.

Rabbi Samson Raphael Hirsch suggests, in commenting on this verse, that there really was enough land for the two of them. Lot's desire, however, for more than what was necessary led him to leave Abraham. Today, there are enough resources to feed every single human being on this earth, yet exploitation and greed lead to global conflicts and national strife.

Judaism condemns a society that tolerates extreme poverty. Rather than retreat into moral callousness by relying on "the markets" as vehicles of inevitable progress, the Book of Proverbs asks us to rise above the myopia of the next payday. Like Abraham, we can leave behind the idol worship of possessions and instead seek spiritual currency by helping others, advocating for the less fortunate, and creating an environment where all people have the opportunity to actualize their fullest selves.

The Strength and Beauty of Our Spiritual Light

The light of the righteous is radiant;
The lamp of the wicked is extinguished.
     —Proverbs 13:9

THE INNER LIGHT that resides in the heart and soul of each human being is precious. The Book of Proverbs teaches that through our righteous deeds and elevated spiritual consciousness, our inner selves can shine forth to create light for us and those around us. We are also warned that our inner light can be extinguished. It is a terrifying thought, and yet it is remarkable that it is virtue alone—self-made, not inherent, virtue—that determines our light. "There are two ways of spreading light," Edith Wharton writes, "to be the candle or the mirror that reflects it."[14]

In some cultures, across a wide swath of history, a murderer became obligated to pay a price to a victim's family, with the size of that payment set based on the victim's social status. The Torah, on the other hand, does not fathom such calculations; the value of a life does not depend on social status! God's image can be increased or diminished in this world, perceived more clearly or more distantly— but God's image does not increase or decrease within a human being depending on their wealth or social status.

Each of us bears a substantial burden as we carry the image of God within us. This responsibility means that we are obliged to honor the rest of God's creations, thereby pleasing our Creator. When we make another person into an object through abuse or exploitation, the image of God within us suffers through their suffering. Our souls cry at the pain of another, especially when we are the ones who have inflicted the suffering. However, we can choose to ignore the cry of our soul. Samuel Johnson wrote that acting like a beast can free one from the pain of being a human.[15] Indeed, if one completely silences their own soul, they can become capable of great atrocities; and if done frequently enough, they can liberate themselves, partially at least, from the suffering involved with causing suffering to others. They forget that both they and those whose suffering they cause share the same humanity.

The major challenge about living with a soul is that we generally find it impossible to experience our spirituality with our five senses. Consequently, we easily lose a consciousness of our spirituality. It is nearly impossible within a life that is rooted in the physical world of here and now to be fully awake to one's spiritual life. Our yearning to perceive of our lives as one unified whole instead of two separate dimensions makes the task even more difficult. John Keats, the nineteenth-century Romantic British poet, compared such a futile attempt to working to unravel a rainbow where, indeed, the spectrum of light can be perceived but not touched, at one with the sky while entirely separate.[16]

And so, each of us has to face the choice each day: I can measure my value according to my social status in the physical world or, on the other hand, according to the dignity of my life, the light of my soul, and the integrity of my choices. It is exhausting and ultimately futile to constantly seek the approval and adoration of others. In the end, only we ourselves and God know whether we have lived a life of integrity or fraud, courage or cowardice, thoughtfulness or vanity.

In addressing the significance of our spiritual consciousness, the Maggid of Mezeritch teaches that each of us "must be nothing but an ear which hears what the universe of the word is constantly saying within [us]. The moment [we] start hearing what [we ourselves] are saying, [we] must stop."[17] A fundamental part of transcending the needs of our physical bodies is to learn how to silence the ego, the voice emerging from the self, in order to hear an external voice, whether from the other or from the Other.

We all have a gift within ourselves. Each of us has the power to choose, every day, whether to brighten our light or to extinguish it. Each of us has the potential to beautify or destroy our inner and outer worlds. We can give more than we take, or take more than we give. Each of us has the potential to give more than we take, making both the *Other* and the *other* the purpose of Creation. This path to rebuilding a broken world starts within each of us and continues in profound interaction with otherness. The choice is ours—but have we journeyed inward toward the hidden light, toward deeper sources of love and light that will help us to do the work that this world so desperately needs?

The Talmud teaches that it is better to throw oneself into a fiery furnace than to shame another person, since shaming another is akin to murdering them.[18] Here is a story that may be hard for us to relate to but is worth reflecting on:

> Rabbi Y'hoshua Leib Diskin (living in nineteenth-century Jerusalem) was ill with diabetic hypoglycemia. His student went to put extra sugar into his tea to replenish the sugars in his teacher's frail body. When Rav Diskin tasted the tea, he realized that his student had accidentally poured spoons of salt instead of sugar into his tea (which was certainly not what his health needed). Nonetheless, to avoid embarrassing his student, he drank the full cup without mentioning anything.[19]

Many of us might want to tell him that he should have protected himself better—but he really believed that shaming another was akin to murder. Perhaps we wouldn't (and shouldn't!) go as far as he did, but it is worth reflecting on these questions: What level of sacrifice am I actually willing to make for the dignity and wholeness of the other? To sustain the dignity of another?

To Discipline through Fear
Is Not Love

He who spares the rod hates his son,
But he who loves him disciplines him early.
—Proverbs 13:24

WE USUALLY DO NOT ASSOCIATE moral lessons with physical abuse
or other forms of afflictions. Moral lessons should be aspirational
precepts that inspire us and allow us to navigate the world. So, when
interpreting a verse that is clearly from a different sociocultural context, it is often challenging to find a valid and inspiring ethical and
spiritual lesson for us.

The above verse is both famous and infamous. It has been used for
centuries to justify force and violence against children, a method to
ensure that they succumb to the will of any authority. It has been used
by overzealous parents and teachers alike to strike fear into children
and others lacking in power. Seen from our time, it is a troubling
verse to say the least. Yet, if we explore an alternative philosophical
reading here, we may be able to redeem the hidden wisdom of the
verse and apply it to our own lives in a constructive manner.

At an earlier time in Jewish history, this verse was taken at face value.
Even the great Maimonides believed that we should hit children to
instill fear in them.[20] For his part, Maimonides recommended that
we avoid hitting out of anger and that we refrain from carrying out
discipline with sticks or straps. Instead, physical punishment should
be motivated by clear pedagogical goals and executed calmly. Any
aggressive acts that are intended to cause harm or embarrass another
are forbidden.[21] Rather than allowing oneself to engage corporal

punishment as an outlet for real anger, one should merely fake anger for the sake of the student's character development.[22] Still, it's not hard not to perceive Maimonides's prescriptions as the promotion of what we would now call psychological abuse.

Later, the *Shulchan Aruch* also speaks in support of corporal punishment, though only of the most minimal application possible.[23] The great Chasidic master Rebbe Nachman saw things differently and made clear that one should absolutely never hit a child in anger or driven by any other strong, irrational emotion. In apparent parallel with the development of sensitivities in secular society, Jewish perspectives regarding the permissibility of corporal punishment have developed in a direction favoring limitations.[24] More recently, the late twentieth-century Jewish thinker Rabbi Shlomo Wolbe further argued that any type of corporal punishment would create a long-term strained relationship between parent and child and should therefore be avoided.[25] But even other ancient sources suggest an antipathy toward the practice. For example, hitting a young child could be considered a violation of the biblical prohibition of *lifnei iveir* (Deuteronomy 9:14)—literally "before a blind," but understood as "causing another to err"—because hitting the child would likely cause them to hit their parent or teacher back, and thus the child would committed the sin of disrespecting a parental figure.[26]

It is undeniable that disciplining children with force is a widespread social problem. Many of the abusive parents seem to blame their behavior on their "bad" or "stubborn" kids. They'll say, "I had to discipline my child this way because he's so rotten and he won't listen," and they believe that violence is the only way to get their kids to submit.

Catherine A. Taylor of Tulane University and a team of researchers studied the impact of urban mothers' use of corporal punishment on their children.[27] She and her colleagues found that a quarter of mothers who spanked their three-year-old children more than twice in the previous month reported that their children were more aggressive by their next interview two years later, independent of any other factor.

These results positively affirm the findings of numerous previous studies: corporal punishment of children is likely to result in more aggressive behavior as the child grows up. It is also for that reason that the American Academy of Pediatrics continues to oppose corporal punishment for children.[28]

Raising children is a blessing but also a supreme trial of will. Parenting presents many opportunities to get frustrated and upset. We are pushed to the limits of our patience. In these moments, our base human instinct to lash out overtakes our angelic selves, our compassionate side. We use the tools of violence to elicit a reaction. This approach is never appropriate.

The Book of Proverbs seems to suggest adopting a style of child-rearing that entails corporal punishment. However, it also seems worthwhile to wonder whether the author of our verse might have simply been acknowledging what the Rabbis discuss extensively elsewhere: as humans, we have an obligation to control our impulses and not to react with violence. The Torah tells us that humans have a *yetzer hara*, an "evil inclination," from the time that they are born (Genesis 8:21). The Rabbis read another verse (Genesis 2:7) as teaching that we also have a *yetzer tov*, a "good inclination."[29] We are admonished to rule over our impulses rather than have them rule over us.[30] As many Rabbinic thinkers have recognized, both our positive and negative inclinations can lead us in both positive and negative directions.[31] Perhaps our verse is descriptive, not prescriptive, reminding us that we are sometimes inclined to act harshly with our children, convinced as we are that such actions are taken out of love, even as we know—or should know—that real love will be accompanied by an effort to overcome our own violent impulses.

Other texts support the hypothesis that Jewish tradition favors a nonviolent pedagogical approach. The Book of Isaiah emphasizes the superiority of peaceful interaction over violence with the well-known image of the times-to-come as an era when violent animals will act with ultimate passivity toward their erstwhile prey (Isaiah 11:6). Similarly, in discussing punishment in the ancient Jewish equivalent of criminal law, a number of Talmudic rabbis vie for non-violence. One claims that capital punishment should not be meted out more frequently than once every seven years; a second says that it would not be appropriate to use the punishment of execution any more often than once every seventy years; others assert that such ultimate violence should never be used as a punishment.[32] A contemporary example is the perspective of twentieth-century Jewish philosopher Emmanuel Levinas, who writes that our morality involved in the relationship of one person to another requires us to avoid interpersonal violence.[33]

We must reinterpret the ancient words of the Book of Proverbs to reflect a more compassionate view of the world and our children. We are not beholden to any proclivity for viciousness, even if, at the same time, we acknowledge the deep wisdom of the Book of Proverbs at other places. Today, we know that the most effective approaches in education and child-rearing involve the use of positive reinforcement and love, not the "stick" that dominated social norms until the mid-twentieth century. It is never appropriate to use any physical aggression as punishment of a child, and any child abuse must be reported to the authorities. Of course, we must establish rules and structures both in the household and in the classroom, but those should be enforced through nonviolent means. We and our children learn best through encouragement and not through fear. We must encourage our youth and offer constant positive reinforcement to help them actualize their potential and flourish in this life. One of the greatest gifts we can give our children is how to handle our fears through love. Rabbi Karyn D. Kedar writes in her poem "Fear and Hope":

> Inside the human heart is fear.
> There is also hope.
> The two wrestle constantly, like Jacob and his God.
> Sometimes one prevails. Sometimes the other.
> The struggle is sometimes silent, other times loud.
> But it is constant—fear, hope, fear, hope.
> Flashes of light and shadow twirling inside us all the time.

It is so much easier when there is love.
When love is in your life
it becomes the context for it all.
Love is the measure of a life well lived,
it is the beacon of possibility.
When you love, the fear is less harsh,
hope is a bit stronger.[34]

We must teach our children structure and boundaries. Sometimes, this requires strictness. But even more important, we must teach them how to love and how to handle the fear that they inherit and absorb on their journeys.

Chapter 14

1   The wisest of women builds her house,
    But folly tears it down with its own hands.
2   One who walks a straight path fears GOD;
    But one whose ways are devious shows scorn.
3   In the mouth of a fool is a rod of haughtiness,
    But the lips of the wise protect them.
4   If there are no oxen the crib is clean,
    But a rich harvest comes through the strength of the ox.
5   An honest witness will not lie;
    A false witness testifies lies.
6   Scoffers seek wisdom in vain,
    But knowledge comes easily to the intelligent.
7   Keep your distance from a dull man,
    For you will not learn wise speech.
8   It is the wisdom of a clever man to understand his course;
    But the stupidity of dullards is delusion.
9   Reparations mediate between fools,
    Between the upright, good will.
10 The heart alone knows its bitterness,
    And no outsider can share in its joy.
11 The house of the wicked will be demolished,
    But the tent of the upright will flourish.
12 The road ahead may seem right,
    But in the end it can be a road to death.
13 The heart may ache even in laughter,
    And joy may end in grief.
14 Those who are unprincipled reap the fruits of their ways;
    The good man, of his deeds.

פרק יד

1 חַכְמוֹת נָשִׁים בָּנְתָה בֵיתָהּ וְאִוֶּלֶת בְּיָדֶיהָ תֶהֶרְסֶנּוּ:

2 הוֹלֵךְ בְּיָשְׁרוֹ יְרֵא יְהֹוָה וּנְלוֹז דְּרָכָיו בּוֹזֵהוּ:

3 בְּפִי־אֱוִיל חֹטֶר גַּאֲוָה וְשִׂפְתֵי חֲכָמִים תִּשְׁמוּרֵם:

4 בְּאֵין אֲלָפִים אֵבוּס בָּר וְרָב־תְּבוּאוֹת בְּכֹחַ שׁוֹר:

5 עֵד אֱמוּנִים לֹא יְכַזֵּב וְיָפִיחַ כְּזָבִים עֵד שָׁקֶר:

6 בִּקֶּשׁ־לֵץ חָכְמָה וָאָיִן וְדַעַת לְנָבוֹן נָקָל:

7 לֵךְ מִנֶּגֶד לְאִישׁ כְּסִיל וּבַל־יָדַעְתָּ שִׂפְתֵי־דָעַת:

8 חָכְמַת עָרוּם הָבִין דַּרְכּוֹ וְאִוֶּלֶת כְּסִילִים מִרְמָה:

9 אֱוִלִים יָלִיץ אָשָׁם וּבֵין יְשָׁרִים רָצוֹן:

10 לֵב יוֹדֵעַ מָרַּת נַפְשׁוֹ וּבְשִׂמְחָתוֹ לֹא־יִתְעָרַב זָר:

11 בֵּית רְשָׁעִים יִשָּׁמֵד וְאֹהֶל יְשָׁרִים יַפְרִיחַ:

12 יֵשׁ דֶּרֶךְ יָשָׁר לִפְנֵי־אִישׁ וְאַחֲרִיתָהּ דַּרְכֵי־מָוֶת:

13 גַּם־בִּשְׂחֹק יִכְאַב־לֵב וְאַחֲרִיתָהּ שִׂמְחָה תוּגָה:

14 מִדְּרָכָיו יִשְׂבַּע סוּג לֵב וּמֵעָלָיו אִישׁ טוֹב:

15 The simple believe anything;
   The clever ponders their course.

16 A sage is diffident and shuns evil,
   But a dullard rushes in confidently.

17 A hothead commits folly;
   A man of intrigues will be hated.

18 Folly is the lot of the simple,
   But the clever glory in knowledge.

19 Evildoers are brought low before the good,
   So are the wicked at the gates of the righteous.

20 The poor are despised even by their peers,
   But the rich have many friends.

21 Those who despise their fellows are wrong;
   Those who show pity for the lowly are happy.

22 Surely those who plan evil go astray,
   While those who plan good earn steadfast love.

23 From all toil there is some gain,
   But idle chatter is pure loss.

24 The ornament of the wise is their wealth;
   The stupidity of dullards is stupidity.

25 A truthful witness saves lives;
   A lying witness [spreads] deceit.

26 Fear of GOD is a stronghold,
   A refuge for one's children.

27 Fear of GOD is a fountain of life,
   Enabling one to avoid deadly snares.

28 A numerous people is the glory of a king;
   Without a nation a ruler is ruined.

29 Patience results in much understanding;
   Impatience gets folly as its portion.

30 A calm disposition gives bodily health;
   Passion is rot to the bones.

15 פֶּתִי יַאֲמִין לְכָל־דָּבָר וְעָרוּם יָבִין לַאֲשֻׁרוֹ:

16 חָכָם יָרֵא וְסָר מֵרָע וּכְסִיל מִתְעַבֵּר וּבוֹטֵחַ:

17 קְצַר־אַפַּיִם יַעֲשֶׂה אִוֶּלֶת וְאִישׁ מְזִמּוֹת יִשָּׂנֵא:

18 נָחֲלוּ פְתָאיִם אִוֶּלֶת וַעֲרוּמִים יַכְתִּרוּ דָעַת:

19 שַׁחוּ רָעִים לִפְנֵי טוֹבִים וּרְשָׁעִים עַל־שַׁעֲרֵי צַדִּיק:

20 גַּם־לְרֵעֵהוּ יִשָּׂנֵא רָשׁ וְאֹהֲבֵי עָשִׁיר רַבִּים:

21 בָּז־לְרֵעֵהוּ חוֹטֵא וּמְחוֹנֵן (עניים) [עֲנָיִים] אַשְׁרָיו:

22 הֲלוֹא־יִתְעוּ חֹרְשֵׁי רָע וְחֶסֶד וֶאֱמֶת חֹרְשֵׁי טוֹב:

23 בְּכָל־עֶצֶב יִהְיֶה מוֹתָר וּדְבַר־שְׂפָתַיִם אַךְ־לְמַחְסוֹר:

24 עֲטֶרֶת חֲכָמִים עָשְׁרָם אִוֶּלֶת כְּסִילִים אִוֶּלֶת:

25 מַצִּיל נְפָשׁוֹת עֵד אֱמֶת וְיָפִחַ כְּזָבִים מִרְמָה:

26 בְּיִרְאַת יְהֹוָה מִבְטַח־עֹז וּלְבָנָיו יִהְיֶה מַחְסֶה:

27 יִרְאַת יְהֹוָה מְקוֹר חַיִּים לָסוּר מִמֹּקְשֵׁי מָוֶת:

28 בְּרָב־עָם הַדְרַת־מֶלֶךְ וּבְאֶפֶס לְאֹם מְחִתַּת רָזוֹן:

29 אֶרֶךְ אַפַּיִם רַב־תְּבוּנָה וּקְצַר־רוּחַ מֵרִים אִוֶּלֶת:

30 חַיֵּי בְשָׂרִים לֵב מַרְפֵּא וּרְקַב עֲצָמוֹת קִנְאָה:

31 One who withholds what is due to the poor affronts their Maker;
   One who shows pity for the needy shows honor.

32 The wicked fall by their own evil;
   The righteous find security in their death.

33 Wisdom rests quietly in the mind of a prudent person,
   But among dullards it makes itself known.

34 Righteousness exalts a nation;
   Sin is a reproach to any people.

35 The king favors a capable servant;
   He rages at an incompetent one.

31 עֹשֵׁק דָּל חֵרֵף עֹשֵׂהוּ וּמְכַבְּדוֹ חֹנֵן אֶבְיוֹן:

32 בְּרָעָתוֹ יִדָּחֶה רָשָׁע וְחֹסֶה בְמוֹתוֹ צַדִּיק:

33 בְּלֵב נָבוֹן תָּנוּחַ חָכְמָה וּבְקֶרֶב כְּסִילִים תִּוָּדֵעַ:

34 צְדָקָה תְרוֹמֵם־גּוֹי וְחֶסֶד לְאֻמִּים חַטָּאת:

35 רְצוֹן־מֶלֶךְ לְעֶבֶד מַשְׂכִּיל וְעֶבְרָתוֹ תִּהְיֶה מֵבִישׁ:

Holy Skepticism and Uncertainty: What Does "Truth" Mean in Times of Upheaval?

The simple believe anything;
The clever ponders their course.
    —Proverbs 14:15

IN 1927 WERNER HEISENBERG revolutionized modern science with his uncertainty principle and, by doing so, disrupted millennia of normative philosophical perspectives on the operations of the universe. Heisenberg stated that the more precisely we measure the location of a subatomic particle—the electron of an atom, let's say— the more imprecise becomes our calculation of its momentum, and vice versa. Thus, because we can never be sure where the electron is at any given moment in time, the attempt to measure both the electron's location and its momentum simultaneously is doomed to fail.

In practical terms, Heisenberg's uncertainty principle relates to whether we can know either where an object is or where it is going in the future. We can calculate exactly where something is in the present moment, but then, as a result, our knowledge of where it is going (that is, its momentum) is completely elusive.

Can we, as humans, be cognizant of the present and simultaneously be aware of our future, or does the uncertainty principle tell us something about how we can—or cannot—predict the future trajectory of our lives? If so, which deserves more of our attention: being present in the moment or being prepared for the future? We would like to fully embrace both options, but our human experience seems to demonstrate that the more "present" we are, the less aware we will be about where we are going, and vice versa. Both of these mindsets are important, but should we give more weight to being present-minded or future-minded? Or might there be an entirely different third possibility?

One might think that we should take a "blind faith" approach to religion, seeing the past as more essential than the present or future. After all, some remind us, do not the teachers and the sages of old understand everything better than we do?[1] Judaism's primary thrust, however, is different: think critically. Indeed, holy skepticism is wiser than acceptance in blind faith.[2] To be sure, there is a role for faith regarding that which cannot be understood, but for regular issues that deserve our full attention and focus (intellectually, emotionally, morally, and spiritually), we shouldn't sell ourselves short. Judaism has struggled to integrate its relationship with the past (memory, *zachor*) and the present (observing and protecting, *shamor*) into its relationship to and responsibility for the future. We carry significant responsibilities to consider the future in addition to the past and present. In fact, to consider the future outcome of our actions is morally essential for all of us.[3]

Science can guide us when we consider the future implications of our actions. Rabbi Joshua Stanton, a Reform rabbi, explains how he understands the relationship between science and religion and the moral implications for such an understanding:

> Evidence for God's existence lies not in juxtaposition to scientific inquiry, but precisely because of it: it is uncanny that there is so much order in our universe if (as in the second law of thermodynamics) it should theoretically be devolving and increasing in entropy. The Ordering Force of the universe that I call God compels us as humans to pursue justice as the highest form of order to which we can aspire. In our own modest way, we connect with the elements of the Force that lies within us and harness it to foster justice in our communities and societies.[4]

God Godself models for us what it means to be fully present and conscious of past, present, and future, as is learned from the divine name (*yod-hei-vav-hei*; "to be" in past, present, and future). However, this presence is one of God's attributes we cannot emulate or truly understand. The blessings recited during Jewish weddings remind us that the era of the Garden of Eden (the past) and the messianic times (the future) are connected.[5] That moment of creating a new union between two people is also a moment of temporal transcendence between past, present, and future. Only love makes such transcendence possible.

However, in less exceptional moments, we are unable to focus simultaneously on our current position and our possible trajectory. We strive, however, to consider the future implications of our actions today to achieve a balance between our thinking about the present and the future.

An imbalance can create problems. Some people are constantly late because they get so caught up in current activities that they neglect future commitments. Others struggle with present obligations because they are so consumed with upcoming events. A better way is to alternate our focus on the present and the future.[6]

The cognitive act of alternating focus between the present and the future teaches us how to create social change. We must attend to the needs of those who are suffering right now (*chesed*, acts of lovingkindness). However, if we focus only on the here and now, we miss the paradigm shifts necessary to cut the roots of systemic injustice (*tzedek*, justice). As moral agents, we must consider both our current situation and the future outcome of our actions. We must not focus exclusively on either our current obligations (deontology) or our future expectations (consequentialism). Our moral lives transcend these clear temporal distinctions.

We must admit that we cannot fully live in the present and the future simultaneously. We are limited in our capability to grasp the different temporal realities of the world we inhabit. Therefore, skepticism is vital to us. Because nobody can ever think of everything, the best we can do is *t'shuvah*: returning to the core lessons of tradition, actively changing ourselves and our world in the present, and working to achieve a moral future.

Rabbi Yisrael Salanter (1809–83, Lithuania), the founder of the Mussar (virtue-based ethics) movement, believed that every person must hold on to three qualities to lead a life suffused with meaning: not to despair, not to get angry, and not to expect to finish the task. We need to seek truth and make it tangible in a broken world. The quest for truth is neither simple nor straightforward, and it must be cultivated for years before it leads to fruition—and we should never expect to reach that point. Because the truth is nebulous, we may never be able to make it tangible in the world. Yet we must strive to ensure that a semblance of truth—a healing variety of it, anyway—can flourish and influence the world.

One of the features of the human mind is that it ceaselessly searches for patterns in the void. It craves logical explanations for the phenomena that we witness. To better understand the world around us, the mind seeks to solve the riddles of the universe through an ontological construction of the *truth*, allowing us to filter out the things that we deem to be "untrue." We quickly realize, however, that it is impossible to discover the entirety of truth. I think that precisely because of the limitations placed upon us are we able to progress and to grow as people. We must constantly strive to learn. The pursuit of truth enables us to also pursue our collective and individual destinies. Seeking the truth is the engine that allows humanity to move forward perpetually, with intentionality, with compassion, with patience, and with the knowledge that meaning is found through navigating the tribulations of living a full, active life.

But how does the search for truth affect humanity? Human beings were blessed with the gift of speech and with the burden of reflection. Whenever our minds and souls are absorbed in an action, a passion, or a cause, we need speech to convey the importance of such a pursuit. A crucial part of our pursuit of our spiritual truths is our ability to speak up when we see them betrayed, even if it is terrifying to do so; being morally confrontational is embedded into our spiritual DNA that yearns for revelation. The challenge is to simultaneously learn how to speak up to the most powerful and how to quiet down and listen to the least powerful. Jewish tradition teaches that we should not seek consensus but aim for respectful disagreement—argument for the sake of heaven—and that decency precedes the laws themselves.[7]

But how does one learn right from wrong and truth from lies? The answer for the Jewish people seems easy: the Torah, our Tree of Life, leads us on our way. And for people of other faiths (or for those of no specific faith), there are manifold paths leading to an understanding of the universe. However, discerning lies from truth is not a simple task. As Maimonides teaches:

> It is impossible to mention in the Torah every detail of a person's conduct with his neighbors and friends, all of his business dealings and the policies of towns and countries, but after it (the Torah) mentioned many (individual laws) . . . it went back to state generally that we should do the right and the good in everything.[8]

Inevitably, society evolves and new definitions of truth and lie arise. Religious laws and norms that used to guide many have been broken and changed considerably; today, many do not turn to religion to solve complex moral dilemmas. We often weigh competing values and priorities to determine the appropriate response to any given situation. Therein lies the challenge we face today: there are multiple definitions and approaches to truth, and each version of truth claims exclusivity. The ideological struggle that most plagues our world today is the struggle between two of those approaches: absolutism and relativism.

Let's take a moment to define the terms and to contrast their ideological presuppositions:

- For **absolutists,** there is but one truth, and beliefs and actions are deemed either right or wrong, regardless of their circumstances. While this appears to be a noble approach, the myopia of absolutist positions is that they make no space for self-critique, doubt, humility, or reinterpretations. It is certainty and fidelity to unquestioned norms that sustain an absolutist individual.

- **Relativists** believe that there are no unconditional morals or truths; everything seems to be determined and made relative by particular personal, social, cultural, or religious circumstances. Scottish philosopher David Hume, considered to be the founder of moral relativism,[9] distinguished between matters of fact and matters of value. He argued that moral judgments are value judgments, as they do not deal with issues of fact.[10] Thus, he rendered the concept of morality itself subjective.

Both the Jewish and modern Western traditions believe that corruption and brokenness occur in a world devoid of both moral standards and humble doubt and self-critique. In the Torah, the lack of standards and self-reflection leads to the horrific crimes of murder, rape, and oppressive regimes, such as at the end of the Book of Judges, a time when "there was no king in Israel" (Judges 21:25). However, the psychology of moral development suggests that we should restructure the way in which our rules are formed. A purely top-down, vertical system of laws and morals favors the powerful and the privileged, because laws favor the lawmaker. Instead of leaving power solely in the hands of the privileged, power—including legislative power—should be shared by all.

The laws of our Torah are written for the Jewish people, and our Rabbis made clear that there is wisdom to learn from the broader world, too[11]—wisdom that might lead us to critical self-reflection. We must consider alternative truths of people of other faiths and even within nature itself. For example:

> Rabbi Yochanan said: If the Torah had not been given, we could have learned about modesty from the cat, honest labor from the ant, marital fidelity from the dove, and good manners from the rooster—who first coaxes his hen and then copulates with her.[12]

We should take an analytic and open, yet also caring and interested approach to every possible truth. Rabbi Kook's definition of an open intellectual life is one to consider:

One must carefully distinguish between a holistic perspective, which succeeds in penetrating the roots of every opinion, enabling it to appreciate every opinion for its intrinsic worth, and the cold tolerance resulting from the difficulty of integrating the spiritual world into life. The later must retreat in its confrontation with the light and energy of life.[13]

Courage, the primary constituent of truth, is the trait that underlies every other. Now, this may seem counterintuitive. If one was to look at the classical character traits (what we refer to in Hebrew as *midot*), courage is not listed among them. Courage does not necessarily foster humility (*anivut*); it is only tangentially related to joy (*simchah*); it may actually be counterproductive to inculcating patience (*savlanut*), but we would not be able to go out into the world and fulfill our soul's potential without courage. Without the spark of courage illuminating the challenging path called experience, would we be able to satiate our desire to learn and grow and follow our calling to better the world? No, we would not.

However, our yearning for truth does not require putting our lives at risk. We do not need to show the boldness of someone like Nachshon ben Aminadav, who walked into the Red Sea as the Egyptians were rapidly approaching his people, hoping that God might intervene and bring a miracle to save all of them.[14] What was Nachshon's truth? Was he truly brave? Was he naïve? The Rabbis teach that we may not rely solely on miracles if we are to be present in the world.[15] There is no virtue in taking senseless risks, but there is also great risk in staying too comfortable and not changing.[16]

One way to discern truth is to live within the discomfort of uncertainty, grappling with questions before jumping to answers, and continuing to seek truth outside our own ideologies. The substance of truth is understanding that each of us is unique and owner of our own truth. Our uniqueness is a mandate to do extraordinary feats that will, in some way, change the world. While we possess an unfathomable ability to unlock our innermost strengths, we must also accept that we will never fully actualize these strengths if we do not recognize our own value. The desires to fit in and to be loved are powerful. Our wish to conform to the truths of others leaves us susceptible to negative influences. On the other hand, taking the time to let a truth wash over us allows it to reveal its power for transformation. Before we take any type of action, it is important to strive to align our inner life with our outer life. At the center of this quest for enthusiastic earnestness is *ratzon* (will). We must have the desire to seek truth; otherwise we cannot reach our respective potentials. We must desire to cultivate a burning passion and a lasting energy to overcome internal and external obstacles. We must desire to overcome our fear of pain, failure, and loss.

Having the foresight to restrain oneself is an under-explored avenue of courageous behavior. The courage to seek our own truths calls upon us not only to speak up publicly, but also to be silent when the times call for silence. Not every situation requires our voice; not every pursuit needs our opinion. Knowing when to back off is as important, maybe even more so, than standing up. To be sure, we learn in the Torah (Leviticus 19:17) that there is a mitzvah to provide constructive feedback to our peers. However, there is also a mitzvah not to speak up when we will not be heard or when our words might make situations worse. As is written in the Talmud:

> Just as there is a mitzvah for a person to say words (of rebuke) that will be accepted, so to there is a mitzvah for a person not to say words [of rebuke] that will not be accepted. Rabbi Abba said: It's an obligation [not to give rebuke that won't be accepted]. As it says: "Do not rebuke scoffers, for they will hate you / Rebuke the wise, and they will love you" (Proverbs 9:8).[17]

Another Talmudic passage suggests that we should still speak up even when what we argue for won't be heard:

> Rabbi Zeira said to Rabbi Shimon, "Master should rebuke these [officials] of the House of the Exilarch." [Rabbi Shimon] said to him, "They do not accept (reproof) from me." [Rabbi Zeira] said to [Rabbi Shimon], "Even though they do not accept it, master should nonetheless rebuke them."[18]

Our strengths are greater than we realize. A person really has the ability to reach much more than his natural [physical] strengths [we think we are limited to one level, we can move this, lift that, only stay awake for so long etc.]. It appears that this is the explanation that our Sages give on the sentence "The daughter of Pharoah stretched her arm and she took the basket that Moses was in. Her arm actually extended many "*amot.*" It's not intended to be understood that her arm physically got longer and then her arm shrunk back to its original state. Because through the gathering of all her energy and her will to save this child, in the merit of that it was in her ability to achieve even the strength of Adam prior to the sin even though the basket was far way. There is no measure to the strength of someone when they arm themself with *ometz* [fortitude] and *gevurah* [strength]. If they do it's in their hand to reach much more than their natural strengths would dictate.[19]

We arrive at our truths through constant spiritual work. This should be both a comfort and a challenge.

Rabbi Abraham Joshua Heschel encourages us to view the recitation of prayer as a vehicle for the cultivation of our truths:

> Prayer is meaningless unless it is subversive, unless it seeks to overthrow and to ruin the pyramids of callousness, hatred, opportunism, falsehoods. The liturgical movement must become a revolutionary movement, seeking to overthrow the forces that continue to destroy the promise, the hope, the vision.[20]

Our tradition teaches us that we should not cling to our "moral clarity." Instead, it argues that we should seek to change, to renew ourselves, to grow, and to compromise. This is the path of the wise:

> Truth and peaceful judgment should you judge in your gates. It would seem that where there is judgment there is no peace, and where there is peace there is no judgment. What is the judgment that incorporates peace? Compromise.[21]

For the Jewish people, it would seem that the dynamics of revelation should offer some insight into the process of true learning, change, and compromise toward a greater spiritual and moral truth. There is a fascinating Talmudic debate regarding how the Israelites responded to the revelation at Sinai:

> And Rabbi Y'hoshua ben Levi said: With every single statement that emanated from the mouth of the Holy One be blessed, the souls of the Jewish people departed [from their bodies], as it is stated: "My soul departed as God spoke" (Song of Songs 5:6). Now, since their souls departed after the first statement, how could they have received the second statement? [God] brought down the dew with which [God] will resurrect the dead in the future, and God resurrected them, as it said: "A generous rain did You lavish, O God, when Your heritage was weary You established it firmly" (Psalm 68:10).[22]

Another Talmudic section on revelation reads:

> And Rabbi Y'hoshua ben Levi said: With every single statement that emanated from the mouth of the Holy One . . . the Jewish people retreated twelve miles, and the ministering angels helped them to totter back, as it is said: "The angels of legions totter, they totter" (Psalm 68:13). (Do not read this [as] . . . *they lead* . . . but as *help others to lead*.)[23]

At moments of revelation, we learn something we did not know before, something new and powerful. Furthermore, in religious revelation, we do not only walk away with new knowledge—rather, our learning leads to emotional transformation. We cannot continue to live the same way after attaining this new knowledge.

Language is limited, making the expression of truth limited as well. The words leaving someone's mouth often do not match the words entering our ears—and even if we truly hear what was intended, we might often reject a truth foreign to us. Pluralism is an approach that enables us to maintain our own truths while honoring the claims of others. To live with an appreciation for pluralism allows us to seek our own truth with intellectual rigor, but also in solidarity and with humility. Everyone is called to pursue their own truth. Rabbi Lord Jonathan Sacks elaborates on this point eloquently:

> There is no life without a task; no person without a talent; no place without a fragment of God's light waiting to be discovered and redeemed; no situation without its possibility of sanctification; no moment without its call. . . . When God calls, [God] does not do so by way of universal imperatives. Instead, [God] whispers our name.[24]

An interesting and contrasting voice to Rabbi Sacks is Immanuel Kant, a well-known relativist. Kant believed that due to the difference between our individual perception and the objective world, we cannot know objective truths. We simply are not capable of accessing unmediated direct knowledge of the external world. Therefore, we have to structure the world not according to our individual experiences of it, but according to fundamental and universal concepts and categories, which we can use to make moral judgments. Since we never know things as they truly are in their essence, we cannot judge them. Kant taught that Abraham should have reflected in the wake of God's commandment to sacrifice Isaac (the *Akeidah*) and concluded that anyone who asked him to kill his son could not actually be God.[25] This notion is compelling since by the Torah's own truth, a malevolent God is not possible.

There are limits to the Kantian approach, of course. When one is in doubt about a moral decision, Kant suggests that we resolve the issue by, essentially, inhabiting the role of "God." His categorical imperative (a moral obligation that is binding in all circumstances) is an invitation to re-create the world. Essentially, every time we have to make a moral decision, we have the opportunity to start the world over by creating a new imperative that all must live by. We are all bound to the same universal standards—however, we all have to find our own paths toward them.

Often, we get stuck in language, especially when it appears to present us with a paradox. Hindus may say they believe in many gods, but unless someone truly understands the Hindu theology of an ultimate source, this would be totally misunderstood. When people say they believe that the "Torah is not from heaven," they might mean widely different things. Rabbi Abraham Isaac HaKohen Kook explains this concept well:

> There is denial that is like an affirmation of faith, and an affirma-
> tion of faith akin to denial. A person can affirm the doctrine of the
> Torah coming from "heaven," but with the meaning of "heaven" so
> strange that nothing of true faith remains. And a person can deny
> Torah coming from "heaven" where the denial is based on what
> the person has absorbed of the meaning of "heaven" from people
> full of ludicrous thoughts. . . . Although that person may not have
> reached the point of truth, nonetheless this denial is to be consid-
> ered akin to an affirmation of faith.[26]

The Rabbis of the Talmud explain that the Torah was revealed not
in divine but in human language so that it could properly be understood.[27] For the Sages, the origin of the Torah is divine, but when
revealed it enters the world as ordinary language. This invariably
renders perfect interpretation or textual consistency impossible;
truths become opaque. This is not a problem unique to Torah. Our
mystical and psychological insights also can never adequately be captured in language. Human experience is more complex than human
language. Our primary grasp of the Divine, albeit elusive, is experiential. Rabbi Samson Raphael Hirsch explains the importance of
the concept *dibrah Torah kilshon b'nei adam*, which literally means "the
Torah speaks in the language of human beings":

> Jewish scholarship has never regarded the Bible as a textbook for
> physical or even abstract doctrines. In its view the main emphasis
> of the Bible is always on the ethical and social structure and devel-
> opment of life on earth; that is, on the observance of laws through
> which the momentous events of our nation's history are converted
> from abstract truths into concrete convictions.[28]

Friedrich Nietzsche and Michel Foucault both taught that we must
analyze the historical relationship between knowledge, truth, and
power. While truth and knowledge are often presented as universal
and eternal, they are actually products of the struggles within and
between institutions and disciplines of thought. Foucault explains
that we gain "power-knowledge" when we make sense of ourselves
and become subjects through the acquisition of knowledge. No

single individual or group holds all the power; power is, rather, a complex and changing flow between different groups and relationships throughout society. Foucault, based upon Nietzsche, explains that our social rules, discourses, sets of meaning, and truths do not merely emerge naturally but are produced to support particular groups and causes. All truths are formed through power struggles.[29]

While Martin Heidegger critiqued "modernity" for forgetting the importance of being, postmodern philosophers have argued that it is language that has been forgotten. "Language" refers not to English, Spanish, Hebrew, etc., but to the systems of differences. The way we think and speak is conditioned by the particular "language" in which we dwell, the pattern of distinctions and connections that makes up our individual human experiences. Language is neither objective nor universally understood, but subjective and tied to context and experience. Postmodern philosophy has made us aware of the constructed nature of all systems of meaning and truth (i.e., has enabled us to understand language and truth in its context and system of power).

In reverse, the Torah's language has to be reinterpreted in changing contexts and systems of power. The Torah was given to be interpreted and to inspire debate. The Holy Scriptures were not meant to be revered in a vacuum, but to be studied at length and within any given context so that the reader understands its changing nuances and depths and, through this understanding, fully internalizes the absence of one ultimate interpretation and truth. According to this hermeneutical practice, we choose how to interpret the world, an experience, a person, or a text. This practice allows us to experience pluralism in our own experience as readers. Rabbi Dr. Irving Yitz Greenberg, a revered teacher of mine, provides a wonderful explication of pluralism and its dynamics in a reading and learning experience:

> Pluralism means more than accepting or even affirming the other. It entails recognizing the blessings in the other's existence, because it balances one's own position and brings all of us closer to the ultimate goal. Even when we are right in our own position, the other

who contradicts our position may be our corrective or our check against going to excess. . . . Pluralism is not relativism, for we hold on to our absolutes; however, we make room for others' as well.[30]

We need to stop pretending that there are no serious moral problems within our traditions, and we need to stop offering false apologetics. We cannot afford to view any form of skepticism as an affront to the inerrable tenets of our faiths. Religious institutions must be honest about the countless problems inherent in their textual traditions and take responsibility for them. We should beware any school of thought that asserts that the Rabbis necessarily express the will of God. Indeed, Jewish theology insists on the fact that all human beings are fallible. Were the Rabbis wiser and more pious than the average person? I most certainly think so. Were they imperfect and also products of their time? Of course. Will each of us, as fallible beings, make more mistakes when we take responsibility for our religious and moral lives instead of outsourcing that responsibility? Perhaps. But that is why we were given free will and one shot at life. We dare not sacrifice this opportunity to cultivate our inner world and learn how to make the best choices we can.

The world is divided and broken. But that doesn't mean we have to give up the struggle to see the light in an increasingly dark world. What we need to do is separate innuendo, bravado, and ideological puffery from truth. The world is in desperate need of deeper moral truths and for individuals to wrestle autonomously with moral problems, in dialogue with text and community. We must break free from the bondage of spiritual conformity and routine thinking about moral quandaries.

Though we may feel that society is being torn asunder, we must echo that simple yet profound reply that Abraham uttered when put to the test: *Hineini*, "Here I am" (Genesis 22:1). We must realize that life is, ultimately, about living the values that renew the spirit of the individual and of the broader society. We cannot look to any outside authority to awaken our religious spirit or to arouse our heart to our own moral calling. We must do that work on our own, albeit through community and with a healthy infusion of holy skepticism.

Gaining from Sorrow

In every sadness there will be profit.
    —Proverbs 14:23

THE BOOK OF PROVERBS is a sad book. It does not focus on lamenting the Jewish people. It doesn't dwell on the horrible tragedies that befell the ancient Israelites and their progeny. Yet, the Book of Proverbs does not shy away from acknowledging the reality that sadness—call it depression, melancholy, lassitude—is a powerful force. The Chasidic tradition, which emphasizes the intimate connection between humanity and divinity frequently teaches about the spiritual value of sadness. Consider this passage from the *Tanya*:

> "In every sadness there will be profit" [Proverbs 14:23].
>
> What is the profit in sadness?
> A broken heart shatters the self
> and the glittering shell of selfishness
> that seems to separate you from God.
>
> "A broken spirit, a broken heart . . .
> You will not despise" (Psalm 51:19).
>
> When your heart is broken
> over the suffering you have caused,
> your sense of otherness is shattered,
> and you can no longer ignore the suffering of others,
> and you are able to "hear joy and gladness" (Psalm 51:10).
>
> "Just as you recite a blessing for good fortune
> so you must recite a blessing for misfortune."[31]
> Why?
> Because your suffering
> attunes you to the suffering of others,

and being so attuned breaks your heart,
allowing the light of God to pierce
the iron ball of isolated self.

Hence it is written,
"The Most High abides in secrecy" (Psalm 91:1).[32]

As we can see in this moving poetic passage, the *Tanya* understands sadness to be breaking our hearts so we allow God to enter it.

Working off of this teaching, Rabbi Kalonymus Kalman Shapira, the Piaseczner Rebbe, who was tragically orphaned at a young age and ultimately murdered by the Nazis, offered quite a bit of spiritual wisdom on sadness. One of his primary teachings was that members of the Jewish people should distinguish between *sh'virat halev*, "the breaking of the heart," which has spiritual depth and sadness to it, and *atzvut*, also "sadness," which is just paralyzing and debilitating. Our holy work should be to elevate our inner sadness to the spiritual level of a broken heart. A broken heart leads to existential reflection, closeness with God, and deeper empathy for others. Indeed, sadness can be a transformative gift.[33]

However, even if sadness can be a gift to us, many others of the negative emotions truly are and remain damaging and dangerous to us, and it is all too easy to "catch" them from others because of the language they speak and we listen to. Language affects the heart. When we're surrounded by others who speak negatively, they can truly affect our mood. Are we aware of how much negative language there is around us?

A generation ago, psychologist James R. Averill analyzed nearly six hundred words for emotions with negative meaning (every one that he could find in the English language) and he found that 62 percent of them had a negative connotation, versus 38 percent that had a positive connotation. He concluded that "in everyday discourse as well as in psychological disquisitions, there appears to be a relative neglect of positive emotions."[34] Legend tells us that Eskimos have one hundred different words for snow. What does it say about us

Americans that we have an abundance of words for negative emotions? How does this affect us?

A story near the end of Tractate *Makot* illustrates one way positivity is understood in the Jewish tradition:

> Rabbi Elazar ben Azaryah, Rabbi Akiva, Rabban Gamliel, and Rabbi Y'hoshua were ascending to Jerusalem after the destruction of the Temple. When they arrived at Mount Scopus and saw the site of the Temple, they rent their garments in mourning, in keeping with traditional practice. When they arrived at the Temple Mount, they saw a fox that emerged from the site of the Holy of Holies. They began weeping, and Rabbi Akiva was laughing. They said to him, "For what reason are you laughing? "Rabbi Akiva said to them, "For what reason are you weeping?" They said to him, "This is the place concerning which it is written: 'Any outsider who approaches shall be put to death' (Numbers 1:51), and now foxes walk in it; and shall we not weep?"
>
> Rabbi Akiva said to them, "That is why I am laughing, as it was written when God revealed the future to the prophet Isaiah: 'And I will take to Me faithful witnesses to attest: the priest Uriah and Zechariah son of Jeberechiah' (Isaiah 8:2)." Now what is the connection between Uriah and Zechariah? He clarifies the difficulty: "Uriah prophesied during the First Temple period, and Zechariah prophesied during the Second Temple period, as he was among those who returned to Zion from Babylonia. Rather, the verse established that fulfillment of the prophecy of Zechariah is dependent on fulfillment of the prophecy of Uriah. In the prophecy of Uriah, it is written: 'Because of you, Zion shall be plowed as a field, and Jerusalem shall become heaps of ruins, and the Temple Mount a shrine in the woods' (Micah 3:12), where foxes are found. There is a Rabbinic tradition that this was prophesied by Uriah. In the prophecy of Zechariah, it is written: 'There shall yet be old men and women in the squares of Jerusalem' (Zechariah 8:4). Until the prophecy of Uriah with regard to the destruction of the city was fulfilled, I was afraid that the prophecy of Zechariah would not be fulfilled, as the two prophecies are linked. Now that the prophecy of Uriah was fulfilled, it is evident that the prophecy of Zechariah remains valid." . . . The Sages said to him, employing this formulation: "Akiva, you have comforted us; Akiva, you have comforted us."[35]

A moving story about redemption from sadness. Rather than seeing the fox as a sign that the Temple Mount, one of the holiest Jewish sites, was in a desolate condition, Rabbi Akiva interprets the situation positively and expresses the conviction that even though things might be difficult for the Jewish people in the present, the fox is already hinting at a future redemption. Tapping into his wisdom, Rabbi Akiva was able to improve the morale of his fellow rabbis.

Another story, this one from around eighteen hundred years later, further illustrates the importance of striving hard to cultivate a positive attitude in one's life:

> A young scholar completed his learning of the entire Talmud for the third time. Full of pride, he ran to tell his teacher about his accomplishment. Strutting into the room where his teacher was diligently learning from a thick tome with a font the size of termites, he exuberantly exclaimed, "Rabbi, I've just been through the whole Talmud for the third time." "That's wonderful," replied his teacher, looking up from his large book, "but let me ask you one question: how many times has the Talmud been through you?" The rabbi then returned to his book while the flabbergasted student went back to his desk to understand the depth of what his rabbi had just told him. For this rabbi, the important part was not the volume of material that his student learned, but rather the way the student internalized the material that he worked so diligently day and night to master.[36]

We are not to merely understand Jewish wisdom, but to allow it to transform us. Even though on the surface the rabbi appears to be criticizing the student for his positivity, I think that we should understand the rabbi in the story as challenging his student to become more aware of the deeper meaning of the text and to achieve deeper happiness and a more substantial satisfaction.

To apply this story to the contemporary moment, we must learn to choose the words we speak and listen to or read with great care. We should pause to consider the language we use to describe our world, allowing for positive hearing and speaking to penetrate our hearts. The Torah, as well as the Book of Proverbs, teaches that we should cultivate positive emotions and use positive speech as much as possible. It takes effort to embrace the deep spiritual and positive wisdom of the Torah. The reward, however, is sublime.

Spiritual Intimacy
or Packed Community

A numerous people is the glory of a king;
Without a nation a ruler is ruined.
—Proverbs 14:28

THERE IS A SIGNIFICANT amount of power in large groups and numbers of people, but there can also be, as a result, myriad problems like fractionalizations and break offs. The Jewish tradition emphasizes the strength of large communities. We can understand the verse from the Book of Proverbs to describe God as that king (or a ruler of some kind). If a member of a royal family is being honored, the royal would probably want to see the masses standing before them; similarly, God wants to see all of God's children—that is, Creation—united in prayer and love.

The phrase "A numerous people is the glory of a king" (*B'rov am hadrat melech*) is generally interpreted to mean that when faced with the choice of doing a mitzvah privately or in a community, one should choose the latter, striving to sanctify God's name with the largest group possible. Drawing on this interpretation, Rabbi David ben Solomon ibn Abi Zimra, a fifteenth-century rabbi also known as the Radbaz (Safed, 1479–1573) writes, "Praising and glorifying the King in a multitude of people cannot be likened to praising God among the few."[37] This principle has been applied to discourage not only small factions but even large groups from breaking away from the main community, as it is written in the *Mishnah Berurah*:[38]

> Even if a person has one hundred people in his home at the *M'gillah* reading with him, but the community is reading it at the same time

in the main synagogue, it is still a mitzvah for him to hear it in the synagogue with the larger group.[39]

At the same time, we know that trying to fit into the masses can lead to extreme discomfort. Sometimes the unity of the masses can lead to conformity and the devaluing of individuality and diversity. Furthermore, shouldn't Jewish leadership be more concerned with quality than with quantity? Rather than show that we were able to crowd two hundred people into an auditorium but leaving few of them impacted, wouldn't we want only a dozen to attend who are truly transformed?[40]

After the Book of Proverbs tells us that masses are needed to secure a nation, we learn just a few verses later: "Righteousness exalts a nation; / Sin is a reproach to any people" (Proverbs 14:34). We might suggest that our second verse is a corrective of the first. Ideally, numbers are great. We want twenty people at the program, two hundred, and perhaps even two thousand! But let's not get so caught up with numbers that we forget our values, purpose, and mission. It is better to be righteous and have a smaller budget, building, and turnout than chasing dirty money in order to grow.

It's interesting to note, for example, that for our gatherings on Rosh HaShanah, Yom Kippur, or Purim, the community gathers in very large groups. But on other holidays like Passover and Sukkot, we retreat to smaller spaces. However, in theory, synagogue could have become the primary place to celebrate a Passover seder and to dwell in a sukkah. Instead, Jews tend to make seder with their families, and maybe some friends and guests, at home; some even build their own sukkah for their family.[41] Ironically, it is those two holidays—Passover and Sukkot—that celebrate the birth of the Jewish nation at large! It might be that this small-group approach developed as a response to the collectivism built into those holidays. For the Jewish people to remain strong at large, we need to strengthen each single home and each single small community. There is not "one community"; rather, there are many different communities with differing customs and approaches, drawing from each other to strengthen the collective. Love and justice start at home. Even in recognizing the value of the crowd, Judaism starts at home.

Being alone is not the ideal. In fact, only twice does the Torah say *lo tov*, "it's not good":

1. "It's not good that the man be alone" (Genesis 2:18).
2. It's not good to lead alone (based on Exodus 18:17–18).

We should neither live nor lead alone.[42] We are here in this world together, connected, mandated to hold each other through the bumpy rides of life. Loneliness is linked to depression and a decline in mental health at large. For our physical health and our spiritual health, we need others.

Of course, it is also worth noting that solitude is a wonderful spiritual practice. We must strike the right balance, for each of us, between being in community and being by ourselves to foster personal growth.

Being Slow to Anger

Being slow to anger (demonstrates) much (wise) understanding,
But a short-spirited person elevates foolishness.
　　—Proverbs 14:29

ANGER IS VERY OFTEN CONSIDERED a vice.[43] We are asked to emulate the Divine, who is *erech apayim*, "slow to anger" (Exodus 34:6; Deuteronomy 11:22). The Rabbis, in fact, place much greater value on appeasement than on fury, referring to anger as a form of idolatry in which one worships oneself.[44] Furthermore, according to Rabbi Nachman of Bratslav, "There is no peace in the world because there is too much anger. You can only make peace with joy."[45] The Rabbis teach us, "One who sees an idol that has not been destroyed pronounces the blessing 'Blessed is God, who is slow to anger.'"[46] I would suggest that this wording was chosen because God should be angry at how much evil there is in the world that remains unchallenged, yet God has humbly allowed us humans to be the ambassadors of truth and the defenders of justice on earth. By mediating between the divine anger and its object, we allow God to achieve the goal of God's anger in an effective but calm manner.

In a brilliant midrash, we learn that God abstains from expressing anger not only to the just but also to the wicked: "Rav Sh'muel bar Nachman said in the name of Rav Yochanan: 'It does not say here *erech af*, but rather *erech apayim* [pluralizing the Hebrew term used to denote the kinds of anger]; as God delays God's anger with the righteous, God delays God's anger with the wicked.'"[47] As humans created in the divine image striving to walk on a righteous path, we are to abstain from quickly expressing anger to any person, good or bad. However, expressing anger can also be useful. Maimonides taught that while people should never get truly angry, we should pretend to be angry to educate young children when they are doing something wrong in order to support them in reaching their goal of inner formation.[48]

Not only can contrived anger be useful in educating the young, but real anger can be effective as well. Visible anger can be particularly useful for social justice activists and leaders. Professor Jeff Stout, the great religion scholar at Princeton University, writes in *Blessed Are the Organized*:

> Anger is one of the most important traits they [organizers] look for in potential leaders. Someone who professes love of justice, but is not angered by its violation, is unlikely to stay with the struggle for justice through thick and thin, to display the passion that will motivate others to join in, or to have enough courage to stand up to the powers that be.[49]

Anyone involved in social justice work must be sure to respond quickly to social problems and injustices—and yet, they must also be sure not to let anger dominate their psyche or persona. Sustained anger takes up an extraordinary amount of energy, and as activists we must preserve our energy as best as we can to ensure that we are effective. The Chasidic rabbis, therefore, teach that we must not subdue our anger, for that leads to losing potential and momentum. Rather, we should channel our anger into constructive organizing. Mohandas Gandhi, who led the fight for independence in India, observed that "anger controlled can be transmuted into a power that can move the world."[50]

To clarify further the effectiveness of anger, Professor Stout describes his concept of "just anger" as anger that

> stands midway between despairing rage and liberal squeamishness about the vehement passions. A politics of just anger aims to restore the spirit of democracy to democratic culture, a spirit disposed to become angry at the right things in the right way and use this passion to motivate the level of political involvement essential to striving for significant social change.[51]

To Stout, "elites" who proclaim their impartiality too often support social injustice by insisting that "victims" remain passive and viewing any righteous anger of the oppressed as a violation of "the elite code of decorum."[52] The proper role of social organizers, Stout notes, is to "oppose that code" and to disrupt the calm of oppression.[53]

Finally, Stout explains that anger can facilitate the creation of a communal feeling of empowerment:

> The experience of anger can reveal to us that we do indeed care about being treated as citizens. If we did not think of ourselves as bound together to some extent by mutual respect, then we would not be angered by the behavior and negligence of elites. To feel anger is to have the importance of the relationship and its demands drawn to our attention. Accordingly, the individual who rarely experiences anger in response to injustices . . . [shows] slavishness and apathy. A central task of a leader . . . is to help others transform themselves from slavish or apathetic victims into people who behave and feel as citizens do.[54]

To put this differently, as the French existentialist (and Resistance member) Albert Camus writes, "I rebel—therefore we exist."[55]

Rabbi Mari Chernow, a Reform rabbi in Phoenix, Arizona, writes that anger enables movements to grow:

> On a societal level, too, anger can indicate that transformative change is necessary. Consider social movements, such as Me Too and Black Lives Matter. The issues at their heart, sexual violence and racial inequality, have long been critical and worthy of our attention. However, they did not gain the national spotlight until anger fueled a sense of urgency. . . . The teachings of the Talmud, Ibn Hasdai, *Orchot Tzadikim*, Proverbs, and *Ki Tisa* itself guide us to identify anger and give it healthy space to breathe. They warn of the danger of unmanaged rage. They invite us to learn from anger as we strengthen our emotional and spiritual health. Anger contains great wisdom. Our task is to give it honor but not too much power, to listen to it carefully without wholly deferring to it, and to find within it sparks of holiness.[56]

Rabbi Abraham Joshua Heschel, in his "A Prayer for Peace," writes:

> O Lord, we confess our sins, we are ashamed of the inadequacy of
> our anguish, of how faint and slight is our mercy. We are a gener-
> ation that has lost its capacity for outrage. We must continue to
> remind ourselves that in a free society all are involved in what some
> are doing. *Some are guilty, all are responsible.*[57]

We must feel outrage, as our prophets once did, when we encounter
oppression and injustice. This is what it means to be Jewish and alive.

Similarly, Rabbi Joseph B. Soloveitchik, a contemporary of
Heschel, argues:

> Of course, love is a great and noble emotion, fostering the social
> spirit and elevating man, but not always is the loving person capa-
> ble of meeting the challenge of harsh realities. In certain situations,
> a disjunctive emotion, such as anger or indignation, may become
> the motivating force for noble and valuable action.[58]

Thus, some among the greatest Jewish and non-Jewish philosophers of the last century recognized the importance of this truth:
controlled and righteous anger, in defense of social justice, is no vice.

Anger can be unhealthy, but it is also human. Two Hebrew words
used in connection with the anger point in two divergent modalities
of the emotion. *Chema* comes from a root word meaning heat. *Af*
means nose, signifying that breath as a lifeforce is related to anger as
an animating feeling. We should dismiss rage (*chema*) when it comes
from hot-headedness or self-righteousness; but when anger (*af*) is
experienced as a healthy response to the pain of others, we should
harness the emotion in order to minimize that pain with all the
breath we possess.

Chapter 15

1 A gentle response allays wrath;
   A harsh word provokes anger.

2 The tongue of the wise produces much knowledge,
   But the mouth of dullards pours out folly.

3 The eyes of GOD are everywhere,
   Observing the bad and the good.

4 A healing tongue is a tree of life,
   But a devious one makes for a broken spirit.

5 A fool spurns a parent's discipline,
   But one who heeds reproof becomes clever.

6 In the house of the righteous there is much treasure,
   But in the harvest of the wicked there is trouble.

7 The lips of the wise disseminate knowledge;
   Not so the minds of dullards.

8 The sacrifice of the wicked is an abomination to GOD,
   But the prayer of the upright is pleasing.

9 The way of the wicked is an abomination to GOD,
   But those who pursue righteousness are loved.

10 Discipline seems bad to whoever forsakes the way;
   One who spurns reproof will die.

11 Sheol and Abaddon lie exposed to GOD,
   How much more the minds of mortals!

12 The scoffer, who dislikes being reproved,
   Will not resort to the wise.

13 A joyful heart makes a cheerful face;
   A sad heart makes a despondent mood.

14 The mind of a prudent person seeks knowledge;
   The mouth of dullards pursues folly.

פרק טו

1 מַעֲנֶה־רַּךְ יָשִׁיב חֵמָה וּדְבַר־עֶצֶב יַעֲלֶה־אָף:

2 לְשׁוֹן חֲכָמִים תֵּיטִיב דָּעַת וּפִי כְסִילִים יַבִּיעַ אִוֶּלֶת:

3 בְּכָל־מָקוֹם עֵינֵי יְהֹוָה צֹפוֹת רָעִים וְטוֹבִים:

4 מַרְפֵּא לָשׁוֹן עֵץ חַיִּים וְסֶלֶף בָּהּ שֶׁבֶר בְּרוּחַ:

5 אֱוִיל יִנְאַץ מוּסַר אָבִיו וְשֹׁמֵר תּוֹכַחַת יַעְרִים:

6 בֵּית צַדִּיק חֹסֶן רָב וּבִתְבוּאַת רָשָׁע נֶעְכָּרֶת:

7 שִׂפְתֵי חֲכָמִים יְזָרוּ דָעַת וְלֵב כְּסִילִים לֹא־כֵן:

8 זֶבַח רְשָׁעִים תּוֹעֲבַת יְהֹוָה וּתְפִלַּת יְשָׁרִים רְצוֹנוֹ:

9 תּוֹעֲבַת יְהֹוָה דֶּרֶךְ רָשָׁע וּמְרַדֵּף צְדָקָה יֶאֱהָב:

10 מוּסָר רָע לְעֹזֵב אֹרַח שׂוֹנֵא תוֹכַחַת יָמוּת:

11 שְׁאוֹל וַאֲבַדּוֹן נֶגֶד יְהֹוָה אַף כִּי־לִבּוֹת בְּנֵי־אָדָם:

12 לֹא יֶאֱהַב־לֵץ הוֹכֵחַ לוֹ אֶל־חֲכָמִים לֹא יֵלֵךְ:

13 לֵב שָׂמֵחַ יֵיטִב פָּנִים וּבְעַצְּבַת־לֵב רוּחַ נְכֵאָה:

14 לֵב נָבוֹן יְבַקֶּשׁ־דָּעַת (ופני) [וּפִי] כְסִילִים יִרְעֶה אִוֶּלֶת:

15 All the days of a pauper are wretched,
  But contentment is a feast without end.

16 Better a little with fear of GOD
  Than great wealth with confusion.

17 Better a meal of vegetables where there is love
  Than a fattened ox where there is hate.

18 A hot-tempered man provokes a quarrel;
  A patient person calms strife.

19 The way of a sluggard is like a hedge of thorns,
  But the path of the upright is paved.

20 A wise son makes his father happy;
  A fool of a man humiliates his mother.

21 Folly is joy to one devoid of sense;
  A prudent man walks a straight path.

22 Plans are foiled for want of counsel,
  But they succeed through many advisers.

23 One's ready response brings joy to oneself,
  And how good is a word rightly timed!

24 For the intelligent the path of life leads upward,
  In order to avoid Sheol below.

25 GOD will tear down the house of the proud—
  But will establish the homestead of the widow.

26 Evil thoughts are an abomination to GOD,
  But pleasant words are pure.

27 Whoever pursues ill-gotten gain makes trouble for the household;
  One who spurns gifts will live long.

28 A righteous person's heart rehearses the answer,
  But the mouth of the wicked blurts out evil things.

29 GOD is far from the wicked—
  But hears the prayer of the righteous.

30 What brightens the eye gladdens the heart;
  Good news puts fat on the bones.

כָּל־יְמֵי עָנִי רָעִים וְטוֹב־לֵב מִשְׁתֶּה תָמִיד: 15

טוֹב־מְעַט בְּיִרְאַת יְהֹוָה מֵאוֹצָר רָב וּמְהוּמָה בוֹ: 16

טוֹב אֲרֻחַת יָרָק וְאַהֲבָה־שָׁם מִשּׁוֹר אָבוּס וְשִׂנְאָה־בוֹ: 17

אִישׁ חֵמָה יְגָרֶה מָדוֹן וְאֶרֶךְ אַפַּיִם יַשְׁקִיט רִיב: 18

דֶּרֶךְ עָצֵל כִּמְשֻׂכַת חָדֶק וְאֹרַח יְשָׁרִים סְלֻלָה: 19

בֵּן חָכָם יְשַׂמַּח־אָב וּכְסִיל אָדָם בּוֹזֶה אִמּוֹ: 20

אִוֶּלֶת שִׂמְחָה לַחֲסַר־לֵב וְאִישׁ תְּבוּנָה יְיַשֶּׁר־לָכֶת: 21

הָפֵר מַחֲשָׁבוֹת בְּאֵין סוֹד וּבְרֹב יוֹעֲצִים תָּקוּם: 22

שִׂמְחָה לָאִישׁ בְּמַעֲנֵה־פִיו וְדָבָר בְּעִתּוֹ מַה־טּוֹב: 23

אֹרַח חַיִּים לְמַעְלָה לְמַשְׂכִּיל לְמַעַן סוּר מִשְּׁאוֹל מָטָּה: 24

בֵּית גֵּאִים יִסַּח | יְהֹוָה וְיַצֵּב גְּבוּל אַלְמָנָה: 25

תּוֹעֲבַת יְהֹוָה מַחְשְׁבוֹת רָע וּטְהֹרִים אִמְרֵי־נֹעַם: 26

עֹכֵר בֵּיתוֹ בּוֹצֵעַ בָּצַע וְשׂוֹנֵא מַתָּנֹת יִחְיֶה: 27

לֵב צַדִּיק יֶהְגֶּה לַעֲנוֹת וּפִי רְשָׁעִים יַבִּיעַ רָעוֹת: 28

רָחוֹק יְהֹוָה מֵרְשָׁעִים וּתְפִלַּת צַדִּיקִים יִשְׁמָע: 29

מְאוֹר־עֵינַיִם יְשַׂמַּח־לֵב שְׁמוּעָה טוֹבָה תְּדַשֶּׁן־עָצֶם: 30

31 One whose ear heeds the discipline of life
   Lodges among the wise.
32 Those who spurn discipline hate themselves;
   But those who heed reproof gain understanding.
33 The fear of GOD is the discipline of wisdom;
   Humility precedes honor.

31 אֹזֶן שֹׁמַעַת תּוֹכַחַת חַיִּים בְּקֶרֶב חֲכָמִים תָּלִין׃

32 פּוֹרֵעַ מוּסָר מוֹאֵס נַפְשׁוֹ וְשׁוֹמֵעַ תּוֹכַחַת קוֹנֶה לֵּב׃

33 יִרְאַת יְהֹוָה מוּסַר חָכְמָה וְלִפְנֵי כָבוֹד עֲנָוָה׃

The Prayer of the Righteous

God is far from the wicked—
But hears the prayer of the righteous.
　　—Proverbs 15:29

DOES PRAYER ABSOLVE the wicked? Does God listen to the prayers of the righteous and only the righteous? What about the sinners, transgressors, murderers, and thieves? Do they deserve the same spiritual attention that a person who has never violated the law deserves? These are complicated ethical questions that have been ever present in Jewish thought for millennia.

But let's step back for a moment. For many people all over the world—Jewish and gentile—the normative function of prayer is to forge a connection to God. Rabbi Leon of Modena (1571–1648, Italy, originally Spain), a noted Jewish thinker of the early Renaissance period, once offered a powerful parable to explain our relationship to God in prayer. He suggested that a person rowing a rowboat might think that he is rowing the shore closer to himself. In reality, he is pulling himself closer to the shore.[1]

In prayer too, we do not pull God closer to us. Rather, we pull ourselves closer to God.

A traditional goal of prayer is to reach for God's presence. God is here and waiting for us. Rabbi Y'hudah HaLevi (ca. 1075–1141, Spain), the foremost poet in (relatively) modern Jewish history and the author of the *Kuzari*, contrasted the "God of the philosophers" with the "God of Abraham, Isaac, and Jacob."[2] For the philosophers, God is unknowable, far away, and impossible to talk to. In this conception, God is an ungraspable idea. However, for our ancestors and the prophets of Israel, God is close, accessible, reachable; God is knowable.

Another goal of prayer is to cleanse ourselves spiritually. Each of us carries our own spiritual and moral baggage. Consider how Thích Nhất Hạnh, a Vietnamese Buddhist Zen monk and peace activist, understands our need to find answers to our inner struggles:

> If we're overloaded with fear, anger, regret, or anxiety, we're not free, no matter what position we hold in society or how much money we have. Real freedom only comes when we're able to release our suffering and come home. Freedom is the most precious thing there is. It is the foundation of happiness, and it is available to us with each conscious breath.[3]

Prayer allows us the freedom to change ourselves. It makes us pause. It helps us to purify ourselves of the psychological barriers we face as we try to grow and heal. Freedom is indeed crucial here. We must believe that we are free and able to change and grow. Maimonides—who held views that HaLevi might well have rejected in the same terms he used in discussing the philosophers—explains that freedom is a foundational element of a person's ability to connect with divinity:

> Free will is granted to all. If one desires to turn oneself to the path of good and be righteous, the choice is that person's. Should one desire to turn to the path of evil and be wicked, the choice is that person's. This is [the intent of] the Torah's statement "Behold, a human being has become unique as ourselves, knowing good and evil" [Genesis 3:22], that is, the human species became singular in the world with no other species resembling it in the following quality: that one can, on one's own initiative, with one's knowledge and thought, know good and evil, and do what one desires. There is no one who can prevent one from doing good or bad. Accordingly, [there was a need to drive that human being from the Garden of Eden] "lest the human being stretch out a hand [and take from the Tree of Life]" [Genesis 3:22]. This principle is a fundamental concept and pillar [on which rests the totality] of the Torah and mitzvot, as [Deuteronomy 30:15] states: "Behold, I have set before you today life [and good, death and evil]." Similarly, [Deuteronomy 11:26] states, "Behold I have set before you today [the blessing and the curse]," implying the choice is in your hands.[4]

We human beings are free to choose how to live, and we can certainly choose a moral path. However, we can also reject that path. The luxury of freedom is also a burden. In Jewish tradition, we pursue *halachta bidrachav* (literally "go in God's ways," a concept also expressed as *imitatio Dei*) as the path to moral growth. We learn from the perfect model of God. The Rabbis explain:

> Rabbi Simlai said: "We find that the Holy One, blessed be God, blesses bridegrooms, adorns brides, visits the sick, buries the dead, and recites the blessings for mourners.
>
> God blesses bridegrooms, as it is written, 'And God blessed them';
>
> God adorns brides, as it is written, 'And the Eternal God built the rib . . . into a woman';
>
> God visits the sick, as it is written, 'And the Eternal appeared unto him . . .';
>
> God buries the dead, as it is written, 'And God buried him in the valley. . . .'"
>
> Rabbi Samuel ben Nachman said: "God also visits mourners, as it is written, 'And God appeared unto Jacob again . . . and blessed him.' How did God bless him? With the blessing of mourners."[5]

The following is a related teaching from the same teacher:

> Rabbi Simlai taught: "The Torah begins with deeds of lovingkindness and ends with deeds of lovingkindness. It begins with deeds of lovingkindness, as it is written, 'And the Eternal God made garments of skins for Adam and his wife and clothed them' (Genesis 3:21). It ends with deeds of lovingkindness, as it is written, 'And God buried Moses in the valley in the land of Moab' (Deuteronomy 34:6)."[6]

On the role of prayer in our lives, Rabbi Karyn D. Kedar writes:

> Prayer is an articulation of our highest desires, our yearnings, our dark places, a reflection of the light we hold within. It is a conversation with the invisible, an acknowledgment of the mystery, a query into the ineffable. When we pray, we reach for clarity, for strength beyond what we know. Praying is at once an intense self-examination and a dialogue with the sacred, representing the seam of a very

fine fabric where the physical is joined to the metaphysical, and where, no matter our reason for praying, we touch a bit of heaven.[7]

"No matter our reason for praying"! Indeed, each of us will have our own virtues and vices and our own reasons to open our hearts to the heavens. Rather than judge one another and judge another's prayers, we should find humility under the starry night, standing before the vast seas.

What does the Book of Proverbs have to say about prayer? Is prayer supposed to bring us closer to God? To change God's mind? To change our own mind? Whatever conclusion we come to, one thing is clear: through prayer, we should grow in our virtue. As our passage from Proverbs explains, God hears the prayers of the righteous. This does not only mean that if one is righteous, then God hears one's prayer; it also means that one is becoming more righteous in one's commitment to pray and in one's prayer itself. We do not have be perfect to approach God. We are all inherently imperfect. Rather, we need to be committed to a path of growth and to standing before the Creator with full integrity.

Chapter 16

1 Mortals may arrange their thoughts,
But what they say depends on GOD.

2 Every person's ways seem right in their own eyes,
But GOD probes motives.

3 Entrust your affairs to GOD,
And your plans will succeed.

4 GOD made everything for a purpose,
Even the wicked for an evil day.

5 Everyone haughty is an abomination to GOD;
Assuredly, they will not go unpunished.

6 Iniquity is expiated by loyalty and faithfulness,
And evil is avoided through fear of GOD.

7 GOD, when pleased with someone's conduct,
May turn even their enemies into allies.

8 Better a little with righteousness
Than a large income with injustice.

9 Mortals may plot out their course,
But it is GOD who directs their steps.

10 There is magic on the lips of the king;
He cannot err in judgment.

11 Honest scales and balances are GOD's,
Whose work includes all the weights in the bag.

12 Wicked deeds are an abomination to kings,
For the throne is established by righteousness.

13 Truthful speech wins the favor of kings;
They love those who speak honestly.

14 The king's wrath is a messenger of death,
But a man who is wise can appease it.

פרק טז

1 לְאָדָם מַעַרְכֵי־לֵב וּמֵיהֹוָה מַעֲנֵה לָשׁוֹן:

2 כָּל־דַּרְכֵי־אִישׁ זַךְ בְּעֵינָיו וְתֹכֵן רוּחוֹת יְהֹוָה:

3 גֹּל אֶל־יְהֹוָה מַעֲשֶׂיךָ וְיִכֹּנוּ מַחְשְׁבֹתֶיךָ:

4 כֹּל פָּעַל יְהֹוָה לַמַּעֲנֵהוּ וְגַם־רָשָׁע לְיוֹם רָעָה:

5 תּוֹעֲבַת יְהֹוָה כָּל־גְּבַהּ־לֵב יָד לְיָד לֹא יִנָּקֶה:

6 בְּחֶסֶד וֶאֱמֶת יְכֻפַּר עָוֹן וּבְיִרְאַת יְהֹוָה סוּר מֵרָע:

7 בִּרְצוֹת יְהֹוָה דַּרְכֵי־אִישׁ גַּם־אוֹיְבָיו יַשְׁלִם אִתּוֹ:

8 טוֹב־מְעַט בִּצְדָקָה מֵרֹב תְּבוּאוֹת בְּלֹא מִשְׁפָּט:

9 לֵב אָדָם יְחַשֵּׁב דַּרְכּוֹ וַיהֹוָה יָכִין צַעֲדוֹ:

10 קֶסֶם | עַל־שִׂפְתֵי־מֶלֶךְ בְּמִשְׁפָּט לֹא יִמְעַל־פִּיו:

11 פֶּלֶס | וּמֹאזְנֵי מִשְׁפָּט לַיהֹוָה מַעֲשֵׂהוּ כָּל־אַבְנֵי־כִיס:

12 תּוֹעֲבַת מְלָכִים עֲשׂוֹת רֶשַׁע כִּי בִצְדָקָה יִכּוֹן כִּסֵּא:

13 רְצוֹן מְלָכִים שִׂפְתֵי־צֶדֶק וְדֹבֵר יְשָׁרִים יֶאֱהָב:

14 חֲמַת־מֶלֶךְ מַלְאֲכֵי־מָוֶת וְאִישׁ חָכָם יְכַפְּרֶנָּה:

15 The king's smile means life;
His favor is like a rain cloud in spring.

16 How much better to acquire wisdom than gold;
To acquire understanding is preferable to silver.

17 The highway of the upright avoids evil;
Those who would preserve their lives watch their way.

18 Pride goes before ruin,
Arrogance, before failure.

19 Better to be humble and among the lowly
Than to share spoils with the proud.

20 One who is adept in a matter will attain success;
Happy is the one who trusts in GOD.

21 The wise-hearted are called discerning;
Those whose speech is pleasing gain wisdom.

22 Good sense is a fountain of life to those who have it,
And folly is the punishment of fools.

23 The mind of the wise makes their speech effective
And increases the wisdom on their lips.

24 Pleasant words are like a honeycomb,
Sweet to the palate and a cure for the body.

25 The road ahead may seem right,
But in the end it can be a road to death.

26 The appetite of laborers labors for them,
Because their hunger forces them on.

27 A worthless man plots evil;
What is on his lips is like a scorching fire.

28 A shifty man stirs up strife,
And a querulous one alienates his friend.

29 A lawless man misleads his friend,
Making him take the wrong way.

30 He closes his eyes while meditating deception;
He purses his lips while deciding upon evil.

15 בְּאוֹר־פְּנֵי־מֶלֶךְ חַיִּים וּרְצוֹנוֹ כְּעָב מַלְקוֹשׁ:

16 קְנֹה־חָכְמָה מַה־טּוֹב מֵחָרוּץ וּקְנוֹת בִּינָה נִבְחָר מִכָּסֶף:

17 מְסִלַּת יְשָׁרִים סוּר מֵרָע שֹׁמֵר נַפְשׁוֹ נֹצֵר דַּרְכּוֹ:

18 לִפְנֵי־שֶׁבֶר גָּאוֹן וְלִפְנֵי כִשָּׁלוֹן גֹּבַהּ רוּחַ:

19 טוֹב שְׁפַל־רוּחַ אֶת־(עניים) [עֲנָוִים] מֵחַלֵּק שָׁלָל אֶת־גֵּאִים:

20 מַשְׂכִּיל עַל־דָּבָר יִמְצָא־טוֹב וּבוֹטֵחַ בַּיהֹוָה אַשְׁרָיו:

21 לַחֲכַם־לֵב יִקָּרֵא נָבוֹן וּמֶתֶק שְׂפָתַיִם יֹסִיף לֶקַח:

22 מְקוֹר חַיִּים שֵׂכֶל בְּעָלָיו וּמוּסַר אֱוִלִים אִוֶּלֶת:

23 לֵב חָכָם יַשְׂכִּיל פִּיהוּ וְעַל־שְׂפָתָיו יֹסִיף לֶקַח:

24 צוּף־דְּבַשׁ אִמְרֵי־נֹעַם מָתוֹק לַנֶּפֶשׁ וּמַרְפֵּא לָעָצֶם:

25 יֵשׁ דֶּרֶךְ יָשָׁר לִפְנֵי־אִישׁ וְאַחֲרִיתָהּ דַּרְכֵי־מָוֶת:

26 נֶפֶשׁ עָמֵל עָמְלָה לּוֹ כִּי־אָכַף עָלָיו פִּיהוּ:

27 אִישׁ בְּלִיַּעַל כֹּרֶה רָעָה וְעַל־(שפתיו) [שְׂפָתוֹ] כְּאֵשׁ צָרָבֶת:

28 אִישׁ תַּהְפֻּכוֹת יְשַׁלַּח מָדוֹן וְנִרְגָּן מַפְרִיד אַלּוּף:

29 אִישׁ חָמָס יְפַתֶּה רֵעֵהוּ וְהוֹלִיכוֹ בְּדֶרֶךְ לֹא־טוֹב:

30 עֹצֶה עֵינָיו לַחְשֹׁב תַּהְפֻּכוֹת קֹרֵץ שְׂפָתָיו כִּלָּה רָעָה:

31 Gray hair is a crown of glory;
   It is attained by the way of righteousness.
32 Better to be forbearing than mighty,
   To have self-control than to conquer a city.
33 Lots are cast into the lap;
   The decision depends on GOD.

31 עֲטֶרֶת תִּפְאֶרֶת שֵׂיבָה בְּדֶרֶךְ צְדָקָה תִּמָּצֵא:

32 טוֹב אֶרֶךְ אַפַּיִם מִגִּבּוֹר וּמֹשֵׁל בְּרוּחוֹ מִלֹּכֵד עִיר:

33 בַּחֵיק יוּטַל אֶת־הַגּוֹרָל וּמֵיְהֹוָה כָּל־מִשְׁפָּטוֹ:

Everything Has a Purpose

GOD made everything for a purpose,
Even the wicked for an evil day.
　　—Proverbs 16:4

CAN WE UNDERSTAND EVIL? Should we? These are questions that have rattled philosophers for eons. Let's begin the analysis of this verse from Proverbs by looking at its closing line. There is a significant ethical lesson contained in this brief section of text, one that should give us pause and reorient our perspectives about the nature of reality. The most challenging part of this verse is the conclusion—the lesson that even the wicked have a purpose. It seems counterintuitive, perhaps even sacrilegious. Why should evil have purpose? Aren't we supposed to avoid evil at all costs?

At first glance, the obvious read of the verse is that everything happens for a reason, which is a platitude that we often hear used to describe the indescribable. We turn away from the reality of evil because, to the average mind, evil is nearly impossible to comprehend. Human nature wants to see the good in everything, even when times are bleak. Yet, the desire to ascribe positive elements to any occurrence is an epistemological fantasy, at best. The verse reminds us that purpose—whether for good or ill—is an extension of all of creation. Both good purpose and evil have their roles to play in and on this world.

Now, of course, we might take exception with those who have made poor moral choices or who support those who act immorally. Yet, the verse buttresses the notion that God has created even those who have made terrible moral mistakes. This does not mean, certainly, that we reject the idea and the practice of criminal justice or that we should allow evil to flourish. Rather, it means that we never forget the truth that nothing and no one is irredeemable.

Maimonides comments on this moral reality. In his philosophical work *Guide for the Perplexed*, he provides elucidation on creation's purposes and the choices that each human, as an element of the created world, makes:

> Now if the spheres exist for the sake of a human being, all the more is this the case for all the species of animals and of plants. However, if this opinion is carefully examined, as opinions ought to be carefully examined by intelligent human beings, the flaw becomes clear. . . . It should not be believed that all the beings exist for the sake of the existence of a human being. On the contrary, all the other beings too have been intended for their own sakes and not for the sake of something else.[1]

Here Maimonides rejects the anthropocentric worldview that the human being is the center of all existence and the purpose of all creation. No doubt, in Jewish theology, the human is the pinnacle of creation—the last act of creation imbued with the gift of being created in God's image—but that reality doesn't mean that humans can exploit creation. Everything is created with its own purpose; everything has its own inherent value. This is to say that every being in the created universe is not merely instrumental, only holding value in relationship to human enjoyment, but rather that each has its own inherent value. We care about climate justice and animal rights not only because of human sustainability, but also because we are responsible for the upkeep of creation. We know that factory farming has the greatest impact on deleterious effects on the climate today. Why isn't the issue of animal rights more front and center in liberal America—if not to reduce animal suffering, if not for human health, then for environmental justice?

After all, Maimonides explains in another passage, all evil is due to ignorance. This is to say that evil is not innate but rather something learned (or perhaps that it exists because its opposite is not learned):

> These great evils that come about between the human individuals who inflict them upon one another because of purposes, desires,

opinions and beliefs are all of them likewise consequent upon privation. . . . Just as a blind person, because of absence of sight, does not cease stumbling, being wounded, and also wounding others, because there is nobody to guide that person on the way, the various sects of human beings—every individual according to the extent of one's ignorance—does to oneself and to others great evils from which individuals of the species suffer. If there were knowledge, whose relation to the human form is like that of the faculty of sight to the eye, they would refrain from doing any harm to themselves and to others. For through cognition of the truth, enmity and hatred are removed and the inflicting of harm by people on one another is abolished. It holds out this promise, saying: "And the wolf shall dwell with the lamb, and the leopard shall lie down with the kid," and so on (Isaiah 11:6-8). Then it gives the reason for this, saying that the cause of the abolition of the enmities, these discords, and these tyrannies will be the knowledge that human beings will then have concerning the true reality of the Deity. For it says: "They shall not hurt or destroy in all My holy mountain; for the earth shall be full of the knowledge of the Eternal, as the waters cover the sea" (Isaiah 11:9).[2]

The Book of Proverbs delves into the ambiguous states of human nature. That is its greatest contribution to the Hebrew literary canon. When matters concern the balance of good and evil, it seems apparent that we, as people who strive for valor and ethical truth, should always follow the path of good. Yet, without there being an oppositional force—in this case, evil in any of its multitudinous forms—then there is no progression.

The world is broken because evil is allowed to fester. Every day, we see news of evil acts perpetrated all over the world. Lamentably, religion is often a factor in these acts. But we shouldn't stand idly by and let evil linger. God gives us the ability, the holy ability, to use our talents to make the world a less broken place. An act of charity, no matter how small, repairs a fissure in the world. A simple kind act heals a rift in the heart. A word of praise can lift the soul. Evil is easy, but pursuing a life of empathy and compassion is difficult work. But those are the values that will prevail in the end.

The work and words of Torah aren't about stasis, about being stuck in a certain mode of thinking. The Torah displays for us the dynamics of the human spirit. Leaders seen as good can perform absolutely wicked acts, and scoundrels can act nobly if the circumstances call for it. Though the ink and parchment may be black and white, the Torah—along with the Jewish wisdom that originates from it—presents itself to be understood and lived in shades of gray.

People of Violence

A lawless man misleads his friend,
Making him take the wrong way.
  —Proverbs 16:29

THE JEWISH TRADITION is no stranger to violence. The Torah records many violent acts, from war and murder to rape and conquest, plagues and genocide. Later in Proverbs, we read, "Blood-thirsty people detest the blameless, but the upright seek them out" (Proverbs 29:10). Yet, the overall message of Jewish wisdom has always been to support the antithesis of violence: a world filled with peace. In the Mishnah, Hillel was known to say, "Be of the disciples of Aaron—a lover of peace, a pursuer of peace."[3] Indeed, the message for the Jewish people to chase after peace is so essential to our spiritual genetics that the Rabbis even taught that the Hebrew word for peace—*shalom*—is one of the names of God.[4]

Yet, for all the calls for it, has peace ever truly been achieved? Can violence ever be eradicated from the earth? While it would be great to answer in the affirmative, the answer is of course not. However, experts in the field of peace studies have suggested that violence, on a global scale, is actually on the decline. According to data compiled by Professor Steven Pinker of Harvard University, a smaller percentage of people die today in battle than ever before.[5] He notes that about 1.2 million deaths are referenced in the Bible and that the percentage of people killed in battle today is less than one-thousandth of what it was before the era of nation-states, from 500 per 100,000 population then to about 1 person per 300,000 today. As for genocide, today the rate has gone down fourteen hundred times from its most recent height during World War II. Professor Andrew Mack of

Simon Fraser University in Canada has documented a similar trend.[6] He found that although the number of wars has increased, the number of people killed in these wars has declined by about 90 percent over the past sixty years.

Consider, for example, a famous ancient war, Julius Caesar's conquest of Gaul. When the Gauls resisted his efforts to engage in open battle, Caesar retaliated by annihilating a city of nearly forty thousand people. When he finally cornered the Gauls, he deliberately starved the women and children who tried to leave the war zone, and after his victory, he murdered one million Gauls and sold another million into slavery. We should also remember that although Caesar was an extraordinarily cunning political strategist, he was not regarded as especially cruel for his time.

Apart from war, Professor Pinker maintains that violent crime in general is also on the decline. Murder rates in Europe are now about 1 percent of the murder rates in the fourteenth and fifteenth centuries. In the United States, a much more violent society, rape has declined 80 percent in the past forty years.[7] The domestic murder rate, while receiving more media attention, has actually declined by nearly half in the past four decades as well.[8] In addition, some significant past crimes, such as lynching, have virtually disappeared.[9]

What are the possible reasons behind these positive developments? Professor Pinker suggests that a more educated population and more numerous democratic states support these trends.

His theory is supported by many examples. In America, about 620,000 soldiers died during the Civil War (nearly half of all American war dead in its history), when the United States had a population of about 31 million. Thus, nearly 2 percent of Americans were killed in that war. Similarly, while England suffered heavy losses during World War I, its rate of death was far lower than during its own Civil War in the mid-seventeenth century.

Despite Pinker's insightful work, his claims do not quite line up with what we are observing regarding religious persecution. In 2007, 24 percent of minority religious groups suffered from religious discrimination and persecution; in 2011, that number rose to 38 percent, and in 2012, to 47 percent. However, religion is not only the reason some religious groups are victimized; it is also the reason some religious groups become violent themselves. We have seen an explosion of violence in the Middle East, especially in the context of the rise of the Islamic State, which engages in a considerable amount of religious persecution.

The history of much of the twentieth century does not seem as peaceful as Pinker and Mack describe. Europe, after the relative peace following the defeat of Napoleon at the Battle of Waterloo in 1815, was traumatized by the seventeen million who died in World War I and, a generation later, by the costliest war in history, World War II, where sixty to seventy million people, primarily civilians, lost their lives. In addition to the unspeakable horrors of the Holocaust, the Second World War featured coordinated armor and air offensives, the firebombing of cities, and the only use of nuclear weapons in wartime. If we expand the time range slightly, the decreased violence thesis seems less convincing.

Perhaps our perception is deceiving in our relationship to violence. Most of us pay special attention to school shootings—a horribly American phenomena—but many suggest that schools overall may actually be safer than they were two decades ago.[10] Similarly, many Americans are fearful of terrorism, even though statistics show that the chances of an American dying in a terrorist attack are 1 in 20 million.[11] School shootings and terror attacks are rare occurrences, but the pall of violence hangs heavily over our society, especially as more deadly weapons present an increasing potential threat. When John Wilkes Booth assassinated President Abraham Lincoln, he used a derringer, a small pistol that fired a single shell.[12] In contrast, in the January 2011 assassination attempt against Representative Gabby Giffords, six people were killed and wounded with a pistol that had a thirty-one-round magazine.[13]

We also shouldn't only be concerned with the volume of violence executed by individuals or armies in wartimes, but should also consider the destructive nature of collective violence. It is not entirely clear if it was ever God's plan to destroy the city of Nineveh, found in the Book of Jonah. Both in the Abraham narrative about the destruction of Sodom and Gomorrah (Genesis 19:25, 19:29) and in the Jonah narrative about the impeding destruction of Nineveh, the destruction of the wicked city is referred to as an "overturning." Rashi notes, however, that this verb "overturn" means "transform" rather than "destroy."[14] Indeed, the city of Nineveh was not destroyed but was "overturned" through its moral transformation and its embrace of peace.

Sodom, however, was destroyed because of the way its residents mistreated strangers. The Sodomites detested kindness and hospitality. In fact, one Rabbinic teaching shares that God decided to destroy the city after the people of Sodom discovered that a young girl had fed a starving beggar; they smeared honey all over her and tied her to the city wall, so that she died from beestings.[15] God shows the same sensitivity to a lack of morals and the same decisiveness when it comes to judging violent behavior in the story of Noah when God says to Noah, "The end of all flesh has come [to mind] before Me, because the earth is full of violence on their account; look now—I am going to wipe them off the earth" (Genesis 6:12–13). The Rabbis make the point that God decided to bring destruction because the people committed the sins of theft and violence (Genesis 6:13; Jonah 3:7–8, 3:10), which all people should know is inherently wrong.[16] And yet, people stray. People commit harmful acts all over the world even though they know better.

Sadly, throughout history, violence has disproportionately been brought by men upon women. It is worth reflecting on this particularly timeless moral crisis. When I was studying to be a rabbi, I spent several years doing volunteer service work in India, Thailand, El Salvador, Ghana, and many other countries, where I heard many wrenching stories from women who had been the victims of violence. They told me they felt powerless, vulnerable, and scared. I pledged on each encounter that I would commit my life to giving voice to their cries. I prayed for an end to this epidemic and sought ways to take action to fulfill the biblical mandate to pursue justice. I still feel this call.

The statistics are staggering and devastating: An estimated one out of every three women worldwide will be physically, sexually, or otherwise abused during her lifetime. Every year, ten million girls under the age of eighteen enter into forced marriages, making them very vulnerable to domestic violence. Six thousand girls a day (more than two million a year) undergo genital cutting. In every corner of the globe, girls, women, and LGBTQ people suffer domestic abuse, rape, and hate crimes.[17]

We can overcome and eradicate violence throughout the world if we do not allow ourselves to become inured to images of violence. Videos and images of violent acts shared online but also simple video games and "action" movies do translate into physical violence or a callous disregard for suffering. Never should we descend to the depths of the Roman Coliseum, where the killing of humans and animals became the leading sport for spectators. A world that allows atrocities to take place on a regular basis and in which not all people are treated with dignity is deeply flawed and, as we saw in the stories of the Flood and the destruction of Sodom and Gomorrah, worthy of divine destruction. Thankfully though, there are always ways in which every one of us can contribute to repairing it.

Do we want to be people of peace or people of perpetual violence? Ultimately, it is up to us to decide what our fate shall be. Yet, what this verse in the Book of Proverbs prompts us to consider is that violence is not the only solution to complicated problems—and that when we decide to look for another solution, others will follow us. It might seem easy to take up arms and defeat our enemies with violence, but it might be more effective to use communication and dialogue.

To learn from history means to see where violence led to more challenges and to work proactively to end this violence. The love of peace is deeply rooted in Judaism's spiritual foundation. However, each of us must take responsibility for ourselves and our communities too—at any given moment in history. The fact that we seem to live in an era with less violence relative to human history should give us the strength to march forward. May we not dare to deceive ourselves: we have not yet reached national or global peace. Often it is clear that violence is merely transformed into a different form rather than being eradicated. For example, it used to be that Black men were lynched in America. Today, lynching, as we knew it, is very rare. However, we might ask, is it possible that it has been replaced with police brutality? Black men are still killed disproportionately. Racism is systemic. Being personally responsible for the state of the world we inhabit, we must ask ourselves: Is it time to pass slave reparations? Is it time to move this issue to the front and center of our communal agendas? The Black Lives Matter movement has raised awareness and momentum. And yet, we still have so far to go.

Proverbs tells us that our own behavior will be perpetuated by many who follow our example—where will you lead the ones who follow yours?

Chapter 17

1 Better a dry crust with peace
Than a house full of feasting with strife.

2 A capable servant will dominate an incompetent son
And share the inheritance with the brothers.

3 For silver—the crucible,
For gold—the furnace,
And GOD tests the mind.

4 An evildoer listens to mischievous talk;
A liar gives ear to malicious words.

5 One who mocks the poor affronts their Maker;
One who rejoices over another's misfortune will
not go unpunished.

6 Grandchildren are the crown of their elders,
And the glory of children is their parents.

7 Lofty words are not fitting for a villain,
Much less lying words for a noble.

8 A bribe seems like a charm to its user;
It brings success at every turn.

9 One who seeks love overlooks faults,
But one who harps on a matter alienates friends.

10 A rebuke works on an intelligent person
More than one hundred blows on a fool.

11 Evildoers seek only to rebel;
A ruthless messenger will be sent against them.

12 Sooner meet a bereaved she-bear
Than a fool immersed in nonsense.

13 Evil will never depart from the house
Of one who repays good with evil.

פרק יז

1 טוֹב פַּת חֲרֵבָה וְשַׁלְוָה־בָהּ מִבַּיִת מָלֵא זִבְחֵי־רִיב:

2 עֶבֶד־מַשְׂכִּיל יִמְשֹׁל בְּבֵן מֵבִישׁ וּבְתוֹךְ אַחִים יַחֲלֹק נַחֲלָה:

3 מַצְרֵף לַכֶּסֶף וְכוּר לַזָּהָב וּבֹחֵן לִבּוֹת יְהוָה:

4 מֵרַע מַקְשִׁיב עַל־שְׂפַת־אָוֶן שֶׁקֶר מֵזִין עַל־לְשׁוֹן הַוֹּת:

5 לֹעֵג לָרָשׁ חֵרֵף עֹשֵׂהוּ שָׂמֵחַ לְאֵיד לֹא יִנָּקֶה:

6 עֲטֶרֶת זְקֵנִים בְּנֵי בָנִים וְתִפְאֶרֶת בָּנִים אֲבוֹתָם:

7 לֹא־נָאוָה לְנָבָל שְׂפַת־יֶתֶר אַף כִּי־לְנָדִיב שְׂפַת־שָׁקֶר:

8 אֶבֶן־חֵן הַשֹּׁחַד בְּעֵינֵי בְעָלָיו אֶל־כָּל־אֲשֶׁר יִפְנֶה יַשְׂכִּיל:

9 מְכַסֶּה־פֶּשַׁע מְבַקֵּשׁ אַהֲבָה וְשֹׁנֶה בְדָבָר מַפְרִיד אַלּוּף:

10 תֵּחַת גְּעָרָה בְמֵבִין מֵהַכּוֹת כְּסִיל מֵאָה:

11 אַךְ־מְרִי יְבַקֶּשׁ־רָע וּמַלְאָךְ אַכְזָרִי יְשֻׁלַּח־בּוֹ:

12 פָּגוֹשׁ דֹּב שַׁכּוּל בְּאִישׁ וְאַל־כְּסִיל בְּאִוַּלְתּוֹ:

13 מֵשִׁיב רָעָה תַּחַת טוֹבָה לֹא־(תמיש) [תָמוּשׁ] רָעָה מִבֵּיתוֹ:

14 To start a quarrel is to open a sluice;
   Before a dispute flares up, drop it.

15 To acquit the guilty and convict the innocent—
   Both are an abomination to GOD.

16 What good is money in the hand of a fool
   To purchase wisdom, when that person has no mind?

17 A friend is devoted at all times;
   A sibling is born to share adversity.

18 Devoid of sense are the people who give their hand
   To stand surety for their fellows.

19 One who loves transgression loves strife;
   One who builds a high threshold invites broken bones.

20 Crooked minds come to no good,
   And the double-tongued fall into trouble.

21 One begets a dullard to one's own grief;
   The father of a villain has no joy.

22 A joyful heart makes for good health;
   Despondency dries up the bones.

23 The wicked draw bribes out of their bosom
   To pervert the course of justice.

24 Wisdom lies before the intelligent;
   The eyes of dullards range to the ends of the earth.

25 A stupid son is vexation for his father
   And a heartache for the woman who bore him.

26 To punish an innocent is surely not right,
   Or to flog the great for their uprightness.

27 One who is knowledgeable is sparing with words;
   A man of understanding is reticent.

28 Even fools who keep silent are deemed wise;
   Intelligent, while their mouth is shut.

14 פּוֹטֵר מַיִם רֵאשִׁית מָדוֹן וְלִפְנֵי הִתְגַּלַּע הָרִיב נְטוֹשׁ:

15 מַצְדִּיק רָשָׁע וּמַרְשִׁיעַ צַדִּיק תּוֹעֲבַת יְהֹוָה גַּם־שְׁנֵיהֶם:

16 לָמָּה־זֶּה מְחִיר בְּיַד־כְּסִיל לִקְנוֹת חָכְמָה וְלֶב־אָיִן:

17 בְּכָל־עֵת אֹהֵב הָרֵעַ וְאָח לְצָרָה יִוָּלֵד:

18 אָדָם חֲסַר־לֵב תּוֹקֵעַ כָּף עֹרֵב עֲרֻבָּה לִפְנֵי רֵעֵהוּ:

19 אֹהֵב פֶּשַׁע אֹהֵב מַצָּה מַגְבִּיהַּ פִּתְחוֹ מְבַקֶּשׁ־שָׁבֶר:

20 עִקֶּשׁ־לֵב לֹא יִמְצָא־טוֹב וְנֶהְפָּךְ בִּלְשׁוֹנוֹ יִפּוֹל בְּרָעָה:

21 יֹלֵד כְּסִיל לְתוּגָה לוֹ וְלֹא־יִשְׂמַח אֲבִי נָבָל:

22 לֵב שָׂמֵחַ יֵיטִב גֵּהָה וְרוּחַ נְכֵאָה תְּיַבֶּשׁ־גָּרֶם:

23 שֹׁחַד מֵחֵק רָשָׁע יִקָּח לְהַטּוֹת אָרְחוֹת מִשְׁפָּט:

24 אֶת־פְּנֵי מֵבִין חָכְמָה וְעֵינֵי כְסִיל בִּקְצֵה־אָרֶץ:

25 כַּעַס לְאָבִיו בֵּן כְּסִיל וּמֶמֶר לְיוֹלַדְתּוֹ:

26 גַּם עֲנוֹשׁ לַצַּדִּיק לֹא־טוֹב לְהַכּוֹת נְדִיבִים עַל־יֹשֶׁר:

27 חוֹשֵׂךְ אֲמָרָיו יוֹדֵעַ דָּעַת (וקר) [וְיְקַר־]רוּחַ אִישׁ תְּבוּנָה:

28 גַּם אֱוִיל מַחֲרִישׁ חָכָם יֵחָשֵׁב אֹטֵם שְׂפָתָיו נָבוֹן:

Peace in the Home

Better a dry crust with peace
Than a house full of feasting with strife.
　　　—Proverbs 17:1

THE HOME is where we find comfort, an oasis from the tribulations of the outside world. In the home that each of us inhabits, we feel as if everything is under control. It is a prime spot for reflection and relaxation, but it is also a location in which we actualize holiness. We can see *the home* writ large—and the individual spot that each of us identifies as our personal home as well—as a portal to another realm, a more spiritual realm.

A focal purpose of our homes is to provide a place to prepare and enjoy food. With restaurants on nearly every street, large supermarkets, and constant advertising for new fast-food products, one might suspect that contemporary American culture defines happiness by the quality (or vast quantity) of its food consumption. Yet, the Jewish tradition, through its emphasis on kashrut, does not allow us to eat all types of foods. How can we apply ancient Judaism's eating rules to the modern (and capitalist) cuisine ecology?

It is pertinent here to look carefully at this chapter's highlighted verse from Proverbs: "Better a dry crust with peace / Than a house full of feasting with strife." The author of this sentence—traditionally understood to be King Solomon—ruminates about the most desired food in ancient Israel, a substance called *zivchei riv*, which is best described as a special cut of meat from the animal sacrifice. This meat was sanctified and highly desirable. However, the Book of Proverbs warns us: *Do not get too eager with the appetite.* In other words, the meat from the sacrifice is not meant to be enjoyed with garnish and flair, and maybe it should not be consumed at all!

More important than tasting the flesh of the sacrifice is enjoying a feast that fosters peace in the home. The fight for scraps of the sacrificial bounty decreases peace and elevates strife. We are called not to nourish ourselves through violence, but to reorient our souls inwardly. Our sacrifice should be a sacrifice of redemption, not destruction. Indeed, people who struggle against each other will not enjoy anything together; a person doesn't succeed in a house of fighting. Rather, we should strive to live more modestly, focus on relationships, and bring people together. This will bring peace, stability, and enjoyment to our lives.

Of course, there is also a broader message at play here: the Children of Israel should never act solely on their base needs. Instead, we should act with deepest intentionality and care. Rashi's commentary on this verse suggests that the verse refers to Israel at large.[1] The Jewish people are strong when they are united in the face of injustice, and weak when their communities are riled by petty rancor. Thus, in this context, it is better to have a responsible Jewish people without the Temple than to have a Temple, with its sacrifices and ritual, desecrated by rigidity and disputation.

Peace in the home (sh'lom bayit) can have many forms. Generally, bringing people together is better than living in an atmosphere of contention. One might even relate this verse to a divorce hearing: better, often, to get less money out of the deal while maintaining a peaceful relationship with a soon-to-be-former spouse with whom we share children. Similarly, one might relate the verse to a legal battle over an inheritance where one sacrifices a portion of their share to make sure that all sides are happy.

Like any virtuous concept though, the concept of sh'lom bayit can be misinterpreted. For example, some generally oppose divorce in the name of peace in the home. Why would you disrupt the lives of your spouse and your children by getting divorced? However, this is a misunderstanding. A peaceful home is built on love and trust. It would be a false peace to remain in a marriage where one or both partners were miserable and the relationship was irreparably damaged. This is most certainly true in tragic cases of domestic violence. No one should ever suggest that peace in the home is a higher priority than the health of anyone involved.

Bracketing extreme cases, we generally seek to work out conflicts in the home through communication. Our homes are precious. Everything of value resides in them. As the soul is the domicile of the divine essence, our homes are manifestations of our dreams, desires, and domestic needs. We must tend to them carefully, while also keeping them open. The heart of a healthy home is the boundless love nurtured within it. An unhappy home affects every aspect of a person's life: career, relationships, spiritual life, and even health. Therefore, our homelife must be peaceful and healthy, even though this vision can never be realized completely at all times. If a person must cut back on enjoyment to help bring peace to the home, the emotional investment will be worthwhile.

A Friend's Love

A friend is devoted at all times;
A sibling is born to share adversity.
　　　—Proverbs 17:17

THE WORD FOR FRIENDSHIP in Aramaic is *chavruta*, and this word refers to more than just a relationship; it is the primary model of Jewish learning. A *chavruta*, in its truest sense, is a challenger—a *bar plugta* (literally, "an offspring of a disagreement")—not a person who merely supports a friend, but someone who challenges us, helping us to become more learned and forthright. The Talmud teaches that in religious learning and growth, a friend is even more important than a teacher: "I have learned much from my teachers, but from my friends more than my teachers."[2] A friend of virtue is more connected to our intimate life pursuits than any teacher will ever be. Thus, the Rabbis teach that "one is not to part from one's friend without exchanging words of Torah."[3] A true friend is primarily a partner in learning, a partner in life. Later in the Book of Proverbs, we learn, "There are companions to keep one company/And there is a friend more devoted than a sibling" (Proverbs 18:24).

The necessity for deep friendships is so central in Jewish thought that living a good happy life without deep friendships was unfathomable to the ancient Sages. According to one Talmudic story, Choni, the legendary miracle worker, was depressed from bouts of social isolation. He yearned and prayed for death so that he would be released from his crushing despondency. Rava, a great Talmudic sage of the fourth century, comments tersely on this story that one must choose "either friendship or death."[4] The lesson contained in these heart-wrenching anecdotes is that people cannot thrive in their life missions without companionship.

Yet today, we witness increased individualism, decreased institutional affiliation, and more involvement with social networks than with actual relationships. While this helps our emerging microcommunities, it diminishes the stability and support provided by traditional groups and affiliations. True friendship, sad to say, is on the decline. For example, in 2011, sociologists reported that adults, on average, have only two friends with whom they can discuss "important matters"—down from three in 1985. Half of those surveyed said they had only one, and 4 percent had none.⁵ We know a lot of people, but our friendships are less confidential and intimate.

The fast-paced, self-interested nature of most contemporary relationships has become more transactional. For example, one can "friend" or "defriend" someone with the click of a finger on Facebook. Such online friendships are formed quickly, but ensuing social bonds are weak.

Without deep friendships, we begin to lack adequate self-knowledge and awareness of our blind spots. That, in turn, can lead to arrogance. The Book of Proverbs relates to this point: to acquire knowledge, we must rely upon others. Web-based friendships may be interesting, entertaining, and productive, but they rarely create strong bonds that foster a more moral and spiritually inspired life. Friendships become more about the taking than the giving.

Friendships can be cultivated best in safe spaces created for personal reflection, the sharing of one's most intimate thoughts, and trust-building activities. When relationships are built through meaningful discussions, shared spiritual yearnings, and social activism, people connect with each other more authentically. Jewish programming looking to foster deeper relationships should be more mission-driven. Real connection can occur through serving and sharing. However, often friends are more social buddies than life partners. We prefer to see them during our "time off" rather than our "time on." For many people, a friend is less of a rock to rely upon than an opportunity to find a social voice and identity. As a campus rabbi, I saw that most students struggled to turn a social buddy into a lasting personal confidant. Of Aristotle's three kinds of friendship—pleasure, utility, and virtue—people tend to understand friendships of virtue the least.[6]

What do we expect when we attempt to "make a friend"? What do we look for? What do we seek? In a friend, we find not only comfort and companionship but also someone to hold us morally accountable. The Scottish moral philosopher Alasdair MacIntyre (b. 1929) who frequently references Aristotle and other classical philosophers, explains, "In achieving accountability we will have learned not only how to speak to, but also how to speak for the other. We will, in the home or in the workplace or in other shared activity, have become—in one sense of that word—friends."[7]

There is something to be said for natural socialization, but we should not underestimate the role spiritual leaders can play in bringing about friendships. Too often, we focus on building communities at large and forget to create individual friendships.

Through dialogue and care for others, we can best engage in the necessary learning of creating long-lasting bonds with others. When a relationship no longer merely serves an instrumental purpose but becomes a bond of truth through mutual self-disclosure, we cultivate intimacy, solidarity, and reciprocal transformation. We come to love one another; in the co-construction of values and discovering a shared conception of how best to live—*eudaemonia*—our identities become intertwined.

The Torah consistently reminds us to protect the stranger. In friendship, we can move the other and ourselves from being strangers to being familiar, known, and loved. Friendship obviously has a crucial role in child development, and it does not lose its significance in adulthood when virtuous living may be actualized every day. Maimonides explains that "people require friends all their lifetime."[8] Likewise, the Rabbis strongly advise us to "acquire for yourself a friend."[9] And the Book of Ecclesiastes elucidates: "Two are better off than one because they have greater benefit from their earnings. For should they fall, one can raise the other; but woe to those who are alone and fall without a companion to raise them up" (4:9–10).

Rabbi Joseph B. Soloveitchik valued both a *"haver li-de'agah*, a person in whom one can confide both in times of crisis, when distress strikes, and in times of glory, when one feels happy and content," and a *"haver le'de'ah*, a friend in whom he or she has absolute trust or faith."[10] A friend is an emotional partner in our highs and lows. Sometimes friendships manifest in lifelong commitments. Other times, we offer moments of the gift of friendship. We are never lonely if we are willing to connect with whomever we encounter. Every moment is an opportunity for spiritual presence and support.

Rabbi Soloveitchik explains that in addition to spiritual support, there is another vital spiritual purpose to friendships. He writes, "Job certainly did not grasp the meaning of friendship. At this phase, even communal and social relations served the purpose of utility and safety. True friendship is possible only when people rise to the height of an open existence, in which they are capable of prayer and communication. In such living, the personality fulfills itself."[11] It is not until Job realizes the importance of opening himself spiritually to others that he truly comes to understand the virtue of friendship: "The Eternal restored Job's fortunes when he prayed on behalf of his friends, and the Eternal gave Job twice what he had before" (Job 42:10).

The Book of Proverbs wants us to understand that a friend is more than someone who shares our experiences and narratives. A friend is someone to whom we have no biological connection, but who shares an emotional genome. To friends, we have special duties. To become an individual committed to moral and religious excellence, life partners are crucial; friends are crucial. The meaning of friendship is the cultivation of virtue, the opportunity to pursue the good, the exploration of life, and the search for meaning. True friendship is both transformative and enduring. As the Rabbis teach, "Any love that is dependent upon a specific cause, when the cause is gone, the love is gone; but if it does not depend on a specific cause, it will never cease."[12] Friendships of pleasure and utility are fun but end as our needs and wants evolve. Friendships of virtue are part of our pursuit of the just, the holy, and the good.

When I think about the need for authentic friendship, I always turn back to the story of Joseph: "[There] a man happened on him as he was wandering in the countryside. The man asked him, 'What are you looking for?' He said, 'I am looking for my brothers'" (Genesis 37:15).

This story about Joseph strikes me deeply. As a child, I used to move to different cities every few years. I constantly felt like I was seeking "my brothers." To some degree, we are all wandering in search of our "brothers." In an age in which we are increasingly interdependent, we must encourage real companionship. Ultimately, cultivating spiritual friendships will ensure that we remain grounded in the virtues of love and respect—virtues we need to see the world thrive.

Rabbi Jay Henry Moses argues that it is precisely our human capacity for love, care, and generosity that makes us godly.[13]

Finally, our capacity to love is the most unique and profound aspect of humanity being created in God's image. God's love is understood to be expressed through the gift of Torah (see *Ahavah Rabbah*, in the morning liturgy). The highest expression of our humanity is when we feel love for another human being and that love motivates us to share selflessly and to put someone else's needs above our own.

Chapter 18

1 Those who isolate themselves pursue their desires;
   They disdain all competence.
2 Fools do not desire understanding,
   But only to air their thoughts.
3 Along with the wicked comes derision,
   And with rogues, contempt.
4 The words a person speaks are deep waters,
   A flowing stream, a fountain of wisdom.
5 It is not right to be partial to the guilty
   And subvert the innocent in judgment.
6 The words of fools lead to strife;
   Their speech invites blows.
7 The fools' speech is their ruin;
   Their words are a trap for them.
8 The words of a grumbler are bruising;
   They penetrate one's inmost parts.
9 One who is slack at work
   Is akin to a vandal.
10 The name of GOD is a tower of strength
   To which the righteous run and are safe.
11 The wealth of the rich is their fortress;
   In their fancy it is a protective wall.
12 Before ruin a person's heart is proud;
   Humility goes before honor.
13 To answer before listening—
   This is foolish and disgraceful.
14 A person's spirit can endure an illness;
   But low spirits—who can bear them?

פרק יח

1 לְתַאֲוָה יְבַקֵּשׁ נִפְרָד בְּכָל־תּוּשִׁיָּה יִתְגַּלָּע:

2 לֹא־יַחְפֹּץ כְּסִיל בִּתְבוּנָה כִּי אִם־בְּהִתְגַּלּוֹת לִבּוֹ:

3 בְּבוֹא־רָשָׁע בָּא גַם־בּוּז וְעִם־קָלוֹן חֶרְפָּה:

4 מַיִם עֲמֻקִּים דִּבְרֵי פִי־אִישׁ נַחַל נֹבֵעַ מְקוֹר חָכְמָה:

5 שְׂאֵת פְּנֵי־רָשָׁע לֹא־טוֹב לְהַטּוֹת צַדִּיק בַּמִּשְׁפָּט:

6 שִׂפְתֵי כְסִיל יָבֹאוּ בְרִיב וּפִיו לְמַהֲלֻמוֹת יִקְרָא:

7 פִּי־כְסִיל מְחִתָּה־לוֹ וּשְׂפָתָיו מוֹקֵשׁ נַפְשׁוֹ:

8 דִּבְרֵי נִרְגָּן כְּמִתְלַהֲמִים וְהֵם יָרְדוּ חַדְרֵי־בָטֶן:

9 גַּם מִתְרַפֶּה בִמְלַאכְתּוֹ אָח הוּא לְבַעַל מַשְׁחִית:

10 מִגְדַּל־עֹז שֵׁם יְהֹוָה בּוֹ־יָרוּץ צַדִּיק וְנִשְׂגָּב:

11 הוֹן עָשִׁיר קִרְיַת עֻזּוֹ וּכְחוֹמָה נִשְׂגָּבָה בְּמַשְׂכִּתוֹ:

12 לִפְנֵי־שֶׁבֶר יִגְבַּהּ לֵב־אִישׁ וְלִפְנֵי כָבוֹד עֲנָוָה:

13 מֵשִׁיב דָּבָר בְּטֶרֶם יִשְׁמָע אִוֶּלֶת הִיא־לוֹ וּכְלִמָּה:

14 רוּחַ־אִישׁ יְכַלְכֵּל מַחֲלֵהוּ וְרוּחַ נְכֵאָה מִי יִשָּׂאֶנָּה:

15 The mind of an intelligent person acquires knowledge;
   The ears of the wise seek out knowledge.

16 A gift eases a person's way
   And gives access to the great.

17 The first to speak in court seems right
   Till the other party cross-examines.

18 The lot puts an end to strife
   And separates those locked in dispute.

19 A sibling offended is more formidable than a stronghold;
   Such strife is like the bars of a fortress.

20 A man's belly is filled by the fruit of his mouth;
   He will be filled by the produce of his lips.

21 Death and life are in the power of the tongue;
   Those who love it will eat its fruit.

22 He who finds a wife has found happiness
   And has won the favor of GOD.

23 The pauper speaks beseechingly;
   The rich person's answer is harsh.

24 There are companions to keep one company,
   And there is a friend more devoted than a sibling.

לֵב נָבוֹן יִקְנֶה־דָּעַת וְאֹזֶן חֲכָמִים תְּבַקֶּשׁ־דָּעַת: 15

מַתָּן אָדָם יַרְחִיב לוֹ וְלִפְנֵי גְדֹלִים יַנְחֶנּוּ: 16

צַדִּיק הָרִאשׁוֹן בְּרִיבוֹ (יבא) [וּבָא־]רֵעֵהוּ וַחֲקָרוֹ: 17

מִדְיָנִים יַשְׁבִּית הַגּוֹרָל וּבֵין עֲצוּמִים יַפְרִיד: 18

אָח נִפְשָׁע מִקִּרְיַת־עֹז (ומדונים) [וּמִדְיָנִים] כִּבְרִיחַ 19
אַרְמוֹן:

מִפְּרִי פִי־אִישׁ תִּשְׂבַּע בִּטְנוֹ תְּבוּאַת שְׂפָתָיו יִשְׂבָּע: 20

מָוֶת וְחַיִּים בְּיַד־לָשׁוֹן וְאֹהֲבֶיהָ יֹאכַל פִּרְיָהּ: 21

מָצָא אִשָּׁה מָצָא טוֹב וַיָּפֶק רָצוֹן מֵיְהֹוָה: 22

תַּחֲנוּנִים יְדַבֶּר־רָשׁ וְעָשִׁיר יַעֲנֶה עַזּוֹת: 23

אִישׁ רֵעִים לְהִתְרֹעֵעַ וְיֵשׁ אֹהֵב דָּבֵק מֵאָח: 24

The Resilience of the Human Spirit

A person's spirit can endure an illness;
But low spirits—who can bear them?
   —Proverbs 18:14

HUMANITY HAS LEARNED throughout history that our bodies and minds can be quite resilient. But can the spirit, the heart, be resilient too? Nothing is harder to endure than a broken heart. And yet, we read about a teaching by Menachem Mendel of Kotzk: "There is nothing more whole," he says, "than a broken heart."[1]

Rabbi Karyn D. Kedar writes, "If my heart is already broken, cracked open, / why not spend some time looking inside?"[2] The broken heart is a window into our souls! She continues this theme in a moving prayer: "God of grace, / teach me / that the layers / of brokenness / create a whole."[3] And another prayer: "To take what is shattered, piece by piece, / and build a vessel of beauty, of compassion."[4] Her words on brokenness are not only descriptive but also prescriptive, indeed a moral mandate: "Send me forth that I may / restore what is broken, / heal what is wounded, / and engage in acts of love / with great and unrelenting determination."[5]

It is our imperfection, not our quest for perfection, that makes us human. It is our growth, not our stagnation, that makes us great. It is our brokenness, not our wholeness, that so often enables us to reach further and break barriers. In our imperfection, growth, and brokenness, we have the ability to emulate God, as a midrash suggests:

> When a person uses a broken vessel, they are ashamed of it, but not so God. All the instruments of God's service are broken vessels as it is said, "The Eternal is close to the brokenhearted" (Psalm 34:19) or "God heals their broken hearts" (Psalm 147:3).[6]

Similarly, another midrash states:

> A person of flesh and blood, if they have a vessel, as long as the vessel is whole, he is happy with it; broken they do not wish it. But not so the Holy One, blessed be God. So long as the vessel is whole, God does not wish to see it, rather God wants it to be broken. And what is the favorite vessel of God? The heart of the human. If the Eternal sees a proud heart, God does not want it; as it says, "The Eternal is close to the brokenhearted" (Psalm 34:19).[7]

Not only can a broken heart lead us to spiritual introspection and radical self-inquiry, but it also takes us closer to the Divine. A story is told of the Baal Shem Tov:

> The Baal Shem Tov of blessed memory commanded Rabbi Zev Kitzes of blessed memory that he should learn the *kavanot* [special mystical intentions] of each shofar blast, because he would be the one to blow shofar on Rosh Hashana. Rabbi Zev learned the *kavanot* and wrote them down on a piece of paper to look at when the shofar was being blown. He then put the paper in his pocket. When it came time for shofar, he began to look for the paper, but he was not able to find it. He looked to and fro, and realized that he did not know what mystical intentions should be done. He became very upset. He cried out with a broken heart, and the shofar was blown without the *kavanot*. After this, the Baal Shem Tov said to him, "In the King's palace there are many rooms and chambers and different keys for each door. But an axe has the capability of all the keys. An axe can open the lock of any door. So, it is true with the *kavanot*. Each heavenly gate has a different *kavanah*. But a broken heart can open them all. When a person breaks their heart before God, it is possible for them to enter through all the gates in the palace of the King of Kings, the Holy One Blessed be He."[8]

Humility awakens within us when we realize our limitations. This humility opens our souls to be receptive to new experiences and philosophies. As Leonard Cohen, a modern-day prophet, famously sang in "Anthem," "There is a crack, a crack in everything. / That's how the light gets in." Indeed, we can persevere through challenges because they provide us with new information and revelation.

Part and parcel of embracing humanity as it is, is the realization that we suffice in spite of our imperfections. We are sufficient because we are all imperfect. We are imperfect and also perfect. We are broken and also whole. We are lonely individuals and yet interdependent and in community. We live in scarcity but also, hopefully, have everything we need.

Everyone is alone in their own existential crisis, but a moment of crisis confronts everyone and calls upon us all. As individuals, we see our crushed spirits and broken hearts as opportunities for spiritual growth, for building community, and for new insights, and if we do not directly experience such brokenness ourselves, our role is to ensure that others experiencing a tragedy do not feel alone. Rather, we must bring them closer to us and to God and care for them.

The Power of Words

Death and life are in the power of the tongue;
Those who love it will eat its fruit.
　　—Proverbs 18:21

NOT ONLY CAN WE BE LIFTED UP by the power of the tongue, we can also be deeply hurt, even destroyed, by this power—especially in the form of *lashon hara* (evil speech). Reputations can be hurt, livelihoods can be ruined, even relationships can be destroyed through powerful and destructive kinds of language. Proverbs teaches about our responsibility to guard our tongues and use our words wisely: "There is blunt talk like sword-thrusts, / But the speech of the wise is healing" (Proverbs 12:18).

The power of speech unfolds in our professional lives, our social lives, our family lives, and on social media. At work, we consistently offer positive reinforcement and constructive feedback to others to improve the quality of our collective efforts. From a Jewish perspective, we are concerned not only with our efficiency but also with the ethics of our workplace. All Jewish workers have a sacred obligation to be a moral presence, which goes all the way back to the Torah. There is a biblical mitzvah to offer rebuke (*tochachah*) to each other: "You shall not hate your kinsfolk in your heart. Rebuke your kin but incur no guilt on their account" (Leviticus 19:17). The verse teaches that we offer reproof for two reasons: so that our resentments do not lead to hate, and so that wrongs are not carried out for which we too would be responsible. Rather than speaking *lashon hara* and *r'chilut* (speaking negatively about another and spreading gossip), we are to confront an individual who warrants gentle rebuke directly. We are to care about the moral and spiritual welfare of others, making it vital to give feedback when we see others going astray.

As explored earlier, according to one position articulated in the Talmud, this mitzvah should only be fulfilled when we think the other will be receptive to hearing the reproof. If not, it is considered counterproductive. "Just as there is a mitzvah for a person to say words of rebuke that will be accepted, so too there is a mitzvah for a person not to say words of rebuke that will not be accepted."[9] Offering rebuke is only a mitzvah if we know that the other has the integrity and emotional intelligence to truly see their blind spot and correct their wrongs. The goal of rebuke, according to this position, is not just to express righteous indignation but to create change and stop a wrong or abuse occurring before our eyes.

As already indicated, Rabbi Zeira, another Talmudic scholar, taught that we should offer rebuke whether or not we believe it will be accepted.[10] We simply cannot stand idly by while others do wrong in our midst. The Rabbis teach, "Everyone who can protest a wrong in one's midst and does not, is responsible for those people. For the people of one's city, one is responsible for the people of the city. For the whole world, one is responsible for the whole world."[11] If we do not speak up, our own moral integrity is in jeopardy. The Rabbis teach *sh'tikah k'hodaah*[12]—"when we stay silent, we are considered to be in agreement." According to this position, we do not necessarily need to correct a wrong that we witness, but we cannot stand idly by. Regardless of whether our voices will be heard, we cannot remain indifferent or even let our silence signal indifference. As Rabbi Abraham Joshua Heschel taught, "We are a generation that has lost its capacity for outrage. We must continue to remind ourselves that in a free society all are involved in what some are doing. *Some are guilty, all are responsible.*"[13] We must express outrage at wrongs.

The obligation to give *tochachah* is not a simple command. One Rabbinic view holds that no one today is on a spiritual level sufficiently high to engage in rebuke properly, as few are self-aware and humble enough to give *tochachah* properly, and few are humble enough to properly hear and accept it.[14] For this reason, *Sefer Chasidim*, an early medieval pietist work, suggests that we can only really give rebuke to a person for whom we feel love. Clearly, we have to carefully check our motives before criticizing another's conduct.

Of course, any feedback should be given gently, in private, at the right time, and in the appropriate environment. Most important is not to shame another. This is the most difficult aspect of offering *tochachah*.

One very important place for rebuke is the workplace. We have moral influence upon coworkers; we must establish clear ethical boundaries. We cannot live in a world where wrongs are ignored, nor can we work in environments where there is indifference toward the welfare of others. Abuses must be addressed. Some acts require whistleblowing when they reach a level of harm or illegality. This applies to corruption, harassment, or any other form of abuse or deception.

We should create an open work culture and communities in which giving and receiving feedback is acceptable and encouraged, especially when boundaries are crossed. We must learn the art and ethics of critique in order to build a stronger society committed to truth, human dignity, and transparency. We can start by checking our own practices, engaging in our own self-accounting, and inviting others to approach us if we ourselves ever cross boundaries.

"The words a person speaks are deep waters, / A flowing stream, a fountain of wisdom" (Proverbs 18:4). All speech causes change, just as silence does. It is a gift we should cherish and care for with great responsibility.

Chapter 19

1   Better a pauper who lives blamelessly
    Than one who speaks perversely and is a dullard.
2   A person without knowledge is surely not good;
    One who moves hurriedly blunders.
3   Mortals' folly subverts their way,
    And their hearts rage against GOD.
4   Wealth makes many friends,
    But a pauper is left friendless.
5   A false witness will not go unpunished;
    One who testifies lies will not escape.
6   Many court the favor of a noble,
    And all are the friends of a man who dispenses gifts.
7   The poor are despised even by their kin;
    How much more are they shunned by their friends!
    One who pursues words—they are of no avail.
8   Those who acquire wisdom are their own best friend;
    They preserve understanding and attain happiness.
9   A false witness will not go unpunished;
    One who testifies falsely is doomed.
10 Luxury is not fitting for a dullard,
    Much less that a servant rule over princes.
11 People show intelligence by their forebearance;
    It is their glory when they overlook an offense.
12 The rage of a king is like the roar of a lion;
    His favor is like dew upon the grass.
13 A stupid son is a calamity to his father;
    The nagging of a wife is like the endless dripping of water.

פרק יט

1 טוֹב־רָשׁ הוֹלֵךְ בְּתֻמּוֹ מֵעִקֵּשׁ שְׂפָתָיו וְהוּא כְסִיל:

2 גַּם בְּלֹא־דַעַת נֶפֶשׁ לֹא־טוֹב וְאָץ בְּרַגְלַיִם חוֹטֵא:

3 אִוֶּלֶת אָדָם תְּסַלֵּף דַּרְכּוֹ וְעַל־יְהֹוָה יִזְעַף לִבּוֹ:

4 הוֹן יֹסִיף רֵעִים רַבִּים וְדָל מֵרֵעֵהוּ יִפָּרֵד:

5 עֵד שְׁקָרִים לֹא יִנָּקֶה וְיָפִיחַ כְּזָבִים לֹא יִמָּלֵט:

6 רַבִּים יְחַלּוּ פְנֵי־נָדִיב וְכָל־הָרֵעַ לְאִישׁ מַתָּן:

7 כָּל־אֲחֵי־רָשׁ | שְׂנֵאֻהוּ אַף כִּי מְרֵעֵהוּ רָחֲקוּ מִמֶּנּוּ מְרַדֵּף אֲמָרִים (לֹא) [לוֹ־]הֵמָּה:

8 קֹנֶה־לֵּב אֹהֵב נַפְשׁוֹ שֹׁמֵר תְּבוּנָה לִמְצֹא־טוֹב:

9 עֵד שְׁקָרִים לֹא יִנָּקֶה וְיָפִיחַ כְּזָבִים יֹאבֵד:

10 לֹא־נָאוֶה לִכְסִיל תַּעֲנוּג אַף כִּי־לְעֶבֶד | מְשֹׁל בְּשָׂרִים:

11 שֵׂכֶל אָדָם הֶאֱרִיךְ אַפּוֹ וְתִפְאַרְתּוֹ עֲבֹר עַל־פָּשַׁע:

12 נַהַם כַּכְּפִיר זַעַף מֶלֶךְ וּכְטַל עַל־עֵשֶׂב רְצוֹנוֹ:

13 הַוֹּת לְאָבִיו בֵּן כְּסִיל וְדֶלֶף טֹרֵד מִדְיְנֵי אִשָּׁה:

14 Property and riches are bequeathed by fathers,
But an efficient wife comes from GOD.

15 Laziness induces sleep,
And a negligent person will go hungry.

16 Those who have regard for their lives pay regard to
commandments;
Those who are heedless of their ways will die.

17 Those who are generous to the poor make a loan to GOD—
They will receive their due.

18 Discipline your son while there is still hope,
And do not set your heart on his destruction.

19 A hot-tempered man incurs punishment;
If you try to save him you will only make it worse.

20 Listen to advice and accept discipline
In order that you may be wise in the end.

21 Many designs are in a person's mind,
But it is GOD's plan that is accomplished.

22 Greed is a reproach to a man;
Better be poor than a deceitful man.

23 One who fears GOD earns life,
And shall abide in contentment,
Free from misfortune.

24 A sluggard buries a hand in the bowl,
And will not even bring it to the mouth.

25 Beat scoffers and the simple will become clever;
Reprove the intelligent and they gain knowledge.

26 A son who causes shame and disgrace
Plunders his father, puts his mother to flight.

27 My son, cease to stray from words of knowledge
And receive discipline.

28 A malicious witness scoffs at justice,
And the speech of the wicked conceals mischief.

29 Punishments are in store for scoffers
And blows for the backs of dullards.

14 בַּ֫יִת וָה֗וֹן נַחֲלַ֥ת אָב֑וֹת וּ֝מֵיְהֹוָ֗ה אִשָּׁ֥ה מַשְׂכָּֽלֶת׃

15 עַ֭צְלָה תַּפִּ֣יל תַּרְדֵּמָ֑ה וְנֶ֖פֶשׁ רְמִיָּ֣ה תִרְעָֽב׃

16 שֹׁמֵ֣ר מִ֭צְוָה שֹׁמֵ֣ר נַפְשׁ֑וֹ בּוֹזֵ֖ה דְרָכָ֣יו (יומת) [יָמֽוּת]׃

17 מַלְוֵ֣ה יְ֭הֹוָה ח֣וֹנֵֽן דָּ֑ל וּ֝גְמֻל֗וֹ יְשַׁלֶּם־לֽוֹ׃

18 יַסֵּ֣ר בִּ֭נְךָ כִּי־יֵ֣שׁ תִּקְוָ֑ה וְאֶל־הֲ֝מִית֗וֹ אַל־תִּשָּׂ֥א נַפְשֶֽׁךָ׃

19 (גרל) [גְּדׇל־]חֵ֭מָה נֹ֣שֵׂא עֹ֑נֶשׁ כִּ֥י אִם־תַּ֝צִּ֗יל וְע֣וֹד תּוֹסִֽף׃

20 שְׁמַ֣ע עֵ֭צָה וְקַבֵּ֣ל מוּסָ֑ר לְ֝מַ֗עַן תֶּחְכַּ֥ם בְּאַחֲרִיתֶֽךָ׃

21 רַבּ֣וֹת מַחֲשָׁב֣וֹת בְּלֶב־אִ֑ישׁ וַעֲצַ֥ת יְ֝הֹוָ֗ה הִ֣יא תָקֽוּם׃

22 תַּאֲוַ֣ת אָדָ֣ם חַסְדּ֑וֹ וְטֽוֹב־רָ֝֗שׁ מֵאִ֥ישׁ כָּזָֽב׃

23 יִרְאַ֣ת יְהֹוָ֣ה לְחַיִּ֑ים וְשָׂבֵ֥עַ יָ֝לִ֗ין בַּל־יִפָּ֥קֶד רָֽע׃

24 טָ֘מַ֤ן עָצֵ֣ל יָ֭דוֹ בַּצַּלָּ֑חַת גַּם־אֶל־פִּ֝֗יהוּ לֹ֣א יְשִׁיבֶֽנָּה׃

25 לֵ֣ץ תַּ֭כֶּה וּפֶ֣תִי יַעְרִ֑ם וְהוֹכִ֥יחַ לְ֝נָב֗וֹן יָבִ֥ין דָּֽעַת׃

26 מְֽשַׁדֶּד־אָ֭ב יַבְרִ֣יחַ אֵ֑ם בֵּ֝֗ן מֵבִ֥ישׁ וּמַחְפִּֽיר׃

27 חֲֽדַל־בְּ֭נִי לִשְׁמֹ֣עַ מוּסָ֑ר לִ֝שְׁג֗וֹת מֵאִמְרֵי־דָֽעַת׃

28 עֵ֣ד בְּ֭לִיַּעַל יָלִ֣יץ מִשְׁפָּ֑ט וּפִ֥י רְ֝שָׁעִ֗ים יְבַלַּע־אָֽוֶן׃

29 נָכ֣וֹנוּ לַלֵּצִ֣ים שְׁפָטִ֑ים וּ֝מַהֲלֻמ֗וֹת לְגֵ֣ו כְּסִילִֽים׃

On Laziness

Laziness induces sleep,
And a negligent person will go hungry.
    —Proverbs 19:15

As a CONCEPT, Jewish wisdom dismisses laziness and sloth as qualities that ethical people should avoid.[1] In Greek philosophy, laziness is assumed to comprise two components: *acedia*—a lack of caring or indifference; and *tristitia*—sadness, sorrow, or despair. What is fascinating about the verses regarding laziness found in the Book of Proverbs is that the book presents a definition of laziness solely based on *acedia*, a lack of motivation, and does not mention anything related to sadness or despair. It could be argued that the high level of individualism led to a lack of care for the welfare of others (*acedia*). Already nearly half a century ago, the sociologist Robert Bellah wrote the following about American individualism:

> The individualism that's on the rise recently in the U.S. is one of "What's in it for me?" with immediate gratification of one's needs coming before all other loyalties. Commitments like marriage only hold while they pay off. . . . In earlier days the individualism in America was one that also honored community values. . . . We have an ideology of individualism that simply encourages people to maximize personal advantage. . . . Considerations of the common good are increasing irrelevant.[2]

A brilliant teaching found in the *Orchot Tzaddikim*, a text from the Middle Ages, explains how laziness and commitment to one's self over anything else affect one's learning:

> They tell the sluggard, "Your teacher is in a nearby city, go and learn Torah from him." He responds, "I fear a lion on the highway."

"Your teacher is in your own city." "I fear a lion in the streets."
"Your teacher is near your home." "I am afraid a lion is outside."
"Your teacher is in a room inside your home." "I am afraid that if I
rise from the bed the door will be locked." "But the door is open."
"I need a little more sleep."[3]

How many of us only want "a little more sleep" rather than facing the
day with vigor and a commitment to help others? There is no viable
excuse for anyone to avoid addressing global poverty for at least five
minutes each week (the time it takes to clip our nails or order a cup
of coffee). Yet, we manage to find any number of excuses to get rid of
that responsibility. We praise ourselves for a single soup-kitchen volunteer experience or picking up random litter, instead of responding
to our calling in a continuous and effective manner.

Rabbi Moshe Chayim Luzzatto, one of Judaism's foremost ethical
teachers and thinkers, paints a clear picture of laziness and how it
affects human potential:

> We see with our own eyes, on numerous occasions, how a person
> who is already cognizant of their duty and who already knows what
> is appropriate for the salvation of their soul and what their obliga-
> tion is to their Creator can nonetheless neglect their duty, though
> not because of a lack of awareness of their obligation or for any
> other reason. Rather, their lethargic indolence dominates them.
> And this is what it says (to them): "I'll eat a bit" or "I'll sleep a bit"
> or "It's hard for me to get out of the house," "I took off my shirt,
> how can I put it back on?" "It's very hot outside," "It's very chilly,"
> or "rainy" and all such other pretexts and excuses that the mouths
> of the indolent are filled with.[4]

It is, of course, not only the privileged and powerful who struggle
with the challenge of energizing themselves to transform the world.
The oppressed are also plagued with this complex problem. Paulo
Freire, a Brazilian educator and author, noticed this phenomenon
among the oppressed:

> The oppressed, having internalized the image of the oppressor
> and adapted his guidelines, are fearful of freedom. Freedom would
> require them to eject this image and replace it with autonomy and

responsibility. Freedom is acquired by conquest, not by gift. It must be pursued constantly and responsibly. Freedom is not an ideal located outside of man; nor is it an idea which becomes myth. It is rather the indispensable condition for the quest for human completion.[5]

This is not the sort of sloth embodying *acedia* I discussed above. Instead, Freire describes the other side of laziness: *tristitia*, the fear, sadness, and hopelessness that prevent an oppressed individual from fighting for autonomy and a complete life.

Thomas Aquinas examined the elements of sloth by explaining that sloth is sinful in two situations: when our despair keeps us from doing what is spiritually good and when our regrets keep us from doing what is ethically right.[6] We may imagine a number of other psychological reasons for people not to meet a moral challenge with alacrity and motivation.

Psychologists have found that satisfaction and happiness in life is 22 percent higher for those who enjoy and work for consistent minor accomplishments—what we may call little victories—than for those who express interest only in massive accomplishments and refuse to work for the smaller ones.[7] Laziness therefore needs to be battled at every moment of our existence. To sustain a life without laziness, we must seek to define concrete meaning in all moments.

To this effect, the Vilna Gaon argued that the reward of doing mitzvot is much greater than the effort invested:

> How difficult it is to leave this world. In this world . . . a person can purchase tzitzit, and as a reward for that simple mitzvah merit to experience the Divine Presence in the world-to-come. But in the upper world, he can no longer earn anything, even if he exerts all his energies.[8]

Laziness is a great force in our modern age, but it doesn't have to be the one that dominates us. Every day, countless people wake up to face the day with the ability to combat the forces inside them that tempt them to lay in bed (or on the couch) for five minutes more. Those five minutes turn into ten minutes, and then suddenly an hour has gone by. Two hours. Twelve hours. A whole day wasted. Being lazy is easy, which makes it appealing. However, we know that laziness breeds apathy and that apathy leads to the destruction of our minds, of the environment, and at the most extreme levels, of other people. The Book of Proverbs reminds us to nourish our souls to stave off laziness in all of its forms.

Chapter 20

1 Wine is a scoffer, strong drink a roisterer;
  None who is muddled by them will ever grow wise.
2 The terror of a king is like the roar of a lion;
  Whoever provokes it forfeits life.
3 It is honorable for a man to desist from strife,
  But every fool becomes embroiled.
4 In winter sluggards do not plow;
  At harvesttime they seek, and find nothing.
5 The designs in a person's mind are deep waters,
  But a man of understanding can draw them out.
6 He calls many a man his loyal friend,
  But who can find a faithful man?
7 The righteous live blamelessly;
  Happy are their children who come after them.
8 The king seated on the throne of judgment
  Can winnow out all evil by his glance.
9 Who can say, "I have cleansed my heart,
  I am purged of my sin"?
10 False weights and false measures—
  Both are an abomination to GOD.
11 Children may be dissembling in their behavior
  Even though their actions are blameless and proper.
12 The ear that hears, the eye that sees—
  GOD made them both.
13 Do not love sleep lest you be impoverished;
  Keep your eyes open and you will have plenty of food.
14 "Bad, bad," says the buyer,
  Then goes away in self-congratulation.

פרק כ

1   לֵץ הַיַּיִן הֹמֶה שֵׁכָר וְכָל־שֹׁגֶה בּוֹ לֹא יֶחְכָּם:

2   נַהַם כַּכְּפִיר אֵימַת מֶלֶךְ מִתְעַבְּרוֹ חוֹטֵא נַפְשׁוֹ:

3   כָּבוֹד לָאִישׁ שֶׁבֶת מֵרִיב וְכָל־אֱוִיל יִתְגַּלָּע:

4   מֵחֹרֶף עָצֵל לֹא־יַחֲרֹשׁ (ישאל) [וְשָׁאַל] בַּקָּצִיר וָאָיִן:

5   מַיִם עֲמֻקִּים עֵצָה בְלֶב־אִישׁ וְאִישׁ תְּבוּנָה יִדְלֶנָּה:

6   רָב־אָדָם יִקְרָא אִישׁ חַסְדּוֹ וְאִישׁ אֱמוּנִים מִי יִמְצָא:

7   מִתְהַלֵּךְ בְּתֻמּוֹ צַדִּיק אַשְׁרֵי בָנָיו אַחֲרָיו:

8   מֶלֶךְ יוֹשֵׁב עַל־כִּסֵּא־דִין מְזָרֶה בְעֵינָיו כָּל־רָע:

9   מִי־יֹאמַר זִכִּיתִי לִבִּי טָהַרְתִּי מֵחַטָּאתִי:

10   אֶבֶן וָאֶבֶן אֵיפָה וְאֵיפָה תּוֹעֲבַת יְהֹוָה גַּם־שְׁנֵיהֶם:

11   גַּם בְּמַעֲלָלָיו יִתְנַכֶּר־נָעַר אִם־זַךְ וְאִם־יָשָׁר פָּעֳלוֹ:

12   אֹזֶן שֹׁמַעַת וְעַיִן רֹאָה יְהֹוָה עָשָׂה גַּם־שְׁנֵיהֶם:

13   אַל־תֶּאֱהַב שֵׁנָה פֶּן־תִּוָּרֵשׁ פְּקַח עֵינֶיךָ שְׂבַע־לָחֶם:

14   רַע רַע יֹאמַר הַקּוֹנֶה וְאֹזֵל לוֹ אָז יִתְהַלָּל:

15 Gold is plentiful, jewels abundant,
   But wise speech is a precious object.

16 Seize his garment, for he stood surety for another;
   Take it as a pledge, [for he stood surety] for an unfamiliar woman.

17 Bread gained by fraud may be tasty to a man,
   But later his mouth will be filled with gravel.

18 Plans laid in council will succeed;
   Wage war with stratagems.

19 Whoever gives away secrets is base;
   Do not take up with a big-mouth.

20 Whoever reviles their father or mother,
   Will be without lamplight when darkness comes.

21 An estate acquired in haste at the outset
   Will not be blessed in the end.

22 Do not say, "I will requite evil";
   Put your hope in GOD and you will be delivered.

23 False weights are an abomination to GOD;
   Dishonest scales are not right.

24 People's steps are decided by GOD;
   What do mortals know about their own way?

25 It is a snare for mortals to pledge a sacred gift rashly
   And after the vows to reconsider.

26 A wise king winnows out the wicked,
   And turns the wheel upon them.

27 A mortal's lifebreath is the lamp of GOD
   Revealing all their inmost parts.

28 Faithfulness and loyalty protect the king;
   He maintains his throne by faithfulness.

29 The glory of young men is their strength;
   The majesty of elders is their gray hair.

30 Bruises and wounds are repayment for evil,
   Striking at one's inmost parts.

יֵשׁ זָהָב וְרָב־פְּנִינִים וּכְלִי יְקָר שִׂפְתֵי־דָעַת: 15

לְקַח־בִּגְדוֹ כִּי־עָרַב זָר וּבְעַד (נכרים) [נָכְרִיָּה] חַבְלֵהוּ: 16

עָרֵב לָאִישׁ לֶחֶם שָׁקֶר וְאַחַר יִמָּלֵא־פִיהוּ חָצָץ: 17

מַחֲשָׁבוֹת בְּעֵצָה תִכּוֹן וּבְתַחְבֻּלוֹת עֲשֵׂה מִלְחָמָה: 18

גּוֹלֶה־סּוֹד הוֹלֵךְ רָכִיל וּלְפֹתֶה שְׂפָתָיו לֹא תִתְעָרָב: 19

מְקַלֵּל אָבִיו וְאִמּוֹ יִדְעַךְ נֵרוֹ (באישון) [בֶּאֱשׁוּן] חֹשֶׁךְ: 20

נַחֲלָה (מבחלת) [מְבֹהֶלֶת] בָּרִאשֹׁנָה וְאַחֲרִיתָהּ 21
לֹא תְבֹרָךְ:

אַל־תֹּאמַר אֲשַׁלְּמָה־רָע קַוֵּה לַיהֹוָה וְיֹשַׁע לָךְ: 22

תּוֹעֲבַת יְהֹוָה אֶבֶן וָאָבֶן וּמֹאזְנֵי מִרְמָה לֹא־טוֹב: 23

מֵיהֹוָה מִצְעֲדֵי־גָבֶר וְאָדָם מַה־יָּבִין דַּרְכּוֹ: 24

מוֹקֵשׁ אָדָם יָלַע קֹדֶשׁ וְאַחַר נְדָרִים לְבַקֵּר: 25

מְזָרֶה רְשָׁעִים מֶלֶךְ חָכָם וַיָּשֶׁב עֲלֵיהֶם אוֹפָן: 26

נֵר יְהֹוָה נִשְׁמַת אָדָם חֹפֵשׂ כָּל־חַדְרֵי־בָטֶן: 27

חֶסֶד וֶאֱמֶת יִצְּרוּ־מֶלֶךְ וְסָעַד בַּחֶסֶד כִּסְאוֹ: 28

תִּפְאֶרֶת בַּחוּרִים כֹּחָם וַהֲדַר זְקֵנִים שֵׂיבָה: 29

חַבֻּרוֹת פֶּצַע (תמריק) [תַּמְרוּק] בְּרָע וּמַכּוֹת חַדְרֵי־בָטֶן: 30

Avoid Fighting

It is honorable for a man to desist from strife,
But every fool becomes embroiled.
        —Proverbs 20:3

WHO IS A "FOOL?" The Malbim, in his commentary on Proverbs 1:22, distinguishes between the simpleton (who lacks knowledge), the scorner (who mocks knowledge), and the fool (who holds moral knowledge but rejects it).

Throughout the Jewish tradition, peace is seen as one of the highest Jewish values. Indeed, one might argue that the goal of Jewish tradition in its entirety is to bring about universal peace. Maimonides writes to this point:

> Great is peace, as the whole Torah was given in order to promote peace in the world, as it was stated (Proverbs 3:17): "Her ways are pleasant ways, and all her paths, peaceful."[1]

On this verse, the Rabbis also teach, "The entire Torah exists only to promote ways of peace, for it is written: 'Her ways are pleasant ways, and all her paths, peaceful' (Proverbs 3:17)."[2] This is not only true on a global scale but also nationally and domestically. In fact, peace in the home (*sh'lom bayit*) is a major Jewish value. It is even given as the basis for kindling Shabbat candles on Friday night.[3]

Furthermore, this significance of peace is emphasized in the first chapter of *Pirkei Avot*, where we learn that "Hillel and Shammai received the [Oral Jewish] tradition [from their predecessors in the previous generation]. Hillel says: Be among the disciples of Aaron, loving peace and pursuing peace, loving people, and bringing them closer to the Torah."[4] The Chofetz Chayim, commenting on this passage, writes:

Seek it [peace] for your loved one and pursue it with your enemy. Seek it in your place and pursue it in other places. Seek it with your body and pursue it with your material resources. Seek it for your own benefit and pursue it for the benefit of others. Seek it today and pursue it tomorrow. With reference for "seek it tomorrow," it teaches that one should not despair, thinking that one cannot make peace, but rather one should pursue peace today and also tomorrow and on the day afterwards, until one reaches it.[5]

Each of us has been gifted our own capacities to work toward increasing peace in the world around us.

Another way of understanding our need to promote peace among ourselves and in our communities comes from the end of the Book of Deuteronomy. Rather than congratulating his followers on getting through their forty-year cross-desert trek, Moses tells those present that "the Eternal did not give you a heart to know, or eyes to see, or ears to hear until this day" (Deuteronomy 29:3). In other words, when complete redemption is near, Moses reminds everyone that they must not forget how they all reached this point, suffering countless setbacks and hardships. Only now, by recalling the miraculous wonders of God, are the Israelites able to breathe freely.

To some later commentators, however, the people of Israel did not learn their lesson at this point in the story. For example, Obadiah ben Jacob Sforno (1475–1550) explains in his commentary to this verse in Deuteronomy that "even though God had tried by means of divine teachings and divine miracles to give the people a knowing heart . . . the lesson had not taken hold due to [their] overwhelming quarrelsomeness."[6] This lesson means much for us in these confused times. Because of their internal fighting, the Israelites who stood at the threshold of the Promised Land were unable to truly understand and accept God's teaching. For us, living in a polarized society with social media often disguising the humanity of others, it is easier than ever to find reasons to resent people from halfway across the world in our own backyards. This reality, according to Sforno, blocks us from truly understanding God and actualizing our unique potential.

Now, one might argue that carrying negative feelings toward others is natural to the human condition; do we not all have the right to sometimes feel anger and argue with others? Yes, we have that right and even, at times, that inclination. But the question is what enables us to thrive. If we wish to thrive, to truly "know," "see," and "hear," we will need to figure out how to forgive, how to let go, and how to be slow to anger. We need to figure out how to avoid toxic resentment, unnecessary conflict, and belligerence.

We cannot cultivate peace in our outer worlds if we're not addressing it in our inner world. Rabbi Yerucham Levovitz (1873–1936), a prominent Eastern European teacher of Jewish ethics, writes:

> Why was the Torah given in the wilderness at Mount Sinai and not in the calm and peacefulness of Israel? This is to teach us that true peace of mind doesn't come from physical comforts, but from an awareness of one's ultimate life goals. When you focus on this, you are constantly traveling toward your goal and will never be overly disturbed or broken.[7]

Rabbi Simchah Bunim of Peshischa hammers away at this point as well:

> The Sages said, "'Seek peace' in your place ['and pursue it' in another place]."[8] You cannot seek peace anywhere but within yourself, until you find it there. In Psalms [38:4] it is said, "There is no peace in my bones because of my sin." Only if we find peace inside ourselves can we seek it throughout the world.[9]

Indeed, we must work for universal peace. But it must start from within. We must look within ourselves, within our families, within our communities, and within our hearts. Only then can we work toward peace among the nations and the world.

Allies and Confidantes

He calls many a man his loyal friend,
But who can find a faithful man?
—Proverbs 20:6

CICERO PUT THE MATTER WELL when he offered that friendship makes prosperity more shining and lessens adversity by dividing and sharing it.[10] In life, we need to have friends to sustain us during happy times, dark times, and everything in between. To live without a friend is to wander the world alone. Hopefully, throughout our lives we will befriend different types of people—people who support us on our journeys but also challenge us. The best friends we can ever hope to have are those who accept us for who we are but who aren't afraid to point out our flaws (and who do that lovingly and respectfully). One of the most significant pieces of wisdom that the Scriptures teach us is that human beings are not meant to exist in isolation. When Adam was created, he wandered through Eden alone. He was listless without someone else like him; he was distraught. However, once Eve was formed, Adam was confident enough to explore the greater part of the earth together with his partner. Everyone needs others at their side in order to navigate life. Adam needed a partner to experience the fullness of life and the breadth of the world. Leaving the Garden of Eden, like a child leaving home, is a natural result of our growth in spiritual and romantic partnerships.

We should be mindful, though, of the difference between friendliness and meaningful friendship. We might find that we have companions whom we may like a lot, enjoy a lot, even care a lot about, but cannot trust to share our vulnerabilities. However, for us to be truly productive, to grow, to change, and to learn, sharing our vulnerabilities is essential.

Even though friendships are vital to our mental and spiritual health, we cannot blindly jump into just any friendship. Unfortunately, the world is filled with unsavory people who seek to exploit and use other people. And even among those people who are as well-meaning as can be, not every one of them is a perfect companion. We always have to be cognizant not to let our guard down too quickly simply because someone seems open and transparent.

To keep up our guard is not a detriment to our character. Rather, it is a necessary means to protect ourselves and the ones for whom we are responsible. In social action organizing, spiritual organizing, and general leadership, we use our primordial emotional antennae to distinguish between allies and confidants. An ally is someone with whom we work closely, whom we support and partner with, while at the same time keeping at a distance regarding our personal emotions. Confidants, meanwhile, are people whom we can trust enough to share our inner lives. It is crucial to know the difference between an ally and a confidant and to discern between situations when we can share deeply personal information and situations when we should show restraint and operate on a more professional level. Clearly, internalizing this distinction protects us emotionally, physically, and financially; but being able to intuit the difference between a colleague and a true friend is also essential to accomplish what we should for the world community.

Let us see what some experts say about this distinction. Ron Heifetz and Marty Linsky at Harvard University, in their book about leadership, write:

> Allies are people who share many of your values, or at least your strategy, and operate across some organizational or factional boundary. Because they cross a boundary, they cannot always be loyal to you; they have other ties to honor.[11]

This is especially true in the religious sphere, where Bob Burns, Donald C. Guthrie, and Tasha D. Chapman claim:

> Pastors are constantly working with allies. Yet pastors are always calculating—consciously and unconsciously—whether these allies

in the congregation could or should be party to their more personal concerns.[12]

Interestingly enough, these Christian scholars also draw from another verse in the Book of Proverbs (Proverbs 27:17) in their thinking about relationships: "Finding and forming intimate friendships, in which 'iron sharpens iron.'"[13] It is hard for religious leaders to make friends. They have to constantly discern between potential allies and potential confidants, given their own central role within the whole community. In the Jewish community as well, a rabbi has to be socially aware: who is grieving, who is rejoicing, who needs a shoulder to cry on. It is a heavenly burden, but a burden nonetheless. There is a delicate balance between sharing and restraint that must be found by anyone in a profession tasked to accelerate the growth of the world with alacrity, joyfulness, and an open heart.

In all we do to find and sustain friendships, we need to do the hard work to ensure that *we* are trustworthy allies, that we take the time to listen to the hardships of others, that we celebrate joyously with them whenever that is appropriate, and that we show up when situations become dire. In the end, it is up to us, not others, to determine how we act as friends and confidants. Without trust, we can never overcome adversity. And without friendship, we can never share in the prosperity of love, support, and healing. Let us do all we can to be a friend to someone else. It must be our spiritual priority to heal our broken society, our broken world.

Humans Illuminate the Heavens

A person's soul is the lamp of GOD...
—Proverbs 20:27

WHEN WE STOP TO THINK about it for a moment, lighting candles is indeed quite a significant practice within the Jewish tradition:

- Lighting Shabbat candles on Friday night (for *sh'lom bayit*, "peace in the home").[14]
- *Havdalah* candle on Saturday night (transitioning out of the peaceful private cocoon of Shabbat into the hectic public world).
- Lighting Chanukah candles (for *pirsumei nisa*, "to publicize the miracle").
- Lighting *yahrtzeit* candles (to honor the memories of those who have passed from this world).[15]
- Lighting a *b'dikat chameitz* candle (to look for bread crumbs before Passover).[16]
- In some segments of the Orthodox community today, there is a custom of not blowing out any candles, since it would resemble blowing out a soul. For that reason, they do not even use candles on birthday cakes because they would need to blow them out.[17]

As can be discerned simply through Jewish ritual, the verse in Proverbs about comparing a soul to God's lamp suggests for us just how even a minimal amount of light dispels a great deal of darkness.[18]

The idea that a soul (*n'shamah*) is present within each human being was articulated, according to classical Jewish thought, at the beginning of time as recorded in the Torah. In the Book of Genesis, the text indicates that a life force is inhaled into Adam, the world's first human being, and thus into all of us (Genesis 2:7).

Jewish mysticism (Kabbalah) takes this teaching a step further by designating the soul into five echelons of increasing depth.[19] While we possess cognitive, affective, intellectual, and physical dimensions, it is the spiritual, soul-based dimension of a person (the *n'shamah*) in which our truest selves are rooted. We get into good moods or bad moods (emotional), act poorly or appropriately (behavioral), think deeply or superficially (cognitive), but the light of the soul never dims. As we read in the Book of Proverbs, "A person's soul is the lamp of God" (Proverbs (20:27). As long as we are alive, our deepest inner flame of godliness is lit.

Consider how the *Tanya* interprets this:

"The self is a candle of God" [Proverbs 20:27].

The self is a flickering flame,
striving to separate itself from the wick.

Despite all its attachments
to matter and mood,
once awake to wisdom
the self yearns to abandon itself
and be emptied into God.

Self and selfishness cry, "Feed me!" [Genesis 25:30].
Yet even when fed they are called "dead,"[20]
for they "die without wisdom" [Job 4:21].

Wisdom "gives life" [Ecclesiastes 7:12]
and rests even in the wicked.
Though hidden from them
by their obsession with the self,
wisdom can be found, as it is written,
"Then God awakened as one out of sleep" [Psalm 78:65].[21]

Throughout the Book of Proverbs, we wrestle with momentous questions—questions that propel us to peer into the delicate mysteries of infinity, relationships, love, and sorrow. What does it mean that that the human soul is the lamp of God? There are many possible ways to explain such a profound proposal, but here are several that come to mind for me that may illuminate your path:

1. The teaching here in Proverbs speaks about *moral accountability*: God utilizes the light of the soul to examine individuals' moral conduct and to hold them accountable. One Talmudic passage further explains that the soul is testifying for us in the heavenly court.[22] However, the idea of divine judgment through reward and punishment is not a popular spiritual approach in Jewish liberal circles today. It is a remnant of a time where morality was seen through a black-and-white prism.

2. Another way to understand the metaphor of the soul's light is to compare it to a candle enlightening a person's inner spirituality. The candle is but a humble stick of wax, but when the wick is set aflame, the modest candle becomes a source of warmth and light. We know how dark it is in the world and how dark it can be inside the human being. If the entire world and individuals were brightly lit and radiating with light, then a candle would achieve nothing. Only in the dark does a candle help.

3. Rabbi Abraham Isaac HaKohen Kook cautions the masses against making big changes in the Jewish tradition but then cites our verse to argue that great people can use their reason to understand the deeper values of the Torah and to institute serious new innovations because "a person's soul is the lamp of God" (Proverbs 20:27). Simply put, it is because of this verse, for Rabbi Kook, that great, virtuous, learned scholars can trust their intellectual reasoning and moral intuition to lead.[23]

4. While it could be understood that the candle illuminates human conscience,[24] another explanation is that the humble candle represents the Torah.[25]

5. Another possible way of approaching the verse is to recognize the possibility that God needs human beings on earth because our souls are God's dwelling place among us: pure light in the earthly realm. It is this light—and the human being immersed in it—that enables God to dwell and "see" in the world; what is described here is the symbiotic Divine-human covenant. We work in partnership with God and vice versa. One midrashic interpretation takes this thought even a step further:

> My lamp is in your hands, whereas your lamp (your soul) is in My hands. If you guard Mine, then I will guard yours. But if you extinguish Mine, then I will extinguish yours.[26]

We do not look to God to solve our problems. Instead, we embrace a human-Divine partnership. One midrash explains this concept well:

> What is light made of? Oil is put into a lamp, and then the two together give light as though they were one. Hence, the Holy One will say to Israel, "My children, since My light is your light, and your light is My light, let us go together—you and I—and give light to Zion: Arise, give light, for your light has come."[27]

In this age, spiritual seekers are interested in a God of pure love devoid of any judgment or in a God of energy devoid of personal relationship. This popular take on divinity is not the biblical concept of God as the God of light and justice, nor is it one that satiates our desire to gain more insight into the infinite mind of God. Yet, even if we simply spark some light, we remind ourselves that nestled between every two atoms is an imprint of the Divine waiting to make its way through our retinas into our body and soul.

Together, in harmony with the presence of God, we can light up the world. Together, in harmony with our neighbor, the stranger, the other, and the vulnerable, we can light up the world. Together, through having faith in ourselves, we can light up the world. All it takes is that first step: to find that spark burning within us waiting to hit the air and bring forth its light.

Chapter 21

1 Like channeled water is the mind of the king in GOD's hand—
   For it is directed according to God's wishes.
2 In their own eyes, all of a person's ways seem right,
   But GOD probes the mind.
3 To do what is right and just
   Is more desired by GOD than sacrifice.
4 Haughty looks, a proud heart—
   The tillage of the wicked is sinful.
5 The plans of the diligent make only for gain;
   All rash haste makes only for loss.
6 Treasures acquired by a lying tongue
   Are like driven vapor, heading for extinction.
7 The violence of the wicked sweeps them away,
   For they refuse to act justly.
8 A person's way may be tortuous and strange,
   Though their actions are blameless and proper.
9 Dwelling in the corner of a roof is better
   Than a contentious wife in a spacious house.
10 The desire of the wicked is set upon evil;
   Their neighbors find no favor in their eyes.
11 When scoffers are punished, the simple are edified;
   When sages are taught, they gain insight.
12 The Righteous One observes the house of a wicked person—
   And subverts the wicked to their ruin.
13 One who turns a deaf ear to the cry of the wretched
   Will likewise call and not be answered.
14 A gift in secret subdues anger,
   A present in private, fierce rage.

פרק כא

1 פַּלְגֵי־מַיִם לֶב־מֶלֶךְ בְּיַד־יְהֹוָה עַל־כָּל־אֲשֶׁר יַחְפֹּץ יַטֶּנּוּ:

2 כָּל־דֶּרֶךְ־אִישׁ יָשָׁר בְּעֵינָיו וְתֹכֵן לִבּוֹת יְהֹוָה:

3 עֲשֹׂה צְדָקָה וּמִשְׁפָּט נִבְחָר לַיהֹוָה מִזָּבַח:

4 רוּם־עֵינַיִם וּרְחַב־לֵב נִר רְשָׁעִים חַטָּאת:

5 מַחְשְׁבוֹת חָרוּץ אַךְ־לְמוֹתָר וְכָל־אָץ אַךְ־לְמַחְסוֹר:

6 פֹּעַל אוֹצָרוֹת בִּלְשׁוֹן שָׁקֶר הֶבֶל נִדָּף מְבַקְשֵׁי־מָוֶת:

7 שֹׁד־רְשָׁעִים יְגוֹרֵם כִּי מֵאֲנוּ לַעֲשׂוֹת מִשְׁפָּט:

8 הֲפַכְפַּךְ דֶּרֶךְ אִישׁ וָזָר וְזַךְ יָשָׁר פָּעֳלוֹ:

9 טוֹב לָשֶׁבֶת עַל־פִּנַּת־גָּג מֵאֵשֶׁת מִדְיָנִים וּבֵית חָבֶר:

10 נֶפֶשׁ רָשָׁע אִוְּתָה־רָע לֹא־יֻחַן בְּעֵינָיו רֵעֵהוּ:

11 בַּעֲנָשׁ־לֵץ יֶחְכַּם־פֶּתִי וּבְהַשְׂכִּיל לְחָכָם יִקַּח־דָּעַת:

12 מַשְׂכִּיל צַדִּיק לְבֵית רָשָׁע מְסַלֵּף רְשָׁעִים לָרָע:

13 אֹטֵם אָזְנוֹ מִזַּעֲקַת־דָּל גַּם־הוּא יִקְרָא וְלֹא יֵעָנֶה:

14 מַתָּן בַּסֵּתֶר יִכְפֶּה־אָף וְשֹׁחַד בַּחֵק חֵמָה עַזָּה:

15 Justice done is a joy to the righteous,
   To evildoers, ruination.
16 One who strays from the path of prudence
   Will rest in the company of ghosts.
17 A man who loves pleasure comes to want;
   He who loves wine and oil does not grow rich.
18 The wicked are the ransom of the righteous;
   The traitor comes in place of the upright.
19 It is better to live in the desert
   Than with a contentious, vexatious wife.
20 Precious treasure and oil are in the house of a wise man,
   And a fool of a man will run through them.
21 One who strives to do good and kind deeds
   Attains life, success, and honor.
22 One wise man prevailed over a city of warriors
   And brought down its mighty stronghold.
23 One who watches over mouth and tongue
   Keeps out of trouble.
24 The proud, insolent person, named scoffer,
   Acts in a frenzy of insolence.
25 The cravings of sluggards are fatal,
   For their hands refuse to work.
26 All day long they are seized with craving
   While the righteous give without stint.
27 The sacrifice of the wicked is an abomination,
   The more so when offered in depravity.
28 A false witness is doomed,
   But a man who listens will testify with success.
29 The wicked man is brazen-faced;
   The upright man discerns his course.
30 No wisdom, no prudence, and no counsel
   Can prevail against GOD.
31 The horse is readied for the day of battle,
   But victory comes from GOD.

שִׂמְחָה לַצַּדִּיק עֲשׂוֹת מִשְׁפָּט וּמְחִתָּה לְפֹעֲלֵי אָוֶן: 15

אָדָם תּוֹעֶה מִדֶּרֶךְ הַשְׂכֵּל בִּקְהַל רְפָאִים יָנוּחַ: 16

אִישׁ מַחְסוֹר אֹהֵב שִׂמְחָה אֹהֵב יַיִן־וָשֶׁמֶן לֹא יַעֲשִׁיר: 17

כֹּפֶר לַצַּדִּיק רָשָׁע וְתַחַת יְשָׁרִים בּוֹגֵד: 18

טוֹב שֶׁבֶת בְּאֶרֶץ־מִדְבָּר מֵאֵשֶׁת (מדונים) [מִדְיָנִים] 19
וָכָעַס:

אוֹצָר | נֶחְמָד וָשֶׁמֶן בִּנְוֵה חָכָם וּכְסִיל אָדָם יְבַלְּעֶנּוּ: 20

רֹדֵף צְדָקָה וָחָסֶד יִמְצָא חַיִּים צְדָקָה וְכָבוֹד: 21

עִיר גִּבֹּרִים עָלָה חָכָם וַיֹּרֶד עֹז מִבְטֶחָה: 22

שֹׁמֵר פִּיו וּלְשׁוֹנוֹ שֹׁמֵר מִצָּרוֹת נַפְשׁוֹ: 23

זֵד יָהִיר לֵץ שְׁמוֹ עוֹשֶׂה בְּעֶבְרַת זָדוֹן: 24

תַּאֲוַת עָצֵל תְּמִיתֶנּוּ כִּי־מֵאֲנוּ יָדָיו לַעֲשׂוֹת: 25

כָּל־הַיּוֹם הִתְאַוָּה תַאֲוָה וְצַדִּיק יִתֵּן וְלֹא יַחְשֹׂךְ: 26

זֶבַח רְשָׁעִים תּוֹעֵבָה אַף כִּי־בְזִמָּה יְבִיאֶנּוּ: 27

עֵד־כְּזָבִים יֹאבֵד וְאִישׁ שׁוֹמֵעַ לָנֶצַח יְדַבֵּר: 28

הֵעֵז אִישׁ רָשָׁע בְּפָנָיו וְיָשָׁר הוּא | (יכין דרכיו) 29
[יָבִין דַּרְכּוֹ]:

אֵין חָכְמָה וְאֵין תְּבוּנָה וְאֵין עֵצָה לְנֶגֶד יְהֹוָה: 30

סוּס מוּכָן לְיוֹם מִלְחָמָה וְלַיהֹוָה הַתְּשׁוּעָה: 31

The Ethics of the Human Heart and the Value of Contradiction

GOD resides inside a person's heart.
—Proverbs 21:2

ONE OF THE MOST MISUNDERSTOOD aspects of textual analysis of biblical literature is the issue of seeming contradictions. A major secular criticism of the Torah is that it is disharmonious and contradictory.[1] However, there might be value inherent in those seeming contradictions. Take, for example, Proverbs 21:2, "God resides inside a person's heart."[2] Only a few chapters later, we also read, "One who trusts one's own heart is a dullard" (Proverbs 28:26). Which of those depictions of the human heart is true? Does the heart provide a dwelling place for the Divine, or is the heart simply a vessel of emotions that blind us to truth and reason?

How could the Book of Proverbs, a sacred text, allow for such a contradiction? What are we to believe?

It should be noted that according to Jewish tradition, biblical contradictions are not viewed as problematic. Rather, seeming contradictions are assumed to encourage readers to use their intellectual creativity. According to this view, both verses can be true at the same time. Indeed, God may dwell within both our hearts and our minds. The two verses tell us that the heart, the conventional seat of emotion, has a deeply divine character, but also that we must search for an understanding of the Divine outside the realm of our own emotions. There is enormous value in seeing the divine truth emanating from the heart. However, *that* truth is limited, since divine truth can also be found in a variety of other ways such as through reason, experience, revelation, and dialogue.

However, there is also a deeper, philosophical and psychological lesson to be drawn from those textual contractions. Jonathan Haidt, a professor of ethical leadership at New York University, explains that some of us intuitively follow the approach of David Hume, who believed that humans are beings of emotion who only later justify their beliefs with a faculty called reason.[3] However, others follow the approach of Immanuel Kant, who suggests the opposite, that we are beings of reason. However, for the purpose of understanding this verse, we need to look at the work of Jean-Jacques Rousseau. It is often described as an achievement of the Enlightenment that we have cast off what Rousseau called our collective character as *homme sauvage* (humankind at its basest level) and became *homme civilize* (humankind at a level of civilization). Rousseau himself was quite paradoxical: he celebrated the revolution in thought of the Enlightenment, yet famously wrote in *The Social Contract*, "Man is born free; and everywhere he is in chains. One thinks himself the master of others, and still remains a greater slave than they."[4] By learning to live with contradictions, we can discover deeper and more complex truths.

Thus, for example, as creatures of the twenty-first century, we are more self-aware, cultured, and controlled than humans have ever been. But we also have become estranged from our core, free, and natural selves and gotten stuck in a web of complex social conventions and conformist behavioral patterns harming human-to-human and human-to-Divine relationships. By letting our true selves get stifled, we have more difficulty getting our hands dirty doing the work that we are here to do. Can we recover parts of our authentic nature? If our society is guided by a desire for comfortable living and the preservation of the status quo, how can we do the necessary work of living with each other, with ourselves, and with the Divine? How can we even discover what our true causes are?

One of the key rituals of Passover is the search for and removal of *chameitz* (leavened foods) from our homes. But is it only from our homes? When Rav Yisrael of Vizhnitz was walking with his friend on their way to search for the *chameitz*, he stopped and opened his cloak. Uncovering his chest, he said: "You know that the real *chameitz* is the *chameitz* in the heart—check me here!"[5]

God is found in our hearts. This means that not only our positive emotions but also our negative emotions are a part of God. We are given opportunities to own them, refine them, and channel them for good. Rather than feeling ashamed of our negative emotions, we should embrace the opportunity to serve with our full hearts. What aspect of God's manifestation is in our heart? God's judgment? God's comfort? God's love? Each of us must search and discover our true natures, every moment anew.

There are divergent views on how to connect with our true natures. Rousseau believed in pure democracy, where the majority would have unlimited authority. However, in a modern republic, the rights of minorities are protected. Rousseau believed that individuals can only discover the authentic true self if they are educated in isolation, removed from society. For Jews, by contrast, the education and formation process takes place within the community and in partnership. We have to do the difficult work to discover ourselves while remaining immersed in society.

We are creatures of both emotions and reasons. We need to sometimes trust our hearts and at other times be suspicious of them. We must strive to refine our morals and ethics, yet we cannot let civilization undo our deepest and most natural selves: our souls that live in our hearts. Too often, modernity has led to the caging of our souls. While we cannot go back in time, we must find avenues back to deeper insight, discovery, and freedom. What the Book of Proverbs is saying to us, through its holy contradiction, is that when we accept the emotional truth of our hearts, then, and then only, can we truly find God in our souls.

The Ethical over the Pious

To do what is right and just
Is more desired by God than sacrifice.
　　—Proverbs 21:3

AT THE HEART OF THIS BOOK, and of countless others throughout the millennia, is the following question: What is Judaism all about? As is often the case with a question that is seemingly simple, the answer is incredibly complex. Scholars have often argued Judaism is simply *monotheism*. Others suggest it is an ethical path, a set of guidelines guiding a person through life. Many have combined the two streams of thought into one definition: *ethical monotheism*. But which is the primary element: the pursuit of ethics or venerating a single divine presence in our lives?

As the verse in the Book of Proverbs here shows us, God wants justice more than sacrifice.

What drives us toward religion? Fear of death? The need for community? Something else? Rabbi Yehuda Amital writes, "It is not [the Jewish people's] terrible suffering that is the source of its longing for redemption, but rather its striving to do good to mankind, for this is the essence of its soul."[6]

Is Judaism a response to fear or a channel for longing? The same question could be asked about religion at large. The late Ernest Becker (American, 1924–74), one of the prominent cultural anthropologists of the twentieth century, writes:

> We understand the idea of God as a logical fulfillment of the Agape [brotherly love] side of man's nature. Freud seems to have scorned Agape as he scorned the religion that preached it. He thought that a man's hunger for a God in heaven represented everything

that was immature and selfish in man: his helplessness, his fear, his greed for the fullest possible protection and satisfaction. But [Otto Rank, a peer of Freud] understood that the idea of God has never been a simple reflex of superstitious and selfish fear, as cynics and "realists" have claimed. Instead it is an outgrowth of genuine life-longing, a reaching-out for a plenitude of meaning—as James taught us. It seems that the yielding element in heroic belonging-ness is inherent in the life force itself, one of the truly sublime mysteries of created life. It seems that life force reaches naturally even beyond the earth itself, which is one reason why man has always placed God in the heavens.[7]

While Becker asserts that religion is, by definition, an endless search for meaning, he intentionally omits how such meaning is attained. In fact, there are many ways that people find meaning. Those who choose religious life due to ethical ideals have to determine what creates change. Is it prayer? Is it community building? Is it advocating? Do we seek outer change or change from the inside? Karl Marx, following the thought of Hegel, believed that in each new era a new force emerges that destroys the previous status quo. For Hegel, this process leads to various types of freedom. For Marx, this process leads to progress measured economically.

In order implement such a process for the sake of Torah, we must engage in spiritual practices (sacrifices) that deepen our reflection, build community, and refine our moral instincts. But we also must bring about justice. We must ensure that our everyday actions are ethical. And we must ensure that our Judaism leads us to prioritizing social justice over private—or communal—piety.

Rabbi Dr. David Ellenson lays out a Jewish universalistic ethical framework:

> After all, Jewish tradition requires Jews to apply the foundational Jewish values of righteousness and mercy to all humanity. Thus, in *Hilchot Melachim* (Laws of Kings) 10:12, Maimonides writes, "One ought to treat the resident stranger [non-Jew] with *derekh eretz* [civility and humanity] and *hesed* [mercy and kindness] just as one does a Jew." Indeed, he justifies his position by citing a passage

from Psalm 145:9, "God is good to all and God's mercy is on all [God's] works." God is made holy as our community displays a concern for all those in need."[8]

A thesis and its antithesis lead to a clash leading to synthesis.[9] Judaism doesn't suggest that the old must die for the new to thrive. The Torah is not purely Darwinian in its views of progress. Rather, the old and new must live alongside each other. As Rabbi Kook writes, "The old shall be renewed and the new shall become holy."[10] Rather than have the "old" become replaced by the "new," it takes on a new meaning and relevance for the current day and age. That is how Torah should be applied and actualized in any given generation; timeless norms are adjusted to the needs of the day.

There is a story about Rabbi Aryeh Levine (1885–1969) that helps illustrate this prioritization of action over piety. Levine was known as "the Tzaddik" and "the righteous one of Jerusalem" because of his tireless commitment to acts of kindness and ceaseless visiting of prisoners of all backgrounds.

> Once, when Rabbi Levine had to pick an *etrog* for the holiday of Sukkot, he only decided between two, picking the first option in a matter of minutes. Such was odd for many of his ilk who often spent hours choosing between dozens of different *etrogim*, wanting to get the nicest one available. Many of his students who saw him hastily make his decision were in shock that it took him so little time and one even followed Rav Aryeh to see why his teacher was in such a rush. He followed Rav Aryeh for several kilometers and watched him walk into a senior resident home. Ninety minutes later he walked out. The student asked: "Rebbe, it's beautiful to visit the elderly but they'll be there after Sukkot. Today is the one chance of the year to focus on the *etrog*. How come you gave so little time to that?"
>
> Rav Aryeh took his student's hand and smiled with love: "My dear student, there are two mitzvot where the Torah uses the term *hidur* [beautification]; one is the mitzvah of a beautiful *etrog* ["p'ri eitz hadar," Leviticus 23:40] and the second is beautifully honoring the face of the aged ["v'hadarta p'nei zakein," Leviticus 19:32]. But the *etrog* is merely an object and the aged individual is a subject, a

human being and not a fruit. So, I believe one must spend much more time in beautifying the mitzvah relating to the human being than beautifying the mitzvah relating to a fruit."[11]

Each of us has the spiritual potential to shift our priorities from materialism to relationship and connection. Only then can we move religion from a practice of piety to action and the practical application of ethics; only then will it help us to make the world a better place.

Chapter 22

1 Repute is preferable to great wealth,
   Grace is better than silver and gold.
2 The rich and the poor meet;
   GOD made them both.
3 One who was shrewd saw trouble and took cover;
   The simple kept going and paid the penalty.
4 The effect of humility is fear of GOD,
   Wealth, honor, and life.
5 Thorns and snares are in the path of the crooked;
   Those who value their life will keep far from them.
6 Train children in the way they each ought to go;
   They will not swerve from it even in old age.
7 A rich person rules the poor,
   And the borrower is a slave to the man who lends.
8 One who sows injustice shall reap misfortune;
   The rod of wrath shall fail.
9 One who is generous is blessed,
   While giving bread to the poor.
10 Expel the scoffer and contention departs,
   Quarrel and contumely cease.
11 A pure-hearted comrade—
   His speech is gracious;
   He has the king for his companion.
12 The eyes of GOD watch the person who is wise;
   [God] subverts the words of the treacherous.
13 The sluggard says, "There's a lion in the street;
   I shall be killed if I step outside."

פרק כב

1 נִבְחָר שֵׁם מֵעֹשֶׁר רָב מִכֶּסֶף וּמִזָּהָב חֵן טוֹב:

2 עָשִׁיר וָרָשׁ נִפְגָּשׁוּ עֹשֵׂה כֻלָּם יְהוָה:

3 עָרוּם | רָאָה רָעָה (ויסתר) [וְנִסְתָּר] וּפְתָיִים עָבְרוּ
וְנֶעֱנָשׁוּ:

4 עֵקֶב עֲנָוָה יִרְאַת יְהוָה עֹשֶׁר וְכָבוֹד וְחַיִּים:

5 צִנִּים פַּחִים בְּדֶרֶךְ עִקֵּשׁ שׁוֹמֵר נַפְשׁוֹ יִרְחַק מֵהֶם:

6 חֲנֹךְ לַנַּעַר עַל־פִּי דַרְכּוֹ גַּם כִּי־יַזְקִין לֹא־יָסוּר מִמֶּנָּה:

7 עָשִׁיר בְּרָשִׁים יִמְשׁוֹל וְעֶבֶד לֹוֶה לְאִישׁ מַלְוֶה:

8 זוֹרֵעַ עַוְלָה (יקצור) [יִקְצָר־]אָוֶן וְשֵׁבֶט עֶבְרָתוֹ יִכְלֶה:

9 טוֹב־עַיִן הוּא יְבֹרָךְ כִּי־נָתַן מִלַּחְמוֹ לַדָּל:

10 גָּרֵשׁ לֵץ וְיֵצֵא מָדוֹן וְיִשְׁבֹּת דִּין וְקָלוֹן:

11 אֹהֵב (טהור) [טְהָר־]לֵב חֵן שְׂפָתָיו רֵעֵהוּ מֶלֶךְ:

12 עֵינֵי יְהוָה נָצְרוּ דָעַת וַיְסַלֵּף דִּבְרֵי בֹגֵד:

13 אָמַר עָצֵל אֲרִי בַחוּץ בְּתוֹךְ רְחֹבוֹת אֵרָצֵחַ:

14 The mouth of a forbidden woman is a deep pit;
   He who is doomed by GOD falls into it.

15 If folly settles in the heart of a youth,
   The rod of discipline will remove it.

16 To profit by withholding what is due to the poor
   Is like making gifts to the rich—pure loss.

17 Incline your ear and listen to the words of the sages;
   Pay attention to my wisdom.

18 It is good that you store them inside you,
   And that all of them be constantly on your lips,

19 That you may put your trust in GOD.
   I let you know today—yes, you—

20 Indeed, I wrote down for you a threefold lore,
   Wise counsel,

21 To let you know truly reliable words,
   That you may give a faithful reply to those who sent you.

22 Do not rob the wretched because they are wretched;
   Do not crush the poor in the gate;

23 For GOD will take up their cause
   And despoil those who despoil them of life.

24 Do not associate with a hothead,
   Or go about with a hot-tempered man,

25 Lest you learn their ways
   And find yourself ensnared.

26 Do not be one of those who give their hand,
   Who stand surety for debts,

27 Lest your bed be taken from under you
   When you have no money to pay.

28 Do not remove the ancient boundary stone
   That your ancestors set up.

29 See a man skilled at his work—
   He shall attend upon kings;
   He shall not attend upon the lowly.

14 שׁוּחָה עֲמֻקָּה פִּי זָרֹות זְעוּם יְהֹוָה [יִפָּל־]שָׁם:

15 אִוֶּלֶת קְשׁוּרָה בְלֶב־נָעַר שֵׁבֶט מוּסָר יַרְחִיקֶנָּה מִמֶּנּוּ:

16 עֹשֵׁק דָּל לְהַרְבּוֹת לֹו נֹתֵן לְעָשִׁיר אַךְ־לְמַחְסֹור:

17 הַט אָזְנְךָ וּשְׁמַע דִּבְרֵי חֲכָמִים וְלִבְּךָ תָּשִׁית לְדַעְתִּי:

18 כִּי־נָעִים כִּי־תִשְׁמְרֵם בְּבִטְנֶךָ יִכֹּנוּ יַחְדָּו עַל־שְׂפָתֶיךָ:

19 לִהְיֹות בַּיהֹוָה מִבְטַחֶךָ הֹודַעְתִּיךָ הַיֹּום אַף־אָתָּה:

20 הֲלֹא כָתַבְתִּי לְךָ (שלשום) [שָׁלִשִׁים] בְּמֹועֵצֹות וָדָעַת:

21 לְהֹודִיעֲךָ קֹשְׁטְ אִמְרֵי אֱמֶת לְהָשִׁיב אֲמָרִים אֱמֶת לְשֹׁלְחֶיךָ:

22 אַל־תִּגְזָל־דָּל כִּי דַל־הוּא וְאַל־תְּדַכֵּא עָנִי בַשָּׁעַר:

23 כִּי־יְהֹוָה יָרִיב רִיבָם וְקָבַע אֶת־קֹבְעֵיהֶם נָפֶשׁ:

24 אַל־תִּתְרַע אֶת־בַּעַל אָף וְאֶת־אִישׁ חֵמֹות לֹא תָבֹוא:

25 פֶּן־תֶּאֱלַף אֹרְחֹתָו וְלָקַחְתָּ מֹוקֵשׁ לְנַפְשֶׁךָ:

26 אַל־תְּהִי בְתֹקְעֵי־כָף בַּעֹרְבִים מַשָּׁאֹות:

27 אִם־אֵין־לְךָ לְשַׁלֵּם לָמָּה יִקַּח מִשְׁכָּבְךָ מִתַּחְתֶּיךָ:

28 אַל־תַּסֵּג גְּבוּל עֹולָם אֲשֶׁר עָשׂוּ אֲבֹותֶיךָ:

29 חָזִיתָ אִישׁ | מָהִיר בִּמְלַאכְתֹּו לִפְנֵי־מְלָכִים יִתְיַצָּב בַּל־יִתְיַצֵּב לִפְנֵי חֲשֻׁכִּים:

Teach Your Child according to Their Uniqueness

Train children in the way they each ought to go;
They will not swerve from it even in old age.
— Proverbs 22:6

THE OBLIGATION TO TEACH one's children is a biblical mitzvah (Deuteronomy 6:7, 11:19). One might have thought that we would pass on tradition in similar and equal ways to each of our children, but the Book of Proverbs elucidates that each child is unique. Each child needs a different path to learning. Each child is different in their affective, cognitive, and spiritual proclivities. Each child is unique in their background, personality, and interests. Each child is singular in their Jewish knowledge and passion. Each child should be parented and educated differently. Equality is not the absolute. "Feed them on your dreams / The one they pick's, the one you'll know by."[1]

Each child is a blessing, a unique soul, a singular repository of potential wisdom.

The sage Gersonides, known by his acronym Ralbag (1288–1344, France), in his commentary on this verse in Proverbs, suggests that education impacts a human life in two ways. If one teaches a child well in their youth, then even as they grow older, they will retain a great character. However, if one teaches a child by affirming or simply ignoring their bad traits, they will likely preserve those problematic traits.

In another commentary to this verse, Rabbi Menachem Meiri (1249–1306, Catalonia) reminds us that religious education has to be age-specific if it is to be the most effective. The act of teaching esoteric and/or complex theology to a child who yearns for something more relevant to their life is a lost cause.[2]

Another dimension of individual uniqueness and the concomitant need for individually tailored pedagogy is the ability of a child to honor their teacher. One child might show respect, while another may be rebellious; one child may do best in groups, while another is able to focus only in one-on-one settings. The challenge is quite complex as parents and educators work to determine what our kids need to thrive. Additionally, educating a child according to their own path not only means acknowledging that they are different from their siblings and classmates, but also acknowledging that they are potentially different from their parents. Parents should not wish for their children to be their little carbon copies. Each child is created uniquely in the image of God, with their unique gifts and potential to contribute meaningfully to the world.

This acknowledgment should also impact our decisions when we look to hire educators in our communities. Is this teacher knowledge-centered or student-centered? As important as the ideas are, they are only actualized in our focus on the students. Does the educator have enough empathy, patience, and spiritual imagination to enter another's mindset?

However, we should also be concerned with adult education and how it affects adult behavior in the world. As we work to ensure a vibrant Jewish future, we have many priorities among the many fine efforts to ensure Jewish continuity. Hebrew schools, summer camps, and the engagement of young professionals—we focus all our energy on the education of younger generations. However, the group that has perhaps received the least amount of attention and funding and has found itself repeatedly at the end of our priority lists is Jewish adults and their education.

Before readers get up in arms, I acknowledge that nearly every synagogue has adult programming, including adult education. However, most of these classes do not satiate the growing interest in the expanding landscape of intellectual Judaism. Thus, I want to suggest three reasons for Jewish communities to flip priorities and focus more on adult and less on children's education.

Rabbi Rachel Timoner, a Reform activist and rabbi in Brooklyn, writes:

> Without a framework, we flail. So we look to a mix of external norms and institutions from the surrounding culture—the Protestant work ethic, the American dream, parenting trends, to name a few examples—to make choices for us. Shouldn't the wisdom of our own people have at least as strong a voice? Once we realize that we've traded one system of external authority for others, we find that the treasure we are seeking is under our own hearth. We are yearning for guidance. We are yearning for coherence. If chosen, covenant, mitzvah, and Torah are as relevant and sacred to us now as they ever have been.[3]

One of the most frequently asked questions from Jewish parents to rabbis across the denominational spectrum is "Rabbi, how do I get my child (or grandchild) to love Judaism?" Perhaps the most appropriate answer is "*You* must love it!"

Perhaps the most frequent reason why parents do not engage their children in rigorous intellectual and spiritual Judaism is because they themselves aren't engaged in it. Meaningful Jewish experiences for adults have a profound and enduring effect on the psyche and will have a trickle-down effect on their children. Sadly, many such spiritual pathways to excellence have been stunted. Yet, if parents took deep meaning from the words of the Talmudic Sages, if they allowed themselves to be transformed by Chasidic thinkers, if they listened to the rhythms and metaphors of Yiddish poetry, if they evolved ethically by attending Mussar workshops, if they challenged themselves with social justice Torah in order to rethink their identities and their obligations, if Jewish art, music, and film helped cultivate spiritual and moral imagination, if they achieved inner peace through Jewish meditation, if Israel or Hebrew or biblical stories inspired them, there is no doubt they would want their children to engage in the same forms of learning—and they could actually share their interests and passions with them.

There is a telling quote about the prioritization of adult Jewish education for the benefit of the community: "A parent and a child must both study Torah. When possibilities exist for only one, the adult's personal needs take precedence over the child's."[4] What does this quote mean? It means that Judaism is not a children's game. The primary goal of Judaism is not to engage children, but to actualize Jewish values in the world. It is an ever-expanding teaching and actualization of business ethics, medical ethics, relationship development, spiritual growth, personal healing, and so much more. Bringing God down to earth—to our workplaces and into our homes—requires sophisticated thought and deliberation. Many of our children go on to receive advanced secular degrees. It is no wonder they view Judaism as irrelevant and childish when their Jewish education stopped as their teen years began. The Jewish answers they remember are children's answers. More tragically, the questions are children's questions.

It is true that for Judaism to survive, we must ensure that the next generation is engaged and invested—but surviving only matters if the adults who received that education as children are themselves thriving Jewishly. Does Judaism have wisdom to offer about the human condition in the twenty-first century? Are Jews a force of moral development, spiritual advancement, and the improvement of the broader society? Judaism will only thrive (and survive) if Jewish adults are learning Jewish wisdom and apply that wisdom in nuanced ways to their lives.

It will always be true that some will not be interested in synagogue participation, Israel advocacy, Holocaust memory, or even matzah ball soup. However, with a program of rigorous, pluralistic Jewish adult education, our Jewish texts can be shown to be relevant and be used to solve the problems of our society today. Furthermore, this engagement can happen in a variety of spaces ranging from synagogues to cafes to bars, creating a community defined by values and knowledge as opposed to space.

We are not asking others to sacrifice their values or time by learning parochial aspects of Judaism with us. Rather, we are making the case that they will be able to thrive in life more deeply if Jewish wisdom and learning are a part of that life. Their souls, hearts, and minds will benefit greatly from this newly strengthened attention to Jewish wisdom.

Adult Jewish learning need not be relegated to an afterthought, nor does it have to follow a cookie-cutter approach that will inevitably lead to mediocrity and, ultimately, irrelevance. When performed with clarity and vigor, Jewish adult learning can be dynamic and energetic. In my work as the leader of multiple Jewish educational organizations, I work hard to demonstrate that pluralistic adult Jewish learning is a transformative vehicle that is accessible but need not be watered down; it is joyful but also challenging, deeply rooted but also nondogmatic, respectful of the past but looking toward the future.

In this manner of teaching, we not only challenge old routines, but we also create new communities of exploration. We expand beyond the confines of our location, spreading out into the ether of Jewish thought and history. We make the richness of Jewish thought accessible to people who believed it was inaccessible, irrelevant, and dead. And that's how learning, especially for adults, should always be.

On Alacrity

See a man skilled at his work—
He shall attend upon kings;
He shall not attend upon the lowly.
    —Proverbs 22:29

THERE IS A FAMOUS TALE of Rabbi Levi Yitzchak of Berditchev (1740–1809), one of the most venerable of the Chasidic masters. One day, Rabbi Levi looked out his window and watched people hustle to-and-fro across the town square. He leaned out and inquired of one man in a rush, "Why are you running?" The man replied, "I'm running to work to make a living." The rabbi replied, "Are you so sure that your livelihood is running away from you and you have to rush to catch it up?[5] Perhaps it's running *toward* you, and all you have to do is stand still and let it catch up with you." Oftentimes, we may be chasing after what is already waiting for us; we would catch it if we just paused.

Leo Tolstoy writes, "The two most powerful warriors are patience and time."[6]

The Book of Proverbs reminds us that a life spent on never-ending pushes forward without any space for reflection is not a life worth living. Every day, challenges stymie us, frustrate us, make us question ourselves and our achievements. Too often, the rat race of life swallows us whole, consumes every fiber of our being. It is difficult to break out of the mold of constant hurriedness and obligations; we obey as society, family, and employees or entrepreneurs.

But there is another path, a path that the Book of Proverbs lays out in this passage. That path is alacrity, a means by which we can engage in the world without being consumed by it. Alacrity means that we stand up to the challenges facing us with our fullest strength of will. Indeed, *z'rizut*—the Hebrew word for "alacrity"—is a key Jewish virtue.[7] When we know what is right and good, we must act with urgency and determination to bring change. Living in the balance between our desire for swift justice and the reality that lasting change requires long-standing work is a difficult task. We must keep faith that our efforts to build a redeemed world will pay off.

The best Jewish examplar of the notion of alacrity was the venerable Rabbi Akiva. Famously, he did not start learning Torah until he was forty years old and without even knowing the *alef-bet*. Yet, he persisted. In the catalogue of wisdom known as *Avot D'Rabbi Natan*, the Rabbis use a verse from the Book Job (chapter 14:19) to explain Rabbi Akiva's extraordinary growth into a master of Jewish knowledge: "Water wears away the stones." Over time, we are able to create real change if we stay steady, focused, and passionate to fulfill the task—just as water eventually wears down stone. Through consistent learning—learning that was tempered by a lifetime of experience—Rabbi Akiva became one of the greatest sages in all of Jewish history

Yet, humans are stubborn by nature; change is not easy. It takes people a long time to adapt to new realities. Consider, for example, how Maimonides explains why the Israelites needed forty years in the desert to transition from the people enslaved in Egypt to masters of their collective destiny in the Promised Land. As he describes in *Guide for the Perplexed*:

> For a sudden transition from one opposite to another is impossible. ... It is not in the nature of people that, after having been brought up in slavish service . . . one should all of a sudden wash one's hands of the dirt (of slavery). . . . The Deity used a gracious ruse in causing (the people) to wander perplexedly in the desert until their souls became courageous . . . and until, moreover, people were born who were not accustomed to humiliation and servitude.[8]

On this point, Michael Walzer, a contemporary political philosopher, adds:

Physically, the escape from Egypt is sudden, glorious, complete; spiritually and politically, it is very slow, a matter of two steps forward, one step back. I want to stress this is a lesson from the Exodus experience again and again.[9]

Indeed, the characters of Pinchas as exemplified in the Book of Numbers (Numbers 25:8) and Moses as described in early days (Exodus 2:12) serve as our quintessential Jewish models of *kinah* (zealotry) and *z'rizut* (alacrity). Both Moses's own identity and his community are transformed by his courageous decision to protect the abused. Likewise, Pinchas, whose actions are subject to a certain amount of Rabbinic criticism,[10] is nonetheless lauded for being quick to act in support of morality. And by way of further example, the way that Abraham greets his guests in the Book of Genesis (Genesis 18:2–5) teaches us that we must develop the emotional intelligence to be in touch with another's needs so that we can respond to situations that demand immediate concern and care.

As noted by Walzer, one of the lessons gained from the Exodus experience is the importance of patience in achieving lasting change. This mentality has been exhibited by the English physician and lecturer Peter Mark Roget (1779–1861).[11] Although he was a famous medical lecturer and inventor (his most notable invention: the slide rule), it was after he retired that his true calling emerged. In 1852 his obsession led to the publication of his *Thesaurus of English Words and Phrases*, which has since been known as *Roget's Thesaurus*, invaluable to everyone from writers to toastmasters to crossword puzzle enthusiasts. Certainly, this is a work compiled gradually over a lifetime and as a reaction and coping mechanism to life's difficulties.

In the modern era, a deliberate, if not swift, form of alacrity has been used to change society. Signing legislation into law takes only a moment, but social adaptation takes decades. Both in the wake of the Civil War and in the 1960s, America saw legislation passed to further civil rights, yet in the twenty-first century we still have not actualized complete equality. We might even be stumbling backward, with the rapid enactment of voter ID laws, the continuing challenge of de facto school segregation, and the use of racially motivated policing policies. In other words, even though we have achieved much, we have a long way to go to create a just American society. It might not only be that lasting change takes time; more often than not, no real change occurs at all. At times, for real change to occur, we must take a longer path even when a quicker one is right before our eyes. As *Avot D'Rabbi Natan* teaches:

> Rabbi Yochanan ben Zakkai used to say, "If there is a sapling in your hand when they say to you, 'Behold, the Messiah has come!' complete planting the sapling, and then go and welcome the Messiah."[12]

The *M'silat Yesharim*, an eighteenth-century work of Mussar that promotes ethical and spiritual development, adamantly promoted the value of *z'rizut*. When we know what we must do, we are on a mission and must commit to achieving our goal. If we are living with purpose and meaning, we are driven to impact the world with our full enthusiasm. This, of course, does not mean that we should always be busy, but rather that we should feel a strong sense of urgency to achieve our goals.

Then again, urgency is not about enduring a perpetually hectic existence but about rejecting complacency. We should strive to moderate our sense of passion into a life of balance, but sometimes that balance should lack equilibrium. At times, we should feel overburdened with responsibility. We are charged not only to do good acts in the world but also to stand up against the evils in our midst even when we do not have the power or ability to change them. As Nobel Peace Prize winner Elie Wiesel declared after winning the prize, "There may be times when we are powerless to prevent injustice, but there must never be a time when we fail to protest."[13] In some fashion or another, we should be present for all of the most crucial issues of our time.

Social justice activism requires a sensitive balance between patience and alacrity. On one hand, we must have the patience for teaching and engaging the apathetic and uninformed. On the other hand, we must have the alacrity to respond to crises and injustices. Most often the urgency of immediate action precedes the necessity of educating and mobilizing the public. This is one of the reasons why the uninformed often view the activist as radical. As activists, we must have the courage to act in the name of shalom and *tzedek*, peace and justice, while maintaining patience and respect for critics.

Rabbi Dr. Sonja K. Pilz writes about the spiritual work of holding patience (*savlanut*):

> Mussar defines *savlanut* not only as a character trait, but as a practice of endurance over time. Like love, patience can only become manifest in time—what good would it be if we were patient or loving for exactly a second? . . .
>
> Mussar asks: Why are you impatient? Mussar asks: Why can't you take the time? And, finally, once you will have discovered your patience, Mussar asks: Are you waiting with love?
>
> It is not our task to be trusted and loved. It is our task to be patient, and to love.[14]

In the Talmud, Rabbi P'rida used to teach a lesson to a slow-learning student four hundred times in one day so that the student would learn properly.[15] *Savlanut* is required of those who believe in their convictions and the necessity of action and also care about their students and constituents.

I do think we can make a case for urgency. Life is short and we want to live it as fully as we can, to achieve, have impact, and give back before our time comes. With the grind of constant demands and responsibilities, it becomes all too easy to hide behind work, family, finances, health, and societal expectations. Instead of succumbing to our preoccupations, we should try prioritizing times of reflection and recharging to help us refocus our attention.

In my own life, alacrity affects the way in which I experience the world. It allows me to accept change, to be free from fear of change, and to take the reins when the obstacles in front of me push me to my limits. For me, change requires consistent commitment, and quick fixes often become mere stopgap measures that hide systemic problems until they become emergencies. I can recall a time when I was working on three different graduate degrees at once while building the early stages of an emerging nonprofit, in addition to working various jobs, amid other passions and duties. Sleep rarely made it onto the agenda. (I still feel this way, thanks to my blessed family!) While I got through all of the tasks in front of me, that type of a lifestyle certainly is not ideal.

There is a time for *savlanut* and a time for *z'rizut*. Acquiring a balance of these traits requires self-awareness, courage, partnership, and sensitivity. With experience and partnership, we are able to create times of reflection, reorientation, and renewal. Proverbs reminds us that even when we might feel settled, we should always embrace the unsettling reality that peace and security can be eliminated in only a moment. If life were just about our own happiness, it would not be difficult for us to live with the greatest of ease. But life is also about fulfilling our duties and responsibilities to our families and communities, helping others, and supporting societal progress. To this aim, we must at times sacrifice our calm and comfort and embrace the urgency of our mission. We must strike a balance between feeling settled and stable and feeling unsettled by being agitated by injustice and insufficiency (in society and ourselves). To transcend these feelings, we must develop spiritual practices that charge and re-center us to ensure that we can achieve spiritual focus and prevent our moral commitments from dragging us into an abyss of addiction to constant activity.

Chapter 23

1 When you sit down to dine with a ruler,
Consider well who is before you.

2 Thrust a knife into your gullet
If you have a large appetite.

3 Do not crave the dainties,
For they are counterfeit food.

4 Do not toil to gain wealth;
Have the sense to desist.

5 You see it, then it is gone;
It grows wings and flies away,
Like an eagle, heavenward.

6 Do not eat of a miser's food;
Do not crave for his dainties;

7 He is like one keeping accounts;
"Eat and drink," he says to you,
But he does not really mean it.

8 The morsel you eat you will vomit;
You will waste your courteous words.

9 Do not speak to a dullard—
Who will disdain your sensible words.

10 Do not remove ancient boundary stones;
Do not encroach upon the field of orphans,

11 For they have a mighty Redeemer,
Who will surely take up their cause with you.

12 Apply your mind to discipline
And your ears to wise sayings.

פרק כג

1 כִּי־תֵשֵׁב לִלְחוֹם אֶת־מוֹשֵׁל בִּין תָּבִין אֶת־אֲשֶׁר לְפָנֶיךָ:

2 וְשַׂמְתָּ שַׂכִּין בְּלֹעֶךָ אִם־בַּעַל נֶפֶשׁ אָתָּה:

3 אַל־תִּתְאָו לְמַטְעַמּוֹתָיו וְהוּא לֶחֶם כְּזָבִים:

4 אַל־תִּיגַע לְהַעֲשִׁיר מִבִּינָתְךָ חֲדָל:

5 (הֲתָעוּף) [הֲתָעִיף] עֵינֶיךָ בּוֹ וְאֵינֶנּוּ כִּי עָשֹׂה יַעֲשֶׂה־לּוֹ כְנָפַיִם כְּנֶשֶׁר (וְעִיף) [יָעוּף] הַשָּׁמָיִם:

6 אַל־תִּלְחַם אֶת־לֶחֶם רַע עָיִן וְאַל־תִּתְאָו לְמַטְעַמֹּתָיו:

7 כִּי | כְּמוֹ שָׁעַר בְּנַפְשׁוֹ כֶּן־הוּא אֱכֹל וּשְׁתֵה יֹאמַר לָךְ וְלִבּוֹ בַּל־עִמָּךְ:

8 פִּתְּךָ־אָכַלְתָּ תְקִיאֶנָּה וְשִׁחַתָּ דְּבָרֶיךָ הַנְּעִימִים:

9 בְּאָזְנֵי כְסִיל אַל־תְּדַבֵּר כִּי־יָבוּז לְשֵׂכֶל מִלֶּיךָ:

10 אַל־תַּסֵּג גְּבוּל עוֹלָם וּבִשְׂדֵי יְתוֹמִים אַל־תָּבֹא:

11 כִּי־גֹאֲלָם חָזָק הוּא־יָרִיב אֶת־רִיבָם אִתָּךְ:

12 הָבִיאָה לַמּוּסָר לִבֶּךָ וְאָזְנֶךָ לְאִמְרֵי־דָעַת:

13 Do not withhold discipline from children;
   If you beat them with a rod they will not die.
14 Beat them with a rod
   And you will save them from the grave.

15 My son, if your mind gets wisdom,
   My mind, too, will be gladdened.
16 I shall rejoice with all my heart
   When your lips speak right things.
17 Do not envy sinners in your heart,
   But only those who fear GOD, at all times,
18 For then you will have a future,
   And your hope will never fail.

19 Listen, my son, and get wisdom;
   Lead your mind in a [proper] path.
20 Do not be of those who guzzle wine,
   Or glut themselves on meat,
21 For guzzlers and gluttons will be impoverished,
   And drowsing will clothe you in tatters.

22 Listen to your father who begot you;
   Do not disdain your mother when she is old.
23 Buy truth and never sell it,
   And wisdom, discipline, and understanding.
24 The father of a righteous person will exult;
   He who begets a wise child will rejoice in them.
25 Your father and mother will rejoice;
   She who bore you will exult.
26 Give your mind to me, my son;
   Let your eyes watch my ways.
27 A harlot is a deep pit;
   A forbidden woman is a narrow well.
28 She too lies in wait as if for prey,
   And destroys the unfaithful among men.

אַל־תִּמְנַע מִנַּעַר מוּסָר כִּי־תַכֶּנּוּ בַשֵּׁבֶט לֹא יָמוּת׃ 13

אַתָּה בַּשֵּׁבֶט תַּכֶּנּוּ וְנַפְשׁוֹ מִשְּׁאוֹל תַּצִּיל׃ 14

בְּנִי אִם־חָכַם לִבֶּךָ יִשְׂמַח לִבִּי גַם־אָנִי׃ 15

וְתַעְלֹזְנָה כִלְיוֹתָי בְּדַבֵּר שְׂפָתֶיךָ מֵישָׁרִים׃ 16

אַל־יְקַנֵּא לִבְּךָ בַּחַטָּאִים כִּי אִם־בְּיִרְאַת־יְהֹוָה כָּל־הַיּוֹם׃ 17

כִּי אִם־יֵשׁ אַחֲרִית וְתִקְוָתְךָ לֹא תִכָּרֵת׃ 18

שְׁמַע־אַתָּה בְנִי וַחֲכָם וְאַשֵּׁר בַּדֶּרֶךְ לִבֶּךָ׃ 19

אַל־תְּהִי בְסֹבְאֵי־יָיִן בְּזֹלְלֵי בָשָׂר לָמוֹ׃ 20

כִּי־סֹבֵא וְזוֹלֵל יִוָּרֵשׁ וּקְרָעִים תַּלְבִּישׁ נוּמָה׃ 21

שְׁמַע לְאָבִיךָ זֶה יְלָדֶךָ וְאַל־תָּבוּז כִּי־זָקְנָה אִמֶּךָ׃ 22

אֱמֶת קְנֵה וְאַל־תִּמְכֹּר חָכְמָה וּמוּסָר וּבִינָה׃ 23

(גול) [גִּיל] יָגִיל אֲבִי צַדִּיק (יולד) [וְיוֹלֵד] חָכָם 24
(וישמח) [יִשְׂמַח־]בּוֹ׃

יִשְׂמַח־אָבִיךָ וְאִמֶּךָ וְתָגֵל יוֹלַדְתֶּךָ׃ 25

תְּנָה־בְנִי לִבְּךָ לִי וְעֵינֶיךָ דְּרָכַי (תרצנה) [תִּצֹּרְנָה]׃ 26

כִּי־שׁוּחָה עֲמֻקָּה זוֹנָה וּבְאֵר צָרָה נָכְרִיָּה׃ 27

אַף־הִיא כְּחֶתֶף תֶּאֱרֹב וּבוֹגְדִים בְּאָדָם תּוֹסִף׃ 28

29 Who cries, "Woe!" who, "Alas!";
    Who has quarrels, who complaints;
    Who has wounds without cause;
    Who has bleary eyes?
30 Those whom wine keeps till the small hours,
    Those who gather to drain the cups.
31 Do not ogle that red wine
    As it lends its color to the cup,
    As it flows on smoothly;
32 In the end, it bites like a snake;
    It spits like a basilisk.
33 Your eyes will see strange sights;
    Your heart will speak distorted things.
34 You will be like one lying in bed on high seas,
    Like one lying on top of the rigging.
35 "They struck me, but I felt no hurt;
    They beat me, but I was unaware;
    As often as I wake,
    I go after it again."

29 לְמִי אֹוי לְמִי אֲבֹוי לְמִי אָבוי לְמִי (מדונים) [מִדְיָנִים |] לְמִי שִׂיחַ לְמִי פְּצָעִים חִנָּם לְמִי חַכְלִלוּת עֵינָיִם:

30 לַמְאַחֲרִים עַל־הַיָּיִן לַבָּאִים לַחְקֹר מִמְסָךְ:

31 אַל־תֵּרֶא יַיִן כִּי יִתְאַדָּם כִּי־יִתֵּן (בכיס) [בַּכּוֹס] עֵינֹו יִתְהַלֵּךְ בְּמֵישָׁרִים:

32 אַחֲרִיתֹו כְּנָחָשׁ יִשָּׁךְ וּכְצִפְעֹנִי יַפְרִשׁ:

33 עֵינֶיךָ יִרְאוּ זָרֹות וְלִבְּךָ יְדַבֵּר תַּהְפֻּכֹות:

34 וְהָיִיתָ כְּשֹׁכֵב בְּלֶב־יָם וּכְשֹׁכֵב בְּרֹאשׁ חִבֵּל:

35 הִכּוּנִי בַל־חָלִיתִי הֲלָמוּנִי בַּל־יָדָעְתִּי מָתַי אָקִיץ אֹוסִיף אֲבַקְשֶׁנּוּ עֹוד:

The Orphans' Field: Ritual, Ethics, and the Protection of Children

Do not remove ancient boundary stones;
Do not encroach upon the field of orphans.
     —Proverbs 23:10

IN 1997 A YOUNG INFANT was found on the edge of the train tracks in rural China, her parents nowhere to be found and nothing else known about her origins. Like thousands of other young girls in China at the time, she was abandoned by her parents as a result of the Chinese one-child policy. She might have been a second child, or maybe her parents wanted their one child to be a boy. There is no way for us to know. What we do know, however, is that this girl was listed by an adoption agency and later adopted by parents in suburban New York, who gave her the resources to succeed. This girl, now a young woman whom we will call Joan, recently graduated from an Ivy League university and is currently working in New York City.

Yet even though Joan got very lucky, thousands of other young children were—indeed, continue to be—victimized by the one-child policy. While we would like to think that such a policy is an artifact of the past, it was only abolished by China in 2015. It is just one example of our failure to protect the children on this earth. Millions of children fall asleep every night hungry, wearing an unchanged diaper, and with no one to hold them as they cry themselves to sleep. There is perhaps no greater suffering than to feel unloved, unwanted, and uncared for. This is the story of the orphan.

The great French Jewish philosopher and Talmudist Emmanuel Levinas taught about the power of Jewish ritual to inform and to inspire us to make the world more just. He writes, "The Justice rendered to the Other, my neighbor, gives me an unsurpassable proximity to God. . . . The pious person is the just person. . . . For love itself demands justice and my relation with my neighbor cannot remain outside the lines which this neighbor maintains with various third parties. The third party is also my neighbor." Thus, when we pursue justice in a Jewish way, interacting with people in the public sphere, and helping those less fortunate than us, we come closer to God. This is because "the ritual law constitutes the austere law that strives to achieve justice. Only this law can recognize the face of the Other which has managed to impose an austere role on its true nature."[1]

Looking to our verse, one is struck by its focus on orphans, who are normally lumped together with other vulnerable populations in the Torah:

> You shall not wrong nor oppress a stranger, for you were strangers in the land of Egypt. You shall not ill-treat any widow or orphan. If you do mistreat them, I will heed their outcry as soon as they cry out to Me, and My anger shall blaze forth and I will put you to the sword, and your own wives shall become widows and your children orphans. (Exodus 22:20–23)

Our verse in Proverbs makes a point unique to orphans, but these Torah verses emphasize that the orphan is just one member of the marginalized part of society, all of whose members need our love and care.

Rabbi Dr. Yitz Greenberg, a progressive Orthodox teacher, writes:

> Judaism believes that by connecting to God, living as He would want us to live, we can progress along the path to earthly perfection. Since the God of Israel, as the Bible tells us, is on the side of the widow and the orphan, the stranger and the oppressed, the needy and the downtrodden, one of the primary ways of serving Him is to practice justice and righteousness toward all His creatures—but especially toward those in need of help.[2]

Perhaps there is no teaching more essential to Judaism than the ethical imperative to protect the rights and secure the needs of the stranger and the widow along with the orphan. Throughout history, societies that deigned to call themselves civilized would marginalize these populations, often ensuring a systemic lack of access to legal, financial, and social protections. The Jewish moral paradigm, on the contrary, is to focus on populations that are often overlooked. We embrace them, seek them out, hold them close.

We often think of "the observant Jew" as an individual who is most ritually observant. We must stop assessing observance in these categories. We should alter our thinking in this regard: those who are kind, morally reflective, and working to alleviate the plight of others are "observant Jews," as they defend, uphold, and preserve the most crucial axioms of Torah.

God instructs us that to be religious people, the marginalized—rather than the elite—have to be our priority. To be faithful is to orient our lives around the needs of the most vulnerable. The stranger, widow, and orphan can be understood conceptually. The mitzvot that are articulated with reference to widows, orphans, and strangers apply to all those who are marginalized, alienated, oppressed, and suffering.

And yet, the verse in Proverbs does focus on the orphan. Jewish tradition encourages adoption and care for the vulnerable child. Jewish law considers the adoptive parents who care for, raise, and teach their child to be the official parents.[3] Rabbi Yisrael Meir HaKohen Kagan, known as the Chofetz Chayim (1839–1933, Russia/Poland) shared a tale that illustrates the power of adoption. He tells of a childless couple—Moshe and Devorah Leah—who devoted their whole lives to the service of the children of others. Inspired by the axiom that if one teaches a child Torah, it is as if one gave birth to the child, Moshe and Devorah Leah dedicated themselves to improving their community through philanthropy and good deeds. The childless couple raised money to help families with their household expenses, made sure that children had the best teachers, and ensured that all children of the community were provided for, essentially adopting a whole generation of children. However, the story does not end with

Moshe and Devorah Leah simply taking care of the children and helping them on their way. When Moshe and Devorah Leah became elderly, they stipulated in their will that all of their assets should not be distributed among their relatives, but rather should go toward the perpetuation of children's education. After the couple passed away, the community was so grateful to them that the entirety of the next generation of children were named either Moshe or Devorah Leah.[4]

The obligation to ensure that the alienated and powerless are cared for is embedded within Jewish collective memory. Our recollection of our enslavement, which we return to so frequently in Jewish prayer and ritual, defines our narrative, ethical consciousness, and drive to protect those who cannot protect themselves. Therefore, Jewish ritual and its repeated reminders of our former enslavement and obligation to empathy does not have to be empty and stifling; instead, it can promote mindfulness and humility, allow for reflection, and give our souls the possibility to grow. The transformative power of ritual is achieved when we seize the opportunity to explore ourselves, our hearts, and our ideals. We step out of this world and then return to life as changed people. In ritual, we slow down, refocus on the big picture, and reaffirm our core values. Sometimes we do this in sacred privacy, but more often we do it within the spiritual partnership of community.

Of course, the process of adoption is not for everyone. There are serious challenges, risks, and commitments that come with a decision to adopt. At the same time, by taking in someone we do not know, we are doing a divine service.

We must begin our social justice work by finding a way to love and support vulnerable populations. Maimonides, one of the first people to codify Jewish law and to standardize ritual, explains that we must show the highest sensitivity toward orphans: "Whoever irritates them, provokes them to anger, pains them, tyrannizes over them, or causes them loss of money is guilty of a transgression."[5] We must do more than avoid wronging parentless children. We must actively show love and care to this population. The great prophet Isaiah teaches us to "uphold the rights of the orphan" (Isaiah 1:17). May we be able to heed and actualize this prophetic call.

Rabbi Jonah Pesner writes:

> "You shall not ill-treat any widow or orphan" (Exodus 22:20–21). The Torah connects our experience of slavery with a command to have empathy for all those who are least protected by society. Widows, orphans, and strangers lacked ancient patriarchal protections, were almost completely without power, and often suffered terribly. It is worthy to note that the Torah doesn't stop with an obligation to "tolerate" or even to "protect" the stranger. Instead, our obligation, as we are commanded, is to *love* the stranger. Over and over again, the biblical text connects our experience of slavery with a radical empathy for all those who suffer.[6]

When we recite the *Sh'ma*, when we read the Passover Haggadah, or when we engage in Jewish ritual in the broadest sense, we are reinforcing the commitment to stand with the vulnerable. We can start with vulnerable children.

Chapter 24

1 Do not envy the wicked;
   Do not desire to be with them;
2 For their hearts talk violence,
   And their lips speak mischief.

3 A house is built by wisdom,
   And is established by understanding;
4 By knowledge are its rooms filled
   With all precious and beautiful things.

5 A wise man is strength;
   A knowledgeable man exerts power;
6 For by stratagems you wage war,
   And victory comes with much planning.

7 Wisdom is too lofty for an ignoramus;
   He does not open his mouth in the gate.
8 One who lays plans to do harm
   Is called a schemer.
9 The schemes of folly are sin,
   And a scoffer is an abomination to all.

10 If you showed yourself slack in time of trouble,
   Wanting in power,
11 If you refrained from rescuing those taken off to death,
   Those condemned to slaughter—
12 If you say, "We knew nothing of it,"
   Surely the One who fathoms hearts will discern [the truth],
   The One who watches over your life will know it,
   And [God] will pay each person as they deserve.

פרק כד

1 אַל־תְּקַנֵּא בְּאַנְשֵׁי רָעָה וְאַל־תִּתְאָו לִהְיוֹת אִתָּם:

2 כִּי־שֹׁד יֶהְגֶּה לִבָּם וְעָמָל שִׂפְתֵיהֶם תְּדַבֵּרְנָה:

3 בְּחָכְמָה יִבָּנֶה בָּיִת וּבִתְבוּנָה יִתְכּוֹנָן:

4 וּבְדַעַת חֲדָרִים יִמָּלְאוּ כָּל־הוֹן יָקָר וְנָעִים:

5 גֶּבֶר־חָכָם בַּעוֹז וְאִישׁ־דַּעַת מְאַמֶּץ־כֹּחַ:

6 כִּי בְתַחְבֻּלוֹת תַּעֲשֶׂה־לְּךָ מִלְחָמָה וּתְשׁוּעָה בְּרֹב יוֹעֵץ:

7 רָאמוֹת לֶאֱוִיל חָכְמוֹת בַּשַּׁעַר לֹא יִפְתַּח־פִּיהוּ:

8 מְחַשֵּׁב לְהָרֵעַ לוֹ בַּעַל־מְזִמּוֹת יִקְרָאוּ:

9 זִמַּת אִוֶּלֶת חַטָּאת וְתוֹעֲבַת לְאָדָם לֵץ:

10 הִתְרַפִּיתָ בְּיוֹם צָרָה צַר כֹּחֶכָה:

11 הַצֵּל לְקֻחִים לַמָּוֶת וּמָטִים לַהֶרֶג אִם־תַּחְשׂוֹךְ:

12 כִּי־תֹאמַר הֵן לֹא־יָדַעְנוּ־זֶה הֲלֹא־תֹכֵן לִבּוֹת | הוּא־יָבִין וְנֹצֵר נַפְשְׁךָ הוּא יֵדָע וְהֵשִׁיב לְאָדָם כְּפָעֳלוֹ:

13 My son, eat honey, for it is good;
   Let its sweet drops be on your palate.
14 Know: such is wisdom for your soul;
   If you attain it, there is a future;
   Your hope will not be cut off.

15 Wicked ones! Do not lurk by the home of the righteous;
   Do no violence to their dwellings.
16 Seven times a righteous person falls and gets up,
   While the wicked are tripped by one misfortune.

17 If your enemies fall, do not exult;
   If they trip, let your heart not rejoice,
18 Lest GOD see it and be displeased,
   And avert God's wrath from them.

19 Do not be vexed by evildoers;
   Do not be incensed by the wicked;
20 For there is no future for an evildoer;
   The lamp of the wicked goes out.

21 Fear GOD, my son, and the king,
   And do not mix with dissenters,
22 For disaster comes from them suddenly;
   The doom both decree who can foreknow?

23 These also are by the sages:

   It is not right to be partial in judgment.
24 One who says to the guilty, "You are innocent,"
   Shall be cursed by peoples,
   Damned by nations;
25 But it shall go well with them who decide justly;
   Blessings of good things will light upon them.

26 Giving a straightforward reply
   Is like giving a kiss.

אֱכָל־בְּנִי דְבַשׁ כִּי־ט֑וֹב וְנֹ֖פֶת מָת֣וֹק עַל־חִכֶּֽךָ׃ 13

כֵּ֤ן | דְּעֶ֥ה חָכְמָ֗ה לְנַ֫פְשֶׁ֥ךָ אִם־מָ֭צָאתָ וְיֵ֣שׁ אַחֲרִ֑ית 14
וְ֝תִקְוָתְךָ֗ לֹ֣א תִכָּרֵֽת׃

אַל־תֶּאֱרֹ֣ב רָ֭שָׁע לִנְוֵ֣ה צַדִּ֑יק אַֽל־תְּשַׁדֵּ֥ד רִבְצֽוֹ׃ 15

כִּ֤י שֶׁ֨בַע | יִפּ֣וֹל צַדִּ֣יק וָקָ֑ם וּ֝רְשָׁעִ֗ים יִכָּשְׁל֥וּ בְרָעָֽה׃ 16

בִּנְפֹ֣ל (אויביך) [א֭וֹיִבְךָ] אַל־תִּשְׂמָ֑ח וּ֝בִכָּשְׁל֗וֹ 17
אַל־יָגֵ֥ל לִבֶּֽךָ׃

פֶּן־יִרְאֶ֣ה יְ֭הֹוָה וְרַ֣ע בְּעֵינָ֑יו וְהֵשִׁ֖יב מֵעָלָ֣יו אַפּֽוֹ׃ 18

אַל־תִּתְחַ֥ר בַּמְּרֵעִ֑ים אַל־תְּ֝קַנֵּ֗א בָּרְשָׁעִֽים׃ 19

כִּ֤י | לֹא־תִהְיֶ֣ה אַחֲרִ֣ית לָרָ֑ע נֵ֖ר רְשָׁעִ֣ים יִדְעָֽךְ׃ 20

יְרָֽא־אֶת־יְהֹוָ֣ה בְּנִ֣י וָמֶ֑לֶךְ עִם־שׁ֝וֹנִ֗ים אַל־תִּתְעָרָֽב׃ 21

כִּֽי־פִ֭תְאֹם יָק֣וּם אֵידָ֑ם וּפִ֥יד שְׁ֝נֵיהֶ֗ם מִ֣י יוֹדֵֽעַ׃ 22

גַּם־אֵ֥לֶּה לַחֲכָמִ֑ים הַֽכֵּר־פָּנִ֖ים בְּמִשְׁפָּ֣ט בַּל־טֽוֹב׃ 23

אֹ֤מֵ֨ר | לְרָשָׁ֗ע צַדִּ֥יק אָ֑תָּה יִקְּבֻ֥הוּ עַמִּ֗ים יִזְעָמ֥וּהוּ 24
לְאֻמִּֽים׃

וְלַמּוֹכִיחִ֥ים יִנְעָ֑ם וַ֝עֲלֵיהֶ֗ם תָּב֥וֹא בִרְכַּת־טֽוֹב׃ 25

שְׂפָתַ֥יִם יִשָּׁ֑ק מֵ֝שִׁ֗יב דְּבָרִ֥ים נְכֹחִֽים׃ 26

27 Put your external affairs in order,
   Get ready what you have in the field,
   Then build yourself a home.
28 Do not be a witness against your fellow without good cause;
   Would you mislead with your speech?
29 Do not say, "I will do to him what he did to me;
   I will pay the man what he deserves."

30 I passed by the field of a lazy man,
   By the vineyard of someone lacking sense.
31 It was all overgrown with thorns;
   Its surface was covered with chickweed,
   And its stone fence lay in ruins.
32 I observed and took it to heart;
   I saw it and learned a lesson.
33 A bit more sleep, a bit more slumber,
   A bit more hugging yourself in bed,
34 And poverty will come calling upon you,
   And want, like a man with a shield.

הָכֵ֤ן בַּח֨וּץ ׀ מְלַאכְתֶּ֗ךָ וְעַתְּדָ֣הּ בַּשָּׂדֶ֣ה לָ֑ךְ אַ֝חַ֗ר 27
וּבָנִ֥יתָ בֵיתֶֽךָ:

אַל־תְּהִ֤י עֵד־חִנָּ֣ם בְּרֵעֶ֑ךָ וַ֝הֲפִתִּ֗יתָ בִּשְׂפָתֶֽיךָ: 28

אַל־תֹּאמַ֗ר כַּאֲשֶׁ֣ר עָֽשָׂה־לִ֭י כֵּ֤ן אֶעֱשֶׂה־לּ֑וֹ אָשִׁ֖יב 29
לָאִ֣ישׁ כְּפָעֳלֽוֹ:

עַל־שְׂדֵ֣ה אִישׁ־עָצֵ֣ל עָבַ֑רְתִּי וְעַל־כֶּ֝֗רֶם אָדָ֥ם חֲסַר־לֵֽב: 30

וְהִנֵּ֨ה עָ֘לָ֤ה כֻלּ֨וֹ ׀ קִמְּשֹׂנִ֗ים כָּסּ֣וּ פָנָ֣יו חֲרֻלִּ֑ים וְגֶ֖דֶר 31
אֲבָנָ֣יו נֶהֱרָֽסָה:

וָאֶחֱזֶ֣ה אָ֭נֹכִי אָשִׁ֣ית לִבִּ֑י רָ֝אִ֗יתִי לָקַ֥חְתִּי מוּסָֽר: 32

מְעַ֣ט שֵׁ֭נוֹת מְעַ֣ט תְּנוּמ֑וֹת מְעַ֓ט ׀ חִבֻּ֖ק יָדַ֣יִם לִשְׁכָּֽב: 33

וּבָֽא־מִתְהַלֵּ֥ךְ רֵישֶׁ֑ךָ וּ֝מַחְסֹרֶ֗יךָ כְּאִ֣ישׁ מָגֵֽן: 34

Know Your Soul

Know: such is wisdom for your soul;
If you attain it, there is a future;
Your hope will not be cut off.
—Proverbs 24:14

THE B'NEI YISACHAR teaches that the *g'matria* (the numerological value of the Hebrew letters) of the verse "Know: such is wisdom for your soul" is the same as the *g'matria* as the word *Shabbat*—702. Further, it is the same *g'matria* as twenty-seven times the name of God. He then states:

> This alludes to the fact that the oneness and unity of *HaKadosh Baruch Hu*, blessed be God's name, can be discerned and inferred within each of the letters of the Torah. They all demonstrate the oneness of God's name.[1]

Shabbat can be a vehicle to spiritual reflection and the "knowing of our souls." Even more, it can be a vehicle for social progress.

We can interpret the Sabbath in many ways. Its benefits, so insightfully discussed by Heschel, can also extend to themes of social justice. In his book *The Sabbath*, written over sixty-five years ago, Heschel explains:

> To set apart one day a week for freedom, a day on which we would not use the instruments which have been so easily turned into weapons of destruction, a day for being with ourselves, a day of detachment from the vulgar, of independence of external obligations, a day on which we stop worshipping the idols of technical civilization, a day on which we use no money . . . is there any institution that holds out a greater hope for man's progress than the Sabbath?[2]

Heschel describes the Sabbath in quite idealistic terms. While the rest of the week might be dedicated toward making a living, often at the expense of others, the Sabbath is dedicated to taking a day for ourselves to escape from that mentality. Rather than a mitzvah whose violation subjects one to punishment as described in the Torah,[3] Shabbat, in Heschel's view, is a joyful privilege for us to recharge and muster the resources to conquer the week ahead.

Such an interpretation is very much applicable to our modern lives, with social media and smartphones constantly diverting our attention. Each of us should feel challenged to embrace a Shabbat on which we do not work, do not employ others, and refrain from the pressures of consumer capitalism. While many American Jews may not be traditionally observing the Shabbat, what we might all consider, at least, is turning off all of our technology and using that time to talk with family and friends, to read and learn, to pray and meditate. On the seventh day of the week, we can build commitment to one another, reflect upon our lives, and become intellectually and spiritually creative.

We invest much into our bodies (and we should!), but all too often we forget the life of the soul. Rabbi Denise Eger, a Reform rabbi, LGBTQ activist, and a former president of the CCAR, writes:

> When we die, our body stops, but our soul, our mass of energy, does not die. It returns to the Spirit of the universe, the Energy that we call God, the Intellect that we call God, and is absorbed and reunited. The folk custom of opening a window or door when in a room where someone dies is to let the soul fly free to return to God, who gave it. The soul does not remain trapped in the body. The life force of humanity, the soul, is eternal.[4]

We might spend more time at the gym than in service to others. Should we not invest in the eternal life of the soul too?

On Perseverance

Seven times a righteous person falls and gets up,
While the wicked are tripped by one misfortune.
—Proverbs 24:16

THE BOOK OF PROVERBS is also a reflection of the human condition. In essence, life is hard. We all get knocked down. As Thomas Edison once famously said, genius is 99 percent perspiration and 1 percent inspiration. For many, it is often difficult, after being faced with adversity, to get back up. The Kotzker Rebbe teaches that after the Binding of Isaac (known as the *Akeidah*), Abraham never "got up" again. That was his end. It appears to have been Sarah's end as well, as the Torah teaches that she passed away right after this episode (Genesis 22–23).

The most important test of a person's value is how they respond to failure. If they get up with more gentility and humility, their perseverance helps to further refine their character. Jewish tradition describes several characters who persevered through failure. Take, for example, the story of Joseph. As we see in the closing verses of Genesis, Jacob's son Joseph did not live an easy life (Genesis 37–50). Hated by his brothers and sold into slavery, Joseph persevered through his time in prison to become the Egyptian second-in-command, saving his entire family from famine and giving them the most fertile land in Egypt (Genesis 45:10). Also Moses, our forefather, persevered despite his speech impediment and lack of confidence[5] and led the people of Israel both out of Egypt and through the Sinai desert for forty years. Imagine working with so many people for so long, frequently dealing with their myriad complaints, and forgoing any respite for over forty years.[6] We should be grateful for Moses's perseverance, because had the Israelites not made it to Israel, the

Jewish people would most likely not be here, and there would definitely not be such a beautiful tradition for us to draw upon for inspiration and support.

The person who arguably sacrificed even more for the Jewish people is Rabbi Yochanan ben Zakkai, who, during the Roman siege of Jerusalem prior to the destruction of the Second Temple, faked his death and got carried out in a coffin to meet with the Roman general Vespasian. Rabbi Yochanan impressed the general, whom he notified of his future promotion to emperor halfway through their conversation, and Vespasian granted him a request. Rather than asking for the Romans to spare Jerusalem, Rabbi Yochanan requested that the Rabbinic center of Yavneh not be attacked, which preserved the scholarly elite stationed there.[7] There is no telling how many close family members and friends Rabbi Yochanan lost by his decision not to ask that Jerusalem be spared. But by saving Yavneh, Rabbi Yochanan preserved the oral tradition that would later be embodied in the Mishnah. As the Temple was destroyed and the Jewish people were exiled from Israel, these texts became the basis for Jewish practice, forming the Jewish traditions and customs we live today. In other words, Rabbi Yochanan made a strategic decision to save the essence of Jewish peoplehood.

There are many other moral leaders who persevered to overcome challenges. We read about great teachers such as Hillel, who listened to Torah lectures in the falling snow outside of the study hall because he could not afford the entry fee,[8] and Rabbi Akiva, who endured being apart from his beloved wife for years so that he could learn enough to gain the following of thousands of students.[9] Maimonides, who gave much to the world in the fields of practical Jewish living, philosophy, and medicine, kept up such a frenetic schedule that he could barely eat or sleep as he ministered to the physical and religious needs of both Jews and non-Jews of his generation.[10] Rabbi Nachman of Bratzlav overcame an array of psychological trials to leave an intellectual and spiritual legacy that shows how to live a life directed by the Torah and defined by joy.[11]

Such examples are not limited to the past. In December 2019, a rabbi's house in Monsey, New York, was violently attacked during a Chanukah celebration. The rabbi and others were injured. Yet, even though the community at large was shocked, the need to remain committed to living with courage was pervasive. The celebration was continued in another location as a way of demonstrating that the rabbi, his family, his students, and his friends were to live their lives as free Jews. A representative of the rabbi was quoted as declaring, "We will persevere."[12]

Those leading or participating in the #MeToo struggle, the #BlackLivesMatter struggle, combating antisemitism, or fighting for any basic human rights will inevitably sometimes get exhausted. Together, we must work to physically and spiritually endure. Sadly, the bar is set quite low today. Instead of advocating for the greatest and most noble good, we must still fight for Black people to have equal rights, for women to have equal rights, to stop rampant gun violence, for basic standards on public health, for precautions during a pandemic, and for basic protections for the most vulnerable. We will win on these, but the fight is much longer, and after each win there will be more to do together.

On Revenge

Do not say, "I will do to him what he did to me;
I will pay the man what he deserves."
　—Proverbs 24:29

REVENGE HAS THE ABILITY to destroy a person. It is a pernicious emotion, an all-encompassing, infinitely heavy albatross. The Torah demands to avoid revenge: "You shall not take vengeance or bear a grudge against members of your people" (Leviticus 19:18). Interestingly enough, the verse just before that one is "You shall not hate your kinsfolk in your heart" (Leviticus 19:17). This seems to be a hint that one of the goals of removing hate from the heart is to make sure it does not lead us to harmful action. In every action and in each reaction to someone else's action, we should come from a place of measured reason, a commitment to justice, and not from a place of anger. Another passage in Proverbs teaches, "Hatred stirs up strife, / But love covers up all faults" (Proverbs 10:12).

Maimonides writes about destructive anger in the *Mishneh Torah*:

> There are certain character traits that one must distance oneself from in the extreme. In fact, it is forbidden to take [the standard approach of] the "middle path" regarding these character traits. . . .
>
> Anger is an extremely negative character trait, and it is fitting for a person to distance oneself from it to the opposite extreme. One should train oneself never to become angry, even regarding things for which anger might be justified. . . .
>
> Those who frequently become angry have no quality of life; therefore, [the Sages] instructed us to distance ourselves from anger to the farthest degree, until a person acts as though not sensing even those things that would justifiably anger a person.[13]

Indeed, the Talmud says that one loses their wisdom in a state of rage just as a prophet loses their prophecy.[14] The types of acts that emerge from hatred (*sinah*) were considered the basis of the destruction of the Temple: idolatry, sexual immorality, and murder.[15] In reflecting on that baseless hatred (*sinat chinam*), Rabbi Kook suggested we seek to cultivate baseless love (*ahavat chinam*).[16]

Even when we have been hurt, we are to try to emulate God's ways (*halachta bidrachav*), remembering that God is forgiving. When we recite the thirteen attributes of God, we focus on the justice of God's actions. Forgiving others is connected to *tzedek* (justice), because forgiving those who have erred is an act of healing both of individual relationships and of the broader social fabric. To be righteous is to be a forgiver, to understand that humans are fallible, and to be loving to others who stumble. The Talmud distinguishes between two prohibitions here: revenge and holding a grudge;[17] and Rabbi Yisrael of Rizhin distinguishes between the *solei-ach*, the one who occasionally forgives depending on their mood, and the *salchan*, the one who forgives time and time again. To perpetuate opportunities to forgive and to repair relationships means to be a *salchan*. Some people hurt us so much that we cannot merely forgive them just once; rather, we need to forgive them in our hearts time and time again. This helps us, too, to heal.

Just as we are obligated to forgive others, so too are we commanded "not to bear a grudge" (*lo titor*). This mitzvah comes from the same Torah verse as the command to love others like ourselves (Leviticus 19:18). Forgiving another is about the past; removing a grudge, on the other hand, affects the present. To truly love another, we must release our grudges.

How does this apply to our daily lives? To be forgiving is to be courageous. Leaders who try to heal long-standing conflicts often pay with their lives. About a month before his assassination, in his second inaugural address, President Abraham Lincoln famously said, "With malice toward none, with charity for all," but he added that forgiveness entailed much work: "to bind up the nation's wounds, to care for him who shall have borne the battle and for his widow and his orphan, to do all which may achieve and cherish a just and lasting peace."[18]

Another more contemporary example of taking Leviticus 19:18 seriously and pursuing a path of forgiveness can be found in the recent history of South Africa. In 1994, bolstered by its political and religious leaders, Archbishop Desmond Tutu and soon-to-be-president Nelson Mandela, South Africa conducted peaceful elections to elect its first black-majority government. Then, in spite of predictions that this government would unleash a vengeful blood-bath against the former apartheid white rulers, the Truth and Reconciliation Commission, chaired by Nobel laureate Tutu, helped bring healing to the country. Instead of putting all the perpetrators—mostly white—on trial or granting a general amnesty that would do nothing to defuse the hatred, South Africa tried a different course. Archbishop Tutu writes:

> They saw the process of the Truth and Reconciliation Commission, when perpetrators of some of the most gruesome atrocities were given amnesty in exchange for a full disclosure of the facts of the offence. Instead of revenge and retribution, this new nation chose to tread the difficult path of confession, forgiveness, and reconciliation.[19]

As long as the torturers and murderers would acknowledge their crimes and ask for forgiveness, the victims would in turn forgive them, and the state would not pursue them further. This tactic avoided the violence that gripped so many other nations such as Mugabe's Zimbabwe and Mozambique. Of course, while there has been real progress over the last thirty years since Mandela was freed, South Africa's problems (racial, economic, and social) are still enormous, painful, and disastrous.

Forgiveness is hard, and sometimes seemingly impossible. However, before we decide that we cannot forgive, we should consider the destructive potential of holding grudges. We must try to be the *sal-chan* who follows the command of *lo titor*. As Archbishop Tutu points out, "Retribution leads to a cycle of reprisal, leading to counter-reprisal in an inexorable movement, as in Rwanda, Northern Ireland, and in the former nation of Yugoslavia. The only thing that can break that cycle, making possible a new beginning, is forgiveness. Without forgiveness there is no future."[20]

There really is no better way to say it than in Archbishop Tutu's insightful words: without forgiveness there is no future.

Chapter 25

1 These too are proverbs of Solomon,
which the officials of King Hezekiah of Judah copied:

2 It is the glory of God to conceal a matter,
And the glory of a king to plumb a matter.
3 Like the heavens in their height, like the earth in its depth,
Is the mind of kings—unfathomable.
4 The dross having been separated from the silver,
A vessel emerged for the smith.
5 Remove the wicked from the king's presence,
And his throne will be established in justice.
6 Do not exalt yourself in the king's presence;
Do not stand in the place of nobles.
7 For it is better to be told, "Step up here,"
Than to be degraded in the presence of the great.

Do not let what your eyes have seen
8 Be vented rashly in a quarrel;
Think of what it will effect in the end,
When your fellow puts you to shame.
9 Defend your right against your fellow,
But do not give away the secrets of another,
10 Lest someone who hears it reproach you,
And your bad repute never end.

11 Like golden apples in silver showpieces
Is a phrase well turned.
12 Like a ring of gold, a golden ornament,
Is a wise person's reproof in a receptive ear.

פרק כה

1 גַּם־אֵלֶּה מִשְׁלֵי שְׁלֹמֹה אֲשֶׁר הֶעְתִּיקוּ אַנְשֵׁי | חִזְקִיָּה
מֶלֶךְ־יְהוּדָה:

2 כְּבֹד אֱלֹהִים הַסְתֵּר דָּבָר וּכְבֹד מְלָכִים חֲקֹר דָּבָר:

3 שָׁמַיִם לָרוּם וָאָרֶץ לָעֹמֶק וְלֵב מְלָכִים אֵין חֵקֶר:

4 הָגוֹ סִיגִים מִכָּסֶף וַיֵּצֵא לַצֹּרֵף כֶּלִי:

5 הָגוֹ רָשָׁע לִפְנֵי־מֶלֶךְ וְיִכּוֹן בַּצֶּדֶק כִּסְאוֹ:

6 אַל־תִּתְהַדַּר לִפְנֵי־מֶלֶךְ וּבִמְקוֹם גְּדֹלִים אַל־תַּעֲמֹד:

7 כִּי טוֹב אֲמָר־לְךָ עֲלֵה־הֵנָּה מֵהַשְׁפִּילְךָ לִפְנֵי נָדִיב אֲשֶׁר
רָאוּ עֵינֶיךָ:

8 אַל־תֵּצֵא לָרִב מַהֵר פֶּן מַה־תַּעֲשֶׂה בְּאַחֲרִיתָהּ בְּהַכְלִים
אֹתְךָ רֵעֶךָ:

9 רִיבְךָ רִיב אֶת־רֵעֶךָ וְסוֹד אַחֵר אַל־תְּגָל:

10 פֶּן־יְחַסֶּדְךָ שֹׁמֵעַ וְדִבָּתְךָ לֹא תָשׁוּב:

11 תַּפּוּחֵי זָהָב בְּמַשְׂכִּיּוֹת כָּסֶף דָּבָר דָּבֻר עַל־אָפְנָיו:

12 נֶזֶם זָהָב וַחֲלִי־כָתֶם מוֹכִיחַ חָכָם עַל־אֹזֶן שֹׁמָעַת:

13 Like the coldness of snow at harvesttime
Is a trusty messenger to those who send him;
He lifts his master's spirits.

14 Like clouds, wind—but no rain—
Is a man who boasts of gifts not given.

15 Through forbearance a ruler may be won over;
A gentle tongue can break bones.

16 If you find honey, eat only what you need,
Lest, surfeiting yourself, you throw it up.

17 Visit your neighbor sparingly,
Lest he have his surfeit of you and loathe you.

18 Like a club, a sword, a sharpened arrow,
Is a man who testifies falsely against his fellow.

19 Like a loose tooth and an unsteady leg,
Is a treacherous support in time of trouble.

20 Disrobing on a chilly day,
Like vinegar on natron,
Is one who sings songs to a sorrowful soul.

21 If your enemy is hungry, give him bread to eat;
If he is thirsty, give him water to drink.

22 You will be heaping live coals on his head,
And GOD will reward you.

23 A north wind produces rain,
And whispered words, a glowering face.

24 Dwelling in the corner of a roof is better
Than a contentious woman in a spacious house.

25 Like cold water to a parched throat
Is good news from a distant land.

26 Like a muddied spring, a ruined fountain,
Are the righteous fallen before the wicked.

27 It is not good to eat much honey,
Nor is it honorable to search for honor.

28 Like an open city without walls
Is a man whose temper is uncurbed.

כְּצִנַּת־שֶׁלֶג | בְּיוֹם קָצִיר צִיר נֶאֱמָן לְשֹׁלְחָיו וְנֶפֶשׁ 13
אֲדֹנָיו יָשִׁיב:

נְשִׂיאִים וְרוּחַ וְגֶשֶׁם אָיִן אִישׁ מִתְהַלֵּל בְּמַתַּת־שָׁקֶר: 14

בְּאֹרֶךְ אַפַּיִם יְפֻתֶּה קָצִין וְלָשׁוֹן רַכָּה תִּשְׁבָּר־גָּרֶם: 15

דְּבַשׁ מָצָאתָ אֱכֹל דַּיֶּךָּ פֶּן־תִּשְׂבָּעֶנּוּ וַהֲקֵאתוֹ: 16

הֹקַר רַגְלְךָ מִבֵּית רֵעֶךָ פֶּן־יִשְׂבָּעֲךָ וּשְׂנֵאֶךָ: 17

מֵפִיץ וְחֶרֶב וְחֵץ שָׁנוּן אִישׁ עֹנֶה בְרֵעֵהוּ עֵד שָׁקֶר: 18

שֵׁן רֹעָה וְרֶגֶל מוּעָדֶת מִבְטָח בּוֹגֵד בְּיוֹם צָרָה: 19

מַעֲדֶה־בֶּגֶד | בְּיוֹם קָרָה חֹמֶץ עַל־נָתֶר וְשָׁר בַּשִּׁרִים 20
עַל לֶב־רָע:

אִם־רָעֵב שֹׂנַאֲךָ הַאֲכִלֵהוּ לָחֶם וְאִם־צָמֵא הַשְׁקֵהוּ מָיִם: 21

כִּי גֶחָלִים אַתָּה חֹתֶה עַל־רֹאשׁוֹ וַיהֹוָה יְשַׁלֶּם־לָךְ: 22

רוּחַ צָפוֹן תְּחוֹלֵל גָּשֶׁם וּפָנִים נִזְעָמִים לְשׁוֹן סָתֶר: 23

טוֹב שֶׁבֶת עַל־פִּנַּת־גָּג מֵאֵשֶׁת (מדונים) [מִדְיָנִים] 24
וּבֵית חָבֶר:

מַיִם קָרִים עַל־נֶפֶשׁ עֲיֵפָה וּשְׁמוּעָה טוֹבָה מֵאֶרֶץ מֶרְחָק: 25

מַעְיָן נִרְפָּשׂ וּמָקוֹר מָשְׁחָת צַדִּיק מָט לִפְנֵי־רָשָׁע: 26

אָכֹל דְּבַשׁ הַרְבּוֹת לֹא־טוֹב וְחֵקֶר כְּבֹדָם כָּבוֹד: 27

עִיר פְּרוּצָה אֵין חוֹמָה אִישׁ אֲשֶׁר אֵין מַעְצָר לְרוּחוֹ: 28

Rising before Power

Do not exalt yourself in the king's presence;
Do not stand in the place of nobles.
    —Proverbs 25:6

IS THE BOOK OF PROVERBS a political treatise? Multiple meanings can be found in its words. Let's break down the different elements of Proverbs 25:6. The first part of the teaching seems clear: Throughout the centuries, and sadly still today, regimes are often run by despots and dictators with massive egos who wish to be glorified at the expense of the dignity of the people whom they should serve. The selfishness of authoritarian thugs—be they kings, junta leaders, or presidents—ultimately leads to the ruin of vibrant societies. That much of the verse's meaning is easily understood.

The second part of the teaching, however, can be read in a few different ways. The most candid reading is that the second clause complements the first part. We need to make rulers feel that they are the center of the world. Just as we should not glorify ourselves before them, so too should we not stand in their place.

An alternative interpretation, albeit less literal, is that we should not wish to stand in positions of despots. This is to say, we should not join them, support them, or emulate their broken ways of looking at the world. To submit to the will of despotic thought is akin to forgoing one's morality. For example, even in the face of despotic demands, we must avoid oppressing the weak and never stand in blind submission.

Another possible and most radical reading is that we should not stand before cruel leaders at all. We should always resist their might. I find this reading the most persuasive, based on other Jewish texts.

This reading of the verse reflects the position of Mordechai when asked to bow down to Haman (Esther 3:5, 5:9). The Book of Esther as much as says that Mordechai would not bow before Haman simply because he rejected his wickedness and his corrupt power. To be sure, the Talmudic Rabbis took a different approach:

> And the king commanded that they should kneel and bow to him. What did Haman do? He embroidered an image on his clothes and his chest. And anyone who would bow to Haman would bow to an idol.[1]

The Rabbis suggest that Mordechai would not bow to the wicked Haman because Haman was wearing an idolatrous image, and Mordechai refused to bow before a religious image—whereas he would have bowed before a wicked political ruler. In other words, the Rabbis objected to Mordechai's decision to put his own life at risk, not to mention the lives of all Jews, by openly disrespecting a powerful authority. They seem to have considered that approach to have entailed such a dangerous choice that they imagined that Haman must have been wearing an idol for Mordechai to risk his life. They suggest that only to avoid one of the worst sins—idolatry—could Mordechai have decided to engage in such a perilous act.

But the literal reading of the Esther text suggests that Mordechai's act was driven by a political and ethical rejection of Haman's authority. Mordechai teaches us that we dare not stand near, with, or for corrupt leaders at all. It is our obligation to call them out and hold them accountable for their misdeeds. This is certainly not an easy task. But it is a necessary one to save the lives of the vulnerable.

Feed Your Enemy

> *If your enemy is hungry, give him bread to eat;*
> *If he is thirsty, give him water to drink.*
> —Proverbs 25:21

IT IS EASY TO VIEW one's enemies as wicked and dehumanize them. Proverbs cautions us that we should never dehumanize them or deny them their basic needs. Elsewhere in the Book of Proverbs, the text indicates that "the kisses of an enemy are profuse" (Proverbs 27:6). We must be cautious and protect ourselves in order to survive. We should not be naïve. The verse here, however, instructs us that we must meet the basic needs of our enemies even while being cautious; every human being is a creation of the Divine.

The Torah describes the ethical rules of war, demanding that Israelite armies treat their enemies with respect. Deuteronomy 20:13 details those obligations, giving instructions that enemies should live if they surrender to Israelite forces; and even if they do not surrender, the Torah allows the killing of only the males (presumably, the soldiers and the ones who are directly taking lives). Furthermore, the text decrees that the enemy be allowed to retain their sources of sustenance by forbidding the cutting down of their fruit trees (Deuteronomy 20:19–20). In other words, with these detailed rules, the Torah recognizes the universal humanity of even our mortal enemies.

The Torah, however, should not have to remind us to recognize the humanity of those around us. We should know, even without those explicit rules, that all human beings are equal and created in the image of God. History has shown that human beings routinely fail to meet this ideal. While it may be problematic for the average person to engage in an act of cruelty toward another human being under normal circumstances, history shows us that in times of war, systemic dehumanization of the enemy feeds into our instinct toward brutality. Once a group of human beings is no longer viewed as human, then they can be perceived as a threat that must be vanquished at all costs. Rabbi Dr. Rachel Adler reminds us that equality is not enough:

> Treating everyone equally would be a start, but that is only the first part of what prophets like Isaiah, Micah, Amos, and Zechariah envision. They urge us to build a world in which everyone can flourish. Anything less will ultimately produce bloodshed and desolation.[2]

Deplorably, the lineage of cruelty extends to the earliest moments of civilization. Members of minorities have been called animals or worse by political demagogues, even by people of faith. This is no less true in our time. In the years leading to the Holocaust, Jews were commonly referred to as rats. Likewise, in the lead up to the horror of the Rwandan genocide in the 1990s, the majority Hutus referred to the minority Tutsi population as cockroaches. In both cases, the implication is clear: the only way to get rid of pests is to exterminate them.[3]

Words have consequences. David Livingstone Smith, professor of philosophy at the University of New England, writes, "When people dehumanize others, they actually conceive of them as subhuman creatures." Only then can the process begin to "liberate aggression and exclude the target of aggression from the moral community."[4] When the Nazis labeled the Jews as *Untermenschen*, literally "under people," they didn't just mean this metaphorically. Smith writes, "They didn't mean they were like subhumans. They meant they were literally subhuman."

Systemic dehumanization is an unfortunate legacy in the United States. When more than one million Irish immigrants came to America to flee the famines of the mid-1800s, many Americans felt threatened by the large number of (mostly Catholic) newcomers. In response, throughout this period, political cartoonists depicted Irish immigrants as apelike creatures who were inherently drunk, lazy, supportive of corrupt politicians, and prone to bomb throwing. The Know-Nothing Party, with its slogan "Americans Shall Rule America," championed repressive measures toward immigrants. In 1856 this xenophobic party nominated former president Millard Fillmore for president, and he won more than 20 percent of the popular vote. In our contemporary moment, dehumanization has flourished. In May 2018, for example, during a roundtable discussion on sanctuary cities that resist efforts to aggressively deport undocumented aliens, one discussant mentioned the violent gang MS-13. In response to the statement, Donald Trump, then president of the United States, said:

> We have people coming into the country, or trying to come in—and we're stopping a lot of them. . . . You wouldn't believe how bad these people are. These aren't people. These are animals.[5]

While former President Trump and his supporters maintained that he was only addressing MS-13, the prevailing imagery was evident both to his supporters as well as to thinking people. Megan McArdle, writing for the *Chicago Tribune*, noted that the "animals" comment, repeated often in the days following the meeting, had an underlying significance: "[The President used] those words to demote those people from the human race . . . to demote immigrants from the empathy and consideration that decent people extend to other human beings."[6] At the same time, President Trump was careful to avoid denouncing the ostentatious display of white nationalist terror in Charlottesville, Virginia.

The plain meaning of the "animals" comment is easily gleaned from earlier statements. In June 2015, when launching his presidential campaign, Trump said, "When Mexico sends its people, they're not sending their best. . . . They're sending people that have lots of problems, and they're bringing those problems to us. They're bringing drugs. They're bringing crime. They're rapists. And some, I assume, are good people."[7] The intent was to demonize asylum seekers who cross the border from Mexico. The Trump administration changed government policy so that everyone entering the United States from Mexico was scheduled for criminal prosecution instead of being sent to civil courts, and it thus separated parents from their children.[8] When selected populations are rhetorically deprived of their human qualities, the consequences can be horrific. Asylum seekers and refugees should be at the center of our spiritual consciousness. We must open our hearts and borders to those fleeing violence.

Will decency ever be restored to its rightful place in society? Will we ever be able to see our "enemy" as the human beings that they are? It is hard to say. We are often fed propaganda urging us to view enemies as "soul-less." These definitions enable others, perhaps even ourselves, to commit atrocities, such as torture, incarceration without trial, or indiscriminate bombing. When the Book of Proverb reminds us to see our enemies as human beings, we are reminded that it is easy for us to hate other people because emotionally we still live in a tribal world. Political ideology, religious affiliation, and even racial and gender discrimination can create chaos and hatred.

We must be vigilant to never allow ourselves to be consumed by baseless hatred. It is baseless hatred that destabilizes a fragile world. We must speak out against white supremacy and other ideologies that foster antisemitism, racism, islamophobia, and other forms of hatred against other people.

Chapter 26

1 Like snow in summer and rain at harvesttime,
   So honor is not fitting for a dullard.
2 As a sparrow must flit and a swallow fly,
   So a gratuitous curse must backfire.
3 A whip for a horse and a bridle for a donkey,
   And a rod for the back of dullards.
4 Do not answer a dullard in accord with his folly,
   Else you will become like him.
5 Answer a dullard in accord with his folly,
   Else he will think himself wise.
6 One who sends a message by a dullard
   Will wear out legs and must put up with lawlessness.
7 As legs hang limp on a cripple,
   So is a proverb in the mouth of dullards.
8 Like a pebble in a sling,
   So is paying honor to a dullard.
9 As a thorn comes to the hand of a drunkard,
   So a proverb to the mouth of a dullard.
10 A master can produce anything,
   But anyone who hires a dullard is as one who hires transients.
11 As a dog returns to its vomit,
   So a dullard repeats his folly.
12 If you see a man who thinks himself wise,
   There is more hope for a dullard than for him.

13 The sluggard says,
   "There's a cub on the road, a lion in the squares."
14 The door turns upon the hinge,
   And the sluggard upon the bed.

פרק כו

1 כַּשֶּׁלֶג | בַּקַּיִץ וְכַמָּטָר בַּקָּצִיר כֵּן לֹא־נָאוֶה לִכְסִיל כָּבוֹד:

2 כַּצִּפּוֹר לָנוּד כַּדְּרוֹר לָעוּף כֵּן קִלְלַת חִנָּם (לֹא) [לוֹ] תָבֹא:

3 שׁוֹט לַסּוּס מֶתֶג לַחֲמוֹר וְשֵׁבֶט לְגֵו כְּסִילִים:

4 אַל־תַּעַן כְּסִיל כְּאִוַּלְתּוֹ פֶּן־תִּשְׁוֶה־לּוֹ גַם־אָתָּה:

5 עֲנֵה כְסִיל כְּאִוַּלְתּוֹ פֶּן־יִהְיֶה חָכָם בְּעֵינָיו:

6 מְקַצֶּה רַגְלַיִם חָמָס שֹׁתֶה שֹׁלֵחַ דְּבָרִים בְּיַד־כְּסִיל:

7 דַּלְיוּ שֹׁקַיִם מִפִּסֵּחַ וּמָשָׁל בְּפִי כְסִילִים:

8 כִּצְרוֹר אֶבֶן בְּמַרְגֵּמָה כֵּן־נוֹתֵן לִכְסִיל כָּבוֹד:

9 חוֹחַ עָלָה בְיַד־שִׁכּוֹר וּמָשָׁל בְּפִי כְסִילִים:

10 רַב מְחוֹלֵל־כֹּל וְשֹׂכֵר כְּסִיל וְשֹׂכֵר עֹבְרִים:

11 כְּכֶלֶב שָׁב עַל־קֵאוֹ כְּסִיל שׁוֹנֶה בְאִוַּלְתּוֹ:

12 רָאִיתָ אִישׁ חָכָם בְּעֵינָיו תִּקְוָה לִכְסִיל מִמֶּנּוּ:

13 אָמַר עָצֵל שַׁחַל בַּדָּרֶךְ אֲרִי בֵּין הָרְחֹבוֹת:

14 הַדֶּלֶת תִּסּוֹב עַל־צִירָהּ וְעָצֵל עַל־מִטָּתוֹ:

15 The sluggard buries a hand in the bowl,
   And will not even bring it to the mouth.
16 In self-regard, the sluggard is wiser
   Than seven who give good advice.

17 A passerby who gets embroiled in someone else's quarrel
   Is like one who seizes a dog by its ears.
18 Like a lunatic scattering deadly firebrands, arrows,
19 Is the man who cheats his fellow and says, "I was only joking."

20 For lack of wood a fire goes out,
   And without a grumbler contention is stilled.
21 Charcoal for embers and wood for a fire
   And a contentious man for kindling strife.
22 The words of a grumbler are bruising;
   They penetrate one's inmost parts.

23 Base silver laid over earthenware
   Are ardent lips with an evil mind.
24 An enemy dissembles with his speech,
   Inwardly he harbors deceit.
25 Though he be fair-spoken do not trust him,
   For seven abominations are in his mind.
26 His hatred may be concealed by dissimulation,
   But his evil will be exposed to public view.

27 One who digs a pit will fall in it,
   And a stone will roll back upon the one who is rolling it.
28 A lying tongue hates those crushed by it;
   Smooth speech throws one down.

15 טָמַ֣ן עָ֭צֵל יָד֣וֹ בַּצַּלָּ֑חַת נִ֝לְאָ֗ה לַהֲשִׁיבָ֥הּ אֶל־פִּֽיו׃

16 חָכָ֣ם עָצֵ֣ל בְּעֵינָ֑יו מִ֝שִּׁבְעָ֗ה מְשִׁ֣יבֵי טָֽעַם׃

17 מַחֲזִ֥יק בְּאָזְנֵי־כָ֑לֶב עֹבֵ֥ר מִ֝תְעַבֵּ֗ר עַל־רִ֥יב לֹּֽא־לֽוֹ׃

18 כְּֽמִתְלַהְלֵ֗הַּ הַיֹּרֶ֥ה זִקִּ֑ים חִצִּ֥ים וָמָֽוֶת׃

19 כֵּֽן־אִ֭ישׁ רִמָּ֣ה אֶת־רֵעֵ֑הוּ וְ֝אָמַ֗ר הֲ‍ֽלֹא־מְשַׂחֵ֥ק אָֽנִי׃

20 בְּאֶ֣פֶס עֵ֭צִים תִּכְבֶּה־אֵ֑שׁ וּבְאֵ֥ין נִ֝רְגָּ֗ן יִשְׁתֹּ֥ק מָדֽוֹן׃

21 פֶּחָ֣ם לְ֭גֶחָלִים וְעֵצִ֣ים לְאֵ֑שׁ וְאִ֥ישׁ (מדונים) [מִ֝דְיָנִ֗ים] לְחַרְחַר־רִֽיב׃

22 דִּבְרֵ֣י נִ֭רְגָּן כְּמִֽתְלַהֲמִ֑ים וְ֝הֵ֗ם יָרְד֥וּ חַדְרֵי־בָֽטֶן׃

23 כֶּ֣סֶף סִ֭יגִים מְצֻפֶּ֣ה עַל־חָ֑רֶשׂ שְׂפָתַ֖יִם דֹּלְקִ֣ים וְלֶב־רָֽע׃

24 בִּ֭שְׂפָתָו יִנָּכֵ֣ר שׂוֹנֵ֑א וּ֝בְקִרְבּ֗וֹ יָשִׁ֥ית מִרְמָֽה׃

25 כִּֽי־יְחַנֵּ֣ן ק֭וֹלוֹ אַל־תַּֽאֲמֶן־בּ֑וֹ כִּ֤י שֶׁ֖בַע תּוֹעֵב֣וֹת בְּלִבּֽוֹ׃

26 תִּכַּסֶּ֣ה שִׂ֭נְאָה בְּמַשָּׁא֑וֹן תִּגָּלֶ֖ה רָעָת֣וֹ בְקָהָֽל׃

27 כֹּֽרֶה־שַּׁ֭חַת בָּ֣הּ יִפֹּ֑ל וְגֹ֥לֵ֥ל אֶ֝֗בֶן אֵלָ֥יו תָּשֽׁוּב׃

28 לְֽשׁוֹן־שֶׁ֭קֶר יִשְׂנָ֣א דַכָּ֑יו וּפֶ֥ה חָ֝לָ֗ק יַעֲשֶׂ֥ה מִדְחֶֽה׃

On Questioning

Do not answer a dullard in accord with his folly,
Else you will become like him.
     —Proverbs 26:4

THE FOOL IS CERTAIN of the truth. Do not answer to that certainty. Rather, walk the nobler path of humble questioning and inquiry. Madeleine L'Engle writes, "An infinite question is often destroyed by finite answers."[1] We must learn to seek wisdom in questions and not hide within the comfort of easy answers.

The Hebrew word for falsity, *sheker*, is made up of letters that appear adjacent to each other in the Hebrew alphabet. The word for truth, *emet*, on the other hand, is made up of letters spaced out throughout the whole alphabet. This is to say that when we stay too close to any subject, we just see lies. But when we take a step back and assess the bigger picture more objectively, we see truth. A teaching from the Kotzker Rebbe relates:

> Concerning the verse in the Scriptures: "And thou shalt see My back" (Exodus 33:23), the rabbi of Kotzk said: "Everything puzzling and confused people see, is called God's back. But no person can see the face, where everything is in harmony."[2]

Many hide behind lies, but we cannot hide from the truth. The Kotzker Rebbe continues, "Everything in the world can be imitated except truth. For truth that is imitated is no longer truth."[3]

May we seek truth and wisdom with all of our might. May we hold the humility and patience to know how far we will ever be from knowing the full truth. This holy skepticism should not frighten or morally paralyze us, but embolden us to lead with both courage and humility.

Chapter 27

1   Do not boast of tomorrow,
    For you do not know what the day will bring.
2   Let the mouth of another praise you, not yours,
    The lips of a stranger, not your own.
3   A stone has weight, sand is heavy,
    But a fool's vexation outweighs them both.
4   There is the cruelty of fury, the overflowing of anger,
    But who can withstand jealousy?
5   Open reproof is better than concealed love.
6   Wounds by a loved one are long lasting;
    The kisses of an enemy are profuse.
7   A sated appetite disdains honey,
    But to a voracious appetite, even the bitter is sweet.
8   Like a sparrow wandering from its nest
    Is a man who wanders from his home.
9   Oil and incense gladden the heart,
    And the sweetness of a friend is better than one's own counsel.
10 Do not desert your friend and your father's friend;
    Do not enter your brother's house in your time of misfortune;
    A close neighbor is better than a distant brother.
11 Get wisdom, my son, and gladden my heart,
    That I may have what to answer those who taunt me.
12 The shrewd man saw trouble and took cover;
    The simple kept going and paid the penalty.
13 Seize his garment, for he stood surety for another;
    Take it as a pledge, [for he stood surety] for an unfamiliar woman.
14 He who greets his fellow loudly early in the morning
    Shall have it reckoned to him as a curse.

פרק כז

1 אַל־תִּתְהַלֵּל בְּיוֹם מָחָר כִּי לֹא־תֵדַע מַה־יֵּלֶד יוֹם:

2 יְהַלֶּלְךָ זָר וְלֹא־פִיךָ נָכְרִי וְאַל־שְׂפָתֶיךָ:

3 כֹּבֶד־אֶבֶן וְנֵטֶל הַחוֹל וְכַעַס אֱוִיל כָּבֵד מִשְּׁנֵיהֶם:

4 אַכְזְרִיּוּת חֵמָה וְשֶׁטֶף אָף וּמִי יַעֲמֹד לִפְנֵי קִנְאָה:

5 טוֹבָה תּוֹכַחַת מְגֻלָּה מֵאַהֲבָה מְסֻתָּרֶת:

6 נֶאֱמָנִים פִּצְעֵי אוֹהֵב וְנַעְתָּרוֹת נְשִׁיקוֹת שׂוֹנֵא:

7 נֶפֶשׁ שְׂבֵעָה תָּבוּס נֹפֶת וְנֶפֶשׁ רְעֵבָה כָּל־מַר מָתוֹק:

8 כְּצִפּוֹר נוֹדֶדֶת מִן־קִנָּהּ כֵּן־אִישׁ נוֹדֵד מִמְּקוֹמוֹ:

9 שֶׁמֶן וּקְטֹרֶת יְשַׂמַּח־לֵב וּמֶתֶק רֵעֵהוּ מֵעֲצַת־נָפֶשׁ:

10 רֵעֲךָ (ורעה) [וְרֵעַ] אָבִיךָ אַל־תַּעֲזֹב וּבֵית אָחִיךָ אַל־תָּבוֹא בְּיוֹם אֵידֶךָ טוֹב שָׁכֵן קָרוֹב מֵאָח רָחוֹק:

11 חֲכַם בְּנִי וְשַׂמַּח לִבִּי וְאָשִׁיבָה חֹרְפִי דָבָר:

12 עָרוּם | רָאָה רָעָה נִסְתָּר פְּתָאיִם עָבְרוּ נֶעֱנָשׁוּ:

13 קַח־בִּגְדוֹ כִּי־עָרַב זָר וּבְעַד נָכְרִיָּה חַבְלֵהוּ:

14 מְבָרֵךְ רֵעֵהוּ | בְּקוֹל גָּדוֹל בַּבֹּקֶר הַשְׁכֵּים קְלָלָה תֵּחָשֶׁב לוֹ:

15 An endless dripping on a rainy day
   And a contentious wife are alike;

16 As soon repress her as repress the wind,
   Or declare one's right hand to be oil.

17 As iron sharpens iron
   So a man sharpens the wit of his friend.

18 One who tends a fig tree will enjoy its fruit,
   And one who cares for a master will be honored.

19 As face answers to face in water,
   So does one's heart to another's.

20 Sheol and Abaddon cannot be satisfied,
   Nor can the human eye be satisfied.

21 For silver—the crucible, for gold—the furnace,
   And a person is tested by praise.

22 Even if you pound the fool in a mortar
   With a pestle along with grain,
   His folly will not leave him.

23 Mind well the looks of your flock;
   Pay attention to your herds;

24 For property does not last forever,
   Or a crown for all generations.

25 Grass vanishes, new grass appears,
   And the herbage of the hills is gathered in.

26 The lambs will provide you with clothing,
   The he-goats, the price of a field.

27 The goats' milk will suffice for your food,
   The food of your household,
   And the maintenance of your maids.

15 דֶּלֶף טוֹרֵד בְּיוֹם סַגְרִיר וְאֵשֶׁת (מדונים) [מִדְיָנִים]
בְּשֻׁתָּוָה:

16 צֹפְנֶיהָ צָפַן־רוּחַ וְשֶׁמֶן יְמִינוֹ יִקְרָא:

17 בַּרְזֶל בְּבַרְזֶל יָחַד וְאִישׁ יַחַד פְּנֵי־רֵעֵהוּ:

18 נֹצֵר תְּאֵנָה יֹאכַל פִּרְיָהּ וְשֹׁמֵר אֲדֹנָיו יְכֻבָּד:

19 כַּמַּיִם הַפָּנִים לַפָּנִים כֵּן לֵב־הָאָדָם לָאָדָם:

20 שְׁאוֹל וַאֲבַדֹּה לֹא תִשְׂבַּעְנָה וְעֵינֵי הָאָדָם לֹא תִשְׂבַּעְנָה:

21 מַצְרֵף לַכֶּסֶף וְכוּר לַזָּהָב וְאִישׁ לְפִי מַהֲלָלוֹ:

22 אִם תִּכְתּוֹשׁ־אֶת־הָאֱוִיל | בַּמַּכְתֵּשׁ בְּתוֹךְ הָרִיפוֹת בַּעֱלִי
לֹא־תָסוּר מֵעָלָיו אִוַּלְתּוֹ:

23 יָדֹעַ תֵּדַע פְּנֵי צֹאנֶךָ שִׁית לִבְּךָ לַעֲדָרִים:

24 כִּי לֹא לְעוֹלָם חֹסֶן וְאִם־נֵזֶר לְדוֹר (דור) [וָדוֹר]:

25 גָּלָה חָצִיר וְנִרְאָה־דֶּשֶׁא וְנֶאֶסְפוּ עִשְּׂבוֹת הָרִים:

26 כְּבָשִׂים לִלְבוּשֶׁךָ וּמְחִיר שָׂדֶה עַתּוּדִים:

27 וְדֵי | חֲלֵב עִזִּים לְלַחְמְךָ לְלֶחֶם בֵּיתֶךָ וְחַיִּים לְנַעֲרוֹתֶיךָ:

On Moral Proximity

A close neighbor is better than a distant brother.
—Proverbs 27:10

IT HAS TAKEN THE WORLD many millennia to even come close to the ethical precepts outlined in this verse. In the fields of community organizing and positive relationship building, we learn about the importance of proximity; we cannot talk *about* other populations without talking *to* them first. We have to march together, or behind each other, in solidarity, giving others the agency to create change from within their own communities. We must master the art of listening, the art of being present. It is natural to love a sibling more than a neighbor because of our inborn preference for consanguinity. The verse at hand teaches us a truly profound lesson: our relationships are only as strong as our proximity.

In social justice work, we have transitioned from advocating for equality—where everyone is treated the same no matter what—to equity, a principle that tells us not to enforce the same paradigms for all, but rather requires us to meet people within their respective personal or communal contexts. If we advocate for others with the goal of equality, we do not need to know anything specific about them, since we simply advocate that everyone gets the same. Equity, on the other hand, means that we advocate for what others truly need. To advocate for those with needs different from our own means that we must know them. This requires us to listen and to challenge our beliefs. According to the paradigm of equity, Jews, for example, are the ones who get to determine what constitutes antisemitism. People of color determine what constitutes racism. Women determine what boundaries they need and what constitutes sexism and harassment. Impacted populations *must* be listened to.

Proximity matters when it comes to our ethics. The closer we are, the more obligated to one another we feel. For communitarians, we are responsible to those with whom we are in a community. For nationalists, we are more responsible to those within our own nation. It is not only that their face, as Emmanuel Levinas explains,[1] awakens our responsibility. It is also that the culture and society that we know best is the place where we can contribute most. We need to be cautious of cultural imperialism and aware of moral relativism when we reach to impact societies far away from us. Closer to home, where there are established relationships and where there is deeper mutual understanding, we can offer more.

The philosopher and author Alain de Botton (Switzerland/United Kingdom, 1969) writes movingly about the subject of proximity:

> Prejudice and ethnic strife feed off abstraction. However, the proximity required by a meal—something about handing dishes around, unfurling napkins at the same moment, even asking strangers to pass the salt—disrupts our ability to cling to the belief that outsiders who wear unusual clothes and speak in distinctive accents deserve to be sent home or assaulted.[2]

Proximity enables us to see the stranger as less strange, to ensure that others do not become the Other, that outsiders have access to resources inside. When we see another, smell another, hear another, we cannot ignore their humanity anymore. We see them not as beings of a different race or religion, of a different ethnicity or creed, but as fellows and friends.

Chapter 28

1   A wicked person flees though no one gives chase,
    But the righteous are as confident as a lion.

2   When there is rebellion in the land, many are its rulers;
    But with someone who has understanding and knowledge,
    stability will last.

3   A poor man who withholds what is due to the wretched
    Is like a destructive rain that leaves no food.

4   Those who forsake instruction praise the wicked,
    But those who heed instruction fight them.

5   The wicked cannot discern judgment,
    But those who seek GOD discern all things.

6   Better is a poor man who lives blamelessly
    Than a rich man whose ways are crooked.

7   An intelligent son heeds instruction,
    But he who keeps company with gluttons disgraces his father.

8   He who increases his wealth by loans at discount or interest
    Amasses it for one who is generous to the poor.

9   He who turns a deaf ear to instruction—
    His prayer is an abomination.

10   He who misleads the upright into an evil course
    Will fall into his own pit,
    But the blameless will prosper.

11   A rich man is clever in his own eyes,
    But a perceptive pauper can see through him.

12   When the righteous exult there is great glory,
    But when the wicked rise up, everyone makes themselves scarce.

13   No one who covers up faults will succeed;
    One who confesses and gives them up will find mercy.

פרק כח

1 נָ֣סוּ וְאֵין־רֹדֵ֣ף רָשָׁ֑ע וְ֝צַדִּיקִ֗ים כִּכְפִ֥יר יִבְטָֽח׃

2 בְּפֶ֣שַֽׁע אֶ֭רֶץ רַבִּ֣ים שָׂרֶ֑יהָ וּבְאָדָ֥ם מֵבִ֥ין יֹ֝דֵ֗עַ כֵּ֣ן יַאֲרִֽיךְ׃

3 גֶּ֣בֶר רָ֭שׁ וְעֹשֵׁ֣ק דַּלִּ֑ים מָטָ֥ר סֹ֝חֵ֗ף וְאֵ֣ין לָֽחֶם׃

4 עֹזְבֵ֣י תֹ֭ורָה יְהַֽלְל֣וּ רָשָׁ֑ע וְשֹׁמְרֵ֥י תֹ֝ורָ֗ה יִתְגָּ֥רוּ בָֽם׃

5 אַנְשֵׁי־רָ֭ע לֹא־יָבִ֣ינוּ מִשְׁפָּ֑ט וּמְבַקְשֵׁ֥י יְ֝הוָ֗ה יָבִ֥ינוּ כֹֽל׃

6 טֽוֹב־רָ֭שׁ הוֹלֵ֣ךְ בְּתֻמּ֑וֹ מֵעִקֵּ֥שׁ דְּ֝רָכַ֗יִם וְה֣וּא עָשִֽׁיר׃

7 נוֹצֵ֣ר תֹּ֭ורָה בֵּ֣ן מֵבִ֑ין וְרֹעֶ֥ה זֹֽ֝ולְלִ֗ים יַכְלִ֥ים אָבִֽיו׃

8 מַרְבֶּ֣ה הֹ֭ונוֹ בְּנֶ֣שֶׁךְ (ובתרבית) [וְתַרְבִּ֑ית] לְחוֹנֵ֖ן דַּלִּ֣ים יִקְבְּצֶֽנּוּ׃

9 מֵסִ֣יר אָ֭זְנוֹ מִשְּׁמֹ֣עַ תֹּורָ֑ה גַּֽם־תְּ֝פִלָּת֗וֹ תּוֹעֵבָֽה׃

10 מַשְׁגֶּ֤ה יְשָׁרִ֨ים ׀ בְּדֶ֥רֶךְ רָ֗ע בִּשְׁחוּת֥וֹ הֽוּא־יִפֹּ֑ול וּ֝תְמִימִ֗ים יִנְחֲלוּ־טֹֽוב׃

11 חָכָ֣ם בְּ֭עֵינָיו אִ֣ישׁ עָשִׁ֑יר וְדַ֖ל מֵבִ֣ין יַחְקְרֶֽנּוּ׃

12 בַּעֲלֹ֣ץ צַ֭דִּיקִים רַבָּ֣ה תִפְאָ֑רֶת וּבְק֥וּם רְ֝שָׁעִ֗ים יְחֻפַּ֥שׂ אָדָֽם׃

13 מְכַסֶּ֣ה פְ֭שָׁעָיו לֹ֣א יַצְלִ֑יחַ וּמוֹדֶ֥ה וְ֝עֹזֵ֗ב יְרֻחָֽם׃

14 Happy is the person who is anxious always,
But one who is hard-hearted falls into misfortune.

15 A roaring lion and a prowling bear
Is a wicked man ruling a helpless people.

16 A prince who lacks understanding is very oppressive;
One who spurns ill-gotten gains will live long.

17 Anyone oppressed by bloodguilt will flee to a pit;
Let none offer support.

18 One who lives blamelessly will be delivered,
But one whose ways are crooked will fall all at once.

19 Those who till their land will have food in plenty,
But those who pursue vanities will have poverty in plenty.

20 A dependable man will receive many blessings,
But one in a hurry to get rich will not go unpunished.

21 To be partial is not right;
Even one who is valiant may do wrong for a piece of bread.

22 A miserly man runs after wealth;
He does not realize that loss will overtake it.

23 One who reproves a person will in the end
Find more favor than a flatterer.

24 Anyone who robs their father and mother and says,
"It is no offense,"
Is the companion to a vandal.

25 A gaping maw provokes quarrels,
But one who trusts GOD shall enjoy prosperity.

26 Those who trust their own instincts are dullards,
But those who live by wisdom shall escape.

27 Those who give to the poor will not be in want,
But those who turn a blind eye will be roundly cursed.

28 When the wicked rise up, everyone goes into hiding,
But when they perish the righteous increase.

אַשְׁרֵי אָדָם מְפַחֵד תָּמִיד וּמַקְשֶׁה לִבּוֹ יִפּוֹל בְּרָעָה: 14

אֲרִי־נֹהֵם וְדֹב שׁוֹקֵק מֹשֵׁל רָשָׁע עַל עַם־דָּל: 15

נָגִיד חֲסַר תְּבוּנוֹת וְרַב מַעֲשַׁקּוֹת (שנאי) [שֹׂנֵא] 16
בֶּצַע יַאֲרִיךְ יָמִים:

אָדָם עָשֻׁק בְּדַם־נָפֶשׁ עַד־בּוֹר יָנוּס אַל־יִתְמְכוּ־בוֹ: 17

הוֹלֵךְ תָּמִים יִוָּשֵׁעַ וְנֶעְקַשׁ דְּרָכַיִם יִפּוֹל בְּאֶחָת: 18

עֹבֵד אַדְמָתוֹ יִשְׂבַּע־לָחֶם וּמְרַדֵּף רֵיקִים יִשְׂבַּע־רִישׁ: 19

אִישׁ אֱמוּנוֹת רַב־בְּרָכוֹת וְאָץ לְהַעֲשִׁיר לֹא יִנָּקֶה: 20

הַכֵּר־פָּנִים לֹא־טוֹב וְעַל־פַּת־לֶחֶם יִפְשַׁע־גָּבֶר: 21

נִבְהָל לַהוֹן אִישׁ רַע עָיִן וְלֹא־יֵדַע כִּי־חֶסֶר יְבֹאֶנּוּ: 22

מוֹכִיחַ אָדָם אַחֲרַי חֵן יִמְצָא מִמַּחֲלִיק לָשׁוֹן: 23

גּוֹזֵל | אָבִיו וְאִמּוֹ וְאֹמֵר אֵין־פָּשַׁע חָבֵר הוּא 24
לְאִישׁ מַשְׁחִית:

רְחַב־נֶפֶשׁ יְגָרֶה מָדוֹן וּבֹטֵחַ עַל־יְהֹוָה יְדֻשָּׁן: 25

בּוֹטֵחַ בְּלִבּוֹ הוּא כְסִיל וְהוֹלֵךְ בְּחָכְמָה הוּא יִמָּלֵט: 26

נוֹתֵן לָרָשׁ אֵין מַחְסוֹר וּמַעְלִים עֵינָיו רַב־מְאֵרוֹת: 27

בְּקוּם רְשָׁעִים יִסָּתֵר אָדָם וּבְאָבְדָם יִרְבּוּ צַדִּיקִים: 28

When the Marginalized Marginalize

A poor man who withholds what is due to the wretched
Is like a destructive rain that leaves no food.
　　—Proverbs 28:3

WE ARE NOT SURPRISED when the richest, most powerful, and most privileged members of our society oppress minorities. Such dynamics have always been present, whether in the person of a king unfairly taxing his peasants or in the form of large multinational corporations expropriating the land of native peoples. When the marginalized oppress other marginalized populations, however, it startles us: Why would any Jewish person be racist? Why would a person of color be antisemitic? Why would a poor person steal from an even poorer person?

It is an unfortunate reality that human beings seek to oppress others not only to enhance their riches but also to gain access to limited and basic resources such as water, food, and shelter. Most marginalized populations are not well-organized into supportive coalitions and alliances. There is a lot of distrust. They have been exploited and betrayed too many times.

There also seems to be a tendency to cut down members of other groups with slightly more privileges. We often hold resentments toward those who seem to be just slightly better off than us. The need to get ahead and cut others down is destructive. It undermines the potential for relationship building and partnership.

Part of the healing work that brings communities close is the ability to build trust in each other.

In a scarcity model of economics, which is based on the true assumption of having limited resources, a zero-sum game approach will inevitably leave everyone a little more impoverished. As this verse in Proverbs warns us, it will be like a destructive rain that leaves no food for anyone.

When I met the Spinka Rebbe, a leader in the Chasidic community (of the Horowitz lineage), when he visited my hometown, I asked him why God waited until Abraham was seventy-five to say *lech l'cha*, leave your country, family, friends, and everyone you know. The rebbe has a profound spiritual air about him. His face is wise and his mind steeped in Talmudic wisdom. When I had the ability to pray near him, I could feel his radiating energy. After I posited this question to him, the rebbe pulled me close. He whispered, "God waited until Abraham had the *koach*—'spiritual strength'—to handle such a charge."

Secular society teaches that young people possess the greatest strength, beauty, and influence. The Spinka Rebbe, on the other hand, tells us that we need to live a life of constant moral and spiritual growth so that we reach pride, wisdom, and strength as we get older. As elders, we should not be marginalized as fossils and treated as worthless bygones. Rather, we should become the most capable, noble, and wise leaders of our communities.

Marginalization is a real problem found throughout all portions of society. But we do not have to succumb to it, even when it would be to our material advantage. We are called to help others, rather than hurt them. We are called to learn about our interconnectivity with others. Yes, we are different, but our differences should not divide us. We should not strive to gain hegemony over those whose weaknesses we can exploit. If we leave our comfort zone and talk and live with others different from ourselves, we will realize who we truly are.

Chapter 29

1   One oft reproved may become stiffnecked—
    But then will be suddenly broken beyond repair.

2   When the righteous become great the people rejoice,
    But when the wicked dominate the people groan.

3   A man who loves wisdom brings joy to his father,
    But he who keeps company with harlots will lose his wealth.

4   By justice a king sustains the land,
    But a fraudulent man tears it down.

5   A man who flatters his fellow
    Spreads a net for his feet.

6   An evil man's offenses are a trap for himself,
    But a righteous person sings out joyously.

7   The righteous are concerned with the cause of the wretched;
    The wicked cannot understand such concern.

8   Scoffers inflame a city,
    But the wise allay anger.

9   When someone who is wise enters into litigation with a fool
    There is ranting and ridicule, but no satisfaction.

10   Those who are bloodthirsty detest the blameless,
    But the upright seek them out.

11   A dullard gives full vent to rage,
    But a wise person calms it down.

12   A ruler who listens to lies—
    All his ministers will be wicked.

13   The poor and the fraudulent meet;
    GOD gives luster to the eyes of both.

פרק כט

1 אִישׁ תּוֹכָחוֹת מַקְשֶׁה־עֹרֶף פֶּתַע יִשָּׁבֵר וְאֵין מַרְפֵּא:

2 בִּרְבוֹת צַדִּיקִים יִשְׂמַח הָעָם וּבִמְשֹׁל רָשָׁע יֵאָנַח עָם:

3 אִישׁ־אֹהֵב חָכְמָה יְשַׂמַּח אָבִיו וְרֹעֶה זוֹנוֹת יְאַבֶּד־הוֹן:

4 מֶלֶךְ בְּמִשְׁפָּט יַעֲמִיד אָרֶץ וְאִישׁ תְּרוּמוֹת יֶהֶרְסֶנָּה:

5 גֶּבֶר מַחֲלִיק עַל־רֵעֵהוּ רֶשֶׁת פּוֹרֵשׂ עַל־פְּעָמָיו:

6 בְּפֶשַׁע אִישׁ רָע מוֹקֵשׁ וְצַדִּיק יָרוּן וְשָׂמֵחַ:

7 יֹדֵעַ צַדִּיק דִּין דַּלִּים רָשָׁע לֹא־יָבִין דָּעַת:

8 אַנְשֵׁי לָצוֹן יָפִיחוּ קִרְיָה וַחֲכָמִים יָשִׁיבוּ אָף:

9 אִישׁ־חָכָם נִשְׁפָּט אֶת־אִישׁ אֱוִיל וְרָגַז וְשָׂחַק וְאֵין נָחַת:

10 אַנְשֵׁי דָמִים יִשְׂנְאוּ־תָם וִישָׁרִים יְבַקְשׁוּ נַפְשׁוֹ:

11 כָּל־רוּחוֹ יוֹצִיא כְסִיל וְחָכָם בְּאָחוֹר יְשַׁבְּחֶנָּה:

12 מֹשֵׁל מַקְשִׁיב עַל־דְּבַר־שָׁקֶר כָּל־מְשָׁרְתָיו רְשָׁעִים:

13 רָשׁ וְאִישׁ תְּכָכִים נִפְגָּשׁוּ מֵאִיר עֵינֵי שְׁנֵיהֶם יְהוָה:

14 A king who judges the wretched honestly—
   His throne will be established forever.

15 Rod and reproof produce wisdom,
   But a youth out of control is a disgrace to his mother.

16 When the wicked increase, offenses increase,
   But the righteous will see their downfall.

17 Discipline your son and he will give you peace;
   He will gratify you with dainties.

18 For lack of vision a people lose restraint,
   But happy is he who heeds instruction.

19 A slave cannot be disciplined by words;
   Though he may comprehend, he does not respond.

20 If you see a man hasty in speech,
   There is more hope for a fool than for him.

21 A slave pampered from youth
   Will come to a bad end.

22 An angry man provokes a quarrel;
   A hothead commits many offenses.

23 Pride of mortals will bring humiliation,
   But one who is humble will obtain honor.

24 He who shares with a thief is his own enemy;
   He hears the imprecation and does not tell.

25 A person's fears become a trap,
   But one who trusts in GOD shall be safeguarded.

26 Many seek audience with a ruler,
   But it is from GOD that a [wronged] party gets justice.

27 The unjust man is an abomination to the righteous,
   And one whose way is straight is an abomination to the wicked.

מֶ֣לֶךְ שׁוֹפֵ֣ט בֶּאֱמֶ֣ת דַּלִּ֑ים כִּ֝סְא֗וֹ לָעַ֥ד יִכּֽוֹן׃ 14

שֵׁ֣בֶט וְ֭תוֹכַחַת יִתֵּ֣ן חָכְמָ֑ה וְנַ֥עַר מְ֝שֻׁלָּ֗ח מֵבִ֥ישׁ אִמּֽוֹ׃ 15

בִּרְב֣וֹת רְ֭שָׁעִים יִרְבֶּה־פָּ֑שַׁע וְ֝צַדִּיקִ֗ים בְּֽמַפַּלְתָּ֥ם יִרְאֽוּ׃ 16

יַסֵּ֣ר בִּ֭נְךָ וִֽינִיחֶ֑ךָ וְיִתֵּ֖ן מַעֲדַנִּ֣ים לְנַפְשֶֽׁךָ׃ 17

בְּאֵ֣ין חָ֭זוֹן יִפָּ֣רַֽע עָ֑ם וְשֹׁמֵ֖ר תּוֹרָ֣ה אַשְׁרֵֽהוּ׃ 18

בִּ֭דְבָרִים לֹא־יִוָּ֣סֶר עָ֑בֶד כִּֽי־יָ֝בִ֗ין וְאֵ֣ין מַעֲנֶֽה׃ 19

חָזִ֗יתָ אִ֭ישׁ אָ֣ץ בִּדְבָרָ֑יו תִּקְוָ֖ה לִכְסִ֣יל מִמֶּֽנּוּ׃ 20

מְפַנֵּ֣ק מִנֹּ֣עַר עַבְדּ֑וֹ וְ֝אַחֲרִית֗וֹ יִהְיֶ֥ה מָנֽוֹן׃ 21

אִֽישׁ־אַ֭ף יְגָרֶ֣ה מָד֑וֹן וּבַ֖עַל חֵמָ֣ה רַב־פָּֽשַׁע׃ 22

גַּאֲוַ֣ת אָ֭דָם תַּשְׁפִּילֶ֑נּוּ וּשְׁפַל־ר֝֗וּחַ יִתְמֹ֥ךְ כָּבֽוֹד׃ 23

חוֹלֵ֣ק עִם־גַּ֭נָּב שׂוֹנֵ֣א נַפְשׁ֑וֹ אָלָ֥ה יִ֝שְׁמַ֗ע וְלֹ֣א יַגִּֽיד׃ 24

חֶרְדַּ֣ת אָ֭דָם יִתֵּ֣ן מוֹקֵ֑שׁ וּבוֹטֵ֖חַ בַּיהֹוָ֣ה יְשֻׂגָּֽב׃ 25

רַ֭בִּים מְבַקְשִׁ֣ים פְּנֵי־מוֹשֵׁ֑ל וּ֝מֵיהֹוָ֗ה מִשְׁפַּט־אִֽישׁ׃ 26

תּוֹעֲבַ֣ת צַ֭דִּיקִים אִ֣ישׁ עָ֑וֶל וְתוֹעֲבַ֖ת רָשָׁ֣ע יְשַׁר־דָּֽרֶךְ׃ 27

When the Poor and Oppressor Meet

The poor and the fraudulent meet;
GOD gives luster to the eyes of both.
—Proverbs 29:13

THE VERSE AT HAND seems to refer to an encounter between a struggling debtor and a fraudulent creditor, a relationship that embodies the cruel power dynamics at play in times of financial duress. Such a relationship can be likened to that between any type of victim and oppressor. What happens when two people, one with the intent to mistreat the other, meet face-to-face? Will there be violence? Will there be bloodshed? Will there be tears? Will financial exploitation lead to abuse, emotional trauma, or physical harm? Or, perhaps, will the encounter evoke compassion?

There is only One. There is only unity.

This verse from the Book of Proverbs teaches the importance of a face-to-face encounter where people's notions of the other are challenged. This challenging moment allows God to enter the souls of both people, becoming a divine link between them. Whenever one person can truly see another, in their full humanity, in that moment of intersubjectivity, compassion can arise. Empathy emerges in ways that would be more difficult from a distance.

But empathy does not only potentially arise in the oppressor. Potentially, the oppressed can also see the humanity of the oppressor. That softening of the eyes of the oppressed might soften the oppressor's eyes as well. For a moment, they might realize the absurdity of their inequalities and that each of them—each of us—suffers in their own ways.

There is only One. There is only unity.

According to D. H. Lawrence (United Kingdom, 1885–1930), it is only through interacting with the realm of the ineffable and irrational that we are able to live on this earth. As he writes metaphorically:

> Water is H2O
> Hydrogen two parts
> Oxygen one
> But there is also a third thing, that makes it water
> And nobody knows what that is.[1]

Human beings can be right next to each other, seemingly unconnected, but only one spark is needed to transform the moment. Indeed, the skill needed to light that spark of true human interconnectedness is of critical importance today, as we are more connected than ever before but increasingly drifting apart.

The miracle of illuminated eyes, allowing us to truly encounter another, might not always lead to a total reversal of perceptions among conflicting parties, but we can hope at least that their relationship might soften in even the most subtle of ways, removing some stress, tension, and fear.

This point is made by the prophet Isaiah in the first chapter of his work, where he declares that the emphasis should be placed on one's relationship with others, as opposed to one's relationship to God. As the prophet puts it:

> And when you lift up your hands,
> I will turn My eyes away from you;
> Though you pray at length,
> I will not listen.
> Your hands are stained with crime—
> Wash yourselves clean;
> Put your evil doings
> Away from My sight.
> Cease to do evil;
> Learn to do good.
> Devote yourselves to justice;
> Aid the wronged.
> Uphold the rights of the orphan;

Defend the cause of the widow.
  (Isaiah 1:15–17)

Rather than our prayer, God wants our eyes to turn away from the heavens and back down to earth, to the divine image in humanity. Religion must soften our hard spots; religion must weaken our callous spots. Torah must open our eyes to the divine manifestations in this world rather than pushing us to evade the human gaze.

We must see and internalize the godliness within each human being. In the words of the Sufi tradition:

I saw my Lord with the eye of my heart.
He said, "Who are you?" I said, "I am You."[2]

There is only One. There is only unity.

When we see that unity within ourselves, we can start to see it within others as well. We can work together to make our world a better place. "Do not rob the powerless because they are powerless!" (Proverbs 22:22).

Chapter 30

1 The words of Agur son of Jakeh, [man of] Massa; the speech
of the man to Ithiel, to Ithiel and Ucal:

2 I am more brutish than anyone else;
I lack common sense.

3 I have not learned wisdom,
Nor do I possess knowledge of the Holy One.

4 Who has ascended heaven and come down?
Who has gathered up the wind in the hollow of his hand?
Who has wrapped the waters in his garment?
Who has established all the extremities of the earth?
What is his name or his son's name, if you know it?

5 Every word of God is pure,
A shield to those who seek refuge.

6 Do not add to God's words,
Lest you be indicted and proved to be a liar.

7 Two things I ask of You; do not deny them to me before I die:

8 Keep lies and false words far from me;
Give me neither poverty nor riches,
But provide me with my daily bread,

9 Lest, being sated, I renounce, saying,
"Who is GOD?"
Or, being impoverished, I take to theft
And profane the name of my God.

10 Do not inform on a slave to his master,
Lest he curse you and you incur guilt.

פרק ל

1 דִּבְרֵ֤י ׀ אָג֣וּר בִּן־יָקֶה֮ הַמַּשָּׂ֒א נְאֻ֤ם הַגֶּ֨בֶר לְאִֽיתִיאֵ֑ל לְאִיתִיאֵ֥ל וְאֻכָֽל׃

2 כִּ֤י בַ֣עַר אָנֹכִ֣י מֵאִ֑ישׁ וְלֹֽא־בִינַ֖ת אָדָ֣ם לִֽי׃

3 וְלֹֽא־לָמַ֥דְתִּי חׇכְמָ֑ה וְדַ֖עַת קְדֹשִׁ֣ים אֵדָֽע׃

4 מִ֤י עָלָֽה־שָׁמַ֨יִם ׀ וַיֵּרַ֡ד מִ֤י אָֽסַף־ר֨וּחַ ׀ בְּחׇפְנָ֗יו מִ֤י צָֽרַר־מַ֨יִם ׀ בַּשִּׂמְלָ֗ה מִ֭י הֵקִ֣ים כׇּל־אַפְסֵי־אָ֑רֶץ מַה־שְּׁמ֥וֹ וּמַֽה־שֶּׁם־בְּ֝נ֗וֹ כִּ֣י תֵדָֽע׃

5 כׇּל־אִמְרַ֣ת אֱל֣וֹהַּ צְרוּפָ֑ה מָגֵ֥ן ה֝֗וּא לַחֹסִ֥ים בּֽוֹ׃

6 אַל־תּ֥וֹסְףְּ עַל־דְּבָרָ֑יו פֶּן־יוֹכִ֖יחַ בְּךָ֣ וְנִכְזָֽבְתָּ׃

7 שְׁ֭תַּיִם שָׁאַ֣לְתִּי מֵאִתָּ֑ךְ אַל־תִּמְנַ֥ע מִ֝מֶּ֗נִּי בְּטֶ֣רֶם אָמֽוּת׃

8 שָׁ֤וְא ׀ וּֽדְבַר־כָּזָ֡ב הַרְחֵ֬ק מִמֶּ֗נִּי רֵ֣אשׁ וָ֭עֹשֶׁר אַל־תִּֽתֶּן־לִ֑י הַ֝טְרִיפֵ֗נִי לֶ֣חֶם חֻקִּֽי׃

9 פֶּ֥ן אֶשְׂבַּ֨ע ׀ וְכִחַשְׁתִּי֮ וְאָמַ֗רְתִּי מִ֥י יְה֫וָ֥ה וּפֶֽן־אִוָּרֵ֥שׁ וְגָנַ֑בְתִּי וְ֝תָפַ֗שְׂתִּי שֵׁ֣ם אֱלֹהָֽי׃

10 אַל־תַּלְשֵׁ֣ן עֶ֭בֶד אֶל־אֲדֹנָ֑ו פֶּֽן־יְקַלֶּלְךָ֥ וְאָשָֽׁמְתָּ׃

11 There is a breed of people that brings a curse on its fathers
    And brings no blessing to its mothers,

12 A breed that thinks itself pure,
    Though it is not washed of its filth;

13 A breed so haughty of bearing, so supercilious;

14 A breed whose teeth are swords,
    Whose jaws are knives,
    Ready to devour the poor of the land,
    The needy among us.

15 The leech has two daughters, "Give!" and "Give!"
    Three things are insatiable;
    Four never say, "Enough!":

16 Sheol, a barren womb,
    Earth that cannot get enough water,
    And fire which never says, "Enough!"

17 The eye that mocks a father
    And disdains the homage due a mother—
    The ravens of the brook will gouge it out,
    Young eagles will devour it.

18 Three things are beyond me;
    Four I cannot fathom:

19 How an eagle makes its way over the sky;
    How a snake makes its way over a rock;
    How a ship makes its way through the high seas;
    How a man has his way with a maiden.

20 Such is the way of an adulteress:
    She eats, wipes her mouth,
    And says, "I have done no wrong."

21 The earth shudders at three things,
    At four which it cannot bear:

22 A slave who becomes king;
    A scoundrel sated with food;

11 דּ֥וֹר אָבִ֥יו יְקַלֵּ֑ל וְאֶת־אִ֝מּ֗וֹ לֹ֣א יְבָרֵֽךְ׃

12 דּ֭וֹר טָה֣וֹר בְּעֵינָ֑יו וּ֝מִצֹּאָת֗וֹ לֹ֣א רֻחָֽץ׃

13 דּ֭וֹר מָה־רָמ֣וּ עֵינָ֑יו וְ֝עַפְעַפָּ֗יו יִנָּשֵֽׂאוּ׃

14 דּ֤וֹר ׀ חֲרָב֣וֹת שִׁנָּיו֮ וּֽמַאֲכָל֢וֹת מְֽתַלְּעֹ֫תָ֥יו לֶאֱכֹ֣ל עֲנִיִּ֣ים
מֵאֶ֑רֶץ וְ֝אֶבְיוֹנִ֗ים מֵאָדָֽם׃

15 לַֽעֲלוּקָ֨ה ׀ שְׁתֵּ֥י בָנוֹת֮ הַ֤ב ׀ הַ֥ב שָׁל֣וֹשׁ הֵ֭נָּה לֹ֣א תִשְׂבַּ֑עְנָה
אַ֝רְבַּ֗ע לֹא־אָ֥מְרוּ הֽוֹן׃

16 שְׁא֖וֹל וְעֹ֣צֶר רָ֑חַם אֶ֗רֶץ לֹא־שָׂ֥בְעָה מַּ֝֗יִם וְ֝אֵ֗שׁ
לֹא־אָ֥מְרָה הֽוֹן׃

17 עַ֤יִן ׀ תִּֽלְעַ֣ג לְאָב֮ וְתָב֢וּז לִֽיקְּהַ֫ת־אֵ֥ם יִקְּר֥וּהָ עֹרְבֵי־נַ֑חַל
וְֽיֹאכְל֥וּהָ בְנֵי־נָֽשֶׁר׃

18 שְׁלֹשָׁ֣ה הֵ֭מָּה נִפְלְא֣וּ מִמֶּ֑נִּי (וארבע) [וְ֝אַרְבָּעָ֗ה]
לֹ֣א יְדַעְתִּֽים׃

19 דֶּ֤רֶךְ הַנֶּ֨שֶׁר ׀ בַּשָּׁמַ֗יִם֮ דֶּ֥רֶךְ נָחָ֢שׁ עֲלֵ֫י־צ֥וּר דֶּֽרֶךְ־אֳנִיָּ֥ה
בְלֶב־יָ֑ם וְדֶ֖רֶךְ גֶּ֣בֶר בְּעַלְמָֽה׃

20 כֵּ֤ן ׀ דֶּ֥רֶךְ אִשָּׁ֗ה מְנָ֫אָ֥פֶת אָ֭כְלָה וּמָ֣חֲתָ֣ה פִ֑יהָ וְ֝אָמְרָ֗ה
לֹֽא־פָעַ֥לְתִּי אָֽוֶן׃

21 תַּ֣חַת שָׁ֭לוֹשׁ רָ֣גְזָה אֶ֑רֶץ וְתַ֥חַת אַ֝רְבַּ֗ע לֹא־תוּכַ֥ל שְׂאֵֽת׃

22 תַּֽחַת־עֶ֭בֶד כִּ֣י יִמְל֑וֹךְ וְ֝נָבָ֗ל כִּ֣י יִֽשְׂבַּֽע־לָֽחֶם׃

23 A loathsome woman who gets married;
   A slave-girl who supplants her mistress.

24 Four are among the tiniest on earth,
   Yet they are the wisest of the wise:
25 Ants are a folk without power,
   Yet they prepare food for themselves in summer;
26 The badger is a folk without strength,
   Yet it makes its home in the rock;
27 The locusts have no king,
   Yet they all march forth in formation;
28 You can catch the lizard in your hand,
   Yet it is found in royal palaces.

29 There are three that are stately of stride,
   Four that carry themselves well:
30 The lion is mightiest among the beasts,
   And recoils before none;
31 The greyhound, the he-goat,
   The king whom none dares resist.

32 If you have been scandalously arrogant,
   If you have been a schemer,
   Then clap your hand to your mouth.
33 As milk under pressure produces butter,
   And a nose under pressure produces blood,
   So patience under pressure produces strife.

23 תַּחַת שְׁנוּאָה כִּי תִבָּעֵל וְשִׁפְחָה כִּי־תִירַשׁ גְּבִרְתָּהּ׃

24 אַרְבָּעָה הֵם קְטַנֵּי־אָרֶץ וְהֵמָּה חֲכָמִים מְחֻכָּמִים׃

25 הַנְּמָלִים עַם לֹא־עָז וַיָּכִינוּ בַקַּיִץ לַחְמָם׃

26 שְׁפַנִּים עַם לֹא־עָצוּם וַיָּשִׂימוּ בַסֶּלַע בֵּיתָם׃

27 מֶלֶךְ אֵין לָאַרְבֶּה וַיֵּצֵא חֹצֵץ כֻּלּוֹ׃

28 שְׂמָמִית בְּיָדַיִם תְּתַפֵּשׂ וְהִיא בְּהֵיכְלֵי מֶלֶךְ׃

29 שְׁלֹשָׁה הֵמָּה מֵיטִיבֵי צָעַד וְאַרְבָּעָה מֵיטִבֵי לָכֶת׃

30 לַיִשׁ גִּבּוֹר בַּבְּהֵמָה וְלֹא־יָשׁוּב מִפְּנֵי־כֹל׃

31 זַרְזִיר מָתְנַיִם אוֹ־תָיִשׁ וּמֶלֶךְ אַלְקוּם עִמּוֹ׃

32 אִם־נָבַלְתָּ בְהִתְנַשֵּׂא וְאִם־זַמּוֹתָ יָד לְפֶה׃

33 כִּי מִיץ חָלָב יוֹצִיא חֶמְאָה וּמִיץ־אַף יוֹצִיא דָם וּמִיץ אַפַּיִם יוֹצִיא רִיב׃

Is Judaism about the Heavens?

Who has ascended heaven and come down?
  —Proverbs 30:4

THE STRAIGHTFORWARD MESSAGE found in this verse is the awareness that religious humility is a precious trait. We are limited mortal beings. The heavens are limitless. No person has gone up to heaven and come back to tell the tale. We do not know what God looks like. We do not know what radiates from God's being. We do not know anything tangible—indeed, even whether there is anything tangible—about the world-beyond-this-world. All we know regarding the afterlife is based on religious texts (which raise as many questions as they resolve), spiritual insights, and oral traditions, which we hold today with a healthy sense of humble skepticism.[1]

A vital point to be learned from this text is that not only can we not go up to heaven, but we should not. Jewish tradition focuses on our lives here and now. Our sacred role is to work to actualize sacredness in this specific life and to improve this world around us. There may be a heaven, there may be reincarnation, and there may be a soul that journeys, but our primary focus is to do what we can to ensure that our world looks more like what we hope the world-to-come will look like: a world of of kindness and justice.

It is easy to believe that everyone is selfish and all systems of human interaction—be they in the realm of politics, sports, medicine, or even religion—are corrupt. Such cynicism runs rampant. Believing that others around us are fundamentally bad is not merely an innocent, if flawed, perception about them; it also has the power to change us for the worst. "The fear of exploitation by takers is so pervasive," writes the Cornell economist Robert Frank, that "by encouraging us to expect the worst in others it brings out the worst in us: dreading the role of the chump, we are often loath to heed our nobler instincts."[2] When we assume that everyone is greedy, we can become greedy too, bringing out our worst instincts. Mark Twain acknowledged this our tendency by writing sarcastically about "the principle of give and take; that is diplomacy—give one and take ten."[3]

True kindness is acting for another without any expectation of gaining anything at all. As Samuel Johnson purportedly writes, "The true measure of a man is how he treats someone who can do him absolutely no good."[4] In Jewish terms, this sentiment is expressed in the term used for the holy work of preparing a dead body for burial: *chesed shel emet*, "kindness of truth." The term is used to underscore the importance of treating everyone with kindness, even the dead, who cannot return the favor.

At a point when we become cynical about our own neighbors, we have almost certainly become extremely cynical about those in authority not in our presence. Krista Tippett, a journalist and entrepreneur, writes:

> People ask me about the common denominators of the wisest people I've encountered. Alongside all the virtues that accompany and anchor wisdom, there is a characteristic physical presence that Jean Vanier epitomizes with others I've met like Desmond Tutu, Wangari Maathai, Thích Nhât Hanh. Here's what it feels like, what I can report: an embodied capacity to hold power and tenderness in a surprising, creative interplay. This way of being is palpable, and refreshing, and in its way jarring, hard to figure out. Among other things, it transmutes my sense of what power feels like and is there for. This is the closest I can come to describing the sense I have, of wisdom incarnate, and it is an experience of physical presence as much as consciousness and spirit.[5]

There are great people in the world, today and throughout history, and we must cling to stories about them. Judaism is not in the heavens. We do not seek to live like heavenly angels. Rather, we seek to live like earthly angels. Each of us can become like an angel. An earthly angel is someone who shows up for someone else at their time of need. They may save their life. They may simply lift their spirits. They do it without expecting anything in return. That is a great person.

In the Chasidic tradition, we cling to both the living among our masters and to stories about the deceased. As Professor Samuel Heilman, a sociologist who focuses on Chasidic dynasties, writes:

> In line with the Talmudic dictum (BT *Berachot* 18b) that *"zaddikim b'motam nikraim chaim"* (the righteous in their death are called living), some Hasidism tried to maintain their relationships with the departed *zaddik* as if he were still guiding them and acting on their behalf from the world beyond, a continuation of an old tradition of praying at the graves of the righteous and hoping for their intercession on high.[6]

Such a practice, actualizing a deceased person's legacy to influence present events and decisions, is not limited to the Chasidic tradition. For example, the memory of Mahatma Gandhi has the ability to serve as a spiritual wake-up call to each of us. What he meant by his teaching "Be the change that you wish to see in the world!"[7] is that each of us must be radically committed to self-transformation. When we see politicians who lie and cheat, we must not only call them out but also double down on our own commitment to truth and integrity. When we see bullies who oppress and steal, we must recommit ourselves to ethics and justice. When we see others spew hate and marginalize the weak, we must become agents of love.

Souls may return to the heavens, but the moral teachings and modeling of great people must remain present here on earth. We not only fight the darkness; we also bring forth light! Gandhi's memory inspires each of us to call out the evils of our day while engaging in the sacred work of deep inner transformation that will truly lead to the repair of the world. More than a political revolution, we need a spiritual evolution that leads us all to hold a deeper spiritual consciousness of all.

Chapter 31

1 The words of Lemuel, king of Massa,
   with which his mother admonished him:

2 No, my son!
   No, O son of my womb!
   No, O son of my vows!

3 Do not give your strength to women,
   Your vigor, to those who destroy kings.

4 Wine is not for kings, O Lemuel;
   Not for kings to drink,
   Nor any strong drink for princes,

5 Lest they drink and forget what has been ordained,
   And infringe on the rights of the poor.

6 Give strong drink to the hapless
   And wine to the embittered.

7 Let them drink and forget their poverty,
   And put their troubles out of mind.

8 Speak up for the dumb,
   For the rights of all the unfortunate.

9 Speak up, judge righteously,
   Champion the poor and the needy.

10 א How precious is a woman of substance!
   Her worth is far beyond that of rubies.

11 ב Her husband puts his confidence in her,
   And lacks no good thing.

12 ג She is good to him, never bad,
   All the days of her life.

פרק לא

1 דִּבְרֵי לְמוּאֵל מֶלֶךְ מַשָּׂא אֲשֶׁר־יִסְּרַתּוּ אִמּוֹ:

2 מַה־בְּרִי וּמַה־בַּר־בִּטְנִי וּמֶה בַּר־נְדָרָי:

3 אַל־תִּתֵּן לַנָּשִׁים חֵילֶךָ וּדְרָכֶיךָ לַמְחוֹת מְלָכִין:

4 אַל לַמְלָכִים | לְמוֹאֵל אַל לַמְלָכִים שְׁתוֹ־יָיִן וּלְרוֹזְנִים (אוֹ) [אֵי] שֵׁכָר:

5 פֶּן־יִשְׁתֶּה וְיִשְׁכַּח מְחֻקָּק וִישַׁנֶּה דִּין כָּל־בְּנֵי־עֹנִי:

6 תְּנוּ־שֵׁכָר לְאוֹבֵד וְיַיִן לְמָרֵי נָפֶשׁ:

7 יִשְׁתֶּה וְיִשְׁכַּח רִישׁוֹ וַעֲמָלוֹ לֹא יִזְכָּר־עוֹד:

8 פְּתַח־פִּיךָ לְאִלֵּם אֶל־דִּין כָּל־בְּנֵי חֲלוֹף:

9 פְּתַח־פִּיךָ שְׁפָט־צֶדֶק וְדִין עָנִי וְאֶבְיוֹן:

10 אֵשֶׁת־חַיִל מִי יִמְצָא וְרָחֹק מִפְּנִינִים מִכְרָהּ:

11 בָּטַח בָּהּ לֵב בַּעְלָהּ וְשָׁלָל לֹא יֶחְסָר:

12 גְּמָלַתְהוּ טוֹב וְלֹא־רָע כֹּל יְמֵי חַיֶּיהָ:

13 ד She looks for wool and flax,
And sets her hand to them with a will.

14 ה She is like a merchant fleet,
Bringing her food from afar.

15 ו She rises while it is still night,
And supplies provisions for her household,
The daily fare of her maids.

16 ז She sets her mind on an estate and acquires it;
She plants a vineyard by her own labors.

17 ח She girds herself with strength,
And performs her tasks with vigor.

18 ט She sees that her business thrives;
Her lamp never goes out at night.

19 י She sets her hand to the distaff;
Her fingers work the spindle.

20 כ She gives generously to the poor;
Her hands are stretched out to the needy.

21 ל She is not worried for her household because of snow,
For her whole household is dressed in crimson.

22 מ She makes covers for herself;
Her clothing is linen and purple.

23 נ Her husband is prominent in the gates,
As he sits among the elders of the land.

24 ס She makes cloth and sells it,
And offers a girdle to the merchant.

25 ע She is clothed with strength and splendor;
She looks to the future cheerfully.

26 פ Her mouth is full of wisdom,
Her tongue with kindly teaching.

27 צ She oversees the activities of her household
And never eats the bread of idleness.

28 ק Her children declare her happy;
Her husband praises her,

דָּרְשָׁה צֶמֶר וּפִשְׁתֵּים וַתַּעַשׂ בְּחֵפֶץ כַּפֶּיהָ: 13

הָיְתָה כָּאֳנִיּוֹת סוֹחֵר מִמֶּרְחָק תָּבִיא לַחְמָהּ: 14

וַתָּקָם | בְּעוֹד לַיְלָה וַתִּתֵּן טֶרֶף לְבֵיתָהּ וְחֹק לְנַעֲרֹתֶיהָ: 15

זָמְמָה שָׂדֶה וַתִּקָּחֵהוּ מִפְּרִי כַפֶּיהָ (נטע) [נָטְעָה] כָּרֶם: 16

חָגְרָה בְעוֹז מָתְנֶיהָ וַתְּאַמֵּץ זְרוֹעֹתֶיהָ: 17

טָעֲמָה כִּי־טוֹב סַחְרָהּ לֹא־יִכְבֶּה (בליל) [בַלַּיְלָה] נֵרָהּ: 18

יָדֶיהָ שִׁלְּחָה בַכִּישׁוֹר וְכַפֶּיהָ תָּמְכוּ פָלֶךְ: 19

כַּפָּהּ פָּרְשָׂה לֶעָנִי וְיָדֶיהָ שִׁלְּחָה לָאֶבְיוֹן: 20

לֹא־תִירָא לְבֵיתָהּ מִשָּׁלֶג כִּי כָל־בֵּיתָהּ לָבֻשׁ שָׁנִים: 21

מַרְבַדִּים עָשְׂתָה־לָּהּ שֵׁשׁ וְאַרְגָּמָן לְבוּשָׁהּ: 22

נוֹדָע בַּשְּׁעָרִים בַּעְלָהּ בְּשִׁבְתּוֹ עִם־זִקְנֵי־אָרֶץ: 23

סָדִין עָשְׂתָה וַתִּמְכֹּר וַחֲגוֹר נָתְנָה לַכְּנַעֲנִי: 24

עֹז־וְהָדָר לְבוּשָׁהּ וַתִּשְׂחַק לְיוֹם אַחֲרוֹן: 25

פִּיהָ פָּתְחָה בְחָכְמָה וְתוֹרַת חֶסֶד עַל־לְשׁוֹנָהּ: 26

צוֹפִיָּה (הילכת) [הֲלִיכוֹת] בֵּיתָהּ וְלֶחֶם עַצְלוּת 27
לֹא תֹאכֵל:

קָמוּ בָנֶיהָ וַיְאַשְּׁרוּהָ בַּעְלָהּ וַיְהַלְלָהּ: 28

29 ר "Many women have done well,
   But you surpass them all."
30 ש Grace is deceptive,
   Beauty is illusory;
   It is for her fear of GOD
   That a woman is to be praised.
31 ת Give her of the fruit of her hands,
   And let her works praise her in the gates.

29 רַבּ֣וֹת בָּנ֖וֹת עָ֣שׂוּ חָ֑יִל וְ֝אַ֗תְּ עָלִ֥ית עַל־כֻּלָּֽנָה׃

30 שֶׁ֣קֶר הַ֭חֵן וְהֶ֣בֶל הַיֹּ֑פִי אִשָּׁ֥ה יִרְאַת־יְ֝הוָ֗ה הִ֣יא תִתְהַלָּֽל׃

31 תְּנוּ־לָ֭הּ מִפְּרִ֣י יָדֶ֑יהָ וִֽיהַלְל֖וּהָ בַשְּׁעָרִ֣ים מַעֲשֶֽׂיהָ׃

The Will to See the Invisible People among Us

Speak up for the dumb,
For the rights of all the unfortunate.
    —Proverbs 31:8

THERE ARE THE OPEN and loud cries reverberating within the soul, but then there are also the hidden and silent cries. Do we hear them? Do we ever attempt to? In this verse, we are implored to recognize, no matter how much we do not want to admit it, that there are invisible, unheard people among us, victims of deep injustices and oppression. They are the young women who make our hotel beds and the women who serve in our homes. They are the young men who wash our dishes at restaurants and the men who wash our cars. They are the people enslaved by our prison system and the people objectified by sexual appetites. They are the homeless who spend their days in the shadows beyond the field of most people's active vision.

To not see an invisible person is a tragedy. To ignore the plight of the invisible is a violation of our ethical mandates to speak up for those who do not have the ability to speak for themselves. Their cries need to be heard. Rabbi Yehuda Amital, an influential twentieth-century Jewish thinker in Israel, explains why it is so vital to open our ears and hearts: "Every generation has its own cry, sometimes open, sometimes hidden . . . we have to try to be attentive to the hidden cries as well."[1]

While invisibility is initially caused by systems of oppression, shame invariably leads vulnerable individuals to perpetuate their state of invisibility. As legal scholar Martha Nussbaum explains,

"Shame involves the realization that one is weak and inadequate in some ways in which one expects oneself to be adequate. Its reflex is to hide from the eyes of those who will see one's deficiency, to cover it up."[2] Those who lack basic needs often wish not to be seen in their lacking for fear of shame. This dynamic becomes even more destructive by our tendency to look away and not take action. Jewish tradition demands not only that we see but that we show ourselves in Jerusalem on the Pilgrimage Festivals,[3] and also throughout the rest of the year our eyes and hearts must be open to see those among us who are usually unseen and to show ourselves in our own vulnerability. The ability to connect and support the concealed is not a distraction from tradition, but rather a powerful actualization.

One of the goals of Jewish spiritual life is to see beyond the physical, to sanctify the unseen, and to elevate our earthly lives. The Maggid of Mezeritch, a great Chasidic master, helped to introduce us to the idea that *yeish m'ayin*—the concept of "creation out of nothing"—meaning that when helping something come into existence that previously did not exist or when helping something be seen that previously was unseen, we repeat the creation of the universe itself.

Greater than lending money or giving *tzedakah* to someone who is poor, the Rabbis tell us, is providing partnership.[4] It is our responsibility to join the invisible in solidarity. Let us make their voices heard and their humanity seen. We need the courage to see and to make seen the victims of injustice among us. We have been granted the power to make visible the invisible. We need to let the vulnerable know, every time we encounter them, that they are recognized and cherished members of society and of our community.

Proverbs 31:8, particularly as interpreted by Rabbi Amital, challenges us not merely to hear cries but to hear the unique cries of our time.

The Woman of Valor

How precious is a woman of substance!
Her worth is far beyond that of rubies.
　　—Proverbs 31:10

OUR JOURNEY ENDS—as does the Book of Proverbs—with one of the most significant Hebrew poems ever written. *Eishet Chayil*—translated famously as "a woman of valor"—which comprises the epilogue to Proverbs 31, is also one of the most enduring pieces of Jewish liturgy, one that is recited on a regular basis in Jewish homes all over the world. Seemingly a simple alphabetic acrostic poem whose singular presumptive focus is to praise an ideal wife, *Eishet Chayil* hides its complexity by being seemingly straightforward. But closer readings, feminist and mystical, reveal its exquisite mysteries, its delicate splendor, and its enduring portrait of love and affection between the people and the Divine.

The placement of *Eishet Chayil* within the Book of Proverbs raises immediate questions, not only about the content of the poem but also about its intention. Proverbs as a whole, as should be apparent, focuses on men as teachers of younger men. Powerful and well-meaning masculinity is driving the Book of Proverbs and, indeed, most of the Hebrew Scriptures. The patriarchal orientation of the Torah relates to a feature of historical reality where ancient societies (or at least the writings that they produced) focused heavily on male power at the expense of female perspectives. While female figures—both literal and metaphorical—always had a place in the world of Torah, the majority of postbiblical analyses didn't place emphasis on the female perspective. Thus, before the modern and postmodern revolution of close reading of the Bible, it is not surprising that Proverbs focuses on men.

Yet here, at the conclusion of a deep dive into Jewish ethics, we engage with the most remarkable (and subversive) aspect of Proverbs, one that pushes our understanding of Jewish philosophy to places traditionally less traveled. The *Eishet Chayil* poem mirrors everything that Judaism holds up: reverence for the human being, reverence for love as a manifestation of our relationship with the Divine, and an ode to the idea that creation and Creator work in partnership to repair the world.

Eishet Chayil is among the most powerful pieces of biblical litera-ture. It frees us from the notion of women as second-class citizens or even as afterthoughts within Jewish wisdom. In the Bible, men and women are meant to be together, so another text on the value of this relationship is not very interesting at face value (though it is still beautiful, mind you). Traditional texts are often heteronorma-tive. With some minor reinterpretation, a queer couple can poten-tially make this passage relevant and meaningful for themselves as well. The power of *Eishet Chayil* arises when we consider its subject: women. Rabbi Dr. Rachel Adler writes:

> The prophets were not able to understand that it was the social system of patriarchy itself that generated these abuses and made them inevitable, because all over their known world patriarchy was the only gender system. There was no alternative to which to com-pare it, and they were unable to envision another. Some moderns still cannot envision another. They do not understand that in any society in which heterosexual men are awarded the lion's share of social and economic privilege and power, people of other genders and sexualities will suffer economic discrimination, sexual harass-ment, and violence. In order for the prophets' concerns for the marginalized and the powerless to have impact on a sociohistorical situation, a society must be able to envision and shape laws and policies that will embody their understanding of what the prophets wanted them to do.[5]

By concluding a male-centric section of a male-centric book by concentrating on the allure and wisdom of the female, the Book of Proverbs ends on a provocative note. The choice serves as an intertextual critique of other biblical narratives: women are often mentioned in the Torah in a not-so-positive fashion.

However, there is potent feminist critique of *Eishet Chayil*, specifically about its seeming reductive rendering of women into servants to men. Indeed, the poem can be read to describe a woman's support of—or even subservience to—a man whom she provides with support, care, and tenderness in all he does. Clearly, most women don't reach the levels of service described in *Eishet Chayil*, nor do they feel called to fulfill such a role. The poem might create anxiety in some women and anger in others.

Another possible reading can be derived from the context of the poem within the Book of Proverbs. Immediately before this chapter, the book records the teachings of King Lemuel's mother, describing how she educated him to be a fair and equitable ruler (Proverbs 31:1–9). Part of her instructions is the commitment to bring justice to the people of Israel. The king's mother also stresses the need to find a partner who will be a guiding light. It seems likely that the *Eishet Chayim* poem is the king's mother's description of that complementary woman who will never lead the king astray.

Dr. Jacqueline Vayntrub, an assistant professor of the Hebrew Bible at the Yale Divinity School, writes about Lemuel's mother as a forward and practical thinker:

> Her . . . first piece of advice concerns Lemuel's choices in his relationships with the opposite sex: *'al-titten lanashim cheylekha*, "Do not give your vigor (*chayil*) to women" (v 3). This advice, read in conjunction with *Eshet Chayil*, begs an interpretation of the poem as a list of must-haves when shopping for the ideal wife. The second to last line of the poem is what really lends itself to such an interpretation, as a mother's advice to her son: *sheqer hachen vhevel hayofi*, "Grace is a lie and beauty is ephemeral" (v 30). Looks fade, choose a woman of substance![6]

Indeed, the poem might describe a mother's dream woman for her son. However, if it's the mother of a king who shares her advice here, then why does he need a worker for a wife? Presumably, he has countless servants to support the kingdom. Should he not rather look for physical beauty, a trait that the poem specifically downplays? Perhaps this mother is critiquing her son, the king. She tells him: you need an honorable woman of virtue as your partner, someone who can help you build and preserve your kingdom.

Yet another interpretation of this text is that it is not concerned with a matriarch, or indeed any woman at all. Rather, the "woman of valor" is the Torah itself. Proverbs 31:26 reads, "Her mouth opens with wisdom, / An instruction-in-responsibility is upon her tongue." We are reflecting on how one might live Torah in all dimensions of our life; medieval commentator Rashi understands the poem in this manner.[7] The kabbalists explain that we're not referring to a woman or to the Torah but to the *Shechinah*, the feminine Divine Presence. By reciting this poem on Friday night, we celebrate all that God did for us during the workweek in all of God's dimensions.

In the traditional Jewish household on Friday night, *Eishet Chayil* is chanted before the meal, but after the welcoming of the angels at the Sabbath table (*Shalom Aleichem*). The order of the songs speaks to the ideal order of our priorities: first, the members of the heavenly court, and second, women (and in particular, the woman of the house). When the song is chanted, the presiding male of the household will stand in honor of his spouse, dedicating the entire ritual to the woman of his household—as wife, mother, protector, and confidante. It is a way not only to express gratitude to God for the food about to be eaten, but to be grateful to the cook, traditionally the matriarch of the home. Not only is she working hard, but she is filled with wisdom, a particular wisdom that is out of reach for the patriarchal mind. She is not praised for superficial beauty but rather for being a wise person committed to moral responsibility (Proverbs 31:30).

There is a powerful midrash focused on *Eishet Chayil* that provokes me as I wrestle with the text. In this midrash, Rabbi Meir's sons both die on a Shabbat when Rabbi Meir is away from the home. His wife B'ruriah takes the bodies and places them on the bed. After Rabbi

Meir returns, the text records a series of cryptic exchanges between husband and wife about the status of the sons:

> "Where are my two sons?" She said [back], "They went to the study hall." He said to her, "I scanned the study hall and I did not see them." They gave him the cup of *Havdalah*, and he separated the days of the week with the closure of Shabbat. He repeated and said, "Where are my two sons?" She said, "They went elsewhere and they are coming now."

After some time, Rabbi Meir's wife leads him to the room where the bodies are lying on the bed. Rabbi Meir is beside himself with grief. B'ruriah consoles him masterfully, noting that their sons have returned to their "Owner." As the midrash ends, it is noted that after hearing these words of comfort, Rabbi Meir's "mind became composed," and he was soothed by that woman of valor.[8] The power of female wisdom can heal hearts and change minds.

Eishet Chayil's ultimate meaning, of course, will never be settled. As we close the Book of Proverbs, it is incumbent upon us to recognize that Jewish wisdom is often hidden in plain sight. With the text of *Eishet Chayil*, the delicate balance of what is apparent and what is obscure, what is simple and what is complex, and what is holy and what is profane is left for us to find on our own. In all we do, may we have the strength to recognize the infinite wisdom contained within these verses, this book, and these ideas. Through them, we are handed the potential needed to actualize deep and true wisdom throughout the world and in ourselves. How we choose to wield this potential is left entirely up to us.

Conclusion

As we conclude our time with the Book of Proverbs, we should feel inspired to have taken a journey into one of the most life-affirming books of the Hebrew canon. The Book of Proverbs is about relationships, power, humility, truth, and the reconciliation of the manifold complexities of life. As with any Torah commentary, we do not simply read texts, try to absorb them, and then move on. We interpret, we ruminate, we digest. And then we start again. We choose to interpret our tradition gently and charitably. Rabbi Jonathan Sacks writes, "The choice is ours—will the generous texts of our tradition serve as interpretive keys to the rest, or will the abrasive passages determine our ideas of what we are and what we are called to do?"[1]

At its essence, the Book of Proverbs teaches wisdom, which in Hebrew is *chochmah*. Interestingly enough, if you move around the first two letters (*chet* and *chaf*) in the four-letter word, you get *koachmah*, "the power of what." Wisdom is about curiosity. It asks questions, never looking for finality. More than providing answers, the Book of Proverbs inspires us to ask new questions.

In its own way, the Book of Proverbs is ahistorical. Some theologians argue that what we need to know we know already. Scientists, especially of the modern era, argue that we actually do not even have a full grasp of the basics of the universe. Combining these approaches and appreciating the wisdom we've inherited, we can still acknowledge how radically insufficient this wisdom is to fully understand ourselves, our society, and the universe. We can synthesize the wisdom of the past with the present recognition that we must work to fill the gaps existing in that wisdom.

In addition to reading our tradition's texts charitably, we read them critically, with intellectual skepticism and seeking self-transformation. We read them as advocates of social justice, looking to be recharged and to move toward healing in an all-too-broken world. In these postmodern times, we are sometimes plagued by the conflict between moral absolutism and moral relativism. On the one hand, we wish to be respectful of different cultures and norms. On the other hand, we work for a more just world that holds certain values absolute. It is difficult to navigate holding a strong moral compass while also holding a pluralistic ethos. We know ethics are complex, but our postmodern relativism must also have healthy boundaries. We no longer believe in one ultimate redemptive model of universal justice. Yet, we do not give up on global solidarity to support the most vulnerable on the planet.

Rabbi Shimon Gershon Rosenberg, a postmodern Religious Zionist thinker known as Rav Shagar writes:

> The Lord is in everything; as the Hasidim say, "no place is empty of Him."[2] He is omnipresent, including in my own existence and values, which are thus a certainty. True, one can always ask, "But do not other people and other societies have different values?" But that possibility must not diminish the fact that I, too, have a certainty that I am unwilling to relinquish, a truth to which I will dedicate myself, for which I am willing to die, even kill (the last is the most difficult and severe of actions). . . . By combining the universal point of view with doubt in the universality and absoluteness of any individual stance, every culture can accept other cultures as true alternatives that carry a kernel of truth. If more of us humbly acknowledge that limited capacity of the individual to utter absolute statements, perhaps we can establish justice and ethics alongside a renewed human solidarity.[3]

Once we have moral clarity, we can't just discuss it and conceal it in our hearts. We must put our values into action. Eleanor Roosevelt said, "It isn't enough to talk about peace. One must believe in it. And it isn't enough to believe in it. One must work at it."[4] When we learn religious texts, we must debate them. When we debate them, we must add to them the fuel of holy action. However, we should not only learn and act, we should also infuse joy into both! The Talmud teaches, "The Divine Presence will only be found where there is joy."[5] We may find spiritual depth within existential crisis and sadness, but it is joy, we are reminded, where God wishes to meet us. We must built a world of joy founded on kindness.

There is a crucial role for the Jewish community to play in rebuilding this world. Abraham was, perhaps, the most influential person who ever lived. From him and Sarah grew the three Abrahamic faiths: Judaism, Christianity, and Islam. Abraham and those with whom he lived did not hold royal or political positions. They had no corporations, formal authority, or national army. They had ideas. They had hope and faith. They had resilience. Most of all, the Rabbis explain, they were willing to reject conformity. Abraham was called *ha-ivri* because "all the world was on one side and he was on the other.[6] Rabbi Dr. Eugene Borowitz argues, in the spirit of Rabbi Mordecai Kaplan, that "a people is prior to its religion."[7] Indeed, a people of strength and resistance sets the stage for the later actualization of a religious mandate.

Consider how Robert Frost famously described such a courageous orientation to life:

> Two roads diverged in a wood, and I—
> I took the one less traveled by,
> And that has made all the difference.[8]

The goal is not to be different for the sake of being different. The goal is to come out of our comfort zones to explore and discover the deeper moral and spiritual potential that each of us holds in our hearts. The goal is to shut off the noise that distracts us from hearing what is truer and hidden deeper. Rabbi Shlomo Wolbe, a twentieth-century teacher of Jewish ethics, writes:

> Every person needs to know that they have importance. Not an imagined importance that they "consider themself as special" . . . rather a deeply profound importance that is even shocking. The Talmud states, "Each and every person must declare, 'The world was created for me.'"[9] Rashi explains that this means I am

considered as important as the entire world. This is the one-time life experience of a particular person—there was never a person like them and nor will there ever be a person like them throughout history. I, with my special character strengths, the child of my parents, born at a specific time period, and in a certain environment—certainly there is a unique challenge that is placed upon me. I have a special share in the Torah, and the entire world is waiting for me to actualize that which is incumbent upon me. For my role cannot be exchanged with anyone else in the world![10]

Mary Oliver, in her poem "The Pond," writes about how she walks around the same pond over and over in order to see it anew and freshly each day. Indeed, it is the same for our holy texts that we read each year. Proverbs is unique in that parts of it became liturgy,[11] and yet it does not have a place in our annual synagogue reading calendar. There is no holiday dedicated to the Book of Proverbs. Thus, it is upon each of us to continue to circle "the Pond."

As we have seen, the Book of Proverbs does not provide us with answers. It provides us with some simple moral reminders. It provides us with a measure of moral clarity to navigate murky waters. It even provides us with verses to chant to reorient us when we're confused. But it does not provide the path forward. Each of us must find our own path. Each of us is unique with our very own purpose. We must grab every tool we can to help us navigate our respective journeys. May the Book of Proverbs, in a different way for each of us, be one of those tools.

Glossary

Adonai: Lit. "My Lord," an epithet for the name of God.

Akeidah: "Binding"; refers to Genesis 22, the story of the Binding of Isaac.

alef-bet: The Hebrew alphabet.

Ashkenazi: Jews of Eastern and Central European descent. Also the name for their rite of liturgy and folkways.

B'reishit Rabbah: Midrash on the Book of Genesis.

Chasidism: A spiritual Jewish movement started in Eastern Europe during the eighteenth century based on the teachings of the Baal Shem Tov.

chavruta: Study system with pairings of study partners, derived from the Hebrew word *chaver*, "friend."

chesed: "Love, benevolence, kindness, grace"; also the fourth of the ten *s'firot*, the mystical layers of God's emanation.

chochmah: "Wisdom"; also the second of the ten *s'firot*, the mystical layers of God's emanation.

din: "Judgment."

Ehyeh-Asher-Ehyeh: Lit. "I will be who I will be"; one of the Hebrew names of God.

Ein Sof: Lit. "no end"; "divine expansiveness," one of the Hebrew names of God.

Elohim: One of the Hebrew names of God.

El Shaddai: A biblical name for God, often translated as "God Almighty" (Genesis 17:1).

emet: "Truth."

Exodus: The journey of the Israelites from slavery in Egypt to freedom in Canaan; also the name of the second book in the Torah.

g'matria: Numerical system using the letters of the Hebrew alphabet according to which one can calculate the numerical value of each word in Hebrew.

hachnasat orchim: Lit. "bringing in strangers"; the Jewish value of welcoming guests, exemplified by Abraham in Genesis 18.

Haggadah: Lit. "telling, story"; the prayer book used on Passover to accompany the Passover seder, the ritual meal and retelling of the story of the Israelite Exodus from Egypt.

hakadosh: "The holy one."

halachta bidrachav: Lit. "walk in His [God's] ways"; also known as *imitatio Dei*.

HaMalach HaGo-eil: Lit. "the redeeming angel"; blessing traditionally given to children on the festival of Simchat Torah.

HaShem: Lit. "the name"; one of the ways to refer to God to avoid pronouncing God's holy name.

Havdalah: Ritual that takes place on Saturday night to separate Shabbat from the rest of the week; focuses on the division of light and darkness, holy and mundane.

High Holy Days: The colloquial English name for the Yamim Noraim, the Days of Awe, encompassing Rosh HaShanah, the Jewish New Year celebration, through Yom Kippur, the Day of Atonement (a period of ten days). The religious services that occur on Rosh HaShanah and Yom Kippur are filled with imagery of God as sovereign and divine.

Kaddish: A prayer said at multiple times during any given religious service, praising God's name and power. Often "the *Kaddish*," when said colloquially, refers to the *Kaddish Yatom*, the "Mourner's *Kaddish*," said at the end of prayer services by people in mourning.

kadosh: "holy, sacred."

kashrut: Jewish laws concerning food and eating, ranging from which kinds of animals can be eaten to which kinds of dishes may be used for different kinds of food.

kavanah (pl. *kavanot*): Lit. "intention" or "direction"; colloquially, a Jewish value often meaning to set one's intention in the right spiritual and emotional place to be present for the sanctity of prayer.

kosher: "Fitting"; when something fits into the laws of kashrut, it is kosher (see above).

lo titor: "Do not bear grudges"; Jewish law based on Leviticus 19:18.

Maimonides (1138–1204, Spain and Egypt): Philosopher, halachic authority, doctor, and merchant.

Malbim (Meir Leibush ben Yehiel Michel Wisser, 1809–79, Russian Empire): Hebrew grammar expert and Torah commentator.

matzah: Unleavened bread traditionally eaten on Passover.

messianic: Refers to a future redemption led by the Messiah, an anointed person chosen by God. In the messianic time, the world shall be at peace, and all its inhabitants shall worship the one God.

midrash (pl. midrashim): Rabbinic exegesis on or expansion of Torah. Midrashim are documented in Talmud as well as other Rabbinic books of Jewish teachings and interpretations.

minyan: The quorum of ten adult Jews who make up the minimum required for a full prayer service.

Mishnah: A second-century work of Jewish law. The Mishnah is the basis for the majority of the Jewish legal tradition.

Mishneh Torah: The first halachic compilation, by Maimonides (1138–1204).

mitzvah (pl. mitzvot): "Commandment, commandments"; refers to the prescriptions and prohibitions in the Torah, Mishnah, and later Jewish legal works.

m'shalim (**sing.** *mashal*): "Allegory"; rhetoric figure used frequently in Rabbinic and Chasidic literature.

n'divut: "Generosity;" one of the ethical values taught within the Mussar movement, a school of Jewish applied ethics.

n'shamah: One of the Hebrew words for soul.

Passover: Weeklong Jewish holiday in the spring celebrating the Israelite Exodus from Egypt.

Pirkei Avot: Lit. "chapters of the ancestors"; an early Rabbinic compilation of ethical teachings, part of the Mishnah.

rachamim: "Mercy, compassion."

ratzon: "Desire, favor, will."

Rema (Rabbi Moses Isserles, 1530–73, Poland): Famous commentator on the *Shulchan Aruch* (see below).

ruach: Lit. "wind"; one of the Hebrew words for spirit.

salchan: Someone who forgives regularly, not only once.

savlanut: "Patience"; one of the ethical values taught within the Mussar movement, a school of Jewish applied ethics.

seder: Lit. "order"; refers to the ritual meal at the beginning of the Passover celebration, in which the Haggadah is used to structure the meal as a telling of the Israelite Exodus from Egypt.

Sefer HaChinuch: "The Book of Education" discusses the 613 mitzvot; published in the thirteenth century in Spain.

Sefer Mishlei: Hebrew name for the biblical Book of Proverbs.

Shabbat: Observed from Friday at sundown to Saturday at sundown, a day of rest from work that celebrates the seventh day of Creation.

Shalom Aleichem: Lit. "peace be upon you"; a poem sung to welcome angels on Shabbat.

Shechinah: Lit. "dwelling"; the female name and aspect of God. *Shechinah* is associated with exile, as this is the aspect of God that dwells with the Israelite people also outside the Land of Israel. Also the lowest of the ten *s'firot*, the mystical layers of God's emanation, also called *Malchut* (kingdom).

sheker: "Lie, falsehood."

sh'tikah k'hodaah: Lit. "silence is like agreement"; Rabbinic principle warning us not to keep silent in the face of injustice.

Shulchan Aruch: A Jewish legal code written in the sixteenth century by Joseph Caro. It is considered to be the most decisive work of Jewish law to this day.

Sifra: Midrash on the Book of Leviticus.

simchah: Lit. "joy" or "happiness"; a celebration or joyful moment.

sukkah: A temporary hut built outdoors with three sides and a partially open roof, used on the holiday of Sukkot to symbolize the temporality of life, the Israelite Exodus from Egypt, and the autumnal harvest.

Talmud: A work of Jewish law from late antiquity based on Rabbinic discussions of the behaviors prescribed and prohibited in the Mishnah, a compendium of Jewish law compiled in the second century. The Babylonian Talmud has been for centuries the core legal source of Rabbinic Judaism.

Tanach: The Jewish canonical Bible, comprising *Torah* (lit. "Law," the Five Books of Moses), *N'vi-im* (Prophets), and *K'tuvim* (Writings).

Tanya: Lit. "Teaching"; central book of the Chabad movement published by Rabbi Shneur Zalman of Liadi in 1797.

tiferet: Lit. "beauty, glory"; the sixth of the ten *s'firot*, the mystical layers of God's emanation.

tikkun: "repair, correction."

tikkun olam: Lit. "repair the world"; often refers to the Jewish call to social justice. In traditionally Orthodox spaces, *tikkun olam* refers to Jews' doing mitzvot to bring about the Messiah and the messianic redemption. In liberal Jewish spaces, *tikkun olam* can mean anything from social action to performance of mitzvot.

tochachah: "Rebuke."

Torah: Lit. "teaching"; refers to the first five books of the Hebrew Bible (Genesis, Exodus, Leviticus, Numbers, Deuteronomy), also called the Five Books of Moses. Depending on context, *torah* can also refer to the larger compilation of text, the full Hebrew Bible, or to a Jewish teaching in general.

t'shuvah: Lit. "return, repentance"; the act of seeking forgiveness that is emphasized as part of the rituals of the High Holy Days.

tzedakah: "Charity." Comes from the Hebrew root for "justice."

tzedek: "Justice."

Vilna Gaon (Elijah ben Solomon Zalman, 1720–97, Lithuania): Halachic and kabbalistic authority.

yetzer hara: "The evil inclination"

yetzer tov: "The good inclination."

YHVH: The Tetragrammaton, the unpronounceable name of God.

Yom Kippur: The Day of Atonement, one of the Jewish High Holy Days in which Jews engage in cultic rituals surrounding death (most notably by fasting and reciting deathbed confessions), as a way to emphasize the importance of repentance.

zeicher tzaddik livrachah: "The memory of the righteous person is for a blessing"; formula used to respectfully commemorate a Jewish scholar.

z'rizut: "Alacrity"; one of the ethical values taught within the Mussar movement, a school of Jewish applied ethics.

Notes

Introduction

1. "The proverbs of Solomon son of David, king of Israel" (Proverbs 1–9); "The proverbs of Solomon" (Proverbs 10:1–22:16); "The words of the sages" (Proverbs 22:17–24:22); "These also are by the sages" (Proverbs 24:23–34); "These too are proverbs of Solomon, which the officials of King Hezekiah of Judah copied" (Proverbs 25–29); "The words of Agur" (Proverbs 30); "The words of Lemuel, king of Massa, with which his mother admonished him" (Proverbs 31). It is important to note, however, that it is possible to view these other authors as nicknames for Solomon.

2. Two other books are generally included in the genre of the wisdom literature that were excluded from the *Tanach* but included in the Apocrypha: Wisdom of Solomon and Wisdom of Ben Sira (or Ecclesiasticus).

3. A midrash recounts that Solomon wrote Song of Songs in his youth, Proverbs as an adult, and Ecclesiastes in his later years (*Shir HaShirim Rabbah* i. I 1:10).

4. Malbim on Proverbs 1:1.

5. Clearly, the book was not completed by Solomon, but the teachings may have begun with him and continued beyond his lifetime.

6. Of course, Jewish wisdom literature was not the first wisdom literature ever written. The Egyptians had written in this genre a few centuries earlier. Consider, for example, the "Instruction of Amen-em-opet," estimated to have been compiled sometime between the thirteenth and tenth centuries BCE, or the Assyrian text "Words of Ahikar," compiled around the same time as the Book of Proverbs.

7. Babylonian Talmud, *Shabbat* 30b.

8. Robert Alter, *The Wisdom Books* (New York: Norton, 2011), 186–87.

9. Babylonian Talmud, *Sotah* 14a and *Shabbat* 133b, based on Leviticus 19:2.

10. As quoted in Abraham Joshua Heschel, *Heavenly Torah: As Refracted through the Generations* (New York: Continuum, 2005), 780.

11. *Pirkei Avot* 4:24.

12. *Pirkei Avot* 6:3, 6:8.

13. *Pirkei Avot* 6:7.

About the Translation
1. Michael V. Fox, *Proverbs 1–9: A New Translation with Introduction and Commentary* (Anchor Bible vol. 18A; New Haven: Yale University Press, 2000), 16.

Chapter 1
1. Harold Kushner, *Who Needs God* (New York: Fireside, 2002), 58.
2. Jonah Dov Pesner, "In Every Generation: The Obligations of Our Exodus," in *Moral Resistance and Spiritual Authority*, ed. Seth M. Limmer and Jonah Dov Pesner (New York: CCAR Press, 2019), 91–92.
3. *Pirkei Avot* 3:21.
4. Ruth W. Messinger and Rick Jacobs, "On Global Jewish Responsibility: Putting the *Olam* in *Tikkun Olam*," in *Moral Resistance and Spiritual Authority*, ed. Seth M. Limmer and Jonah Dov Pesner, 271–72.
5. *The Kennedys: America's Front-Page Family*, collected by The Poynter Institute (Kansas City: Andrews McMeel, 2009), 112.
6. See also Proverbs 4:1, 6:20, 10:1, 13:1, 13:24, 15:20, 19:18, 19:26, 20:20, 23:13–14, 23:22, 30:11, and 30:17.
7. See also Exodus 21:15, 21:17; Leviticus 19:3; and Deuteronomy 27:16.
8. Celia Hatton, "New China Law Says Children 'Must Visit Parents,'" *BBC News*, July 1, 2013, https://www.bbc.com/news/world-asia-china-23124345.
9. Susan O'Doherty, "Mother's Day Ruminations," *Mama PhD* (blog), Inside Higher Ed, May 12, 2013, http://www.insidehighered.com/blogs/mama-phd/mothers-day-ruminations.
10. "Overview of Major Legislation," Japan Health Policy NOW, http://japanhpn.org/en/legislation/.
11. Francine Russo, "Caring for Aging Parents: Should There Be a Law?," *Time*, July 22, 2013, http://healthland.time.com/2013/07/22/caring-for-aging-parents-should-there-be-a-law/.
12. Russo, "Caring for Aging Parents."
13. Gal Wettstein and Alice Zulkarnain, "How Much Long-Term Care Do Adult Children Provide?," Center for Retirement Research at Boston College, June 2017, no. 17-11, https://crr.bc.edu/wp-content/uploads/2017/06/IB_17-11.pdf.
14. Wettstein and Alice Zulkarnain, "How Much Long-Term Care Do Adult Children Provide?"
15. Marsha Mercer, "Can You Afford a Home-Care Worker?," AARP, updated November 4, 2019, https://www.aarp.org/caregiving/financial-legal/info-2017/afford-a-homecare-worker.html.

16. Christine Benz, "Must-Know Statistics about Long-Term Care: 2019 Edition," Morningstar, November 25, 2019, https://www.morningstar.com/articles/957487/must-know-statistics-about-long-term-care-2019-edition.
17. See *Shulchan Aruch*, *Yoreh Dei-ah* 240:3, which articulates as a legal requirement the obligation to honor a parent even in the face of parental humiliation.
18. Babylonian Talmud, *Kiddushin* 31a.
19. Of course, the case of an abusive or neglectful parent is a different matter altogether. A child must be protected. Even adult children have the right, and even obligation, to protect themselves from such a parent. The assumption in this section, at large, is that we're dealing with non-abusive parents, albeit parents that err, as all do.
20. *Shulchan Aruch*, *Yoreh Dei-ah* 240:10.
21. *Sefer HaChinuch*, mitzvah 33.
22. Babylonian Talmud, *Kiddushin* 30b.
23. Babylonian Talmud, *Nidah* 31a.
24. Laura Geller, "Honoring Your Father and Mother," in *Inscribed: Encounters with the Ten Commandments*, ed. Oren J. Hayon (New York, CCAR Press, 2019), 90.
25. Malbim on Proverbs 1:8.

Chapter 2

1. Abraham Isaac Kook, *Manuscripts, Collection B*, 35, as quoted in Benjamin Ish-Shalom, *Rav Avraham Itzhak HaCohen Kook: Between Rationalism and Mysticism* (Albany: State University of New York Press, 1993), 214.
2 Abraham Isaak Kook, *Orot HaKodesh*, vol. 3, 61, 103.
3. Vilna Gaon, *Even Sh'leimah* 1:1.
4. Maimonides, *Sefer HaMitzvot*, positive mitzvah 8.
5. *P'sikta Rabbati* 14:13.
6. Rabbeinu Asher on *Mishnah Pei-ah* 1:1.
7. Babylonian Talmud, *Y'vamot* 21a and *Bava Batra* 88b.
8. Babylonian Talmud, *Sanhedrin* 108a.

Chapter 3

1. Alter Rebbe, *Tanya*, chapter 18.
2. Craig E. Johnson, *Ethical Decision Making and Behavior: Meeting the Ethical Challenges of Leadership* (Thousand Oaks: SAGE, 2004).
3. Ronald Heifetz, Alexander Grashow, and Marty Linsky, *The Practice of Adaptive Leadership: Tools and Tactics for Changing Your Organization* (Boston: Harvard Business Press, 2009), 195.

4. Joseph B. Soloveitchik, "A Theory of Emotions," in *Out of the Whirlwind: Essays on Mourning, Suffering, and the Human Condition*, ed. David Shatz, Joel B. Wolowelsky, and Reuven Ziegler (New York: Ktav, 2003), 183.

5. Lawrence Kushner, *God Was in This Place and I, I Did Not Know: Finding Self, Spirituality, and Ultimate Meaning* (Woodstock, VT: Jewish Lights, 2016), 52.

6. Maimonides, *Mishneh Torah, Hilchot T'shuvah* 4:4.

7. Sogyal Rinpoche, *The Tibetan Book of Living and Dying* (New York: HarperCollins, 1992), 225.

8. Jonathan Sacks, *Future Tense: Jews, Judaism, and Israel in the Twentieth Century* (New York: Schocken, 2012), 221.

9. Anaïs Nin, *Seduction of the Minotaur* (Chicago: Swallow Press, 1961), 124.

10. For more on Fromm's frame of orientation, see Erich Fromm, *The Anatomy of Human Destructiveness* (New York: Holt, Rinehart and Winston, 1973).

11. Agnes De Mille, *Martha: The Life and Work of Martha Graham* (New York: Random House, 1991), 264.

12. Marianne Williamson, *A Return to Love: Reflections on the Principles of a Course in Miracles* (New York: HarperCollins 1992), 165.

13. Maimonides, *Mishneh Torah, Hilchot Dei-ot* 2:1.

14. Maimonides, introduction to his commentary on *Pirkei Avot*, chapter 5.

Chapter 4

1. See François Raffoul, *The Origins of Responsibility* (Bloomington: Indiana University Press, 2010), 177.

2. Babylonian Talmud, *Bava M'tzia* 30b.

3. Nachmanides on Leviticus 19:2.

4. Immanuel Etkes and Jeffrey M. Green, *The Gaon of Vilna: The Man and His Image* (Berkeley: University of California Press, 2002).

5. See Moshe Halbertal and Avishai Margalit, *Idolatry* (Cambridge, MA: Harvard University Press, 1992).

6. Shulchan Aruch, *Orach Chayim* 151:5.

7. Alan M. Dershowitz, *Chutzpah* (New York: Simon & Schuster, 1992), 194. At that time, Dershowitz was considered a civil rights advocate and liberal. Today, he is generally viewed as a conservative, making the contrast with Meir Kahane less stark.

8. Douglas Murray, "Why We Must Debate the Extremists," *The Guardian*, June 19, 2009, https://www.theguardian.com/commentisfree/belief/2009/jun/19/religion-islam-muhajiroun-choudary.

9. Babylonian Talmud, *Bava M'tzia* 6a.

Chapter 5

1. *Beit HaLevi* explains this in *d'rashah* 18, based on an earlier source in *Yalkut Shimoni*.

2. Yisrael Berger, *Simchat Yisrael* (Pioterkov: Ch.H Publishing, 1909), 49. See also "Reb Eisik's Treasure" in Ellen Frankel, *The Classic Tales: 4,000 Years of Jewish Lore* (NJ: Jason Aronson, Inc., 1989), 545–46.

Chapter 6

1. Y'hudah HaLevi, *Kuzari* 2:48.
2. Y'hudah HaLevi, *Kuzari* 2:48.
3. Babylonian Talmud, *Eiruvin* 100b. Note that the ant is again mentioned in this passage.
4. This notion was declared by many medieval commentators: Saadia Gaon, Rabbi David ibn Zimra, etc.
5. Parts of this model originates from *Zohar* 2:215b.
6. Abraham Isaac Kook, *Orot HaTorah* 12:2–3. Rabbi Kook's teaching calls to mind the midrashic idea that *derech eretz* preceded Torah (*Vayikra Rabbah*, chap. 9).
7. See Samuel Heilman, *Sliding to the Right: The Contest for the Future of American Jewish Orthodoxy* (Berkeley: University of California Press, 2006). Such a claim is further supported by a 2019 Nishma survey on modern Orthodoxy, which puts little emphasis on commitment to morality and social justice as a basis for Orthodox practice: Nishma Research, *The Successes, Challenges, and Future of American Modern Orthodoxy*, November 9, 2014, http://nishmaresearch.com/assets/pdf/Nishma%20 Research%20-%20Future%20of%20American%20Modern%20 Orthodoxy%20Nov%202019.pdf.
8. *S'fat Emet, Tol'dot* 5663.
9. *B'reishit Rabbah* 44:1.
10. Babylonian Talmud, *B'rachot* 19b.
11. Nachmanides on Leviticus 19:2.
12. Babylonian Talmud, *Bava M'tzia* 83a.
13. Rabbi Lichtenstein's wife was the daughter of the esteemed scholar Rabbi Joseph B. Soloveitchik.
14. Aharon Lichtenstein, *By His Light: Character and Values in the Service of God* (Jerusalem: Maggid Books, 2017), 249.
15. Jerusalem Talmud, *Shabbat* 1:4; Babylonian Talmud, *Shabbat* 17a.
16. This appears to be one of the cases where Maimonides was influenced by the Islamic law of his time according to which blasphemy was punished with death. Perhaps Maimonides intended to show that Jews did not show less fidelity to God's law. *Mishneh Torah, Hilchot Rotzei-ach*

Ushmirat Nefesh 4:10.

17. *Mishneh Torah, Hilchot Ishut* 21:10.

18. To be sure, Maimonides does, in a later passage, take back this extreme view (albeit not enough). In *Mishneh Torah, Hilchot Mamrim* 3:3, he limits the punishment of heretics to exclude those who are born into a heretical culture. Other thinkers call this *tinok shenishba* (child captured and raised by idolaters). Nonetheless, we must generally call out and reject such intolerant views as unacceptable worldviews for our Judaism today.

19. Arie Morgenstern, *The Gaon of Vilna and His Messianic Vision* (Jerusalem: Gefen, 2014), 246.

20. Consider this Talmudic teaching: A teacher is not one to submit to but rather one to learn from and one to challenge at times. Rav Y'hoshua ben Korcha taught that the student must point out to the teacher the error he is about to make. We are instructed to fear God, not man! "Do not hold back your words because of anyone" (Babylonian Talmud, *Sanhedrin* 6b).

21. Babylonian Talmud, *Bava M'tzia* 30b.

22. Abraham Isaac Kook, *Orot HaKodesh*, 3:1–35.

23. Abraham Isaac Kook, *Midot HaRAYaH, Torah* #25

24. Babylonian Talmud, *Eiruvin* 100b.

25. Babylonian Talmud, *Yoma* 28b.

26. Levi Yitzchak of Berditchev, *K'dushat Purim* #1.

27. Levi Yitzchak of Berditchev, *K'dushat Levi, Parashat Yitro.*

28. Avery Dulles, *Models of Revelation* (New York: Orbis Books, 1992).

29. See Babylonian Talmud, *M'gillah* 28b, for a discussion of the consequences of relying on external sources.

30. *Pirkei Avot* 4:1.

31. Babylonian Talmud, *P'sachim* 113b.

32. See also *Vayikra* (Leviticus) *Rabbah* (21:8), where Rabbi Shimon bar Yochai (second century CE) states that "God hates four things."

33. Joseph B. Soloveitchik, "A Theory of Emotions," in *Out of the Whirlwind: Essays on Mourning, Suffering, and the Human Condition*, ed. David Shatz, Joel B. Wolowelsky, and Reuven Ziegler (New York: Ktav, 2003), 183.

34. This dichotomy is explored in Friedrich Wilhelm Nietzsche, *Aphorisms on Love and Hate* (London: Little Black Classics, 2015).

35. See Lewis R. Goldberg, "The Structure of Phenotypic Personality Traits," *American Psychologist* 48, no. 1 (January 1993): 26–34, https://doi.org/10.1037/0003-066X.48.1.26.

36. Babylonian Talmud, *B'rachot* 9b and *Sanhedrin* 113b.

37. Babylonian Talmud, *B'rachot* 10a.

38. The term *tikkun olam*, literally "repair of the world," has multiple connotations, ranging from the mystical to the legal. The term is used here in an ethical sense.
39. A prominent contemporary Conservative rabbi based in Los Angeles.
40. David Wolpe, *Why Be Jewish?* (New York: Holt, 1995), 37.
41. A prominent contemporary Reform rabbi based in the San Francisco Bay area.
42. Teaching at Valley Beit Midrash.
43. An Egyptian tablet made of stone, dated to around 1200 BCE.
44. *Sifrei D'varim* 357.
45. *Sifra K'doshim* 4:12.
46. Rabbi Abraham ben David, twelfth century, Provence. Quoted in Yuval Cherlow, *In His Image: The Image of God in Man* (Jerusalem: Maggid, 2016), 118–19.
47. Lisa L. Goldstein, "Fine-Tuning Our *Middot* as a Spiritual Practice," in *The Mussar Torah Commentary: A Spiritual Path to Living a Meaningful and Ethical Life*, ed. Barry H. Block (New York: CCAR Press, 2019), xxxii.
48. Babylonian Talmud, *P'sachim* 54a.
49. Babylonian Talmud, *M'gillah* 16b.
50. *P'sikta Rabbati* 21:17.
51. Daniel Goleman, *Primal Leadership* (Boston: Harvard Business Review Press, 2013), 3.
52. Adapted from Isaac Mayer Wise, "Hebrew Monotheism: A Dedicatory Sermon," in *The American Jewish Pulpit* (Cincinnati: Bloch, 1881), 199–208.

Chapter 7

1. *P'sikta D'Rav Kahana* on Psalm 34.
2. Yehudah Leib Levin, *Chasidim Mesaprim Torah Va'avod*, vol. 1 (Jerusalem: Mosad Har'im Levin, 1968), 134.
3. For more on Rav Kook's interpretation of freedom, see Abraham Isaac Kook, *Ma'amerei HaRe'iyah*, *Celebration of the Soul*, 141–43.

Chapter 8

1. *Tol'dot Yaakov Yosef*, *Chayei Sarah* 23a. See also *Keter Shem Tov* 56. See the Baal Shem Tov, *B'reishit*, *Noach*, note 31.
2. Deepak Chopra, *How to Know God: The Soul's Journey into the Mystery of Mysteries* (New York: Three Rivers Press, 2000), 32–33.
3. Ariana Silverman, in *Lights in the Forest: Rabbis Respond to Twelve Essential Jewish Questions*, ed. Paul Citrin (New York: CCAR Press, 2016), 32.
4. Dana Evan Kaplan, ed., Michael Marmur, "Speaking Truthfully about

God," *A Life of Meaning: Embracing Reform Judaism's Sacred Path* (New York: CCAR Press, 2017), 41–42.

5. The "I" here could refer to the Torah or to Jewish wisdom generally.

6. See *Mishlei Rabbah* 8:9, ed. Buber, 30a.

7. *Tosefta, Sanhedrin* 8:3.

8. *Vayikra Rabbah* 19:1.

9. *Midrash Konen, Beit Hamidrash* II p. 23.

10. *Midrash HaGadol* on Exodus 3:22; *Mishlei Rabbah* 23:1.

11. Babylonian Talmud, *Bava M'tzia* 59b.

12. Babylonian Talmud, *Bava M'tzia* 59b.

13. Yossi Klein Halevi, *Letters to My Palestinian Neighbor* (New York: Harper, 2018), 124.

Chapter 9

1. For similar ideas, see Proverbs 12:1, 13:1, 13:18, 15:12, 15:32, 19:25, 21:11, 27:5, and 28:23.

2. Babylonian Talmud, *Y'vamot* 65b.

3. Babylonian Talmud, *Shabbat* 55a.

4. Abraham Joshua Heschel, "A Prayer for Peace," in *Moral Grandeur and Spiritual Audacity*, ed. Susannah Heschel (New York: Farrar, Straus & Giroux, 1996), 231. Heschel refers to his own generation, those who lived through World War II and the Holocaust. However, we today must recognize the responsibility each of us carries, too.

5. Babylonian Talmud, *Shabbat* 54b.

6. Babylonian Talmud, *Bava M'tzia* 6a.

7. Arthur Green, *Ehyeh: A Kabbalah for Tomorrow* (Woodstock, VT: Jewish Lights, 2004), 1.

8. This rendering of the divine name stands for the four Hebrew letters *yod, hei, vav*, and *hei*, called the Tetragrammaton.

9. Martin Buber, *Moses: The Revelation and the Covenant* (Amherst, NY: Humanity Books, 1988), 51–52.

10. Harold Kushner, *Overcoming Life's Disappointments* (New York: Anchor, 2006), 4–15.

11. *Mishnah Sanhedrin* 6:5.

12. Babylonian Talmud, *B'rachot* 59a.

13. This is not to be confused with the concept of pantheism (from the Greek *pan*, meaning "all"—denoting the belief that God is all things), which suggests that God is everything and, likewise, everything is God; such thinking has not been accepted among traditional Jewish thinkers throughout history.

14. *B'reishit Rabbah* 68:9.

15. Martin Buber, *Hasidism and the Modern Man* (Princeton: Princeton University Press, 2015), 41.

16. Moshe Cordovero, *Sefer Shiur Komah*, commenting on *Zohar* 3:14b (the section of the Zoharic text called the *Idra Rabba*); this translation is by Bradley Shavit Artson, as published in *Panentheism across the World's Traditions*, ed. Loriliai Biernacki and Philip Clayton (New York: Oxford University Press, 2014), 29.

17. Israel ben Eliezer (Baal Shem Tov), *Sefer Tzava'at Harivash* (New York: Kehot Publication Society, 1998), §73, 141.

18. Israel ben Eliezer, *Sefer Tzava'at* Harivash, §73, 141

19. Nachman of Bratzlav, *Likutei Moharan* 21:11; see also Lawrence Kushner, *Eyes Remade for Wonder: A Lawrence Kushner Reader* (Woodstock, VT: Jewish Lights, 1998), 152.

20. Michael Rosen, *The Quest for Authenticity: The Thought of Reb Simhah Bunim* (Jerusalem: Urim, 2008), 135.

21. Meister Eckhart, "Sermon IV: True Hearing," in *Meister Eckhart's Sermons* (New York: Cosimo Classics, 2007), 32.

22. Green, *Ehyeh*, 52.

23. Abraham Isaac Kook, *Orot HaKodesh*, vol. 1, 269.

24. Abraham Isaac Kook, *Igerot HaRaayah*, vol. 1, no. 134, 14.

25. Maimonides, *Guide for the Perplexed* 3:32.

26. Abraham Isaac Kook, *Igerot HaRaayah*, vol. 1, no. 89.

27. Babylonian Talmud, *M'gillah* 29a. The word "God" in the translation here denotes the four-letter name in the Hebrew original. At times, a more restrained approach was taken: "God is like a mirror, which never changes, yet everyone who looks into it sees a different face." God does not change; only our perception does (*P'sikta D'Rav Kahana*, as cited in Harold Kushner, *When Children Ask about God* [New York: Schocken, 1989]), 26.

28. Babylonian Talmud, *Chulin* 60b.

29. *Sifrei D'varim* 33:5.

30. *Sh'mot Rabbah* 3:6.

31. Rabbi Y'hudah Aryeh Leib Alter, *Otzar Michtavim Umaamarim* (Jerusalem: Machon Gachalei Esh, 1986), 75–76.

32. Kalonymus Kalman Shapira, *Conscious Community: A Guide to Inner Work* (Lanham, MD: Jason Aronson, 1977), 84. The title of the original work is *B'nei Machshavah Tovah*.

33. Richard A. Cohen, ed., *Face to Face with Levinas* (Albany: State University of New York Press, 1986), 31–32.

34. In an effort to write in the spirit of engaged pedagogy, I have presented the thoughts discussed here mindful of the responsibility of rabbis and

Jewish educators to present various theologies (not merely the ones they favor) to their congregants and students to provide pluralistic spiritual entry ways into a relationship with God.

35. Rabbi Pinchas of Koretz, *Midrash Pinchas* (Warsaw, 1876), 55.
36. Michael Fishbane, *Sacred Attunement: A Jewish Theology* (Chicago: University of Chicago Press, 2008).
37. Shimon Gershon Rosenberg, as quoted in *Faith Shattered and Restored: Judaism in the Postmodern Age*, ed. Zohar Maor (Jerusalem: Maggid, 2017), 169–70.

Chapter 10

1. *Pirkei Avot* 2:16.
2. A reference to Job 5:7.
3. Maharal of Prague, *Tiferet Yisrael*, chapter 4.
4. For more information about Fowler's hierarchy of faith and human development, see Felicity B. Kelcourse, ed., *Human Development and Faith: Life-Cycle Stages of Body, Mind, and Soul*, 2nd ed. (St. Louis: Chalice Press, 2015), 45–47.
5. Babylonian Talmud, *Avodah Zarah* 19a.
6. Joseph B. Soloveitchik, *Out of the Whirlwind: Essays on Mourning, Suffering, and the Human Condition* (New York: Ktav, 2003), 206.

Chapter 11

1. See also Proverbs 12:28, 13:6, 13:22, 14:34, 15:15, and 21:13.
2. *Tosefta, Sanhedrin* 1:3.
3. Babylonian Talmud, *Bava M'tzia* 83a. Rav quotes twice in this passage from Proverbs 2:20.
4. Malbim on Proverbs 2:20.
5. Rabbi Binyamin of Zlazitz, *Turey Zahav, R'eih*, as quoted in *Sefer Baal Shem Tov, R'ieh* 12.
6. David Jaffe, "N'divut—Generosity: Giving Away, Bringing Close," in *The Mussar Torah Commentary: A Spiritual Path to Living a Meaningful and Ethical Life*, ed. Barry H. Block (New York: CCAR Press, 2019), 153.
7. Babylonian Talmud, *Bava Batra* 10a.
8. "Changes in Basic Minimum Wages in Non-Farm Employment Under State Law: Selected Years 1968 to 2019," US Department of Labor, Wage and Hour Division, www.dol.gov/agencies/whd/state/minimum-wage/history.
9. Paul Krugman, "Would Cutting the Minimum Wage Raise Employment?," *New York Times*, December 16, 2009, krugman.blogs.nytimes.com/2009/12/16/would-cutting-the-minimum-wage-raise-employment/.

10. See Louis Uchitelle, "A Pay Raise's Impact," *New York Times*, January 12, 1995, D1.
11. David Cooper, "Raising the Federal Minimum Wage to $15 by 2025 Would Lift Wages for over 33 Million Workers," Economic Policy Institute, July 17, 2019, www.epi.org/publication/minimum-wage-15-by-2025/.
12. Maimonides, *Mishneh Torah, Hilchot Mat'not Aniyim* 10:7.
13. See the Rema's gloss to *Shulchan Aruch, Choshen Mishpat* 163:1.
14. Babylonian Talmud, *Bava Batra*, 90a; *Shulchan Aruch, Choshen Mishpat* 231:20.
15. Barbara Ehrenreich, "Minimum Wage Rises, Sky Does Not Fall," *Huffington Post*, May 25, 2011, www.huffingtonpost.com/barbara-ehrenreich/minimum-wage-rises-sky-do_b_39255.html.
16. *Shulchan Aruch, Yoreh Dei-ah*, 251:10.
17. *Pirkei D'Rabbi Eliezer* 25.
18. Babylonian Talmud, *Sanhedrin* 109b.
19. *Pirkei D'Rabbi Eliezer* 25.
20. Maimonides, *Mishneh Torah, Hilchot Mat'not Aniyim* 10:1.
21. All three answers can be found: Babylonian Talmud, *Sotah* 30b–31a.
22. Babylonian Talmud, *B'rachot* 50a.
23. Babylonian Talmud, *K'tubot* 7b.
24. *Pirkei Avot* 4:19, quoting Proverbs 24:17.
25. Babylonian Talmud, *Sanhedrin* 39b.
26. Traditional song of gratitude sung on holidays consisting of particular psalms.
27. *P'sikta D'Rav Kahana, P'sachim, parashah bet.*
28. Babylonian Talmud, *Sanhedrin* 113b.
29. Babylonian Talmud, *B'rachot* 9b. See also Psalm 97:10.
30. Babylonian Talmud, *B'rachot* 10a.
31. Rabbi Meir Simcha of Dvinsk on Exodus 12:16.
32. Babylonian Talmud, *Bava M'tzia* 32b.

Chapter 12

1. *Mishnah B'rachot* 9:5.
2. Babylonian Talmud, *B'rachot* 9:2.
3. Babylonian Talmud, *B'rachot* 60b.
4. Adapted from "Perspective," Chabad.org, https://www.chabad.org/library/article_cdo/aid/2262/jewish/Perspective.htm.
5. The apocryphal story is found in Mark Twain, "The Lowest Animal," in *Holt Elements of Literature: Essentials of American Literature*, ed. G. Kylene Beers and Lee Odell (Austin, TX: Holt, Rinehart and Winston, 2005), 469–73.

6. David Brooks, *The Road to Character* (New York: Random House, 2015), 244.

7. See Kook's poem in Noam Zion, "Reinventing Hanukkah: Lubavitch Looks for the Inner and Outer Light," https://www.hartman.org.il/reinventing-hanukkah-lubavitch-looks-for-the-inner-and-outer-light/.

8. Babylonian Talmud, *Sanhedrin* 91b.

9. Babylonian Talmud, *Kiddushin* 30b.

10. Jerusalem Talmud, *B'rachot* 3:5.

11. Aharon Lichtenstein, "Is Anything New under the Sun: Reflections on the First Anniversary of the Attack on the Twin Towers," Torat HaEtzion, September 21, 2014, https://www.etzion.org.il/en/reflections-first-anniversary-attack-twin-towers.

12. Babylonian Talmud, *Bava Batra* 12b.

13. Over half a million Americans are homeless (2019).

14. Based on *Vayikra Rabbah* 4:6.

15. In addition to living for a week mostly at the mercy of the elements, Sukkot presents opportunities to connect with and reinforce a sense of guardianship over the natural world. In taking up the *lulav* and *etrog*, we are reminded of our duty to safeguard nature, with its many blessings. *Mishnah Sukkah* 3:1 says that one cannot fulfill the mitzvah with a stolen *lulav*, making clear that ritual is inextricably ethical.

16. Babylonian Talmud, *Taanit* 23a.

17. Alex Kirby, "Less Meat for the Rich Can Cut Heat and Hunger," *Climate News Network*, September 17, 2019, https://climatenewsnetwork.net/less-meat-for-rich-can-cut-heat-and-hunger/.

18. *Sefer HaChinuch*, mitzvah 429.

19. *Sefer HaChinuch*, mitzvah 529.

20. Roger Harrabin, "UN Climate Talks Extend Kyoto Protocol, Promise Compensation," *BBC News*, December 8, 2012, www.bbc.co.uk/news/science-environment-20653018.

Chapter 13

1. Babylonian Talmud, *Eiruvim* 54b; *Avodah Zarah* 19a.

2. Babylonian Talmud, *Chulin* 49b. See CCAR Responsum 5761.4 for further context.

3. Babylonian Talmud, *Eiruvim* 65b.

4. Jennifer E. Stellar, et al., "Class and Compassion: Socioeconomic Factors Predict Responses to Suffering," *Emotion*, vol. 12, no. 3, 2012, doi:10.1037/a0026508.

5. Michael Kraus, Paul Piff, and Dacher Keltner, "Social Class, Sense of

Control, and Social Explanation," *Journal of Personality and Social Psychology*, 97 (2009), 992-1004, doi:10.1037/a001635. 4.

6. Robert Parry, "Reagan's 'Greed is Good' Folly," *Consortium News*, October 5, 2011, http://consortiumnews.com/2011/10/05/reagans-greed-is-good-folly/.

7. Peter Dreier, "Reagan's Legacy: Homelessness in America," *Shelterforce*, May 1, 2004, https://shelterforce.org/2004/05/01/reagans-legacy-homelessness-in-america/.

8. John Herbers, "Breakup of Housing for Poor Is Backed on Integration Move," *New York Times*, April 28, 1987, https://www.nytimes.com/1987/04/28/us/breakup-of-housing-for-poor-is-backed-in-integration-move.html

9. Dreier, "Reagan's Legacy."

10. Robert Pear, "Reagan Leaving Many Costly Domestic Problems, GAO Tells Bush," *New York Times*, November 22, 1988, https://www.nytimes.com/1988/11/22/us/reagan-leaving-many-costly-domestic-problems-gao-tells-bush.html

11. Babylonian Talmud, *Bava M'tzia* 83a.

12. Rashi on Genesis 1:1.

13. See Torah commentary of Chizkuni (Rabbi Hezekiahv ben Manoah) on Genesis 13:6.

14. Edith Wharton, "Versalius in Zante," *North American Review* 175, no. 552 (November 1902): 625–31, https://www.jstor.org/stable/25119328.

15. Samuel Johnson, "Anecdotes of the Revd. Percival Stockdale," (1809) in *Johnsonian Miscellanies* (1897), vol. 2, 333.

16. John Keats, *Lamia*, http://www.gutenberg.org/files/2490/2490-h/2490-h.htm.

17. David J. Wolpe, *Why Be Jewish?* (New York: Holt, 1995), 72.

18. Babylonian Talmud, *Bava M'tzia* 59a–b.

19. Story adapted from Levi Cooper, "World of the Sages: Fiery Furnaces," in *The Jerusalem Post* (2009).

20. Maimonides, *Mishneh Torah, Hilchot Talmud Torah* 2:2.

21. Maimonides, *Mishneh Torah, Choveil uMazik* 5:1.

22. Maimonides, *Mishneh Torah, Hilchot Dei-ot* 2:3.

23. *Shulchan Aruch, Yoreh Dei-ah* 245:10. The Vilna Gaon seemed to take this approach as well; see *Ulim Litrufa*.

24. Yehiel S. Kaplan, "Corporal Punishment of Children in Israel: A New Trend in Secular and Religious Law," *International Journal of Children's Rights* 14 (2006): 363–421, https://dx.doi.org/10.2139/ssrn.1508691.

25. Kaplan, "Corporal Punishment of Children in Israel," 393.

26. Babylonian Talmud, *Mo-eid Katan* 17a and *Kiddushin* 30a.
27. Catherine A. Taylor, Jennifer A. Manganello, Shawna J. Lee, and Janet C. Rice, "Mothers' Spanking of 3-Year-Old Children and Subsequent Risk of Children's Aggressive Behavior," *Pediatrics* 125, no. 5 (May 2010): e1057–65, https://doi.org/10.1542/peds.2009-2678.
28. Robert D. Sege, "AAP Policy Opposes Corporal Punishment, Draws on Recent Evidence," *AAP News*, November 5, 2018, https://www.aap-publications.org/news/2018/11/05/discipline110518.
29. Babylonian Talmud, *B'rachot* 61a.
30. *Pirkei Avot* 4:1.
31. Jonah Pesner, "Channeling Our Good and Evil Impulses," *Sh'ma Now*, December 13, 2016, https://forward.com/shma-now/yetzer-hara/356653/channeling-our-good-and-evil-impulses/.
32. Babylonian Talmud, *Makot* 7a.
33. Steve Larocco, "The Other, Shame, and Politics: Levinas, Justice, and Feeling Responsible," *Religions* 9, no. 12 (2018): 381, https://doi.org/10.3390/rel9120381.
34. Karyn D. Kedar, *Amen: Seeking Presence with Prayer, Poetry, and Mindfulness Practice* (New York: CCAR Press, 2020), 26.

Chapter 14

1. There are a number of Jewish texts also supporting this sentiment. Consider, for example, the preface to *Shibolei Halleket* by Zedekiah ben Abraham (thirteenth century).
2. On a related theme, to learn more about the idea of challenging God (as a religious practice), see Dov Weiss, *Pious Irreverence: Confronting God in Rabbinic Judaism* (Philadelphia: University of Pennsylvania Press, 2016). This theme also runs throughout Elie Wiesel's works such as *Night* (see the chapter on Yom Kippur), *The Town beyond the Wall*, *The Gates of the Forest*, *A Jew Today* (see especially his essay on saying *Kaddish* for his father), *The Trial of God, Biblical Portraits*, and *Five Hasidic Masters*.
3. *Pirkei Avot* 2:13.
4. Joshua Stanton, in *Lights in the Forest: Rabbis Respond to Twelve Essential Jewish Questions*, ed. Paul Citrin (New York: CCAR Press, 2016), 208–9.
5. The sixth blessing recited during the traditional Jewish wedding ceremony recounts the joy that God's creations experienced in the Garden of Eden, while the seventh blessing speaks of the happiness that will settle upon the world at the end of days.
6. Ron Heifetz and Marty Linsky, Harvard professors of leadership studies, teach that when we "dance" we must also be "on the balcony" watching ourselves. If we are only dancing, we are unaware that the

dance is changing. Yet, if we only observe, then we fail to dance properly in the present. Heifetz and Linsky, "A Survival Guide for Leaders,"
Harvard Business Review, June 2002, https://hbswk.hbs.edu/archive/
leadership-on-the-line-staying-alive-through-the-dangers-of-leading.

7. See, for example, *Pirkei Avot* 5:17.
8. Maimonides on Deuteronomy 6:18.
9. Baruch Spinoza suggested similar ideas centuries before Hume.
10. See George DeMartino and Deirdre N. McCloskey, eds., *The Oxford Handbook of Professional Economic Ethics* (New York: Oxford University Press, 2016), 203.
11. Babylonian Talmud, *Kiddushin* 31a and *Z'vachim* 19a.
12. Babylonian Talmud, *Eiruvin* 100b.
13. Abraham Isaac Kook, *Letters of Rav Kook* (Jerusalem, 5745), 79.
14. See Babylonian Talmud, *Sotah* 37a, for more on Nachshon ben Aminadav.
15. Babylonian Talmud, *Kiddushin* 39b.
16. Another disclaimer: Historically, courage was ascribed to men as a masculine trait. Women were described as their passive supporters but not as agents of change per se. See Rabbi Patricia Karlin-Newmann's feminist critique of the Nachshon narrative in Tamara Cohn Eskenazi and Andrea L. Weiss, eds., *The Torah: A Women's Commentary* (New York: CCAR Press, 2008), 402.
17. Babylonian Talmud, *Y'vamot* 65b.
18. Babylonian Talmud, *Shabbat* 55a.
19. Mussar Institute, "Middah a Month," December 2011. Selections from *Sichot Mussar* by Reb Chaim Shmulevitz.
20. Abraham Joshua Heschel, "On Prayer," in *Moral Grandeur and Spiritual Audacity*, ed. Susannah Heschel (New York: Farrar, Straus & Giroux, 1996), 262–263.
21. Babylonian Talmud, *Sanhedrin* 6b.
22. Babylonian Talmud, *Shabbat* 88b.
23. Babylonian Talmud, *Shabbat* 88b.
24. Jonathan Sacks, *To Heal a Fractured World: The Ethics of Responsibility* (New York: Schocken, 2007), 262.
25. See Omri Boehm, *The Binding of Isaac: A Religious Model of Disobedience* (New York: T & T Clark International, 2007), 115.
26. Abraham Isaaac Kook, *Orot HaEmunah* 25.
27. Babylonian Talmud, *Sanhedrin* 64b; Jerusalem Talmud, *Shabbat* 19:2.
28. Samson Raphael Hirsch, *Collected Writings*, vol. 7 (New York: Feldheim, 1984), 57.
29. Ludwig Wittgenstein, in his earlier years, believed that language had a

purely analytical and logical nature. But his views evolved and he later argued that language is always embedded and can only be understood in relation to its context.

30. Irving Greenberg, *For the Sake of Heaven and Earth: The New Encounter between Judaism and Christianity* (Philadelphia: Jewish Publication Society, 2004), 196.

31. Jerusalem Talmud, *B'rachot* 9:5.

32. Schneur Zalman, *Tanya, the Masterpiece of Hasidic Wisdom*, trans. Rami Shapiro (Woodstock, VT: SkyLight Paths, 2010), 81–83.

33. Kalonymus Kalman Shapira, *A Student's Obligation: Advice from the Rebbe of the Warsaw Ghetto* (Lanham, MD: Rowman and Littlefield, 2004), 214–15.

34. James Averill, "On the Paucity of Emotions," in *Assessment and Modification of Emotional Behavior: Advances in the Study of Communication and Affect*, ed. Kirk Blankstein et al. (Boston: Springer, 1980).

35. Babylonian Talmud, *Makot* 24b.

36. Nathan Lopes Cardozo, *Jewish Law as Rebellion: A Plea for Religious Authenticity and Halachic Courage*, chapter 7 (Jerusalem: Urim Publications, 2019), 115.

37. *Responsa Radbaz* 3:472.

38. Jewish legal code viewed as authoritative among traditionally observant Ashkenazi Jews.

39. *Mishnah Berurah, Orach Chayim* 687:2.

40. It is important to note here that the two are not mutually exclusive. One could have a meaningful program that draws hundreds of people, and a small program could have negative effects on its participants.

41. Of course, many synagogues lead communal Passover seders and build one large communal sukkah. However, even in the Temple era, when Jews traveled in pilgrimage to Jerusalem to celebrate Passover, individual paschal lambs were to be eaten in relatively small groups as if to emphasize the tension found in the relationship between the communal and the familial within Jewish life.

42. *Lo tov* appears in a similar fashion throughout later sections of *Tanach* as well. See, for example, I Kings 19:4; Isaiah 65:2; Nehemiah 5:9; and Ezekiel 20. For a different (justice-related) use of *lo tov* in the Book of Proverbs, see Proverbs 18:5.

43. This interpretation of Proverbs 14:29 is mirrored in several other verses found in Proverbs, notably 14:17, 15:18, 16:32, 17:11, 22:24, and 29:11.

44. *Pirkei Avot* 5:10.

45. As quoted in Avraham Weiss, *Principles of Spiritual Activism* (New York: Ktav Publishers, 2002), p. 156.

46. *Tosefta, B'rachot* 7:2.

47. Jerusalem Talmud, *Taanit* 2:1; Babylonian Talmud, *Eiruvin* 22a.

48. Maimonides, *Mishneh Torah, Hilchot Talmud Torah* 2:2.

49. Jeff Stout, *Blessed Are the Organized: Grassroots Democracy in America* (Princeton: Princeton University Press, 2012), 64.

50. Mohandas Gandhi, quoted in Kathryne Pirtle, "Powerful Words from Gandhi: How to Turn Anger into Effective Action," Performance without Pain, July 18, 2010, http://performancewithoutpain. com/2010/07/18/powerful-words-from-gandhi-how-to-turn-anger-into-effective-action/.

51. Stout, *Blessed Are the Organized*, 65.

52. Stout, *Blessed Are the Organized*, 65.

53. Stout, *Blessed Are the Organized*, 65–66.

54. Stout, *Blessed Are the Organized*, 66–67.

55. Camus, *The Rebel* (London: Penguin Books, 1951), 2.

56. Mari Chernow, "*Kaas*—The Value of Anger," in *The Mussar Torah Commentary: A Spiritual Path to Living a Meaningful and Ethical Life*, ed. Barry H. Block (New York: CCAR Press, 2019), 131–32.

57. Abraham Joshua Heschel, "A Prayer for Peace," in *Moral Grandeur and Spiritual Audacity*, ed. Susannah Heschel (New York: Farrar, Straus & Giroux, 1996), 231.

58. Joseph B. Soloveitchik, *A Theory of Emotions* (New York: Academic Press, 1980), 183.

Chapter 15

1. See Marc Saperstein, *Jewish Preaching, 1200–1800: An Anthology* (New Haven, CT: Yale University Press, 1989), 93.

2. See Naomi E. Pasachoff, *Great Jewish Thinkers: Their Lives and Work* (Springfield, NJ: Behrman House, 1992), 27–29.

3. Thích Nhất Hạnh, *The Art of Communicating* (New York: HarperOne, 2013), 19.

4. Maimonides, *Mishneh Torah, Hilchot T'shuvah* 5:1.

5. *B'reishit Rabbah* 8:13, as quoted in Judith R. Baskin, *Midrashic Women: Formations of the Feminine in Rabbinic Literature* (Waltham, MA: Brandeis University Press, 2002), 63.

6. Babylonian Talmud, *Sotah* 14a.

7. Karyn D. Kedar, *Amen: Seeking Presence with Prayer, Poetry, and Mindfulness Practice* (New York: CCAR Press, 2019), xvii.

Chapter 16

1. Maimonides, *Guide for the Perplexed* 3:13.
2. Maimonides, *Guide for the Perplexed* 3:11.
3. *Pirkei Avot* 1:12.
4. Babylonian Talmud, *Shabbat* 10b.
5. Steven Pinker, *The Better Angels of Our Nature: Why Violence Has Declined* (London: Viking Books, 2012).
6. Patrick Worsnip, "Wars Less Deadly Than They Used to Be," Reuters, January 20, 2010, https://www.reuters.com/article/us-war-casualties-report/wars-less-deadly-than-they-used-to-be-report-says-idUSTRE60J5UG20100120.
7. Pinker, *Better Angels*, 402.
8. Pinker, *Better Angels*, 402.
9. Pinker, *Better Angels*, 385.
10. Scott Neuman, "Violence in Our Schools: How Big a Problem Is It?," National Public Radio, March 16, 2012, https://www.npr.org/2012/03/16/148758783/violence-in-schools-how-big-a-problem-is-it.
11. Brad Plumer, "Nine Facts about Terrorism in the United States since 9/11," *Washington Post*, September 11, 2013, https://www.washingtonpost.com/news/wonk/wp/2013/09/11/nine-facts-about-terrorism-in-the-united-states-since-911/.
12. "Booth's Reason for Assassination," Teachinghistory.org, https://teachinghistory.org/history-content/ask-a-historian/24242.
13. Dennis Wagner et al., "Gabrielle Giffords Shooting Suspect Jared Loughner Charged," *Arizona Republic*, January 9, 2011, http://archive.azcentral.com/news/articles/2011/01/09/20110109gabrielle-giffords-arizona-shooting-charges.html.
14. Rashi on Jonah 3:4. To support this reading, consider Psalm 30:12 and Lamentations 5:15.
15. Rashi on Genesis 18:21, citing Babylonian Talmud, *Sanhedrin* 109b.
16. Babylonian Talmud, *Sanhedrin* 108a.
17. For more information regarding global violence against women, see "Violence against Women," World Health Organization, March 9, 2021, https://www.who.int/news-room/fact-sheets/detail/violence-against-women.

Chapter 17

1. Rashi on Proverbs 17:1.
2. Babylonian Talmud, *Taanit* 7a.
3. Babylonian Talmud, *B'rachot* 31a.
4. Babylonian Talmud, *Taanit* 23a.

5. Matthew E. Brashears, "Small Networks and High Isolation? A Reexamination of American Discussion Networks," *Social Networks* 33, no. 4 (2011): 331–41, https://doi.org/10.1016/j.socnet.2011.10.003.
6. *Nicomachean Ethics*, book 8.
7. Alasdair Macintyre, *Dependent Rational Animals: Why Human Beings Need the Virtues* (Chicago: Carus, 1999), 150
8. Maimonides, *Guide for the Perplexed* 3:49.
9. *Pirkei Avot* 1:6.
10. Joseph B. Soloveitchik, *Family Redeemed* (Jersey City, NJ: Ktav, 2000), 27–28.
11. Joseph B. Soloveitchik, "*Out of the Whirlwind: Essays on Mourning, Suffering and the Human Condition* (Jersey City, NJ: Ktav, 2003), 154.
12. *Pirkei Avot* 5:16.
13. Jay Henry Moses, in *Lights in the Forest: Rabbis Respond to Twelve Essential Jewish Questions*, ed. Paul Citrin (New York: CCAR Press, 2016), 123.

Chapter 18
1. This quote is widely attributed to Chasidic Rabbi Menachem Mendel of Kotzk (1787–1859).
2. Karyn D. Kedar, *Amen: Seeking Presence with Prayer, Poetry, and Mindfulness Practice* (New York: CCAR Press, 2019), 46.
3. Kedar, *Amen*, 14.
4. Kedar, *Amen*, 60.
5. Kedar, *Amen*, 116.
6. *T'hillim Rabbah* 25:158b.
7. *Midrash HaGadol*, Genesis 38:1.
8. *Or Yesharim, Stories of the Baal Shem Tov* (New York: Mishor, 2006), 203.
9. Babylonian Talmud, *Y'vamot* 65b.
10. Babylonian Talmud, *Shabbat* 55a.
11. Babylonian Talmud, *Shabbat* 54b.
12. Babylonian Talmud, *Y'vamot* 87b.
13. Abraham Joshua Heschel, "A Prayer for Peace," in *Moral Grandeur and Spiritual Audacity*, ed. Susannah Heschel (New York: Farrar, Straus & Giroux, 1996), 231.
14. *Sifra, K'doshim* 4:9.

Chapter 19
1. For more on laziness, see Proverbs 3:11, 6:6–8, 6:10, 19:24, 20:4, 20:13, 21:25, 22:13, 24:30, 24:33, and 26:13–14.
2. Robert Bellah, *Habits of the Heart: Individualism and Commitment in*

American Culture (Berkeley: University of California Press, 1985), 155.

3. *Orchot Tzaddikim* 16:5.

4. Moshe Chayim Luzzatto, *M'silat Yesharim* 6:18.

5. Paulo Freire, *Pedagogy of the Oppressed* (New York: Herder and Herder, 1970), 31.

6. *Summa Theologica*, chapter 35, article 1.

7. Terry Orlick, *Embracing Your Potential* (Champaign, IL: Human Kinetics, 1998).

8. Story in full as quoted in Rabbi Joseph B. Soloveitchik, *Halakhic Man* (Philadelphia: Jewish Publication Society, 1983), 30–31: "The story is told about the Gaon of Vilna, how just before his death he clutched the *tzitzit* of his garment, wept, and exclaimed: 'How beautiful is this world—for one penny a person can acquire eternal life.' And when a Polish woman of noble birth proved stubborn and demanded, as the purchase price for the fresh, green, moist myrtles that grew in her garden, the reward that was reserved for the Gaon for the performance of the commandment, he gladly and wholeheartedly fulfilled her request and 'transferred' to her the reward for the commandment of taking the four species. On that Sukkot, so the folk legend relates, he was exceedingly joyful and told his students: 'All my life I grieved, when would I have the opportunity of fulfilling a mitzvah without receiving a reward, in order that I might thereby fulfill the injunction of Antigonos of Socho: 'Be like the servants who minister to their master without the intent of receiving a reward' [Avot 1:31]; and now that I have this opportunity, should I not fulfill this mitzvah with gladness and joy?'"

Chapter 20

1. Maimonides, *Mishneh Torah*, *Hilchot Chanukah* 4:14.

2. Babylonian Talmud, *Gittin* 59b.

3. Babylonian Talmud, *Shabbat* 23b.

4. *Pirkei Avot* 1:12.

5. Chofetz Chayim, *Sh'mirat HaLashon, Shaar Haz'chirah*, chap. 17.

6. Sforno on Deuteronomy 29:3.

7. Yerucham Levovitz, *Daat Torah B'reishit*, 279–83.

8. *Tanchuma, Chukat* 22.

9. Quoted in Martin Buber, *The Way of Man: According to the Teaching of Hasidism* (New York: Kensington, 1964), 32.

10. See Cicero, *De Amicitia—On Friendship*.

11. Ron Heifetz and Marty Linsky, *Leadership on the Line: Staying Alive through the Dangers of Leading* (Cambridge, MA: Harvard Business School Press, 2002), 199.

12. Bob Burns, Donald C. Guthrie, and Tasha D. Chapman, *Resilient Ministry: What Pastors Told Us about Surviving and Thriving* (Downers Grove, IL: InterVarsity Press, 2013), 42.

13. Burns, Guthrie, and Chapman, *Resilient Ministry*, 42.

14. Interestingly enough, the Talmud understands the light within a Jewish woman to be connected to the outer light that she lights on Friday night (Babylonian Talmud, *Shabbat* 31b–32a).

15. This custom is actually based on the verse in Proverbs under discussion.

16. In Babylonian Talmud, *P'sachim* 7b, leavened bread is likened to an evil inclination, and this verse in Proverbs is applied to teach the need to use a candle to find the leavened bread around the home.

17. Most generally understood: lighting the Shabbat candles, a *Havdalah* candle, and Chanukah candles are Rabbinic mitzvot; the lighting of *yahrtzeit* and *b'dikat chameitz* candles are mere customs, but accepted widely.

18. Bachya Ibn Pakuda, *Chovot HaL'vavot, Shaar Yichud HaMaaseh* 95.

19. *B'reishit Rabbah* 14; these are *ruach, nefesh, n'shamah, chayah,* and *y'chidah.*

20. Babylonian Talmud, *B'rachot* 18b.

21. Schneur Zalman, *Tanya, the Masterpiece of Hasidic Wisdom,* trans. Rami Shapiro (Woodstock, VT: SkyLight Paths, 2010), 65.

22. Babylonian Talmud, *Taanit* 11b and *B'rachot* 58a; and the Baal Shem Tov's commentary on *Pirkei Avot* 3:16.

23. Rabbi Abraham Isaac Kook, *Ein Ayah, Shabbat,* vol. 1 (*perek* 1:52).

24. Samson Raphael Hirsch on Proverbs 20:27.

25. *Sh'mot Rabbah* 36:3.

26. *Vayikra Rabbah* 31:4.

27. *P'sikta D'Rav Kahana, Kumi Uri* 21:1.

Chapter 21

1. For a famous example, see the two versions of the Creation story found in the Genesis 1 and Genesis 2.

2. See also Proverbs 24:12.

3. See Jonathan Haidt, *The Righteous Mind: Why Good People Are Divided by Politics and Religion* (New York: Vantage, 2013), 134.

4. Rousseau, *The Social Contract,* book 1, chapter 1. See Jean-Jacques Rousseau, *The Social Contract, and Other Later Political Writings* (Cambridge: Cambridge University Press, 1996), 351.

5. Maggid of Kozhnitz, *Avodat Yisrael, Vayikra/Shabbat HaGadol.*

6. Yehuda Amital, "The Ethical Foundations of Rav Kook's Nationalist Views," trans. B. Caspar and R. Ziegler, *Alei Etzion* 2 (5755): 19.

7. Ernest Becker, *The Denial of Death* (New York: Simon & Schuster, 1973), 153.

8. David Ellenson, foreword to *Righteous Indignation: A Jewish Call for Justice*, ed. Or N. Rose, Jo Ellen Green Kaiser, and Margie Klein (Woodstock, VT: Jewish Lights, 2008), x.
9. The earliest trace of this formula is attributed to Immanuel Kant in his *Critique of Pure Reason* (1871).
10. Abraham Isaac Kook, *Rav Kook's Introduction to Shabbat Haaretz* (New York: Hazon, 2014)
11. Read the widely known story of Rabbi Aryeh Levine and his lesson on beautifying the mitzvah at https://www.jewishedproject.org/news/aspire-inspire-tale-dentures-etrogim-and-sukkot.

Chapter 22
1. Crosby, Stills, Nash, and Young, "Teach Your Children" (Rhino Atlantic, 2009).
2. One might normally think of youth "education" (*chinuch*) as being before 12 for a girl and before 13 for a boy, but the Talmudic Sages explain that the main concern is between the ages of 16 and 24 (Babylonian Talmud, *Kiddushin* 30a).
3. Rachel Timoner, in *Lights in the Forest: Rabbis Respond to Twelve Essential Jewish Questions*, ed. Paul Citrin (New York: CCAR Press, 2016), 212.
4. Jonathan Sacks, *A Letter in the Scroll: Understanding Our Jewish Identity and Exploring the Legacy of the World's Oldest Religion* (New York: Free Press, 2004), 140.
5. Babylonian Talmud, *Kiddushin* 29b; *Shulchan Aruch, Yoreh Dei-ah* 245:2.
6. Leo Tolstoy, *War and Peace* (London: Penguin Random House, 2008).
7. See also Moshe Chayim Luzzatto, *M'silat Yesharim* 17.
8. Maimonides, *Guide for the Perplexed* 3:32.
9. Michael Walzer, *Exodus and Revolution* (New York: Basic Book, 1985), 58.
10. Jerusalem Talmud, *Sanhedrin*, 48b. The Rabbis argue that Pinchas acted against the will of the Sages by acting violently.
11. Thomas Mallon, "Obsessed (Agog, Beset, Consumed, Driven, etc.)," *New York Times*, March 16, 2008, http://www.nytimes.com/2008/03/16/books/review/Mallon-t.html?
12. *Avot D'Rabbi Natan*, version B, 31.
13. Elie Wiesel, "The Nobel Lecture: Hope, Despair, and Memory," nobelprize.org/prizes/peace/1986/wiesel/lecture/.
14. Sonja K. Pilz, "*Savlanut*—To Be Patient and to Love, in *The Mussar Torah Commentary: A Spiritual Path to Living a Meaningful and Ethical Life*, ed. Barry H. Block (New York: CCAR Press, 2019), 232–33.
15. Babylonian Talmud, *Eiruvin* 54b.

Chapter 23

1. Emmanuel Levinas, *Difficult Freedom* (Baltimore: John Hopkins University Press, 1997), 176–77.
2. Irving (Yitz) Greenberg, *Sage Advice: Pirkei Avot* (New Milford, CT: Maggid Books, 2016), xviii.
3. Babylonian Talmud, *Sanhedrin* 19b: "Whoever brings up an orphan in their home, it is as though they gave birth to them."
4. As told to author, from *Ahavat Chesed* by Rabbi Yisrael Meir ha-Kohen Kagan (Chofetz Chaim, 1838-1933).
5. Maimonides, *Mishneh Torah, Hilchot Dei-ot* 6:10.
6. Jonah Dov Pesner, "In Every Generation: The Obligations of Our Exodus," in *Moral Resistance and Spiritual Authority: Our Jewish Obligation to Social Justice*, ed. Seth M. Limmer and Jonah Dov Pesner (New York: CCAR Press, 2019), 92–93.

Chapter 24

1. The Munkatcher Rav, *B'nei Yisachar, maamar* 1.
2. Abraham Joshua Heschel, *The Sabbath* (New York: Farrar Straus Giroux, 2005).
3. See, for example, Exodus 31:15.
4. Denise Eger, in *Lights in the Forest: Rabbis Respond to Twelve Essential Jewish Questions*, ed. Paul Citrin (New York: CCAR Press, 2016), 97.
5. See, for example, Exodus 3:9-14, describing Moses at the Burning Bush.
6. There are countless incidents of the Israelite people complaining to Moses. See, for example, Exodus 16.
7. Babylonian Talmud, *Gittin* 56ab.
8. Babylonian Talmud, *Yoma* 35b.
9. Babylonian Talmud, *K'tubot* 62b-63a.
10. Letter from Moses Maimonides to Samuel ibn Tibbon, quoted in "Maimonides' Letter to a Friend," *Jewish History Blog*, March 13, 2010, https://www.jewishhistory.org/maimonides-letter-to-a-friend/.
11. David Biale et al., *Hasidism: A New History* (Princeton: Princeton University Press, 2018), 113.
12. Scottie Andrew, "After an Attack on His Hannukah Celebration, a Rabbi Moved the Event to His Synagogue," *CNN*, December 30, 2019, https://www.cnn.com/2019/12/30/us/rabbi-hanukkah-event-synagogue-new-york-stabbing-trnd/index.html.
13. Maimonides, *Mishneh Torah, Hilchot Dei-ot* 2:3.
14. Babylonian Talmud, *P'sachim* 66b. On the destructive nature of anger,

see also Babylonian Talmud, *Kiddushin* 40b–41a; Babylonian Talmud, *Sanhedrin* 105b; *Pirkei Avot* 2:11.

15. Babylonian Talmud, *Yoma* 9b.
16. Abraham Isaac Kook, *Orot HaKodesh* 3:324.
17. Babylonian Talmud, *Yoma* 23a–b.
18. "Transcript of President Abraham Lincoln's Second Inaugural Address," March 4, 1865, Our Documents, https://www.ourdocuments.gov/doc.php?flash=false&doc=38&page=transcript.
19. See Desmond Tutu, "Let South Africa Show the World How to Forgive," *Knowledge of Reality* 19, https://www.sol.com.au/kor/19_03.htm.
20. Tutu, "Let South Africa Show the World How to Forgive."

Chapter 25

1. *Esther Rabbah* 7:5; Babylonian Talmud, *M'gillah* 19a.
2. Rachel Adler, "Equality of Social and Political Rights . . . Irrespective of . . . Sex," in *Deepening the Dialogue: Jewish-Americans and Israelis Envisioning the Jewish-Democratic State*, ed. Stanley M. Davids and John L. Rosove (New York: CCAR Press, 2020), 115.
3. "Rawanda Genocide: 100 Days of Slaughter," *BBC News*, April 4, 2019, http://www.bbc.com/news/world-africa-26875506.
4. See David Livingstone Smith, *Less Than Human: Why We Demean, Enslave and Exterminate Others* (New York: St. Martin's Press, 2011).
5. Rebecca Morin, "Trump: 'Animals' Comment Referred to MS-13 Gang Members," *Politico*, May 17, 2018, https://www.politico.com/story/2018/05/17/trump-immigrants-animals-595118.
6. Megan McArdle, "Trump's 'Animal' Comments Were Loathsomely Loaded and Coded," *Chicago Tribune*, May 31, 2019, http://www.chicagotribune.com/news/opinion/commentary/ct-perspec-animals-trump-ms-13-gang-immigrants-0525-story.html.
7. Michelle Lee, "Donald Trump's False Comments Connecting Mexican Immigrants and Crime," *Washington Post*, July 8, 2015, https://www.washingtonpost.com/news/fact-checker/wp/2015/07/08/donald-trumps-false-comments-connecting-mexican-immigrants-and-crime/.
8. Elise Foley and Roque Planas, "Trump's Crackdown on Immigrant Parents Puts More Kids in an Already Strained System," *HuffPost*, May 25, 2018, https://www.huffpost.com/entry/immigrant-children-separated-from-parents_n_5b087b90e4b0802d69cb4070.

Chapter 26

1. Madeleine L'Engle, *The Crosswicks Journal* (Open Road Media, 2016), section 1.9.
2. Martin Buber, *Tales of the Hasidim* (New York: Schocken, 1991), 275–76.
3. Buber, *Tales of the Hasidim*, 284.

Chapter 27

1. Emmanuel Levinas, *Totality and Infinity: An Essay on Exteriority* (Pittsburgh: Duquesne University Press, 1998).
2. Alain de Botton, *Religion for Atheists* (New York: Pantheon, 2012), 41.

Chapter 29

1. D. H. Lawrence, "The Third Thing," in *Pansies: Poems* (New York: Knopf, 1929), 133.
2. See Steven T. Katz, ed., *Mysticism and Philosophical Analysis* (New York: Oxford University Press, 1978), 92.

Chapter 30

1. For a more robust discussion of Jewish views of the afterlife, see Simcha Paul Raphael, *Jewish Views of the Afterlife* (London: Rowman and Littlefield, 2019).
2. Adam Grant, *Give and Take: A Revolutionary Approach to Success* (New York: Penguin, 2014), 23.
3. Grant, *Give and Take*, 1.
4. For a discussion on the source of this quote see the following website: https://www.samueljohnson.com/measure.html.
5. Krista Tippett, *Becoming Wise: An Inquiry into the Mystery and Art of Living* (New York: Penguin Press, 2016), 85.
6. Samuel C. Heilman, *Who Will Lead Us? The Story of Five Hasidic Dynasties in America* (Oakland: University of California Press, 2017), 7.
7. This quote is popularly attributed to Mahatma Gandhi (*Los Angeles Times*, July 30, 1989).

Chapter 31

1. "A Tribute to Rav Yehuda Amital," YouTube video, July 28, 2011, http://www.youtube.com/watch?v=JPxq_p8L-MM (at 12:40).
2. Martha C. Nussbaum, *Hiding from Humanity: Disgust, Shame, and the Law* (Princeton: Princeton University Press, 2004), 183.
3. Babylonian Talmud, *Chagigah* 2a.
4. Babylonian Talmud, *Shabbat* 63a.
5. Rachel Adler, "Equality of Social and Political Rights . . . Irrespective of

. . . Sex," in *Deepening the Dialogue: Jewish-American and Israelis Envisioning the Jewish-Democratic State*, ed. Stanley M. Davids and John L. Rosove (New York: CCAR Press, 2020), 112.

6. Jacqueline Vayntrub, "Who Is the Eshet Chayil?," TheTorah.com, June 26, 2014, https://thetorah.com/who-is-the-eshet-chayil/.

7. Rashi on Proverbs 31:10.

8. *Midrash Mishlei* 31.

Conclusion

1. Jonathan Sacks, *Dignity of Difference: How to Avoid the Clash of Civilizations*, new rev. ed. (India: Bloomsbury Academic, 2003), 207.

2. See *Tikkunei Zohar* 81b. Various Chasidic writings played up this statement and greatly expanded its meaning.

3. Shimon Rosenberg, *Faith Shattered and Restored: Judaism in the Postmodern Age* (Jerusalem: Maggid Books, 2017), 112, 118.

4. Broadcast of Voice of America, November 11, 1951.

5. Babylonian Talmud, *Shabbat* 30b.

6. *B'reishit Rabbah* 24:8.

7. Eugene Borowitz, *Choices in Modern Jewish Thought* (Springfield, NJ: Behrman House, 1995), 103.

8. Robert Frost, *The Road Not Taken* (self-published, 1916).

9. Babylonian Talmud, *Sanhedrin* 37a.

10. Shlomo Wolpe, *Alei Shur*, vol. 1, 168.

11. By way of example, traditionally before the Shabbat meal on Friday night, many people recite verses from the last chapter of Proverbs beginning with the words *eishet chayil*, often translated as "the woman of valor."

About the Author

RABBI DR. SHMULY YANKLOWITZ is the President and Dean of Valley Beit Midrash, Founder and President of Uri L'Tzedek, Founder and CEO of Shamayim: Jewish Animal Advocacy, and Founder and President of YATOM: The Jewish Foster and Adoption Network.

Rabbi Yanklowitz's writings have appeared in outlets as diverse as the *New York Times, Wall Street Journal, Washington Post, Guardian*, and *Atlantic*. Rabbi Yanklowitz is a sought-after educator, social justice activist, and motivational speaker as well as the author of twenty-two books on Jewish spirituality, social justice, and ethics. This is his third book with CCAR Press, following social justice commentaries on *Pirkei Avot* and the Book of Jonah.

Rabbi Yanklowitz has volunteered, staffed trips, and taught across the world, including in Israel, Ghana, India, France, Thailand, El Salvador, England, Senegal, Germany, Switzerland, Ukraine, Argentina, South Africa, and Haiti. Rabbi Yanklowitz has served as a rabbinic representative and speaker at the World Economic Forum in Geneva and Davos. His religious journey was filmed in the PBS/Independent Lens documentary *The Calling*.

Rabbi Yanklowitz earned a master's degree from Harvard University in Leadership and Psychology, another master's from Yeshiva University in Jewish Philosophy, and a doctorate from Columbia University in Moral Development and Epistemology. He obtained rabbinical ordination from the Yeshivat Chovevei Torah Rabbinical School and two private ordinations in Israel. He has twice been named one of America's Top Rabbis by *Newsweek*. In 2016, the *Forward* named Rabbi Yanklowitz one of the Most Inspiring Rabbis in America and one of the fifty most influential Jews.

Rabbi Yanklowitz, his wife Shoshana, and their four children live in Scottsdale, Arizona. They are also foster parents.